THE MUDD CLUB

BY RICHARD BOCH

The Mudd Club © 2017 by Richard Boch

ISBN 978-1-62731-051-2

Feral House
1240 W. Sims Way
Suite 124
Port Townsend, WA 98368

10 9 8 7 6 5 4 3 2 1

Design: Dave Shulman, designSimple
Cover photo by Bob Gruen

For Alice, Mickey, Pete and Ricky

TABLE OF CONTENTS

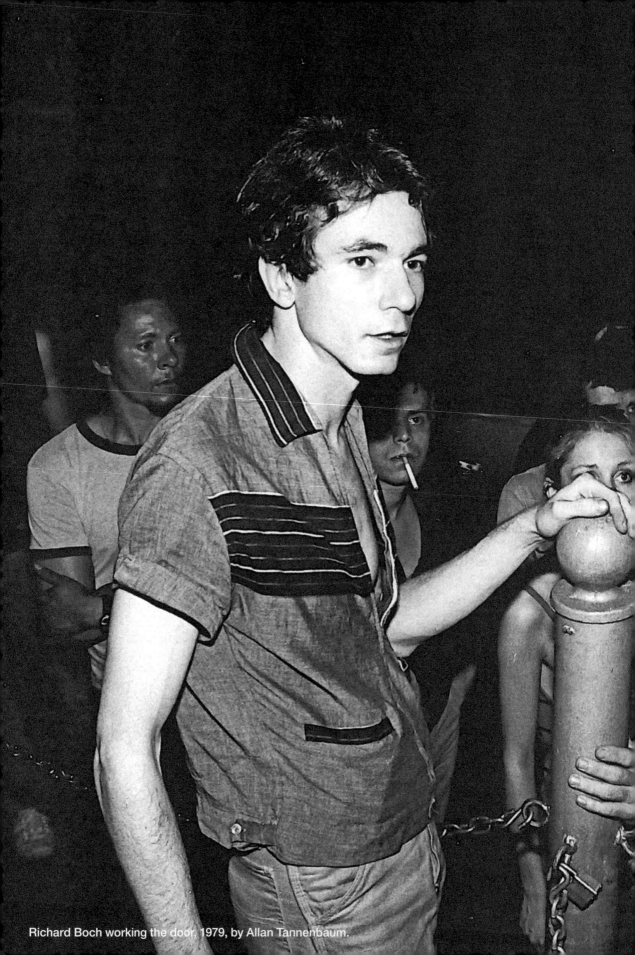

Richard Boch working the door, 1979, by Allan Tannenbaum.

INTRODUCTION/ OUTSIDE WANTING IN

I had less than fifteen minutes, but needed twenty. I stepped off the curb, a taxi pulled over, I told the driver, "Canal and Broadway, left side, far corner." He cruised through every light for the next ten blocks while I dug around in my Marlboro box, searching for a lost Quaalude. When I got out of the cab I ordered a vanilla egg cream and two hot dogs at Dave's Luncheonette, a twenty-four-hour dive that specialized in extra grease and lousy coffee. I drank the egg cream fast and grabbed the hot dogs, walked two blocks and I was there. Standing outside while a dozen people watched me eat the second dog, I checked out some of the faces and swallowed the last bite. I lit a cigarette and I was ready. Midnight came and went. Hours later, the night ran me over and kept on going; after that, no telling what.

It happened on White Street, 1979 and 1980—twenty-one months that seemed to last forever. By then, I'd been living in the city four-plus years, moved twice, and worked different jobs. I met a lot of people, made new friends and fell in love at least five or six times. Before that, I was just another kid from Long Island, trying to figure out what was going on. Now I'm just trying to remember, before the pictures fade and disappear.

I close my eyes and look back on what's left of my earliest memories; the black-and-yellow caterpillar in the road near my grandparents' house in Newton, New Jersey, is one I still see. Holding my father's hand and walking through Forest Park is one I can feel. It was summer 1956 and I was three years old.

Two years later, I started school. I remember standing in a hallway—twenty little kids buzzing and shuffling—waiting for something but not knowing what. When the bell finally rang I was scared and drifted off into another world. Alone in a kindergarten crowd, I cried for a while until the crayons stepped in and saved me. I settled down but it was already time to go home.

An overprotected only child, I was shy and felt outnumbered. I looked like a "normal" kid but didn't feel that way. I was never sure what anyone else thought about me—if they noticed—or if I even cared. That part caught up with me later, and by then, all I wanted was to fit in. I just didn't know where.

Looking back I see a pattern—dreaming and getting ahead of myself—somewhere on the outside, wanting in and feeling alone when I got there. Seventh and eighth grade, Catholic school, a good boy longing for bad; standing around an empty playground or hanging with friends in a strip mall parking lot; going home, hoping not to smell like a cigarette. I was just getting started and already hiding something.

It wasn't long before I got drunk for the first time. Smoking pot and chugging cough syrup weren't far behind. At fifteen, I was too young to know the difference between the fast lane and getting lost. Throw sex into the mix and I was eager but confused. By the time I was sixteen, I put on the headphones, turned up the music and disappeared.

I made it through high school without too much pain. I took lots of LSD and did pretty well in college. I finished school in 1976, moved to the city and wound up living on Bleecker near Sullivan Street. CBGB's was exploding, SoHo was the center of the art world and the soon-to-be ruins of Bohemia were still standing. The West Village bars, trucks and piers were a free-for-all; sex was easy and drugs were everywhere. I looked around, found a job, and made a little money. I shared a studio with my friends, and I was painting every day. I went out every night, came home in the morning and slept for a few hours. I was twenty-two and had no problem keeping up but knew there had to be more. I wanted to find out what. I thought I was ready for anything.

I ran around the Village for over a year when there was still enough room to run. November 1977 I paused for a second, caught my breath, and decided to grab a piece of the city while there was something left to grab. I gave up my apartment on Bleecker for the far-off neighborhood that was becoming Tribeca and became a *postpioneer* in what was still a beautiful, nearly desolate environment. Two thousand square feet of raw space in a twelve-story commercial building on Murray Street became my home. The World Trade Center loomed three blocks south, Chambers Street ran two crosstown blocks north. Surrounded by subway stations and City Hall, an odd lot store called the Job Lot Trading Company was around the corner and the Lower Manhattan Ocean Club a couple blocks away. A mattress on the floor, a makeshift shower and some basic third-hand furniture were all I needed. I had a stereo, boxes of records and a roommate who loved music and liked to get high. I was tending bar in SoHo and I had cash in my pocket. I had my own studio to work in and paper hanging on the wall. I thought I was finally figuring things out and getting some answers. I never saw what was coming.

***

In the fall of 1978, I walked thru the doors of 77 White Street. I saw the address and a phone number printed on a few small posters but had no idea what to expect. It was place called the Mudd Club and it felt like home the moment I stepped inside. I ordered a drink and moved onto the dance floor. I ran into some friends, spotted some familiar faces, hung out for hours and didn't want to leave. The following night I had to go back.

Three months later, I got the phone call that changed everything, and before long, I was working the Mudd Club door. The music was loud and the midnight hour kept coming and going. Standing outside those final days of winter, I stared at the crowd, trying to figure out who or what was coming in—and learning as I went along. Two or three drinks helped me relax; cocaine helped me feel up to the job. It was *out there* versus *in here* and I was on the inside. I never thought about how I got there, and I never thought about leaving.

By early spring of 1979, I felt the whole world was headed for White Street—and that working the door was a big deal. I finally got what I wanted and became part of what was happening. I met *everyone* and the job quickly defined me. I just wasn't sure if I was finding out who I was or forgetting who I was. I'm not sure it was even possible then to know, and I still have doubts. Though it took a once-in-a-lifetime, often crazy, dreamily inspired Mudd Club while, eventually I got the answer.

***

I've always referred to the Mudd Club as the *scene of the crime*, always meant as a term of endearment. It was the night that never ended: the day before never happened and the day after, a long way off. There was nothing else like it and I wound up right in the middle. I thought I could handle it and for a while, I did.

Mudd Club daze, 1980, by Nick Taylor.

1.
QUICKLY SAID AND LEFT UNSAID

"If you've been standing here for more than ten minutes, you're not coming in."

I made that announcement on more than one occasion. I had to do something. No one was leaving, and no one, at least for the moment, was getting in.

I looked around at what passed as Mudd Club security in the summer of 1980. Moonlighting cops, gangster wannabes and one or two guys with a little height and a few extra pounds were doing their best to keep us safe. When I started working the door in early spring of 1979 there was a chain around the front steps but no security at all: just Louie and Joey, Gretchen, Robert and Colter. We made up the rules as we went along and handled whatever came our way. The press, weekend crowds, money and the Hells Angels changed all that. In time, everything changed.

I learned a lot watching Louie, like how to say NO by saying nothing at all. Joey was the everyman, Gretchen was the beautiful blonde and Robert kept things cool. Colter ran around chasing girls and left shortly after I arrived.

When the night got to be too much or not enough, when we wanted to dance or hang out in the bathroom, we'd take turns, head inside and get lost. It was that easy.

Tonight, I'm just staring at faces and by 2 A.M., it's already too much. Aldo's standing behind me handling security and Chi Chi's working the stairs to the second floor. I glance at the crowd and step inside. Chi Chi looks at my face and says, "Oh honey"—the full-syllable version of the *Oh hon* Cookie Mueller gave me an hour ago. It's time to disappear.

I pass Boris Policeband, legendary violinist and pool shark, who's holding up the wall near the door. He's fiddling with a transistor radio, a tape recorder or maybe a Geiger counter—it's hard to tell. Squeezing by, I pull my friend Edward with me and keep walking. We turn the corner and head for the basement. At the bottom of the stairs I take a key from my pocket, we slip into the storage area, walk halfway to the elevator and stop. It's quiet and calm except for the muffled music, the stomping feet and the slapping sound of a security guy fucking some bridge-and-tunnel girl behind a stack of boxes. I pull a cut straw from my pack of Marlboros, unfold the twenty someone handed me at the door and snort up half the half-gram of coke inside. I hand the rest over to Edward, stare at him and smile.

We're able to speak again after a minute or two and hang out a little while more. We get in the elevator, take it for a ride, and step into another world.

The air on the second floor is all cigarettes and alcohol—so thick I can feel it. Phoebe, the sixteen-year-old Westchester wild child dressed in go-go boots and one of her mother's wash-and-wear party dresses, strolls past laughing; Mick Jagger is close behind. Edward heads for the bar while I kick the bottom of the bifold steel door on the "men's" room. Chris Frantz opens it, says hi and keeps on talking to the same person he was talking to an hour ago. No one's paying attention to the girl sitting on the rim of the seatless toilet, and she's not paying attention either. Edward returns with two more drinks and we lock the door. The room's vibrating. There's a rainbow haze around the fluorescent lights. The ceiling looks like it's moving. I lean back against the cool white tile and Edward leans on me—five of us inside, but we might as well be alone.

Ten minutes later, nothing has changed. I try to stay in the moment but I've got to get back to the door. Aldo's alone out there and they'll eat him alive.

I make my way across the second floor. The Russian Punks, crammed onto an old couch in the corner, appear to be melting. My friend's mother, an oddball of a club regular, looks trapped inside one of Ronnie Cutrone's black steel cages. Johnny Thunders hangs on the side of the cage, oblivious to the sixty-year-old woman inside. Everybody seems drunk, even if they're not. I turn around, Edward looks at me, and I tell him I'll catch him later. I'm not exactly sure what that means.

Almost 4 A.M. If I'm lucky, I'll be out of here by 5, home on Murray Street by 5:30 and Penn Station by 7. Gennaro's working the weekend and I'm leaving for Montauk.

***

Six hours and a train ride later I'm sitting on an old redwood chair, halfway in the shade, listening to the ocean. I'm peeling paint off the concrete deck with the sole of my flip-flop and staring at a bright white sky that even my Ray-Bans can't turn down. The phone booth inside is the only connection to 77 White.

Five minutes later, I get up and stick a straw into a small glassine envelope. I haven't slept in over twenty-four hours. I light a cigarette, walk upstairs and lie down. I start to drift, my feet kicking as though I'm swimming in bed. I close my eyes somewhere between asleep and a nod.

The weekends in Montauk are a new thing. I feel I've been doing everything else forever.

It's strange how it all started.

The Phone Call

Winter-springtime 1979. Hanging at home and nothing's going on. I'm scribbling something about Johnny Rotten around the edges of a large sheet of paper hanging on the studio wall, smoking a joint and watching *Taxi* without sound. Roxy Music's *Manifesto* is playing when the black desk model jacked-in phone starts ringing. I pick up and hear my friend Pat say, "Steve Mass is calling you right now." I hang up and it rings again.

"Pat Wadsley tells me you know everyone, I need someone at the door on the weekends. Richard Lloyd, Taylor Mead and some other people couldn't get in. Come see me Friday night after eleven."

Steve Mass is the owner of the Mudd Club. He's talking and I'm listening. Lots more is quickly said and left unsaid. The call lasts ten minutes, more or less.

Roxy Music stopped, the joint went out and I'm just sitting, staring at a silent TV. *What just happened? Did Steve Mass offer me a job? He doesn't even know me.* I light a cigarette and phone Pat to fill her in on the call even though it's too soon to say Thanks or What the fuck?

I roll another joint and make several more calls. I start telling friends I'll be doing the door at the Mudd Club. I have no idea if it's true, but something tells me it is.

The Once-Over Once

I arrive Friday night dressed in jeans, boots and a motorcycle jacket, pretty much what I always wear. Louie Chaban, dressed in silvery sharkskin pants too tight to believe, unhooks the chain. It's heavy-duty steel made for towing or lumbering, ready to handle a serious workload. There's no welcome mat: the chain says *stay out* when it has to, but for the moment, it says *come in*.

I walk toward the door and notice Louie's black Tony Lamas with red piping down the side—the same boots I have on. Joey Kelly and Robert Molnar are both working but no one pays me any attention. I step inside and tell the blonde collecting the money that I'm looking for Steve. She laughs, gets off her stool, turns around and points, all without putting down her drink, her cigarette or the cash.

Steve Mass is at the bar in a slightly rumpled suit paired with an off-season Hawaiian shirt, talking with someone I've seen around but barely know. The guy's rambling and it's hard to cut in. I stand for a minute staring at the two until finally I say, "Hi, I'm Richard." Steve looks at me a few seconds.

"Oh hi, be here tomorrow at midnight."

I say, "Okay," and that's it.

I don't even get the once-over once.

I'm caught off guard and leave quickly and quietly. Twice in one week I'm left thinking, *What was that, what just happened?*

Walking two blocks west to Church Street, I head uptown on Sixth Avenue. I'm not even close to realizing what this job might become.

Steve Mass and Diego Cortez, 1978, by Bobby Grossman.

I'm still trying to figure out what makes this club different; there's a spirit and soul I've yet to define. I live in the neighborhood, the drinks are cheap and I get in easily whenever I show up. Maybe that's what's so important, or maybe there's more.

I cross Canal, grab a cab, and head for West Tenth Street to kill time. Maybe there'll be something going at the Ninth Circle other than the usual hustlers shooting pool and a Cherry Vanilla single on the jukebox.

I walk in, look around and step into the bathroom. From a small amber bottle I dump two lines of coke on my fist. One blast nearly knocks me over. I walk out and wind my way along West Fourth, across Gansevoort to Washington and Little West Twelfth. Just past 1 I wander into The Mineshaft—a half-dozen anonymous, reckless encounters help pass the time and before I know it, it's 5 A.M. I leave alone, cab it home and manage to sleep.

I did as I was told and returned to the Mudd Club the following night. I thought I knew what was happening but truly had no idea. Weeks later, on the heels of Bill Cunningham's White Street photos published in the *New York Times*, Pat Wadsley (who often claims to remember nothing) wrote an article about the Mudd Club for the *SoHo Weekly News*. By then I was deep in the mix.

The Friday and Saturday nights briefly mentioned in that fateful call turned into five or six nights a week for the next twenty-one months. Looking back, it was a lifetime.

***

August 1980. Still Saturday afternoon in Montauk. I come alive after a few hours, burnt from the nightlife and the sun. I can hear the ocean and I'm wondering where the last eighteen months have gone. The room's hot and breezy, the sheets and carpet are sandy. The sleep was deep and the pillow left creases in my face. I splash cold water, light a cigarette and grab a towel. The only thing separating me from the beach is Route 27A, the two-lane Old Montauk Highway. Teri, Gary, Ricky and Ron are already in the water.

The world seemed small and Montauk was as far as I could run. Time was hard to measure; sometimes I felt as if the five of us had known each other our entire lives. They were my friends and like everything else, I thought those friendships would last forever.

I tossed the cigarette and walked across the sand thinking about where I met each one of them. Ricky Sohl was first, back in 1975. He was playing piano the first time I saw Patti Smith and he gave me a note scribbled in bad French on a scrap of paper.

I met Gary Kanner at The Ballroom, a cabaret on West Broadway between Houston and Prince, where we worked in 1978. He moved into the loft on Murray Street two weeks later. Boyfriend, lover, friend— it was hard to decide and harder to describe. Our relationship was based largely on drugs, music, movies and TV; his identity then was his connection to me, while my mixed-blessing identity became *Mudd Club doorman*. Our "partnership" was troubled from the start—doomed by dishonesty and resentment, any chance of love warped by codependence. We stuck it out for two decades, trying and sometimes succeeding to remain friends.

In spring 1979, I met Teri Toye at Mudd. Transcending gender and beyond androgyny, Teri was a beauty, an accessory and accomplice. That same year I met Ron Beckner—a.k.a. Big Ron—at Mickey Ruskin's One University Place. A merchant marine and the only male waitress on the One U staff, he liked it fast and crazy, and found it with the four of us.

I met a lot of people in those years, and most of them came out of nowhere. Some stumbled out of bars on the Lower West Side and some were hanging on the sidewalk outside of CBGB. I woke up next to some others, not sure who they were or where I was. I met everyone else on White Street.

Part of that *everyone*—the friends I came to know.

Meeting Steve Mass was different, and it never really happened until I began working for him. I bumped into him once or twice before but he didn't know me except possibly by sight. I went to the Mudd Club when it opened; after the Richard Lloyd shows in January I started going regularly. Those nights were wild—the sound was incredibly loud and Richard's guitar tore the room apart. I remember walking there after work and hearing the music as I crossed Canal Street. At least I think I did, or think I remember I did.

I was drawn to the place. I felt as though I'd found something. The whole world was there, or what passed for one in my mind in 1979. It was like a new drug but still I had no idea, no clue—and never looked back until now.

End of summer 1980, I was hooked on Montauk. Those last few Sunday afternoons were shaky and heading back to the city was rough. I worked on small paintings, hung out at the beach and coasted along on what always was supposed to be my last line of dope.

When I'd get back to Murray Street I'd pull it together. Drinks at One University and several more at a new club called Danceteria. I'd come in for a landing at the Mudd Club, float around upstairs and see who was going out for breakfast. The only other option was home, and hanging on to the slow burn of Monday morning.

I thought it was the life and for a while it was, until the edges started to fray. Painting was becoming more of a dream and drugs more of a focus. I began drifting away from the heart of what was happening but was too busy to notice.

September 1976 already seemed a distant past—living in the Village and getting settled on Bleecker Street, just the beginning. I found a job and had a short-lived career as a personal assistant to the elderly author and science writer Harland Manchester and his wife, Letitia. They lived in a large apartment above the Cherry Lane Theatre on Commerce Street and he kept an office next door above The Blue Mill Tavern. They were sweet and kind, and the job was easy. I walked to work and was finished by 1 p.m. I stole blue and yellow Valium from their medicine cabinet.

My love life was always more of a sex life. I liked the idea of being involved in a relationship but maintaining one seemed to require more of an effort than I was capable of, or willing to make. When a one-night stand turned into two or three I was ready to move on.

Then I met John, a nice guy who was even more confused than I was. We were both easily distracted and sex eventually became tiresome. He dumped me after six months, in winter 1977. It was done over the phone with a late-night call from San Francisco; he said, "You're a really nice guy, it isn't you." I cried; I was messed up for days and then I got pissed off. I spray-painted *Fuck You* on the wall of his New York City apartment, swiped a few Hawaiian shirts, an old oak file cabinet and a copy of Patti Smith's *Seventh Heaven*. I wore the shirts at the door of the Mudd Club and never once thought about how I got them. I still have the file cabinet and the book became a treasure; the ex-lover, a memory—but a treasure, not so much.

By spring I was fully recovered, spending late nights in the West Side backroom leather bars. Days were spent sharing a workspace on West Fourth with my friends, *New Yorker* cartoonist Michael Maslin and a painter I knew from college named Sarah Heidt. We were working hard, excited to have a large studio to call our own.

Three months later I met a guy wearing a black cowboy hat during the August '77 blackout. I was twenty-three and eager to make bad choices. He was twenty-eight, not quite rough trade and visiting from the Midwest; I called him "Chicago." He stayed for a couple weeks before we said good-bye. I cried again but only for a minute. I thought I got over it and went out that night looking for sex. Nearly forty years past, I still think about Chicago.

In November 1977, I moved to Murray Street, nine blocks south of White, and left a crazy fifteen months on Bleecker Street behind. South of Canal was a different world and I was drawn to the no-man's-land of half-empty buildings and nighttime desolation. Despite the risk, and a fear that no one would ever visit me, I saw opportunity. I took a leap of faith.

Ten months earlier I'd started tending bar at The Ballroom on West Broadway. It's where I met Pat Wadsley when she was writing her "Cabaretbeat" column for the *SoHo News*. I watched battle-axe Broadway legend Ethel Merman get drunk and loud at a table up front and Robert Mapplethorpe occasionally would stop by to meet me after work. Producer Joe Papp, the actress Estelle Parsons and other names, big and small, appeared on stage. The place was an oddball mix of entertainment, insanity, alcohol and drugs; for a while, I fit right in.

A week after the call from Steve Mass, I left a note on the bar. It read simply *Thanks and good-bye*. I'd been working at The Ballroom for over two years and never went back.

Lucky to Be Alive

My friend Steve Miller found his way to Murray Street in November '78. Co-conspirators from high school and college days, Steve and I swam with the Flushing Flyers, the team at the Flushing YMCA. He was one of the first people I went with to the Mudd Club.

Miller was an instigator and inspiration; he remembers the late nights dancing on White Street, followed by early mornings around the kitchen table on Murray. Drugs, alcohol and reckless behavior were nothing new, often taking us to the edge, but one snowy post-Mudd morning I wound up on the lip of my roof listening to Steve play a fiddle at 5 A.M. He refers to some of those experiences as "over the top"—even for him—and placed a few in the "lucky to be alive" category.

Maybe it's true, but at the time we weren't thinking about it and didn't care. Somehow we survived and remember. Not everybody did or can—or wants to.

Rock 'n' Roll

Drifting back more than a decade. Rock 'n' Roll had become a constant. I was always jumping up and down in my bedroom listening to records, informed by the music and the images on the album covers. Staring at the Rolling Stones on the cover of *High Tide and Green Grass*, I wanted the red wide-wale "cords" that Brian Jones was wearing. I wore out my copy of Jefferson Airplane's *Surrealistic Pillow*, the Beatles' *Rubber Soul* and *Sgt. Pepper's Lonely Hearts Club Band*. Big Brother and The Holding Company's *Cheap Thrills* never left my turntable. I peeled back the peel-away banana skin on *The Velvet Underground and Nico* and thought a song called "All Tomorrow's Parties" was a weird song. I knew the words and sang along to "Heroin." I saw Andy Warhol on the news and wanted to know more. I smoked pot and tossed back cough syrup at a neighborhood basement Romilar party. I was staring at my future and didn't know it.

Growing up in New Hyde Park, Long Island, I was the only child of two working parents. I got used to being alone but never got comfortable—always wanting for something I couldn't describe. I saw it and felt it in New York City when I cut school with my friends to hang in Washington Square, on St. Mark's Place or at the free concerts in Central Park. Reading about life in Greenwich Village, I wanted to go for the ride but it was still out of reach.

My first acid trip was a Purple Haze microdot handed to me by my friend Steve in the locker room at the Flushing Y. I took it the next morning before school and laughed my way thru homeroom and the next six periods. Wandering the halls, I believed I found the answers to whatever questions I was asking when it was really just the microdot singing in my ear. I picked up lunch in the cafeteria, holding on to a scoop of instant mashed potatoes when it tried to run away. Then I tried to step inside my locker, laughed too hard, and stepped back out. No one noticed but I wish they had—or maybe they did and I just didn't notice.

I spent over four years at the University of Connecticut, drifting back and forth to New York City, absorbing as much art and music, alcohol and LSD as I could. The experience made me believe I could do anything. I was accepted at NYU for my graduate work (painting and printmaking) and finally said, to no one in particular, "I'm moving to the Village." I registered, set up my courses and schedule, and never saw the inside of NYU again for thirty-five years. I lived at 167 Bleecker Street near Sullivan, on the third floor above a dive called Mill's Tavern. My graduate "work" took place in my apartment, at CBGB's and at Max's. Extra credits, a number of bruises and several cases of the "clap" were all earned at The Mineshaft.

My last acid trip was a '79 vintage orange barrel remake. I split two tabs three ways at the Mudd Club and quickly realized those synthetic sunshine days were gone. Standing on the front steps and winding my way thru the club was a new and different kind of trip.

I was always looking to fit in and stand out at the same time. I was looking for something I couldn't define, some identity specific to me; it was something I wasn't sure I'd ever find simply by going out, hanging out or fucking my brains out—though all of that helped. I needed to find out what other people like me were doing.

The first time I walked into the Mudd Club I knew I was getting close. The music I grew up with was playing alongside sounds that were happening on the spot. The nights spent on the Bowery, Park Avenue South and other joints and dives around town had reopened my eyes, ears and mind. When I got to White Street, lightning struck twice and saved me.

Looking back is a funny thing. The timeline in my mind is faded but linear. I believe what I'm remembering to be true, just a little charred around the edges, worn at the elbows and knees. I was a twenty-five-year-old artist living downtown via Greenwich Village, Long Island, Queens, and Brooklyn (where I was born). I wound up in the thick of it on White Street and Cortlandt Alley, two blocks below Canal—an address nobody knew, yet.

Dark and Golden

Knowing where I wanted to go was one thing; figuring out what to do when I got there was the challenge. Uncomfortable without a drink in one hand and a joint in the other, by the third or fourth drink I was on the way to comfortable but drunk. Hanging out in a club or bar, discovering a new band and listening to new music, I just kept going. I felt myself getting closer.

Hearing a little about the place and reading a few articles in the *Village Voice*—all of it true—was my initiation. CBGB's on the Bowery was Rock 'n' Roll reborn. Patti Smith and Television, Talking Heads and Blondie; along with Richard Hell, the Ramones, and the Dead Boys, they blew the doors off the place. CB's even showcased the new British Invasion featuring The Damned, X-Ray Spex, and The Jam. There were nights I stood near the stage, jaw dropping, mouth open, absolutely stunned. By 1977, the sounds coming out of CBGB's changed everything.

Over a decade earlier, in 1965, Mickey Ruskin gave us Max's Kansas City, the birthplace of hip, cool and beyond. The Velvet Underground became the house band and there was blue chip art on the walls. Emmylou Harris (pre-Gram Parsons) and Debbie Harry waited tables there. Max's showed us all how it was done.

Mickey left in 1975 and by 1978 had moved several times, from The Lower Manhattan Ocean Club and The Locale to One University Place Chinese Chance. Like Max's, One U masqueraded as a bar and

MUD CLUB NEWSLETTER

SCHEDULE JANUARY 26th through FEBRUARY 3:

JANUARY 25th, Thursday night, _ _ _ _ _ _THE **CRAMPS**
10:30 P.M., $4.00

Teenage rockabilly assault on Judeo-Christian
tradition with Bride of Frankenstein.

JANUARY 26th, Friday night, _ _ _ _ _ _ _THE **CRAMPS**
10:30 P.M., $5.00

ditto

JANUARY 27th Saturday night, _ _ _ _ _ _ **D-JAY**   DANCING TIL DAWN
10:30 P.M. $ 2.00

Film Clips

JANUARY 28th, Sunday night, _ _ _ _ _ _ **BIKINI GIRL**   MAGAZINE
10:30 P.M. $4.00

Dance Party with Nervous Rex, Fleshtones
and special guests.

JANUARY 31st, Wednesday night, _ _ _ _ _ **JOE SHOW** JOHN HOLMSTROM
11:00 P.M. $3.00

Unanimated cartoons, Live radio theatre, music.

FEBRUARY 1, Thursday   night _ _ _ _ _ _ **JOE SHOW** JOHN HOLMSTROM
11:00 P.M. $3.00

Ditto

FEBRUARY 2, FRiday night _ _ _ _ _ _ _ **TINA PEEL**   BAND FROM D.C.
10:30 P.M., $4.00

(Teenage accident film to be announced)

FEBRUARY 3, Saturday night _ _ _ _ _ _ _ **D-JAY**
10:30 P.M. $2.00

Dancing

DR. MUDD DECLARES HAWAII NIGHT A SUCCESS:

December 20th saw the B-52's fabulous Freddie Schneider show with Freddie as master
of ceremonies for the Ray Ortiz Royal Hawaiians. Four brown skinned Bronx maidens
demonstrated the native stick dance, twirling batons and moving their grass skirts
seductively. The romantic island atmosphere was disturbed briefly when a Soho artist
enraged at what she took to be Yankee chauvinism directed at the Hawaiian people
shed her fur coat and baring her naked chest stood in front of the four hula dancers as
though to shield them from the morbid stares of the crowd. Then she began screaming and
due to the 20 degree cold could not be removed to the outside. Characteristic quick thinking
by Dr. Mudd located her furs under a pile of beer bottles where she had hidden them. She
was quickly spitited away by an unknown friend. Dr. Mudd noted that he had seen this
trick before at a Vermont Hippie anti-nuclear demonstration where the hippies had entered
the facility in below freezing weather and then hidden their clothing.

MUD [sic] Club Newsletter featuring The Cramps, 1979, courtesy Richard Boch.

restaurant but was totally out of bounds: great art, bad behavior, decent food and lots of drugs—it was all on the menu.

Max's had new owners after Mickey, and its mid- to late-'70s incarnation transformed into a full-on Rock venue. Everybody from Sid Vicious to Devo performed at Max's, and half of everybody still went there.

The city had already wound its way thru a number of dark and golden ages and the club scene kept pace. When Studio 54 opened in April '77 it was the place to go but by 1979 had become a machine. It was crowded and still had its moments but everyone had already been there. Hurrah was a onetime coke bar disco that by the late '70s turned Rock 'n' Roll. Paradise Garage was a dance palace in a machine shop, and DJ Larry Levan and the Paradise sound system— legends in their time. Infinity on Broadway had already burned down and no one I knew was going to 12West. Between The Anvil and The Mineshaft, one was a carnival sideshow, the other a leather-bound inferno. Club 82, New York's oldest drag club, featured a few bands, but kept getting older. Xenon in the West Forties wasn't much; and The Saint, located at the site of the old Fillmore East, was still a year away from opening. Places like The Bottom Line and The Lone Star Café were already becoming institutions. The one thing they all had in common was an ultimate expiration date.

New York's corporate front was on the rise—threatening a take-over—and affecting, infecting and finally eliminating the possibilities and freedom we knew and loved. What many failed to see through the lens of that time was rapidly approaching.

***

I was running around every night and so was everyone I knew. It was easy to find out what was going on, even easier to make friends. Getting high and getting laid was easy. Getting lost was easy too.

I loved the white-light daytime hours of the city, but I was drawn to the weird illuminated darkness of a New York night. I felt anxious getting off work or leaving my apartment, not sure if I was looking for sex, drugs or both. Downtown was an almost gothic Gotham City, parts still desolate. I remember walking alone, late at night, in the middle of the street with no plan and little idea of direction. As screwed up as New York was, I was fearless and ready for anything.

Heading south, Broadway was still a long stretch of empty between Houston and Chambers Street, still a land of opportunity. Walking home in those after-midnight hours, I never passed a single person on the street and there was hardly any late-night traffic below Canal. "Fab 5 Freddy" Brathwaite, a member of the Fabulous 5 crew, remembers those days as "the era before the twenty-four-hour Korean deli." It was a time before containers of cut-up cantaloupe, multicolored bunches of short-stemmed tulips and bottled water drawn from faraway springs. Only a crazy person with a crazy idea would've thought to open a nighttime business below Canal.

The New Club

Performance artist and musician Judy Nylon (whether wrapping people in bandages or vocalizing with Snatch) was a big part of the scene and found most of "the existing venues incorrect for a lot of what was happening." Judy was one of the first to realize the Mudd Club would help correct that.

It wasn't about money, at least in the idea stage, and the concept was simple enough. The new club would be a bar, a place to hang with friends and a venue for art, performance, film and whatever might follow. That's a version of what was told to the building's owner in order to secure a lease. The "whatever might follow" is what made things interesting.

If it sounds easy, it was. In New York City 1978, anything was still possible. The neighborhood south of Canal was rundown, up and coming, or undeveloped, depending on whom you were asking and what they were selling. The space itself was a hole in the wall, minimally transformed by aspiring filmmaker and ambulance service operator Steve Mass, curator and provocateur Diego Cortez, and the incendiary and uncensored Anya Phillips. Years later, when I spoke to Contortions and Bush Tetras guitarist Pat Place, she referred to them as the Radical Three. We laughed but it was true.

Steve, Diego and Anya were on a mission and Steve Mass had the cash to fund it. Legs McNeil, the *Please Kill Me* mastermind and co-founder of *Punk Magazine*, remembered Steve as "the only person at the time with an American Express card," a generous guy who picked up the bar tabs at Phebe's on the Bowery, between sets at CBGB's.

It wasn't long before Steve became the generous guy who gave away a million drinks at Mudd.

The Seeds of an Idea

Steve Mass was born in Macon, Georgia, in 1940, the oldest of three children including a sister and a brother. He was from a southern, liberal, Reformed Jewish family descended from an ultra-Orthodox grandmother. Navigating all that with both ease and discomfort, he was bar mitzvahed and was on his way.

Georgia was the land of golf and nothing was lost on Steve. He was on the high school golf team and his picture appeared in the *Macon Telegraph* acknowledging his talent with a driver, a five iron and a putter. He was also a member of the ROTC. His path to achievement was paved a few years earlier when his scouting career earned him the rank of Eagle Scout, another honor noted in the *Telegraph*. Promise and irony were already in sync.

Steve's college career took him to Northwestern University where he studied anthropology and philosophy; he became interested in the writings of Karl Marx and Søren Kierkegaard. This was deep and direct thought, rooted in sociology, class struggle and a study of the individual. It was also the time of Burroughs, Ginsberg, Kerouac and the Beat Generation. Along with expanded boundaries of acceptability and a lack of conformity, all would eventually play a role at the Mudd Club.

When the fifties ended I was starting first grade, Elvis was "All Shook Up" and the world was getting ready to blow. The Beatles were in Liverpool without a Ringo, Andy Warhol was without a Factory and a Campbell's Soup can was just a can of soup. Marilyn was still alive, filming *The Misfits* with Clark Gable and Montgomery Clift. It was her last film and nearly the end for all three.

The Vietnam conflict was already more than five years old; Castro and Cuba were in revolt and the United States was ready to launch its failed Bay of Pigs Invasion (a great name for such a sad affair). JFK ultimately stared down Khrushchev in a three-way fuck-fest with Fidel Castro in the middle. Just short of nuclear disaster, the standoff became known as the October Missile Crisis and Russia came out of it looking bad. Kennedy was assassinated in

Dallas, Texas, thirteen months later; I was in fifth grade and I remember how everyone cried.

That was the end of 1963. I already knew the words to "Hound Dog" and might've heard "Please, Please Me" or "I Want to Hold Your Hand" on the radio but that was it. I was only ten years old, there was no such thing as a hippie, a Yippie or a Woodstock; a punk was just a punk and the Mudd Club was still fifteen years away.

The seeds of an idea for the club were planted in spring 1978 on a road trip to Memphis where Anya, Diego, Steve and his 16mm movie camera filmed *Grutzi Elvis*. The unreleased phantom, directed by Diego and starring Anya (and as rumor has it, Vernon Presley), was partly shot at Graceland before the crew headed north thru Chicago and began winding their way back east. Diego produced a soundtrack album featuring No Wave stars James Chance, Arto Lindsay, Bradley Field and George Scott. It became one of the obscure pieces of evidence related to the film.

By then everyone was somehow connected; musician and artist Walter Steding called those connections "constellations." In the summer of 1977, when Diego briefly rented a loft below Canal, one of those constellations began to form. The following spring, the Radical Three returned from their road trip and the search for a space began. Within weeks, Steve found a first floor with a basement in the same building where Diego spent the previous summer.

An odd coincidence, another connection and the Walter Steding Constellation Theory was in play. By then I was living just nine blocks away, with less than six degrees between us.

No One Had Any Idea

Independence Day '78 fell on a Tuesday—the endgame of a weekend that seemed to go on forever. Steve Mass, musician John Lurie and his girlfriend Leisa Stroud were out on a joyride, cruising the East Village in an ambulance. The Hells Angels were blocking off East Third Street for a July Fourth celebration, and I was wandering thru SoHo, heading home.

The ambulance turned on the siren, stepped on the gas, and blew thru the barricade. The Angels tossed fireworks and beer bottles. A dozen blocks south I crossed Canal Street thru a cloud of firecracker smoke and kept on walking toward Murray Street. The ambulance headed

B 52's

Halloween
Alert

PARTY
OCT. 31,

Mudd Club
77 White St.
$ 2.52

Opening Night flyer, October 31, 1978: The B-52's for $2.52, courtesy Maureen McLaughlin.

for White Street, and the Angels kept celebrating on East Third. The official opening of whatever Steve, Anya and Diego were planning was just four months away. No one had any idea what to expect.

***

The club found its home at 77 White Street, a nondescript six-story building owned by the artist Ross Bleckner. From Hewlett, Long Island, by way of Cal Arts, Ross arrived in New York City in 1974. Like other young artists before and after, he moved into a loft on Broadway below Canal Street.

MUDD CLUB NEWSLETTER
February 19, 1979

FEBRUARY 21st, WEDNESDAY NIGHT

Crystals
Pick up tips from their lyrics on how to land that special boy. Crystals songs include "Da Doo Ron Ron, Under the Boardwalk, He's A Rebel, Today I Met the Boy I'm Gonna Marry."

Mandy Doll
The current rage of the television kitchen, this smash girl group of the '80's' proclaim shopping mall liberation.

FEBRUARY 22nd, THURSDAY NIGHT
Admission $2.50 for blondes
(not ash or brown)

Blonde Night
Beauty contest judged by Willoughby Sharp (video taped), Debut of new singer, Films including rare, M.M. footage.

FEBRUARY 23rd FRIDAY NIGHT
FEBRUARY 24th, SATURDAY NIGHT

D-JAY DANCING TIL DAWN

FEBRUARY 25th, SUNDAY NIGHT

CLUB CLOSED FOR PRIVATE PARTY

FEBRUARY 26th, MONDAY NIGHT
10:30 P.M. Limited Admission

30 fashion designers from the Soho area. Music by Harold Budd.

FEBRUARY 27th, TUESDAY NIGHT

D-JAY DANCING TIL DAWN

FEBRUARY 28th, WEDNESDAY NIGHT

BLANK GENERATION, film by Amos Poe

*** MUDD CLUB editorial will not be printed this week while Dr. Mudd attends the International Security Conference in Los Angeles. Dr. Mudd hopes to bring back many new security products for testing in the Mudd Club. Dr. Mudd has requested, for purposes of teenage crowd control, that individuals requiring easier entry into the club premesis tear off Dr. Mudd's picture appearing to the right of this paragraph and present it to the doorman.

Newsletter featuring the film *Blank Generation*, 1979, courtesy Marina Lutz.

Just around the corner a "For Sale" was hanging on the front of 77 White, midblock between Broadway and Lafayette. The block was cut in half by Cortlandt Alley, which ran between Leonard Street to the south and Canal Street to the north. The side of Number 77 ran along the alley. Ross saw the sign and bought the building in 1976 for $125,000. When asked why, his answer was simple: "It was for sale."

The lease for the club was signed after Diego reassured Ross that whatever happened, it would be "like a local bar, an art thing." It wasn't the truth but no one, at least yet, had any idea what the truth really was.

Ross' investment came to show unusual, unexpected and lucrative returns but "something like Mickey's One University Place" or a "local bar with low music" wasn't one of them. In September 1978, arriving home after a summer away, Ross couldn't help but notice a new sound system with very large speakers and realized, well before the rest of us, what we were in for.

With a radical aesthetic born of Punk, 77 White was getting ready for something. Diego's later comment that the club was "well-anchored in the art world" was an understatement: roots were everywhere, from Dadaism and the Paris salons to the early days of Max's Kansas City and Andy Warhol's Factories. Steve added his own brand of irony, a twisted sense of humor and the vision to just let it happen.

Punk Magazine *Awards*

On Friday the thirteenth of October, a little more than two weeks before the club's official opening, Steve Mass was busy getting the place ready for the Punk Magazine Awards after-party. Racing against time, a newly assembled crew was trying to turn a stack of plywood and a pile of two-by-fours into a bar and DJ booth. There were still no turntables but there was a sound system—the same one that frightened Ross Bleckner the first time he spotted it. Future star DJ David Azarch was in the basement putting together a mix-tape to provide the music and the beat. The liquor license pending, Punk Magazine cofounder John Holmstrom paid Steve five hundred dollars to stock the bar. The awards were being handed out earlier in the evening at Club Hollywood, a not-very-Punk dive on Second Avenue in the East Village, described by Holmstrom as a "sleaze pit."

There were a lot of loose ends, not to mention the disaster that went down the previous day.

Nancy Spungen's death, allegedly at the hands of her Sex Pistol boyfriend, Sid Vicious, occurred on Thursday, October 12, 1978. It was the kind of nightmare no one saw coming. An accidental overdose maybe—but not murder, and no one knew how to respond or react. I thought it was sad watching the end of that brief era unfold, and even from a safe distance I could sense the tragedy and chaos. Nancy was dead; Sid, beyond redemption or repair.

The awards ceremony went on despite what happened, and presenters, guests and nominees included everyone from Lou Reed and Joey Ramone to Harvey Keitel and Malcolm McLaren. Club Hollywood was nearly destroyed in what turned into a free-for-all, but everyone still made it to the after-party at the not-quite-ready club on White Street. The night that started out as a clusterfuck quickly turned into a huge success. Everybody got drunk, Steve Mass reimbursed John Holmstrom his five hundred and it wasn't long before the place on White Street had a name.

The Line Outside

The Mudd Club officially opened its doors on Halloween 1978. A performance by the Animal X configuration Xerox kicked things off, and a new band from Athens, Georgia, called the B-52's was the headliner. The ongoing citywide newspaper strike that began back in August eliminated any chance of front-page coverage.

The B-52's were the perfect quirk: with a unique look and distinctive sound, they had already played Max's and CBGB to a varied but enthusiastic response. Mudd was a different story and by October the 45 rpm version of "Rock Lobster" on DB Records was an underground hit. Flyers mentioned the two-dollar-fifty-two-cent admission charge and the cartoon-style map on the backside directed people to a neighborhood that barely existed and a club that no one knew. Curiosity and word of mouth did the rest. Opening night the place was packed, the stage makeshift and the line outside ran all the way to Broadway. Everybody remembers being there, whether they really were or not.

Mudd quickly became the place to go if you could find it. Word spread and people started hunting down a deserted little pocket of

New York sometimes referred to as Industrial Chinatown. Taxi drivers started to hear the words *White Street* and the line down the street turned into a mob around the door. The early days passed and there was no stopping the momentum; someone needed to stand outside and get a grip on what was already out of control. Eventually that someone was me.

Whether you were looking to dance, get drunk, be enlightened or get laid, White Street became the next wave-No Wave alternative. We were children of the fifties, the sixties and the Sexual Revolution, fueled by whatever we could consume, including one another. Everyone was willing to try anything at least twice. With little use for the words *no*, *stop* or *enough*, the Mudd Club was perfect.

The Talent Pool

I continued bartending in SoHo and drifted in and out of Mudd. I walked in on filmmaker and actress Tina L'Hotsky and her Crazy Spanish Girls party in early December, picked up on the crazy, while appreciating anything even remotely Spanish. I'd see various Talking Heads, a Blondie or two in the corner and Andy Warhol standing near, but never on, the dance floor. When I spotted Frank Zappa leaning into the DJ booth I wondered, *really*? I walked past, an arm's length away, as our elbows hadn't started rubbing.

January 1979. The Cramps freaked out the Mudd Club with a loud Psychobilly grind that included such hits as "Human Fly" and "Surfin' Bird." A few months later, the "big names" started to appear; a few years later, the Cramps returned and *pussy did the dog* (something everyone, including me, was waiting for).

Joe Jackson performed on Sunday, April 8, but I only liked a couple of songs, and never really got it. The legendary Sam and Dave got onstage a few weekends later, and it was the first time on my watch that I got to see the real deal. By late summer, Talking Heads took the stage while Marianne Faithfull, X, Lene Lovich, and the Brides of Funkenstein waited in the wings.

There were so many great performances: scheduled, impromptu, logical and out of left field. The locals and the regulars were the staple and the stable and performed as part of the White Street experience. They included everyone you could imagine and some you never could. John Cale, Chris Spedding, Judy Nylon and Nico, John

Lurie and Philip Glass were just a few. Writers and poets such as William S. Burroughs, Max Blagg, Cookie Mueller and "Teenage Jesus" Lydia Lunch all wound up on the Mudd Club stage. The talent pool was so deep and occasionally dark that even *Hollywood Babylon*'s Luciferian auteur Kenneth Anger got involved.

Steve's willingness and generosity along with his guarded enthusiasm offered support to a local community of artists, musicians and filmmakers. Together with Diego's early influence and Anya's short-lived but "dominating" spirit, the Mudd Club became an instant happening, a free-for-all with No Wave orchestration and very few rules.

Diego described the Mudd Club as "a container, a vessel, but certainly not the only one in town." What made the place unique was its blank-canvas emptiness. When the space filled up, *it* happened and everybody wanted to be a part. A living, breathing work of art, it was beautiful and way off-center, a slice of golden time.

I was lucky, and soaked it all in.

The Job

By early 1979 the secret was out and someone truly had to start watching the door. Steve Mass briefly hoped performance artist and future femme fatale Joey Arias would be the one whose eye would look after the downtown crowd and get the mix just right.

Joey worked as a "shop girl" at Fiorucci, the hip fashion emporium on East Fifty-ninth Street. Anyone with a sense of cool and a willingness to indulge in dubious taste shopped there. Joey, whose taste remains unquestionable, had an active social life and was out every night, particularly at Studio 54. He knew "everyone," something Steve Mass liked to believe about people who worked the door, which by this time had turned into a nightly round of chaos.

It seemed the perfect fit, and Joey handled the crowd with what he called "thumbs up—thumbs down, Caesar at the Roman Colosseum" decisiveness. The only glitch was that he happened to be working with singer and visionary performer Klaus Nomi, who was concerned that Joey's position would alienate potential fans—a worry that led Joey to give up the door after just two weeks.

Joey Arias set the bar high and paved the way for all who followed. Designer Robert Molnar (boyfriend of B-52 Fred Schneider), working in the Mudd Club "checkroom," was up next, and soon became one of the first official doorkeepers. Joey Kelly, already part of the team, was there at the beginning and helped build the place. Colter Rule came by one night, found Steve, and volunteered his services.

Louie Chaban soon stepped in alongside Robert after artist Ronnie Cutrone and fashion icon Edwige brought him to the Mudd Club. They were at One University when Ronnie said "I found this new place," and for Louie, "that was the beginning." Rebecca Christensen, wife of Contortions drummer Donnie and personal assistant to oil heiress and arts patron Christophe de Menil, told Steve Mass, "Hire him!"

Louie was perfect and did a great job. He had a sexy look, a sense of humor and very little patience. His biggest problem: finding enough time for himself on the dance floor or in the bathrooms.

That's when I came along.

My first night at the door of 77 White was in the cold early spring of 1979. I showed up at midnight, the club was already open, and the place was busy. I stood there, not sure if Steve Mass told anyone to expect me or expected me to tell someone that I was working. I thought, *Okay, I get it*, but really I didn't.

Joey Kelly was one of the people outside with me, and a woman named Gretchen Stibolt was taking money at the door. They were the only ones who talked to me. He was busy handling the crowd, and she was as frazzled as anyone would be collecting three-dollar covers with a cocktail in one hand and a cigarette in the other. Gretchen was my first real friend at the Mudd Club and she was a lifesaver.

A guy named Glenn McDermott seemed to be in charge of something but I was never sure what. He stepped outside, said hello and disappeared. Steve came by, said "Oh hi," the same as during my ten-second interview.

I was on my own, afraid to do much of anything. I felt as I did in high school—I still didn't fit in and just stood there, wondering if this job was really for me.

When I turned around Meat Loaf was behind me talking to Joey. He was wearing a velvet jacket with a ruffled shirt, sweating, his hair stuck to his face. Definitely not something I wanted to get close to, physically or musically. I looked away and remembered Steve Mass telling me he wanted to avoid the bloated "seventies music" and "limo crowd." Maybe he was talking hypothetically or maybe I needed clarification.

Poison Ivy Rorschach, The Cramps, post-performance, Mudd Club, by Alan Kleinberg.

The Loaf lingered but I ignored it, trying not to focus on what came to be considered a prime example of "two cover charge large." When Steve suggested excluding people of a certain size, I just listened and nodded, still apprenticing my role as judge and jury.

I stood around, the night flew by, and the overweight singer left in a cab. I saw people I knew, people I admired, and people I wanted to know. All was a blur and left me wondering what I'd gotten myself into. At 4 A.M., I grabbed a beer and walked home—my head spinning—my ego inflating and deflating a half-dozen times. Steve called the next day and asked me to work that night. I knew I had the job if I wanted it but still wasn't sure what the job really was. Maybe I had to open the chain and start letting people in to figure it out.

Standing on what amounted to a loading dock and facing a crowd that wanted in was both funny and frightening at once. People in the street looked at me and raised a few fingers, letting me know how many they were. Knowing I was the possible opening between where they stood and the front door, I hesitated to respond. Luckily for me, the chain did the talking.

I kept to myself those first few weeks, ignored by the staff but occasionally told what to do. I was somewhere between wanting to be accepted and doing the accepting. I was a stranger but wanted to feel at home. Biding my time without knowing it, I was waiting for something to happen. Then it did.

I was just getting started when I was exiled to the downstairs bar for a night or two. A week later, I was sent upstairs to work the "beer bottle bathtub bar" of the second floor. After two weeks of pouring drinks and opening bottles of Miller and Heineken, I missed Gretchen and Joey and Louie. I was ready to get back outside.

Shuffling Me Around

I'd been at the club barely a month, working the door and filling in at the upstairs bar. The Mudd Club's version of management seemed to think they were in charge and kept shuffling me around; they didn't get why Steve wanted me out front or why I was even hired.

Finally, one night Steve confronted me. He wanted to know what I was doing behind the bar other than making friends and handing out a lot of free drinks. I didn't have an answer even though I was learning the pecking order: figuring out who drank for free, who thought they should, and who got a free drink because it was the easiest way to make them go away. It was like some kind of mad Darwinian process and I assumed the information would come in handy, whether at Mudd or as a life lesson. I also understood who was paying me and knew the club wouldn't be happening were it not for Steve Mass. No matter who did what or which way things went, Steve called the shots. Working behind a bar wasn't what he hired me for and by the next night I was back outside. Management didn't say a word but had to know something was up—like time.

By then I started to settle in, slowly realizing that *fitting in* was more mind over matter. Despite the realization, I often needed a joint to lift my spirits, a drink to grease the conversation and cocaine to numb the fear. At that point I was free to do whatever I wanted as long as I stayed outside and worked the door. I reported only to Steve and didn't answer to anyone else. That was one thing that never changed. Management never interfered with me again and Steve rarely if ever bothered me about anything. If there were a need to brief or debrief me, the wall phone rang in the entryway and I'd be given my orders or asked to come upstairs. It might be as simple as looking out for some behind-the-scenes person from *Saturday Night Live* or making sure his brother Larry got safely inside; other times it might be an off-duty cop and his wife, an obscure foreign journalist, or some underage and unshaven East Village debutante.

Steve's communication style was simple, no frills, few questions and no wasted words. I'd usually try to respond with something amusing, informative or ridiculous. Our conversations were often brief, occasionally interesting and always a little strange. I liked Steve, and in our own way we connected, but I still looked at him as some kind of peculiar underground celebrity. I respected him and believe he respected me but I felt awkward and hesitant to offer either opinion or suggestion (something that plagued me for years to come). Even so, when the nights got crazy, so did I, and to his credit and mine, Steve let me do my thing. Not everyone had it so easy.

Either by accident, necessity or default, it was tall, curly-haired and friendly Glenn McDermott who tried to take on the task of "managing" the Mudd Club. I'm not sure if *manager* was really his title and even less sure anyone could've handled something so expressively free-form. There were hardly any straight lines in the game plan when it came to getting the place open each night and fewer when it came to closing it down at daybreak. I think Glenn scheduled the bartenders and occasionally the DJs, ordered the liquor and tended to minor repairs. He might have scheduled some of the door people but never me. He looked like he was working hard, but maybe it was cocaine that left him out of breath and running around or hiding out in the basement. It was a routine I came to know.

The Cocktail Napkin

I barely knew Brooke Delarco, a sound technician who worked with The Feelies, the B-52's and Richard Lloyd, among others. She was at White Street from the beginning and her contribution was a key element that affected anyone who ever walked thru the doors. When Steve Mass handed her a cartoon schematic doodled on a cocktail napkin by musical superman Brian Eno, she laughed but didn't think very much. When she went ahead and built the Mudd Club sound system on her own, she blew the place away.

Steve understood the importance of a great PA and provided Brooke with a generous budget. She picked out mikes, extremely large speakers, woofers, several Crown amps, and a sixteen-channel deluxe soundboard. Using her experience at Vanguard Records, a bit of formal training from the Institute of Audio Research and her intuitive sense of sound, she put it all together. Joey Kelly helped hoist and hang the speaker stack from the ceiling as Brooke watched nervously. A quick sound check had the room vibrating.

Brooke worked the boards for the bands she knew. She liked a live performance as loud and clear as the system could handle. She didn't last very long on White Street and was gone by the time I got there but that sound system was her Mudd Club legacy.

Maybe Steve Mass liked to think Brian Eno designed the system; who wouldn't? Brooke just thought about the cocktail napkin and kept smiling.

Sound of Mudd

Late April '79. I kept doing my job and the door staff seemed to be functioning in its own appropriate and sometimes inappropriate way. The mix we sent inside helped fuel the fire and White Street became *the* place to dance. DJ David Azarch went from making a mixed tape for a pre-opening event to becoming the Sound of Mudd.

David was already a star and I'd been at the door just five weeks when Anita Sarko arrived from the Motor City by way of Atlanta. A former radio DJ with an eclectic taste in music, Anita knew how to spin and went after a job on White Street. She dropped off tapes that wound up getting lost, gently muscled her way into the club when she had to, and strongly let her opinions be known. That's another thing that never changed.

The night of Anita's "audition" Steve didn't even show up. When he asked her how it went, she said, "Great!" The process seemed even more passive-aggressive than my own trial by fire but in the end it didn't matter. Steve said, "You're hired" and the New York chapter of Anita Sarko's DJ career began. She offered DJ David a worthy partner in crime and her vinyl collection added a new dimension to Mudd's playlist. Despite the games Steve played, and the odd musical requests she endured, Anita became an essential part of the Mudd Club sound.

By now there was no stopping the Mudd Club's dance floor, and the roster of DJs included both the tenured and short-lived. When musician and Punk legend Howie Pyro got behind the turntables he took everybody for a wild ride, splattering the room with Fifties Rock and Las Vegas Grind, some Goo Goo Muck and his own collection of children's records. Encouraged by Steve to play the Chipmunks doing back-to-back Beatles songs, Howie followed up with their squeaky rodent version of "On Top of Old Smokey." Steve urged Howie to keep it up until both he and the dance floor felt uncomfortable and alienated. An inside joke without many insiders, Steve walked away smiling and somewhat amused.

Howie's other contributions to Mudd life and culture came as both a member of The Blessed and Steve's posse of troubled teenage party planners. Behind the scenes or in the middle, Howie helped orchestrate as much mayhem as music.

DJ Sean Cassette had a Mudd moment early on. The club had just opened, I was still a customer, and I remember only his leather jacket with *Cassette* stenciled on the back. The next time I saw him was at a new club on Thirty-seventh Street in summer 1980. Danny Heaps, a future music biz professional, was working the turntables the night I started; he played music I liked but never put a stamp on the Mudd Club sound. Danny was friendly but seemed skeptical or unconvinced of my involvement. I always felt that he was part of Glenn's crew and he was gone by the summer.

Milk 'n' Cookies vocalist Justin Strauss, encouraged by designer and Mudd Club regular Abbijane, returned from the West Coast and within weeks he was spinning records on White Street. Working the nights in between David and Anita, he was a perfect fit.

The multitalented Johnny Dynell got his start under the tutelage of DJ Anita, and by January 1980, he was working the turntables all by himself. I'd be outside, hear the call, leave my post and drift inside. I watched that dance floor move in ways beyond what anyone could have choreographed or even imagined. I jumped in and went with it.

DJ Johnny called the Mudd Club "The Cradle of Civilization."

Reality

For me, the Mudd Club is where I found out what was going on, where I started to figure out what I was doing and where I eventually got lost. Like a childhood memory, it was the place where time began. The world might be spinning out of control, the bad news cycle on endless repeat, but White Street was both shelter and a different kind of storm.

The staff at the door—Joey, Robert, Louie and me—remained in position for the moment. Gretchen was still the cashier, and I was mostly out in front with the exception of a few events on the second floor.

I began to take what I was doing seriously and thought of it as a big deal. I was enthusiastic about being there. If anyone questioned my choices, I had little response and even less need to defend them. It became obvious that together we knew or at least recognized the art, music, fashion and neighborhood crowd. We had the great White Street convergence covered and everything was working fine, up to a point.

Then reality began to set in and Steve wanted a house full of paying customers. That meant the number of people who paid at the door versus those who didn't needed an adjustment.

The party was getting crowded and someone had to pay the rent.

2.
JOAN CRAWFORD, NYQUIL AND FRIED CHICKEN

Jackie Curtis and David Bowie in Ronnie Cutrone's Cage, 1979, by Bobby Grossman.

Costume parties and Halloween always made me uncomfortable. As a kid, costumes left me feeling alone and isolated; as an adult, I refused to wear one. Never understanding the appeal of dressing as a pirate, a clown or Superman, I avoided even the possibility. Mudd Club theme parties were different; here, I felt no more or less estranged from everyone else. Maybe I was making progress or maybe it was the alcohol and cocaine.

The Joan Crawford Mother's Day Celebration took place on Sunday, May 13, 1979. I wasn't frightened or uncomfortable and it didn't disappoint. A greeting card invitation suggested maternal attire, forbade wire coat hangers and offered the lure of a free buffet. Pretty boys with thick arched eyebrows came dressed as the always handsome Joan; a dozen bruised and battered daughter Christinas, plenty of booze and lots of Quaaludes helped turn the evening appropriately tragic. Juvenile, heavy-handed and right on target, it was a real Happy *Mommies Dearest*.

Political incorrectness was part of Mudd's recurring theme and despite any shame or regret there was a demented sense of freedom that came with the ability to speak and act without thinking. Collective memory helps clarify my late-night blackouts and the good or even bad memories at last fall into place. Today I mention a name, you tell me what you remember and maybe it all comes back. Drunken sex in a bathroom might be happily lost but a patriot-themed Combat Love party with the tagline "Nuke 'em till they glow" is unforgettable even thru the blur.

Behind the scenes there was never a shortage of gofers, jail-bait and Mudd Club stars willing to set up and get things started, some even coming up with their own ideas. Tina L'Hotsky's inspired events were one thing, while the whim of a fresh-faced sixteen-year-old with big tits and no underpants was another. In the latter case, Steve generally mumbled a non sequitur response and handed out the money to make it happen.

The Dead Rock Stars Rock 'n' Roll Funeral Ball was already in the works but still a nightmare away. A Soul Night celebration with pimps, hookers and uptown fried chicken was somewhere on the horizon. Three months in, I remained the new guy but I was getting hungry; and no matter how strange and offbeat things got, there was something comfortable if not always familiar about the club's *feels like home* insanity.

Teenage rebellion past its expiration date, 77 White was the house party when your parents were away, smoking pot in the basement or drinking and dropping acid at the dance in the high school gym. Alcohol, drugs and sloppy sex were an adventure at fifteen and by twenty-five, the bad behavior felt new again. The Mudd Club was just darker and louder. I looked around and thought it might last forever.

The Night in Play

Walking the line between awe and detachment was a nightly challenge I didn't see coming. Feeling alone in someone's company confused me and reminded me of my childhood but I was sure this situation was different. Chain in hand and smoking a cigarette, I was surprised to find myself passing what amounted to judgment, considering how unsure I was of myself. Whether you were a troubled teen, a musician or an artist celebrating a Guggenheim retrospective didn't matter.

You are cordially invited to attend

JOAN CRAWFORD
MOTHER'S DAY CELEBRATION

in conjunction with the
INTERNATIONAL YEAR OF THE CHILD

Sunday, May Thirteenth, Nineteen Hundred Seventy-Nine
at the MUDD CLUB, Seventy-Seven White Street

Maternal attire suggested. Abused children admitted free.
There will be a buffet, Joan Crawford films and many
distinguished guests. Pepsi Cola MOTHER OF THE YEAR
Certificate to be awarded to the guest whose attire best captures
the spirt of Miss Crawford's career.

No wire coat hangers permitted

By invitation only
ADMIT TWO

Joan Crawford Mother's Day Celebration invitation, 1979, courtesy Marina Lutz.

My job was to make sure that if you were supposed to get in you did, even though "supposed to" was often arbitrary.

Learning to go with a first impression, avoiding confrontation and working without a guest list was the easy part; reading Steve's mind, or staring at the outsiders who didn't have a chance, was harder. There were times when I felt like those people, despite always having managed to ease my way at least halfway in. Then I surprised myself, suddenly moved past the middle and wound up working the Mudd Club door. Steve trusted me to get it right and most of the time I did. Thankful for that trust, though I never said so at the time, my gratitude for Steve and the job came largely in retrospect.

Standing on those front steps, I watched as 77 White took on a life of its own. The mixed-up soundtrack, the dark No Wave sensibility and a disjointed beat playing at full volume provided the full embrace. The performers and events were as varied and off-kilter as the fit was perfect. The dance floor was a wildfire and the bar, three deep. Whether by strategy or luck, the fruit of inspiration or happy accident, Steve Mass brought *smarts* to the party and the rest just happened. His friendship or acquaintance with such musicians as The Contortions and James Chance, filmmakers such as

Amos Poe and journalists like Legs McNeil was just a beginning: the three-way brainstorm on the road to Memphis pushed things a little further. A Brian Eno connection through Judy Nylon and Diego along with introductions to Talking Heads, Blondie and the B-52's made things interesting. Handing out a free drink to anyone who looked thirsty sealed the deal. Beyond that, it was all about the people who wanted in, and made it past the door.

Once inside, the sound of Mudd, like everything else, remained *anything goes*. Walter Steding's violin could fill the room and make it spin; Screamin' Jay Hawkins rising from a coffin singing "I Put a Spell on You" was tough to beat. Actor and Warhol superstar Jackie Curtis did just that, with an amphetamine crash/vodka-fueled cover of the tried and true: Elvis Presley's "Loving You." I was unsure whether to laugh or cry.

Later, when a smiling David Bowie caught up with Jackie on the second floor, photographer Bobby Grossman snapped a few pictures of them in one of Ronnie Cutrone's steel cages. No one else paid any attention, it was business as usual, but today those pictures place a mark in time. They hold a memory of just another night on White Street.

Things got started around 11:30 or midnight with a few people at the bar and even fewer dancing. Art world legend Billy Kluver, a scientist and engineer turned multimedia creative partner of Robert Rauschenberg, was often first to arrive. After a dinner at One University he and his wife Julie Martin would stop by, take a spin on the dance floor and leave before things heated up. They were in their late fifties, and I thought they were sweet but very old.

The place started getting busy around 1 A.M., some nights earlier. The DJ had the dance floor in a frenzy while inspired scheduling of avant-garde pioneers Philip Glass, Glenn Branca and Dickie Landry added something to the mix that might've been missing elsewhere. The 2 A.M. live performance became the sudden move that kept the night in play, the bar and bathrooms busy and everyone entertained. Despite the distractions and amusement, the door was my job and I tried to focus.

By 3 A.M. it was well past the witching hour but the Mudd Club wouldn't or couldn't stop. When things wound down around 4 or 5, the dance floor had its own stories to tell but was too beaten and battered to come clean. By that time I was either upstairs, dancing somewhere else, or riding the nighttime high toward noon.

***

Fashion show twirl, 1980, by Nick Taylor.

The art world might have been where the Mudd Club was anchored but everyone came to drink and dance. Filmmakers and photographers, painters, sculptors, dealers and patrons either crowded the down-stairs bar or attempted to navigate the second floor. Whether it was the party after an opening, the next stop beyond One University or the pursuit of whatever's happening, everyone was headed this way. They stood side by side with Rock 'n' Roll, from Iggy to the Stones, assorted Sex Pistols and Pretenders, while the soon-to-be-known unknowns stepped in alongside. That was the mix and the moment; the White Street scene perched on the cusp of '79 and '80 was a new and different take on Max's Kansas City's late-'60s so-cial riot. Whatever I missed back then was happening again, and it seemed everyone wanted to be part of it.

Fashion from the streets of London and the Lower East Side was also trickling down and taking shape at the door and inside 77 White. It was downtown couture and retro cool, thrift shop chic, Rock 'n' Roll, Punk and leather. Mary Lemley's painted paper dress-es, Millie David's plastic wraps and the Western wear of Katy K all found a home and audience on White Street. Francine Hunter's Jungle Red Studio style had only a short walk from Desbrosses Street before it hit the dance floor, while British design legend Zandra Rhodes' arrival was a one-night go-round of high-end fashion tourism.

Never a boy Teri Toye could show up wearing anything, look beautiful and keep people guessing. Boy Adrian was all-boy sexy, whether he was platinum blond or brunette. Joey Arias and the kids from Fiorucci were hanging out after a hard day on Fifty-ninth Street, and Klaus Nomi's inspired visions of the future were becoming a now look. Designer Anna Sui and photographer Steven Meisel were just starting to make a move, and Maripol was Polaroiding her way forward, looking for the next big or medium-sized thing. Betsey Johnson, who'd seen it all, was seeing it again. She practically lived around the corner, stopped by nearly every night and staged one of her early namesake collections on the Mudd Club "runway."

Then, now and future, the old guard, pioneers, and next-wave contenders walked up to the door and usually went right inside. When a guy looking like an auto mechanic in a dirty white T-shirt approached I told Gretchen it was the artist Richard Serra. She smiled, stopped asking him for three dollars and let him thru. Painter Brice Marden, handsome, easygoing and wearing a fairly clean shirt, breezed in without a problem. Dead Boy Cheetah Chrome with no shirt at all was right behind him. A minute later I sent in two kids from the neighborhood; they just wanted to dance but didn't have any money. Then I looked at Gretchen and we both laughed. I realized that at least for the moment, I was part of what was happening.

Performance artist, shop girl and Strange Party entertainer Joey Arias called the Mudd Club "one big Petri dish." Walter Steding would consider it a vast new constellation. Photographer Marcia Resnick said it best and filmmaker Eric Mitchell agreed, "It was a democratic society once you got inside."

Today this is one of the precious commodities vanished from New York. The Democratic Society phenomenon, in terms of nightlife or city life in general, is gone. Our culture's become fractured; the mix no longer exists. There's no longer a scene, not to mention a heart.

What Are They Doing Here?

I was still figuring out how to turn a mob in the street into that Democratic Society while Steve was trying to figure out how to keep up with day-to-day, night-to-night repairs. An ad in the *Village*

Voice reading "Wanted—Carpenters High Pay" seemed like it might be the answer.

Charles Patty called the number listed in the ad and in less than an hour the carpenter job turned to plumbing. There were two clogged sinks and a broken toilet at the Mudd Club, conditions that were becoming routine. The new plumber had a full-time job.

Several weeks later, when Steve tried his hand at plunging, Charles stood by, knowing the second-floor toilet needed more. Steve wasn't giving up when one of the bartenders ran into the bathroom exclaiming, "Steve, Princess Caroline is downstairs!" Keeping his eye on the clog and without missing a beat, Steve calmly responded, "Maybe she can help."

From where I stood I could see everything, and between the buzz and word of mouth, White Street became the number-one after-midnight destination. With a half-dozen cabs, two or three limos and a crowd around the door, Princess Caroline of Monaco had to wait until we introduced ourselves across the chain. She brought along her own personal dance partner, while husband Philippe Junot and Peppo Vanini from Xenon (the club, not the planet) stayed at the bar and never broke a sweat. Polite and almost charming, the princess didn't need anything special—she danced while Junot and Peppo drank. When I checked back it seemed as if they were having fun, though it was hard to tell. I can't remember if I rolled my eyes or smiled.

The following weekend, a face in the crowd looked at me from across the chain and said, "Hi, I'm Caroline Kennedy." Along with her cousin Kerry, the children of America's "royalty" were friendly and without pretense—ready to drink, dance and run around. I brought them inside and introduced Caroline to Steve, who ordered her a beer and gave her a playing card as a VIP pass so she could get upstairs. (She didn't need it, but it was the thought.) Caroline walked away with a thank you and a smile and Steve wondered out loud, "What are *they* doing here?" Still pulling up my Long Island roots and easily impressed, I responded, "Steve, it's the Mudd Club."

A minute later I was back outside unsure whether I was a Kennedy associate or just hired help holding a chain.

When the Hollywood hotshots came and went no one really cared. Stallone walked in, looked around and quickly exited what he considered a dump. The place was happening, but Rocky didn't get it. I preferred the big-name clowns who stuck around and made themselves at home. Dan Aykroyd was already living in a loft on the fourth

DR. MUDD ACHIEVES FLOOR CARE BREAKTHROUGH:

After 6 months of experimentation Dr. Mudd has come much closer to finding a solution to disco floor abuse. After inspecting many uptown disco floors he came to the conclusion that all they were doing was applying layers over an existing surface. The fragile surface was easily scuffed especially by lethal stiletto heels. Through careful research Dr. Mudd found a floor similar to the Mudd Club at the Bergen Shopping Mall in Paramus New Jersey and located the mall manager. Dr. Mudd spent days watching vital young teenagers abuse the shopping center floors with chewing gum, broken glass, urination and other unmentionable perversions that tested the wood to its limits. The mall manager had been using a special technique which impregnated the fibers of the wood itself with a prophylactic substance. The substance requires further testing but Dr. Mudd is confident that it will be suitable for the Mud Club.

RESEARCHING OF APPROPRIATE DRESS CODE CONTINUES AT MUD CLUB:

Dr. Mudd is trying to arrange for private screenings of films that would help Mud Club patrons in hair styling and clothing selection. To date he has selected "They Came From Beyond Space , Barbarella, Daughter of Dracula and Bride of Frankenstein."

DR. MUDD DESIGNATES FEBRUARY 2nd AS TEENAGE AUTO SAFETY NIGHT:

Sensitive to the tragedy of parents whose teenagers have mangled themselves in thrill-seeking joy rides Dr. Mudd is trying to obtain films such as THE LAST PROM AND DRIVING DRINKING & DRUGS from government sources for showing on Feb. 2. The sight of vital young bodies crushed in fast cars, bloodied short shorts, muscular young jocks who will never see the locker room again has moved Dr. Mudd's sense of civic responsibility and he has decided to forbid playing songs promoting auto speed. Such songs as LEADER OF THE PACK by the Shangri-Las would be deemed appropriate. Dr. Mudd intends to commission an artist to paint a mural depicting the Jayne Mansfield tragedy for permanent display in the Mud Club basement. To make his point absolutely clear Dr. Mud has engaged a teenage band with a perfect driving record. They are Tina Peel from Washington, D.C. and they have commuted scores of times between Washington and New York without incident.

MUDD CLUB

77 WHITE STREET

NEW YORK CITY

227-7777

Newsletter featuring notes on dress code, floor care and teen auto safety, 1979.

floor with writer Rosie Shuster when John Belushi, Bill Murray and Brian Doyle-Murray were letting loose and getting looser downstairs. Even after Dan and John opened their own Blues Brothers Bar on Hudson Street, Mudd was still one of the places where the *Saturday Night Live* crew tossed around the crazy in their spare time. They were nice guys, though I did think Belushi was a bit more passionate than the rest of us. Running wild, he was upstairs and down, with my friend Phyllis in a blonde wig and hot pursuit. Sweating, out of breath, and carrying on about the girl that was chasing him, Belushi pounded the bar and rattled a few bottles but not much else.

Then Gilda Radner stopped by wearing a pleated skirt cut below the knee, saddle shoes and ankle socks while I stood there, just short of starstruck. She went inside and joined the familiar fray. The real revelation: seeing saddle shoes at the Mudd Club.

Another night, a soft cackle from somewhere in the crowd was coming from Bella Abzug, one of New York's great activist voices of freedom. The outspoken United States Congresswoman came by wearing one of her famous hats with her husband Martin on her arm. Hanging with me at the door before going inside, she kept talking and asking questions. I kept working, trying to explain why the club was so popular while no one outside could figure out what the fuck was going on. I was honored to have had the opportunity and happy that Bella became part of the mix.

Inside Out Upside Down

I looked at the crowd inside the club and out on the street. I was part of it but at times felt more outside than in. Everyone was young, some very, and some just at heart. I was just a few months short of twenty-six, and I loved everything about New York City in the '70s. There was hardly a condo below Canal, barely a tourist, and not a Century 21 shopping bag in sight. New York City, along with the Mudd Club, were leaving one decade behind and moving toward a period of seismic change. Sixties response to fifties conservatism brought about the excess of the seventies. The chaos was still reactionary but different—the tripped-out dream nearly ten years past, having crashed mid-nightmare. The Kennedy and King assassinations combined with seven years of escalation in Vietnam nearly destroyed the country's morale if not the country itself.

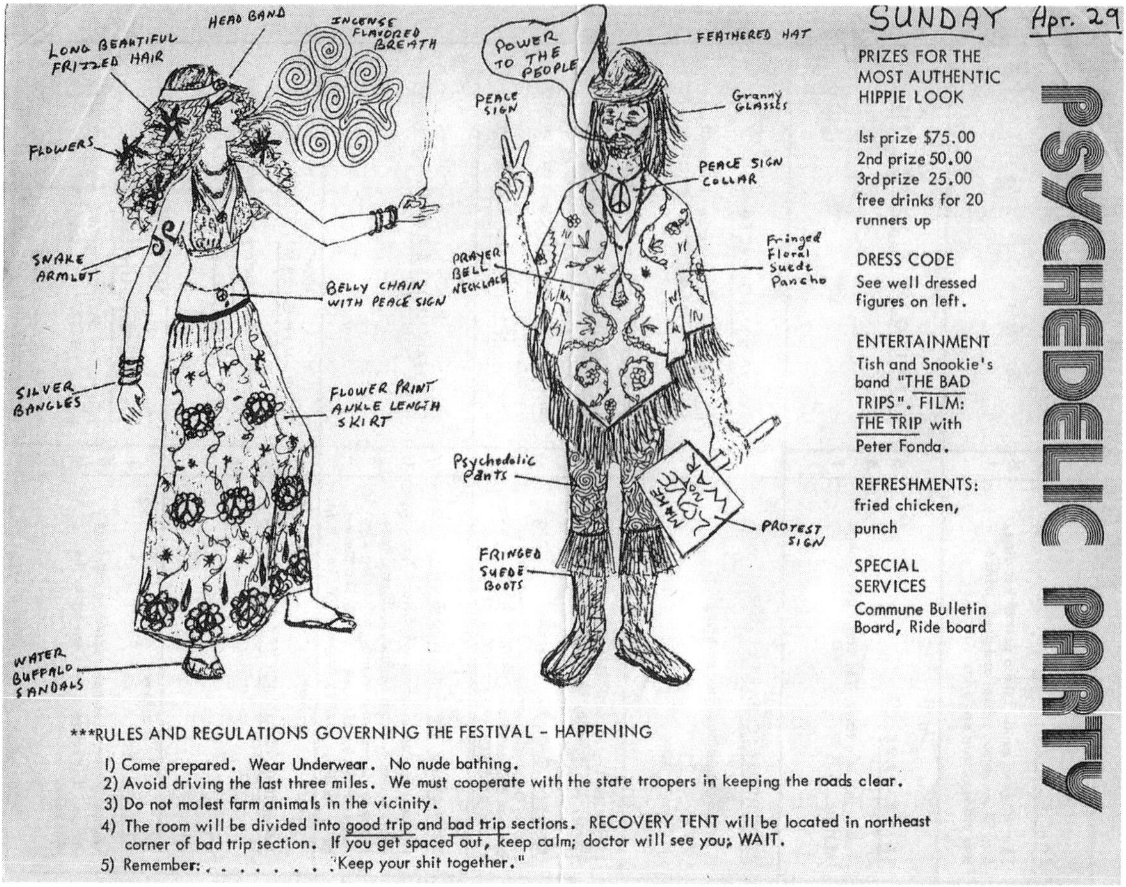
SUNDAY Apr. 29
PSYCHEDELIC PARTY
PRIZES FOR THE MOST AUTHENTIC HIPPIE LOOK
Ist prize $75.00
2nd prize 50.00
3rd prize 25.00
free drinks for 20 runners up
DRESS CODE
See well dressed figures on left.
ENTERTAINMENT
Tish and Snookie's band "THE BAD TRIPS". FILM: THE TRIP with Peter Fonda.
REFRESHMENTS:
fried chicken, punch
SPECIAL SERVICES
Commune Bulletin Board, Ride board
LONG BEAUTIFUL FRIZZED HAIR
HEAD BAND
INCENSE FLAVORED BREATH
FLOWERS
SNAKE ARMLET
BELLY CHAIN WITH PEACE SIGN
SILVER BANGLES
FLOWER PRINT ANKLE LENGTH SKIRT
WATER BUFFALO SANDALS
POWER TO THE PEOPLE
PEACE SIGN
FEATHERED HAT
Granny GLASSES
PEACE SIGN COLLAR
PRAYER BELL NECKLACE
Fringed Floral Suede Pancho
Psychedelic Pants
PROTEST SIGN
FRINGED SUEDE BOOTS
***RULES AND REGULATIONS GOVERNING THE FESTIVAL - HAPPENING
1) Come prepared. Wear Underwear. No nude bathing.
2) Avoid driving the last three miles. We must cooperate with the state troopers in keeping the roads clear.
3) Do not molest farm animals in the vicinity.
4) The room will be divided into good trip and bad trip sections. RECOVERY TENT will be located in northeast corner of bad trip section. If you get spaced out, keep calm; doctor will see you; WAIT.
5) Remember: . . . . "Keep your shit together."

Psychedelic Party flyer, good trips and bad trips, 1979, courtesy Marina Lutz.

The scars left by Manson and Altamont, not to mention Kent State, never quite healed. Updike and Vonnegut, along with Thompson and Wolfe, were zeroing in, turning our lives into stories. Taking a cue from both Duchamp and Warhol's mixed message on life and death, visual artists began working with concepts, sending new messages. The language everyone was speaking became disillusion and repetition. By 1975, the music scene, centered on CBGB, began to echo that feeling and moved toward anarchy. London jumped in and everyone began screaming for change.

When the Mudd Club opened in late '78, *change* found a home.

When I looked again the crowd outside was winding down. It was getting late and I walked upstairs. Diego was still hanging out but I couldn't remember the last time I saw Anya. She'd already become a phantom—living in what became just legend. Her falling out with Steve just as the club was opening seemed largely irrational given the free-for-all and occasional *in your face* attitude of Mudd. Still, when people started coming and the place got crowded, Anya had already disappeared. She stopped by one night to see Debbie

Harry, and I spotted her on the street a few times with her boy-friend, musician and Contortions leader James Chance. Later, I ran into them when James Brown performed at Studio 54. That was late March 1980, and the last time I saw Anya Phillips.

I nodded at Diego, kept walking and headed for the bathroom. Ten minutes later I was back outside. I stood there thinking, *This is it? I can handle it. It's what I want, so what's the problem?* I knew I was part of what was happening, though where and how I fit in was still the question on my mind. I'd move closer to whatever or whom-ever I thought was important, insinuating myself rather than speak-ing truth, saying yes rather than no because it's what I thought people wanted to hear. Maybe I wasn't talented or strange enough to fit; maybe I just opened the door and bought you a drink. Maybe you gave me cocaine in return or maybe not. So much seemed surface, little of it real. Then I looked at the crowd waiting to dance and drink and fuck around and knew I was thinking too much—that the extra bullshit was all mine. I lit a cigarette, picked up my beer and reached for the chain.

The closer-to-norm worktime-playtime schedule I kept before that initial *Steve Mass phone call* had been turned upside down, stood back up and spun around. The steps in front of 77 White started to feel like solid ground and the chain felt lighter in my hand. Louie was inside, Joey had the night off and Gretchen was either dancing or missing in action. Only four or five people were waiting so I sent them in. I tossed the cigarette, finished the beer and tried to stop thinking.

Dave's Luncheonette, Mudd Club outpost.
Egg creams, lousy coffee and extra grease, 1980, by Lisa Genet.

3.
SPRINGTIME

DAVE'S

LUNCHEON

COOK

NEER

46

ette

L BEEF
FRANKFURTER

BOW
TILES

DONT
WALK

What's next is anyone's guess. The crowd around the door keeps getting bigger.

    Deep breath.

    Pour what's left of a Heineken down my throat.

    Everything's fine.

    At the club full-time, I'd occasionally arrive as early as 9 P.M.
and finish as late as 6 the next morning; other nights I show up
at 11, some nights trying to keep it midnight to 5. I'm supposedly
off duty at 4 A.M. but it's still a full house and nobody's going
anywhere, including me. The music's slowing down but everybody's
still looking for that *something* they never find. Slow motion or
hyperdrive, there's no middle ground; it's last-call desperate:
romper room crazy, cigarette smoke mixed up in a liquor, cocaine
and Quaalude haze. Another ten minutes, it's a spontaneous burn,
the aftermath, but it's hard to leave. I look around one more time.
Where do I go now?

Life Was Still That Simple

My before- and after-hours routine keeps changing. I'm moving away from the bars and clubs of Chelsea and the West Village. I'm stepping away from the trucks, the piers and a Meat Packing District that still packs meat. CBGB's on the Bowery and Max's on Park Avenue South are both going strong but they've become the places to go *before*.

At some point I have to eat, and One University Chinese Chance, Mickey Ruskin's social mecca, is the place to be. Familiar faces, a crowded bar with a jukebox and a well-lit dining room with Serious Art on the walls; the food fills you up but sometimes lets you down. Most important, the place has that feels-like-home thing going on—cutting enough slack for anyone to indulge in bad behavior when necessary. Everyone I know eats and drinks there and half of them find their way to White Street between 2 and 4 A.M. Most important, Mickey likes me and we've become friends.

Last resort: if I'm running late or just running, Dave's Luncheonette on the corner of Canal and Broadway is a food-on-the-fly kind of place. It's all about eggs or hot dogs for dinner—and more coffee please. Wash it down with an egg cream and I'm ready for work.

The other end of the night, another story, and there's no schedule or plan after 5 A.M. I'm guided thru the after-hours by instinct, drugs and sex. Going home to sleep and stepping out of the late-night/morning mindset is nearly impossible. Piling into a Checker Cab with Gary, Gretchen and future temporary Murray Street resident Teri Toye is fun—but hardly a safe bet. Still, a full-out A.M. club crawl was a weekend favorite.

Crisco Disco became the Sunday morning special and anyone who could keep up or willing to try was welcome. If you had coke or Quaaludes it was a plus and if you had a car it was even better. The ever-changing cast of characters might include a Pop, a Pallenberg or a Pretender—famous, infamous or notorious—but mostly just us. Arrive at 7 A.M., get checked for weapons and leave by 11— four hours gone missing. The place was a slow-motion train wreck, lights flashing, lost in the fog. The vibe, if we still had a sense of one: past the point of no return. We'd hang in the DJ booth that sat perched on a giant can of Crisco, drink, dance and snort our way thru the morning. I'd take a break, have sex in the stairway and pass out in the VIP room. I'd wake up refreshed, order another drink and dance some more. I either thought I was unwinding after a

S U N	**DANCE TO DAWN** 1 Club closed for private party until 12:30 a.m. Pajama Party postponed. After 12:30 there will be film clips and dancing with D-Jay.	**S U N**	**JOE JACKSON** 8 Hot new A & M Recording star makes his New York debut.
M O N	**DANCE TO DAWN** 2 Dance til dawn. Film clips	**M O N**	**JOHN HASSEL** 9 Rhys Chatham presents an evening of experimental music.
T U E S	**NICO** & JUDY NYLON 3 Famed chanteuse Nico does songs of lost souls. Judy will do new performance piece centered around flesh and money.	**T U E S**	**DANCE TO DAWN** 10 Dance til dawn. Film clips.
W E D	**WILLIAM BURROUGHS** & JOHN GIORNO 4 Burroughs will read new unpublished work to an an assemblage of appropriately attired Nova criminals. Admission by ticket only ($5.00). Tickets on sale beginning April 1, at 6:00 P.M. Reading begins promptly at 9:00 P.M.	**W E D**	**MANDY MIAMI** 11 The female Brian Ferry.
T H U R S	(I wanna be your dog) **RICHARD HELL** 5 The lower East Side Jonny Ray will give the girls one last glimpse before returning to his European tour.	**T H U R S**	**THE ANGELS** 12 One of the great teen romance girl groups. "My Boy Friend's Back." Think of your goose bumps when your boy friend peeled rubber in your driveway. Thrill to "Till" and "I Adore Him." The Angels recently appeared on Midnight Special.
F R I	**DANCE TO DAWN** 6 Dance til dawn. Film Clips	**F R I**	**DANCE TO DAWN** 13 Dance til dawn. Film Clips.
S A T	**Le Dance Avec Le Deesk Shock-kee** 7 Dance til dawn. Film Clips	**S A T**	**Le Dance Avec Le Deesk Shock-kee** 14 Dance til Dawn. Film Clips

Mudd Club Newsletter, April '79.

hard night at work or I wasn't thinking at all. Other than running fast and searching for some unknown, I'm not sure what I was doing.

Existing in the lost netherworld fade of reality, Crisco's was far removed from the energy of White Street. We eventually escaped, vertical but semi-comatose, and headed into the sunshine hustle bustle of Fifteenth Street and Tenth Avenue. The key to survival was a pair of sunglasses, cab fare and a cigarette. Life was still that simple—but also offered choices.

The Nursery on Third Avenue near Thirteenth Street was the easy alternative: equally reckless but more of a workingman's morning out. Sleep-deprived but unwilling to surrender, I barely remember arriving and have no memories of leaving. The first time I showed up there, a big guy named Big Mike turned to Joey Kelly and asked, "You know this guy?" A quick frisk later and I was in. Dim and dirty, red light and cigarette smoke spread out over a few floors, The Nursery was at once benign and scary. For some it was home, but for me it was someone else's home and most of the time I stayed too long.

New in town Krystie Keller worked nearby. She loved The Nursery and remembers Rolling Stones guitarist Ronnie Wood wandering around at 8 A.M. just like everybody else. An early-morning night out was always the great equalizer and the place seemed to suit everyone's need for excess. From Iggy to Belushi, Bowie and even Cher (innocently slumming with a new boyfriend), the hour and the vibe quickly diminished the pecking order. With a second floor dark enough to conceal any residual rock star wreckage, the club was safe harbor for acting out and passing out. Eyes half closed, I drifted around looking for drunken sex, cheap drugs and one more drink that was always the last. I played a slow-motion black-and-white Atari game— one of the very first, called Pong—and it hypnotized me. I got up and leaned against the wall of a tiny bathroom built for pissing and getting high, yet distinctly lacking the clubby feel of a Mudd Club toilet. I remember warm beer, cocaine and Mudd Club DJ David Azarch among the barely standing midmorning crowd. Along with off-duty bouncers and bartenders, a few Hells Angels and drug dealers running out of drugs, it was anyone riding the train to the last stop. The only place left to go was home or the curb.

Early morning or early evening, wherever I went didn't matter. My calling card became *I work the door at the Mudd Club*, now show me yours. It felt like a bit of a pickup line and it worked.

The Dark Ages

Never sure when it began, the morning appeared to end sometime tomorrow. Time itself seemed anxious, almost confused; trying to sleep and turning daylight into night was a challenge nearly perfected on Murray Street. I kept the steel shutters on the north-facing windows closed. The phone stayed unplugged until midafternoon or whenever I got out of bed. It was the Dark Ages: the days of limited technology, busy signals and jacked-in phones on long cords. There was no doorbell or intercom and if you wanted to stop by, you'd call from the payphone on the corner. Answering machines were around but I didn't have one, making it easy to avoid anyone who might ask "Are you working tonight?" If I wanted to talk, I'd plug in the phone, make the call and unplug it again. There was a system for everything.

Waking up well past late, I plugged in and called Sunny the pot dealer. She lived at 105 MacDougal Street above Panchito's Restaurant and we met when I lived on Bleecker. She sold decent pot at a fair price and sold subway slugs on the side. My friend Richard Sohl bought the slugs but I used real tokens and just went for the pot. Sunny was the best pot-dealing slug peddler in town.

I'd buy an ounce and leave MacDougal, duck into the West Fourth Street subway station and take any downtown train on the upstairs tracks to Chambers Street. I'd be home in ten minutes, roll a joint, put on a record and paint in the studio; I was serious about making art and still pretending I just worked late. Facing off with large sheets of paper on the wall of my studio, I'd start playing. Watching oils and acrylics resist one another, I moved in close with a rag or paint stick, never sure where I'd wind up. Loving the feel of paper, big beautiful pages, I'd start writing at the edges and across the middle: memories and lost thoughts, sometimes words, sometimes not.

I made believe I had a real day-and-night, light-and-dark existence. Never sure if it was time for breakfast or dinner, time to sleep or wake up, I just kept painting, tried to stay out of trouble and make it to White Street on time. It seemed to be working out fine.

Nova Criminals and the Remarkable Parade

Arriving at 11 P.M., I always found two or three people waiting but by 1 A.M. the crowd often surprised me. Strangers sometimes looked familiar while the faces I knew began to look like everyone else. Old friends and college friends occasionally showed up; there were even chance encounters with my suburban past. When a girl I knew in high school looked at me from across the chain, the only words she could manage were "Oh my God … Richard?" Apparently, I wasn't the only one who didn't see it coming.

Friends, acquaintances and strangers—every night I witnessed a remarkable parade. Some were finding their way, some were ready to explode and a few already had. Waiting outside, lined up at the bar, drinking or *begging* for a drink, the faces changed but the parade marched on. When author Lynne Tillman arrived she stood next to me as we talked, and watched it go by.

A young, underappreciated Jean-Michel Basquiat "vandalized" the Mudd bathroom with his logo-like *SAMO Was Here* sloganized poetics. Tossed out the door, he came back every night. The SAMO stuff was all over neighborhood; the vandalism was debatable.

Artists Jeff Koons and Christopher Wool were part of the parade and the future, while musician Johnny Thunders was the hero lost, staggering toward the door. Cheetah Chrome was easy to like and if we had to throw him out, he'd apologize and get back in. Richard Lloyd (ex-Television) was still almost beautiful: he could pick up his guitar, turn up the volume and make it sing. Some of us kept listening; others looked away.

Artists and writers, drunk Punks and Punks on dope. Out of control, unavoidable, bandaged and lost—predictably, by 2 A.M. someone was always getting the bum's rush. I opened the chain and closed it behind them. I played diplomat depending on who was getting tossed and let them back in if they promised to behave. I thought it was the right thing to do.

Looking past *lost*, I stared into Cortlandt Alley. I thought about Wednesday, April 4, and a different kind of "Punks on dope." I'd been working the club just two weeks when Steve called me at home and asked me to come in early; I was eager and agreed. Writer Max Blagg had arranged for William S. Burroughs and poet John Giorno to do a reading that was set to start at 9 P.M. The Mudd newsletter anticipated a room filled with "appropriately attired Nova criminals," and negotiating a five-dollar cover charge with the I-never-

William S. Burroughs reading, Allen Ginsberg and Peter Orlovsky watching and listening, Mudd Club, 1979, by Marcia Resnick.

pay-to-come-in crowd was going to keep me busy. I waited outside, hand on the chain, ready for the challenge.

Burroughs wasn't known for his readings but was a legend for *Naked Lunch*, *Junkie*, *Wild Boys* and the Nova Trilogy. White Street was out of the way, nighttime desolate, the Mudd Club a dark set piece, weird and perfect. When Giorno finished there was an awkward moment and a minor tussle over who'd do the Burroughs introduction. Blagg had a hand in setting up the evening but author-biographer Victor Bockris got involved. Finally resolved, Max introduced William to the crowd.

Burroughs sat at a desk: gray metal, scratch-and-dent, office furniture salvage. The only thing missing was the typewriter. I remember his voice sounded proper but strange, like an old radio broadcast. He was wearing a three-piece suit, very considered and nearly impeccable. The PA hissed but Burroughs kept reading. I picked up my beer, moved closer and took a ride on the Nova Express.

The Burroughs reading by now seems long past but that strange voice still speaks. I'm outside working and the street's getting busy when a *Fuck you* gets lobbed in the direction of the door. Club regulars Hal and Roxanne ask "What was that?" as they step inside. I either say "Nothing" or say nothing and the remarkable parade continues.

I open the chain for painter and underground film star Duncan Hannah accompanied by Contortions model and *The Correct Sadist* author Terence Sellers. He's cool and calm on the surface and offers a quiet hello; she's chilly, offers nothing.

It's another few rounds of *nothing* until Spandex-clad porn star Sharon Mitchell arrives. Decades away from a second calling as Doctor Mitchell, the *Wanda Whips Wall Street* and *Load Warrior* actress shimmies her way thru the door with a wide-open smile and a deep throaty hello.

Art world fixture Christophe de Menil is already inside drinking and tipping heavily or maybe the other way around. She got out of a limo a half-hour ago calling "Mark, Mark!" as in Benecke, the Studio 54 doorman. Either her driver took a wrong turn or she thinks we all look alike.

By now the crowd is filling the sidewalk but I'm in no hurry to open the chain. We're just getting started. There's no end in sight.

"I'm a Friend of Steve"

When I first began working the door, 77 White was already becoming the only game in town. Studio 54 had a running start but by the spring of 1979, the Mudd Club was ascending. The seventies were winding down and Disco was becoming more of a cliché, a punch line or point of reference at best. Still, if you couldn't get into Mudd, you could always grab a cab and head back uptown.

Deciding who or what, yes or no; I still couldn't believe I was working the Mudd Club door. As for the crowd in front of me, you relate to some and deal with others. Starting with the basics, like *How many?* or *Hold on*, was simple enough. Telling someone *It's going to be a few minutes* gave people hope without getting them upset. *Sorry, I can't right now* only made things worse, and a bullhorn-like delivery of *The club is now closed* had little or no effect. Don't look them in the eye and don't engage, keep moving and don't turn your back, cut your losses and head inside—that's what Fridays and Saturdays were like. The rest of the week was a close second: some people pushed too hard, dropped names, offered business cards. Lots of people tried using the "I'm a friend of Steve" routine, which usually meant they weren't. Others mentioned names I'd never heard

The crowd outside, good kids, bad kids, 1980, by Nick Taylor.

and a few even told me, "I'm a friend of Richard's." I smiled and told them, "Richard's off tonight."

In the end no one really cared about anything once they got inside. People who didn't get in went somewhere else, went home or threw something at me. Some stopped me on the street and wanted to know why I wouldn't let them in. Sometimes I ignored them and other times I told them I was sorry. Occasionally I told them to *fuck off*; once I went home and fucked one of them. That person came in the next time he showed up—but he paid five dollars.

I learned people are just people. Nothing is personal and a bad attitude is worth very little. It took a while but I learned.

Freaks and Beauties

New Yorkers, suburban kids and escapees from Middle America along with West Coast immigrants and a contingent of Europeans: those were the new faces showing up every night. Freaks and beauties, often one and the same, all wanted to get thru the door. I did my best to pass gentle judgment, occasionally wondering if I'd let *my-*

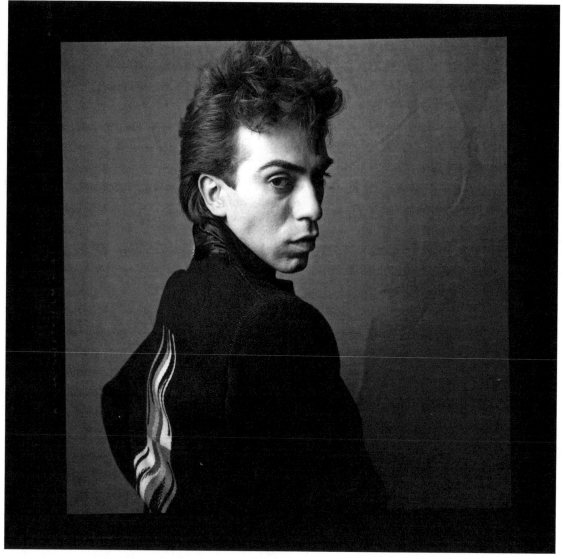

Mudd Club portrait series, *Punks of New York* by William Coupon.
Left to right: Joey Arias, 1979; Colette, 1979.

self in were the situation reversed. Sometimes I might have, other times, maybe not.

Some club regulars were difficult but a lot of them were easy; most I was happy to see. Self-proclaimed Queen of the Mudd, Tina L'Hotsky was a full-figured blonde in a cocktail dress. She was a feminist of sorts, a creative force in the spirit of White Street. Writer, actress and Mudd denizen Vicki Pedersen referred to her as a "great conceptualizer." A bigger-than-life Barbie doll (she once cooked a Barbie in a frying pan for her 1977 short film *Barbie*), Tina had Steve's ear. She was a star somewhere in the middle of the Mudd Club constellation, and the Crazy Spanish Girls, Cha Cha, and Joan Crawford Mother's Day parties wouldn't have happened without

her. I liked Tina, and she always stopped to say hello before heading to the bar. Not everyone was that easy.

Unsure if saying *hello* is part of the conversation, I only hear the question, "Who are you?" I try not to appear frightened and do my best to say, "I'm Richard; I just started working here." She rolls her eyes, takes another drag on her cigarette and starts telling me how things work.

Leisa Stroud was one of the first people I met the first night I worked the door. Short bleached hair and a tight party dress, a pair of heels and a pocketbook, Leisa wasn't shy about standing outside and making sure I knew the people I was supposed to know. She kept tabs on who was inside and always let me know who was important—to her.

This page: Leisa Stroud and pocketbook in a booth on the second floor, 1979, by Alan Kleinberg. Opposite: Tina L'Hotsky, 1980. *Hidden Identities* series by Marcus Leatherdale.

I'd watch Leisa work the room and it seemed she had Steve wrapped around her finger. Actor, artist and Lounge Lizard John Lurie even called her *a fucking tornado*—he meant it in a good way. In 1979, John was Leisa's boyfriend but he knew that everyone from Brian Eno to Larry Rivers to David Byrne was crazy about her.

Leisa was there from the beginning and deserves some credit for helping to turn the Mudd Club into the indelible madhouse it became. I deserve some credit for letting attitude and beauty pass for charm.

Portrait photographer William Coupon was well versed in beauties and freaks. He saw it at Studio 54, where he shot some "classy black and whites" on the sly. Truman Capote even suggested Coupon put together a photo book about Studio, visions far removed from *In Cold Blood*'s "high plains of western Kansas." That idea ended quickly when 54 owner Steve Rubell got wind of it.

The Mudd Club was next and the photographer was ready. Coupon's first paid assignment: photograph the new place on White Street for *Interview* magazine. Three months later in February '79, he told Steve Mass he wanted to take more pictures and Steve was agreeable. He set himself up on the second floor of Mudd and over the next several weeks shot portraits of various Mudd Club regulars. He photographed Talking Head David Byrne dressed in pajamas and Walter Steding with violin in hand. Images of Joey Arias, Klaus Nomi, Tina L'Hotsky and Marcia Resnick were serious but playful and equally stylish. Coupon calls the Mudd portraits his "first in a long series of subcultures." Future stars, ghosts and survivors, their photos soon hung on the wall opposite the first-floor bar.

Don't Leave Yet

Back outside I stood at the chain and thought, *Oh no, not this one.* By the next night I was thinking, *I love this one.*

Abbijane was a fashion designer, a Mudd Club regular and a lover of Rock 'n' Roll. She came on strong, greeting me with a loud sustained *Hi* and a dose of genuine in-your-face enthusiasm. Her early fashion shows, staged at locations like the Forty-second Street Horn & Hardart Automat, were not-to-be-missed events. There was never any question of Abbijane coming in; the only question, when could I come in and dance?

I remembered Abbijane as one of the girls who screamed and jumped up and down in front of the stage at CBGB's for the band Milk 'n' Cookies. Hard to forget based on decibels alone, now she was screaming *Hold this!* and tossing her jacket at DJ David Azarch. The toss and scream became a mating ritual. Abbijane and David fell in love.

Abbi and I became friends at the Mudd Club and our friendship lasted thirty years. She was the first to wag her finger disapprovingly when I started spinning out of control. She told it, or more accurately, *screamed it* to me straight, "Stop what you're doing, I've seen it destroy too many people I care about." I didn't listen and we kept on dancing.

Klaus Nomi is looking at you, 1979, by Alan Kleinberg.

The last time I saw Abbijane I said "Good night" and gave her a kiss. She said "I can't believe you're leaving, don't leave yet."

Nomi, Nobody and Night School

It's difficult to remember if it was the same night I met Abbi, but the moment remains unforgettable. Regardless of who or what was passing thru the door it was hard not to stop and stare.

Operatic vocalist and performer Klaus Nomi crossed the street wearing a shiny, cropped jacket with a satin collar, looking like a cross between an intergalactic bellhop and a toy soldier. His hair was blue-black with a high widow's peak and twisted into a small point on top of his head. His skin was pale, his lips pursed and painted blackish red. He carried himself with a jittery grace and an understated sense of *politesse* (a funny little word I've heard Mick Jagger use). No one looked, sang or did anything like Nomi.

He soon wound up sardined in the center of a crowd that was backed up onto the street. I can still hear Joey Kelly yelling, "Klaus, get in here!" as he opened and closed the chain. It seemed one minute Klaus was in the crowd, the next he was in the door and the moment in between disappeared. I looked around wondering if anyone else noticed but Joey was already busy and the disappearing moment came and went. Then I turned around and that weird blond-haired guy with horn-rimmed glasses was headed for the door.

Bob Williamson was the polar opposite of Klaus Nomi. A blend of middle-age prep school nerd and way too many Heinekens, he was the Lauren Hutton pseudo Svengali and the only guy who wore Topsiders to the Mudd Club. Bob was the person Steve Mass was listening to ramble on and on the night of my ten-second interview; he was at the club nearly every night—still talking when the sun came up. Even I listened to him drone about everything from the art scene and Public Image Ltd.'s *Metal Box* to the fuckable waitresses at One University Place. He was Zelig—here, there and everywhere. With a good hustle and a good eye he fooled anyone who took him seriously. Years later, people figured out he was nobody.

Bob stopped as I opened the chain. He asked how I was doing but I'm not sure I responded. That's when Francine arrived, squeezed my hand and said, "Hi doll." I smiled and said *ouch*.

Francine Hunter opened Jungle Red Studios on Desbrosses Street in 1977. The Mudd Club opened a year later six blocks away. She had her eye on White Street from the beginning.

Shortly after I started working at Mudd, Francine brought *Night School* to 77 White. It was an Invitation Only event, meaning only the people we let in, got in. For the high price of six dollars a person, Francine gave the crowd a "fashion performance to teach you a lesson." The ensemble cast featured Cookie Mueller, future Mudd employee Gennaro Palermo, photographer Nan Goldin and a host of desperate nightlife denizens hungry for fame. An over-the-top, under-the-radar smash, the show was a comedic take on the world of fetish, leather bars, bondage and discipline. Whether or not you dabbled in that world, got taken down a notch, and learned from the experience, you still needed *Night School*. I had, I did, but I needed more.

A few months earlier, Francine's character, Mrs. Frontporch, came to life on the Mudd Club stage in a Honey Walters production called *Sleazy Living*, a loving tribute to old-school burlesque. With no better setting than the ready-for-anything world of White Street, *Night School* and *Sleazy* were beloved by the regulars, amused the curious, and sent more than a few running for the bar. When *Sleazy*'s giant vagina began dancing to Donna Summer's "Hot

Stuff," the line was drawn and crossed, and the Mudd Club was on its way to becoming the Farthest Off of the Off-Off Broadway world.

Whether it was the crowd buying drinks or a *vaginormous* spectacle, Steve Mass liked what he saw and purchased Francine's mailing list for two hundred fifty dollars. The Mudd Club was already the new watering hole-in-the-wall for the "Downtown 500" and by late spring-early summer 1979 there was simply nothing like it.

I try and keep up with Francine Hunter when she talks about New York in the late '70s but it's hard to get in a single word. When the subject turns to Mudd she's clear on one thing—"It was a love story." When she squeezes my hand we can still feel it.

Class of '79

White Street was a last stand of *do it yourself* and *let it happen* nightlife. It was a comfort zone filled with what were fast becoming familiar faces, seemingly like minds and the pursuit of creative endeavor. There was a sense of community and camaraderie—a connection based solely on being there—a connection that remains to this day. That's how it was for me, and it seemed the same for Lisa Rosen and her brother, Danny.

A fashion icon without even trying, Lisa often arrived with stylist and photographer Sophie VDT. Eighteen years old, born in New York Hospital and proud of it, Lisa helped define everything that was possible, beautiful and insane about the Mudd Club Class of '79.

Danny Rosen was only sixteen but played the field like he was seventeen and a half. He hung out with Ken Compton and Boris Policeband, was jazz-cool and he owned it. He briefly appeared in the early Lounge Lizards lineup and made a little noise with Basquiat's band Gray. Like his sister, Danny was an accidental icon and carried a thrift shop suit with an easy swagger and bespoke style. Lisa's smile was mile-wide while Danny worked a grin or a scowl with bad-boy charm. Both were hard to resist—Mudd Club heart and soul.

Hal Ludacer was another one of the kids. Seventeen when the club opened, he was hard to miss and one of the prettiest people in the room. He grew up on Long Island and lived on South Street with his brothers Randy and Kenneth. I spotted him and Randy at the bar a few months before I started working at the club, and I tried not to stare. They both had on white T-shirts and Hal wore dress trousers,

The Offenders poster, Super 8mm and misfit Mudd Club movie stars, 1980, courtesy Lisa Genet.

a look made famous by Brando and Belmondo twenty-five years earlier: beauty rechanneling beauty and it still worked.

The brothers had a band called Ludacer and I'd seen them play at Max's. They went on after a screening of Scott and Beth B's film *The Offenders* that featured a host of misfit Mudd Club movie stars. The band looked and sounded high school-era garage and when they finished I headed for White Street. The film didn't seem much more than a bunch of kids and one or two adults in trench coats making a movie and acting like kids. Despite what it was or wasn't, I had respect for the work as well as the effort. I had the chance to say it then but instead I just watched. Today *The Offenders* marks the time and vice versa; it points a direction forward and brings back memories, most of them good.

I called Hal recently and he told me Mudd was just "a continuation of high school" but quickly realized "it was more like junior high, the formative years." I told him based on our behavior alone it often was. He remembers the "amazing convergence and a special time" on White Street. I remember the connection everyone shared— along with the drugs and the drinking and the sex. Then I thought about actual high school, Class of '71, and started laughing.

The Most Interesting People

Those school days gone, five years passed. I got to the city in 1976 and I never thought about leaving. James Nares left London in 1974, landed in New York and felt the same way. He was twenty-one and remembers, "The moment I arrived I knew I was home." He looked around thinking that "the streets were like Rauschenberg paintings," the urban *combine* of surface, ruin and discard becoming something else, something beautiful. By 1978, walking from White Street to Murray, I saw those Rauschenberg paintings too. I couldn't wait to put some paper on the wall and start working.

There was a sense of great comfort in that rubble and chaos. James made his way downtown, found a place on Jay Street not far from 77 White and wound up living in the little bridge that connected two buildings several stories above the ground. I was south on Murray, and Diego was busy with Steve and Anya just a few blocks north. The neighborhood crowd included Richard Serra, photographer Allan Tannenbaum, Donnie Christensen, actor Lindzee Smith and artist Jo Shane. Boris Policeband was living nearby in a basement apartment, heating up his nightly can of spaghetti and watching a half-dozen television sets simultaneously. Painter, filmmaker and future Academy Award winner Katherine "Kathy" Bigelow was a few blocks east living in the same building as the Ludacers. Almost everyone could be found hanging at Magoo's or Barnabas Rex, the local art bar dives. Showing up for a drink was the only means of communication other than telegraph, mail or a corded phone.

James started making films, mini-movies and the almost feature-length *Rome '78*, a sword-and-sandal epic with a Lower East Side vibe. He did a performance piece at The Kitchen, an alternative space in SoHo. Steve Mass was there, saw the work and was anxious to do something with his ambulance service dollars. He told James he was opening a new place on White Street and was interested in sponsoring some projects. When the "new place" opened, James fit right in.

James Nares always thought, "Mudd was the place with the most interesting people, the place where it was happening." He met Lisa Rosen there the same night he met Edwige, the Parisian Punk icon. Lisa spotted James from across the room and wanted to know more. Knowing more turned into love and marriage.

The scene below Canal Street now centered on White: another new constellation, another spin on the Walter Steding Theory.

James Nares and Diego Cortez, 1978, by Bobby Grossman

Meeting of the Minds

Standing outside the club was what I did, or was supposed to be doing; meeting people and getting to know a few was inevitable. Despite my inability to look closely at myself, I could see things in others, often from half a block away. If I liked what I saw, I opened the chain. It was a big responsibility.

Michael Holman is walking down White Street wearing a continental-cut iridescent sharkskin suit. He sees me, steps up to the chain and smiles. He's handsome, polite and secure in the knowledge that he won't have to wait. Our camaraderie in that moment is based solely on the Mudd Club and my ability to say yes or no at the door.

Holman had left San Francisco in 1978. He arrived in New York and began working as a courier. (His van from that job was the same that eventually ran errands and helped put together the legendary Mudd Club Soul party.) Before long Michael was hanging out at Max's, Studio 54 and Galaxy West. He checked out the Canal Zone parties at artist Sam Peskett's Canal Street loft where he met SAMO graffiti writer and artist Jean-Michel Basquiat. In late April 1979, the earliest version of the industrial noise, jazz and space band formed by Holman and Basquiat was born. Originally named Channel Nine, the band quickly became Bad Fools, then Test Pattern. It would take another year before this meeting of the minds stepped onto the Mudd Club stage as Gray.

Right now it's 1 A.M. Michael says hi, I unhook the chain and the door opens. James Brown's "Sex Machine" screams. I turn around and Michael's already inside dancing. A minute later, so am I.

Who Do You Love

Back at the door I smiled thinking of Alice Himelstein. She never really danced but she saw the Beatles perform at Carnegie Hall in 1964 and ran around London during Punk's heyday. Alice lived in a duplex on Central Park West with her father, the renowned Doctor Theodore Himelstein. She came to Mudd every night but stayed near the bar until a band was ready to play. She laughed a big laugh, powered by an even bigger heart. I felt like we knew each other before we even met.

Michael Holman, Mudd Club boogaloo, 1980, by Nick Taylor.

Alice often got out of the cab at Broadway and I'd see her coming down the block. She carried a giant tote bag when pocketbooks were still small and wore an arm full of black rubber bracelets years before someone put them on Madonna. Her hair was a Goth shade of black until she added a touch of purple. The braided tail that started at the hairline on the back of her neck was a beautiful detail. I can't believe I never pulled on it when I had the chance.

If she could stop laughing, Alice would be proud that I'm the one writing this story. Alice was my friend and I loved her. I know she loved me.

"Who do you love?" is always a difficult question; just ask Bo Diddley—but when Lynette Bean turned on her million-dollar smile the answer came easy. I'd see her at CBGB's or The Bottom Line but White Street was where we became friends. She was guitarist Ivan Kral's girlfriend, she knew everyone, and she loved Rock 'n' Roll.

In late 1979, when Ivan started touring with Iggy Pop's band, Lynette and I went out on a tour of our own. We ran the circuit midnight to noon, winding our way thru concerts, clubs and early-morning parties; looking for fun and trouble, we were *all area access all the time.*

Alice Himelstein, 1980, *Hidden Identities* series by Marcus Leatherdale.

When a new band or a new player came to town, Lynette showed them around, brought them to Mudd and introduced us. I became friends with some, while others just picked up a free drink and kept walking. Meeting more people than I could keep track of, fun and trouble occasionally crashed head on.

When legendary photographer Kate Simon strolled up to the door with the artist Carl Apfelschnitt, I could never tell if they were trouble, fun or funny but I took a chance and let them in anyway. They'd start out at the first-floor bar, charm a few drinks out of Steve Mass and move on from there.

Kate was born and raised in Poughkeepsie, New York. She escaped, studied in Paris, moved to London in '72 and lived and worked there until 1977. She was around for the mayhem, when the Sex Pistols and

Kate Simon, glamour girl photographer at large, Mudd Club 1979, courtesy Kate Simon.

The Clash tore the town apart and when the Heartbreakers, Patti Smith and the Ramones invaded. London was calling and burning at the same time and Kate shot the pictures.

During my time at the door and through our mutual friends, Richard Sohl and Andi Ostrowe of the Patti Smith Group, I got to know Kate. She's the one who started calling me *RB* and I'm the one who's always reminding her that she's Kate Simon. We remain friends.

Mudd Every Night

Words like *friends* and *love* can be hard to understand, finding out what's real and what isn't. Drifting apart and reconnecting, most of us remember where we came from. Certain childhood friends become family, while high school—with few exceptions—is little more than a connection to time and place. The friends I made in college left a mark and still matter. Everyone I met on White Street will in some way always be part of me.

When I met Jo Shane, the artist, future surfing fanatic and sometime educator, she was a soft-spoken party girl and I was a painter working at the Mudd Club. She arrived on White Street in late 1978; Mudd was still on the down low and "artist Ronnie Cutrone and his wife, Gigi Williams, were the conduit." Before long Jo knew her way around the dance floor, the bathrooms and Cortlandt Alley. Her realization that "the fabric of art and life were tightly interwoven" happened fast, and "if you didn't want to miss anything, you couldn't blink and you had to be at the club every night."

We'd walk home together in the early morning daylight, smoking cigarettes and talking about art, life and the Mudd Club. We laugh about it today, but love the fact we had a crush on each other back then. All these years later, it's still there.

I ask Jo, "What made Mudd different?"

Without pause she answers, "From the minute I walked in it changed my life."

I know what she means: that connection from then till now, being there and never leaving.

All I can say is, "It changed mine too."

Jean-Michel Basquiat, smiling and dancing, 1980, by Nick Taylor.

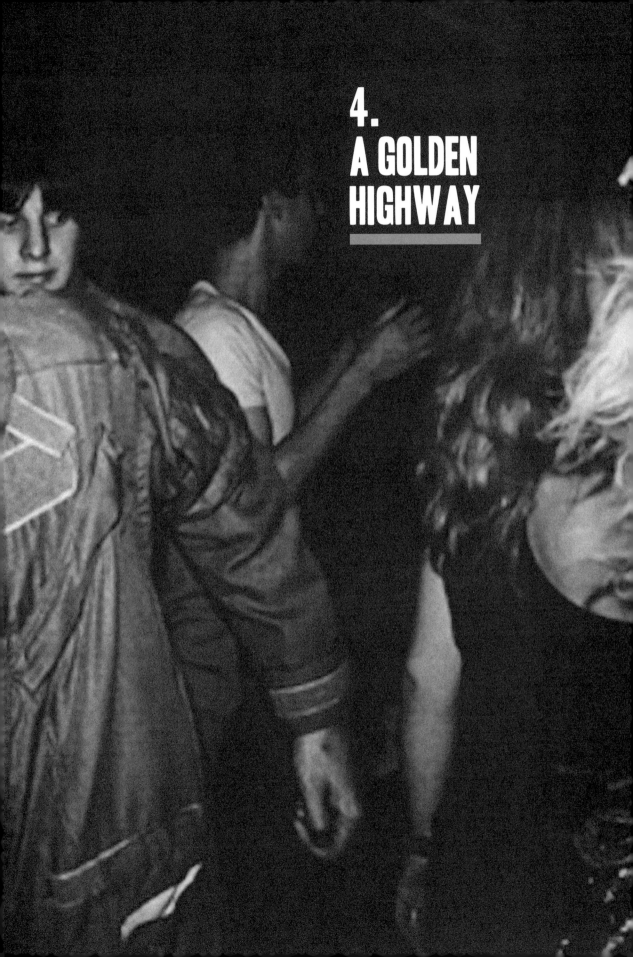

4.
A GOLDEN
HIGHWAY

Everything stops when David Bowie gets out of a cab. No bodyguard, no entourage; he's alone and we head inside. I have a little coke but feel a bit awkward offering just a few lines. I find Hal Ludacer for a dose of moral support, grab Bowie and we escape to the basement. The cocaine disappears quickly.

Back upstairs an old reel-to-reel projector perched on a shelf flickers out-of-sync images of Motown. Jean-Michel Basquiat stands under the projector, his back to the wall, looking out at the dance floor grinning. Choppy waves of light fly around the room and DJ David has the crowd going Supremes crazy. It's a trip—a throwback thrown forward. It's getting late and the place is packed.

Bowie leaves around 4 A.M. He isn't alone. Hal's hanging out on the second floor and I'm sitting on the downstairs bar drinking a beer when the lights come on.

New York was always a small town: anywhere south of Fourteenth Street, familiar territory. You never knew who you might run into, though working the Mudd Club door surely changed the odds.

I'd been running around downtown for almost three years; after nearly three months at the door I know who people are without actually knowing them. Whether it's the locals Richard Serra, Jenny Holzer or James Rosenquist, or a visiting West Coast crazy like Chris Burden, no one gets left outside. Artist and art critic Walter Robinson doesn't have to ask; the chain just opens. Pioneering conceptualist Dennis Oppenheim lives around the corner and walks right thru the door. Artist Kiki Smith lives across the street and has no problem getting in. Belushi blubber-shoves everyone out of the way and Teri Toye just shoves without the blubber.

Back inside, one of the DJs is excited by a rumor that the guys from Van Halen are coming. They sort of creep me out and I'm not interested; besides, I can't even name one of their songs. I'm more amused by the ridiculousness of Leif Garrett's arrival. After that, and considering my chaotic but measured crowd orchestration, I need a break and a hot dog from Dave's.

***

Every now and then I left work alone and walked to Murray Street. Broadway south of Canal was a golden highway with a lot to offer. The 6 A.M. streets were a pre-rush hour wasteland of cardboard-wrapped, metal-banded bales of fabric scrap waiting for pickup. The odd roll of backdrop paper or discarded canvas stretchers were the good garbage that I could use. Along the way I found old wooden doors, pieces of plywood, buckets of paint and a double-basin stainless steel sink. The sink became part of my kitchen. The rest of it became art.

North of Canal and south of Houston had the same vibe of lost and found, litter and debris, the streets even darker and narrower. The offices of the *SoHo Weekly News* were located just east of Broadway on Crosby Street, not far from White. Senior editorial staff, gossips and entertainment columnists emptied out into Mudd nearly every night. *SoHo* music editor and author Peter Occhiogrosso and future *Paper* Magazine founders Kim Hastreiter and David Hershkovits wandered in, got lost, and were eventually found. Nightlife scribe Stephen Saban, and the legendary tattler and social indicator Michael Musto (often in the company of actress and *SoHo News* contributor Sylvia Miles) arrived after 1 A.M. and poured themselves out the door a few hours later. Writer, critic and *SoHo News* columnist and contributor Pat Wadsley (whose résumé includes everything from *16* Magazine to the *New York Post*) usually arrived early and stayed late. Even publisher Michael Goldstein, dressed in a brass-button navy blazer and looking like a country club admiral, wasn't immune to the charms of White Street.

Allan Tannenbaum, the *SoHo News* photographer, shot everything from the parties to the performances and the crowd outside. His visual account of the city, chronicled in his book *New York in the 70s,* includes a photo of me working the door in 1979. My thoughts and words, *the Mudd Club ushering out the decade and moving into a new one, being part of the phenomenon and celebration that happened on White Street,* introduce images of New York nightlife.

The seventies were turning eighty and I had no idea how long I'd be standing out front but as summer slowly approached I knew this was a moment I'd never forget. Within three or four years the eighties would be full swing and full-on; the need to be entertained met with a new take on nightlife. With few exceptions that vision became purely surface. By then the *SoHo Weekly News* was gone.

During the newspaper's run, nearly everyone involved generously chronicled events and nonevents at the Mudd Club. Columnist Stephen Saban even reported that Richard Sohl and Andi Ostrowe were at Murray Street after hours, cleaning my kitchen. No photographs were taken of the event but by 8 A.M. my stove, refrigerator and sink were spotless—just another perk of working the door.

Tales of Mudd are vague but numerous, and the photo coverage is limited. Many tried and some succeeded but freelance photographer Alan Brand—whom Steve often stopped from taking pictures inside the club—was relentless when it came to capturing nearly every fleeting Mudd moment. Brand became a ghost years ago but his archive, if it exists, would be a goldmine. Thankfully, Tannenbaum's images, along with those of David Armstrong and Nan Goldin, Bobby Grossman, Alan Kleinberg, Dustin Pittman, Eileen Polk, Ebet Roberts, Kate Simon, Nick Taylor and Harvey Wang speak for a perilously undocumented time.

The Right Direction

Despite the fact that there was neither a time card nor similar documentation, Vicki Pedersen called it *the office* and checked into Mudd every night. Like Jo Shane, she knew you had to or you might miss something. At the door, I tried to point everyone in the right direction.

There were two floors, two bars, a stage and a dance floor. The bathrooms were functioning but in constant need of repair. If you were hungry, Dave's Luncheonette was just around the corner. Mudd had everything you needed but mail delivery, a toothbrush and clean underwear, though for some the latter was meaningless.

The door policy kept getting tighter and Steve let me do my thing, though I do remember Rebecca Christensen reminding me, "If people aren't bringing something to the *party*, they shouldn't get in"—a suggestion that always rings true.

If someone questionable or nonassessable arrived, I'd do my best to find Steve. If he had no idea who or what I was talking about, his response was usually "Let them in." He'd disappear, reappear later and ask me to point out the person in question. He'd say "Oh" and disappear again.

Back at the door I check out the crowd, ask how many and open the chain. When Louie asks "Who's that?" my response is simply, "I like them." He rolls his eyes, I shrug and we let in a few more people. Then Steve steps outside and mumbles something. It's an inscrutable, low-talking 1 A.M. mumble that occasionally turns into a semi-serious mindfuck. *No beards, no fat people, no limos* are a few of the favorite grenades he likes to lob at the door people. *No black leather* is the worst. Tonight's mumble translates as *no guys with long hair*.

I'm standing there in front of one hundred people and none of the guys have long hair. My hair's short and Louie's is even shorter. Then Brice Marden arrives and his is nearly at the shoulder but neither of us cares. Between Louie, Joey and me, we're the ones holding the chain and Steve's already back inside. The final takeaway: artists (but not all), some musicians and Mudd Club regulars trump belly fat, beards, limos and long hair.

Still, it wasn't *always* that much fun at the door and there was always someone behaving like an asshole, demanding recognition. There was always someone copping an attitude and wanting to know my name so they could report me to a higher authority.

Do you know who I am, whether coming from a hero like Paul Simon (obviously challenged by his diminutive stature and resulting arrogance) or some freak claiming to be a member of Earth, Wind & Fire was more sad and wrong than funny. Not letting them in was part of the genius of Mudd.

Another beguiling tactic was *Hi, you don't remember me, do you?*
It was less aggressive, conveyed less of an attitude, but still an-
noying. All anyone had to do was extend his hand or introduce herself, and give me a fucking break.

In spite of it all, almost everyone either said hello or didn't
and went inside. It was pop culture versus high art with me in the
middle, happy but occasionally confused and often surprised. Taken
aback that Mr. Simon didn't turn out to be a nice guy, I was amazed
to find myself giving a thumbs-up or down to anyone. Snap judgment
was part of my job; it followed me home and never left.

Never About the Money

No real system for a lot of things was how the place operated; in
a way a reflection of a beautiful but broken New York City. I offered chain-wielding hospitality, with a cigarette in one hand and
a drink in the other. I'd step into the alley to take a piss or hang
inside getting almost famous for fifteen minutes at a time. Who
knows what went on behind the bar, how the liquor was inventoried,
how the cash was reconciled or if it even was? Where the night deposit wound up and how it got there was a mystery—until my friend
Marina filled me in.

The cover charge was rarely more than five dollars and usually two, three or free during the week. I remember Diego saying the
original idea for the club "was never about the money" but by late
spring '79 that idea became impossible.

Word was well out and the club started attracting a larger per-
centage of a bridge-and-tunnel crowd on weekends. Today it's no
big deal, but back then *everybody* lived in Manhattan. New Jersey
and Long Island, Brooklyn and Queens were a world away while the
Bronx and Staten Island, except for the zoo and the ferry, were
the unknown frontiers. Despite the stigma of another borough, the
bridge-and-tunnel suburban mix soon became unavoidable and lucrative. The Friday and Saturday crowds were getting bigger by the
week and if you looked good and had a little patience, chances were
you got in. Boy or girl, Upper East Side or Bayside, Queens, didn't
matter—but young, pretty and single always helped. A Punk costume
from the Trash and Vaudeville boutique didn't help, and was always

MUDD CLUB NEWSLETTER

APRIL 27	**F R I**	May 4
SAM & DAVE		DANCING DISC JOCKEY FILMS
The kings of soul. Like a pair of hot dice, they'll make you wheel and deal, dance and prance, spin and win.		
April 28	**S A T**	May 5
SAM & DAVE		DANCING DISC JOCKEY FILMS
Two nights in a row. You can't get enough of them.		
April 29	**S U N**	May 6
PSYCHEDELIC PARTY		TO BE ANNOUNCED
Limited admission. (see reverse side)		(Information on this event be obtained by calling 227-7777 on the day of the performance.)
April 30	**M O N**	May 7
RHYS CHATHAM: with Glenn Branca, Nina Canal, Joe Hannan, Garrett List with Robert Longo's film "Pictures for Music". JEFFREY LOHN: Music for amplified string sextet, percussion,and chorus, with Julius Eastman and ensemble. 9:00 P.M. and 11:00 p.m ROCK AND ROLL AT '1:00 A.M.		ELECTRIC MUSIC Short electric music pieces by 20 composers coming out of fringe rock, jazz and classical contexts. 9:00 P.M. ROCK AND ROLL DANCING 12 MIDNIGHT
MAY 1	**T U E S**	May 8
DREAMERS OF THE ABSOLUTE		SPECIAL GUEST BAND from Boston
Conceptual Performances - Political Transmission Jean Quinn & Ralph McRae....Marty West.... Margaret Dewys and friends performing electric shorts. Films by Lindzee Smith & Tim Burns Betsy Sussler. STARTS PROMPTLY 9:00 P.M.		
May 2	**W E D**	May 9
DANCING DISC JOCKEY FILM CLIPS		SCREAMING JAY HAWKINS Conceptual Artist before the word was coined PIANO ——— COFFIN COFFIN ———PIANO
May 3	**T H U R S**	May 10
TIN HUEY		TO BE ANNOUNCED
Warner Brothers hot new recording act from Akron. The rubber city's answer to the Monkees.		Information on this event may be obtained by calling 227-7777 after May 9th.

Mudd Club Newsletter, Spring '79.

a bit of an eyesore. A tourist looking to see somebody dressed in one was even worse.

Drunk on arrival or just impatient usually meant NO and people with a lot of questions didn't fare much better. My response to *How long is the wait?* or *Is this the line?* depended on the hour, the amount and type of drugs in my system and the person asking. Stepping back and saying nothing was the best option.

There were always self-imposed guidelines to follow or not: two or three single women were usually okay, but a party of three or more straight single men was a problem to avoid. The teenage Sons of Mulberry Street, the unavoidable exception—young, handsome and a lot to deal with—were a time bomb. Their fathers would stop by too and greet me with a *Hey Richie*, a wink and a slap on the back. One of them, Joe the Crow, told me to let him know if his son ever caused any trouble. I smiled, thought *okay,* but avoided getting anywhere near the middle and just laughed when Steve told me not to let them in. I played along, didn't fuck with them and they didn't fuck with me. They treated me with respect and shook my hand when I'd pass thru Little Italy on a drug or pizza run. That respect would prove to come in handy.

We did our best to keep trouble outside. I stuck to people I knew or recognized and took my chances based on a good or gut feeling; I felt responsible for getting it right.

The club wasn't big, the legal capacity of the first floor under under 300. The sign, informing anyone who cared, was posted somewhere above the basement staircase, and near the ceiling—impossible for the crowd of 400 or more to see. There was no bottle or weapons check and no real security. If a problem came up, anyone willing to dive in helped us out. It was still the age of fearless innocence; we didn't even keep a baseball bat behind the bar. A lawless respect prevailed and for the most part we got away lucky.

***

Steve Mass wanted the same thing we all wanted—drinks, drugs, sex and entertainment, all wrapped up in a place that felt like home. He was *Dr. Mudd* and his sense of irony, anarchy and point-specific open-mindedness was what the place was all about. When you crossed it with a bit of semi-intellectualized political incorrectness and a heavy anchor in the worlds of art, music and fashion, you had

Mudd Club magic. New York City and its seventies-era ambient disorder was icing on the cake.

Remaining aloof had already become a dubious exercise. Jo Shane accurately recalls how "enthusiasm was not an affect that shone kindly at Mudd," and wonders "how we accounted for the ironic re-creation of teen dreams" that played out on the dance floor. If enthusiasm wasn't the answer, maybe it was cigarettes and alcohol, too many drugs or not enough. Maybe some people were just too cool—but I was never one of them. In the thick or working outside, I made my way; the edge still hadn't sharpened and the chill hadn't set in. Keen and eager, I stopped short of gush. I opened the chain and without fully realizing, I was putting my stamp on the job.

Through the blur of memory and forward to now, Jo winds up answering her own question. "It was the zeitgeist." She might be right but I still think drugs and alcohol had a lot to do with it.

Some of the nightly arrivals were cash-poor. They got by on looks, attitude and instinct with a few willing to do anything to get what they needed. It was No Wave Darwinism—survival of the fittest, Mudd Club-style—and there were a lot of ins and outs.

Getting thru the door for free was part of the game and drinking for free was one of the prizes. There were no drink tickets at the time and it was all about Steve, me, or even the DJs *buying* people drinks. The bartenders, whether it was a friendly gesture, small-scale deal or part of some late-night agenda, had their own thing going on. Up your nose, down your throat or in your pants, there was a lot of motivation coming from every direction—and at that point rich or poor didn't matter.

By 3 A.M., people were talking or still trying to talk, dancing, standing around or trying to stand. You'd get lost in the bathroom and leave with someone you found. The first floor, chaos set to music, the unedited reel; the second floor, a late-night fever dream. By closing time nearly everything was free.

Jo Shane always reminds me, "There were so many Mudds, each with its own hierarchy and dysfunctional family genealogy." Between the Punks and No Wave, the Mickey Ruskin art world spillover and the new guard—the likes of which included Basquiat, Cortez, Brathwaite and Goldin—each faction or "Mudd" was identified by how they dressed, where they lived and the company they kept. Cocaine and heroin became identifying markers. The Europeans, Russians and Rockabillies were ever-present while a core group of true Mudd blood included Lurie and Stroud, the Rosens, L'Hotsky, Pedersen, Phoebe, Pyro and

David Bowie and Dee Dee Ramone, Ramones Party, Mudd second floor, 1979, by Bobby Grossman.

Jo. Who was fucking whom was merely gossip but occasionally interesting; straight or gay seemed to have little bearing in a still pre-AIDS awareness world. I was the "doorkeeper" free to join any of those coalitions. I tried being part of them all but I kept losing track—too busy at the door or heading for the bathroom.

Slumming

Mudd Club regulars or one-night stands, nightlife legend Steve Lewis referred to those I considered tourists as "the uptown crowd slumming for sex and drugs." If the hour was late enough and my own drugs stopped working, I wound up slumming too. Maybe we all did.

I'd look around and laugh. I'd sit in a booth upstairs and nurse a beer, talking to almost anyone. Running for the basement, sucking face or getting my dick sucked, the highs and lows seemed even keel. Taking a break, I'd go for a drive in Dr. David's late-model Rolls. Privacy, comfort and pharmaceutical cocaine were gifts, payback for free drinks and priority treatment at the door. It felt wrong but I did it anyway and by the sometimes 5 a.m. very last call I tried not to think about it. I'd pull two beers from behind the bar and split.

Another night feels better and just after midnight the regulars start showing up. Hal's already inside dancing, Tina L'Hotsky and Steve are at the bar and my friend Roxanne Jefferies, wearing a black eye patch and nearly black lipstick, is outside keeping me company. Cookie Mueller and her girlfriend, fellow John Waters actress Sharon Niesp, arrive. Jean-Michel swings around the corner and Lisa Rosen gets out of a cab. There's either a party emptying out or some higher state of consciousness sending White Street a mini-convergence; either way, I'll take it. Now I just have to wait and see who's in the limo pulling up out front.

A road-tested former Bond Girl, ex-wife of comedian great Peter Sellers and recent ex-girlfriend of Rod Stewart is parked at the curb. Her driver gets out, asks me to come to the car; whether she's shopping or slumming is hard to tell.

Britt Ekland is slouched in the back seat behind a pair of shades looking like a character from *Saturday Night Live*. She offers a quick hello, then cuts to the chase, asking, "Who is inside?" I take the question to mean young, famous or nearly, plays Rock 'n' Roll and looking to get laid, but all I can come up with is David Bowie. Following me in, she has a drink and disappears. It's the closest I'll ever get to Peter Sellers or James Bond.

The rest of the night is a blur and at 4 A.M., upstairs is still crowded; it's the anything-can-happen hour and everyone's guard is way down. I'd been going full speed since midnight, couldn't wait till 4 and dropped mine in the basement a few hours ago. Now I want more.

Thought-Provoking

The following night, Ronnie Cutrone was talking to me outside. He worked for Andy Warhol, knew even more people than I did, and introduced at least half of them to the Mudd Club. In November '78 he brought artist Neke Carson to White Street to meet Steve Mass.

Neke moved to New York in 1970 and settled in a loft on Broome Street, six blocks from 77 White. He hung out at Max's Kansas City and spent a little time at Warhol's Factory on Union Square. Carson's one-man art movement, rectal realism, was uniquely radical and equally obscure. Warhol, intrigued as anyone would be by the idea of a rectally held paintbrush, agreed to sit for a portrait. Neke remembered how his "eye-ass coordination was in sync" and things proceeded smoothly. The *end* result was stunning and forty years later, the painting's history—including its theft, return and eventual exhibition at the Warhol Museum in Pittsburgh, PA—is both thought-provoking and exciting.

It made sense that Neke would wind up on White Street. He was at Mudd for the Rastafari roots Reggae star Burning Spear and, like Kate Simon, was blown away when Percy Sledge took the stage. He even remembers "runway legend" Pat Cleveland's long-forgotten performance. Fearless and fun-loving, Neke was soon tossing back shots of NyQuil at the NyQuil party on the Mudd Club's second floor. I couldn't help recalling my wayward teenage Romilar experience and took a pass.

Ronnie headed inside; Neke showed up shortly after. It's 1 A.M. and the place is just getting started. My friend Ray Adams walks up to the door with Marion Pinto, the artist, SoHo pioneer and Punk enthusiast; they look like twins in matching motorcycle jackets. He gives me a hug, looks at the crowd and asks, "How do you do this?" I ignore the question but sometimes wonder the same thing.

I've known Ray since my college days in Connecticut and Marion's one of the first friends I met when I moved to the city. We order drinks, go downstairs and smoke a joint before Ray and Marion hit the dance floor. I try to sit still for a few minutes and breathe before going back outside. Half a minute later I head for the door, DJ Anita cues up "Public Image" and John Lydon starts screaming. The place goes crazy and the night disappears.

By 5 A.M., the club empties out, the sun's coming up but I have no idea where I'm going. Home seems an almost logical choice.

Best Known Missing Child

I tried to sleep but couldn't. I turned on the TV, turned off the sound and put on Blondie's *Blondie* album. Debbie Harry started singing about an X Offender; I went into the studio and picked up a paintbrush (with my hand). I played both sides of *Blondie* twice and crashed. I woke up late afternoon but had no idea what was happening in SoHo.

Friday, May 25, 1979. Etan Patz was walking to catch the school bus on West Broadway, his first time doing it on his own. He disappeared on the short two-block stretch and was never seen again. Etan was six years old and lived on Prince Street, five blocks north of Canal. The Ballroom where I once worked was just steps away from the bus stop.

There were posters on every lamppost, every corner and in every doorway. Sadly, Etan Patz became the first face to appear on a milk carton and was soon to become the world's best-known missing child. The neighborhood was long to recover; his parents never did. Decades later his family still lives on Prince, and people still wonder.

Puffy Coat

Nearly a week went by but the story of a missing six-year-old kept getting bigger. I passed at least half a dozen posters on the way to work and stopped to stare at one on the corner of Franklin Street. I walked three more blocks to Dave's Luncheonette and passed two more. The kid was gone but his face was unforgettable.

Heading into June, White Street never slowed down and I was at the door working with Joey, Louie and Robert. The crowd was usually six deep and closing in. The DJ was playing "Heart of Glass" and we could hear it thumping outside. The song, as Chris Stein later confided, was a goof or a fluke but the dance floor ate it up. I kept the chain in my hand, movin' to the groove. It was a catchy song.

Blondie was touring constantly and it seemed like months since Chris and Debbie Harry were at the Mudd Club. It was a late winter night and Debbie was still wearing a full-length black puffy coat. Discreetly obvious behind dark glasses, they huddled in a corner near the windowsill with *Interview* editor Glenn O'Brien. Now, the weather's warmed and the band's on the verge of selling a million records; the success of *Parallel Lines*, a big deal. Debbie's already an icon without any formal acknowledgment, and the boys from Blondie, when they're not on the road, are always at the club. Drummer Clem Burke's a friendly guy who knows everyone, and songwriter and keyboard player Jimmy Destri often arrives with Bowie. The puffy coat came and went but never said good-bye.

Fear of Music

Across the East River but avoiding the bridge-and-tunnel stigma, Talking Heads were recording *Fear of Music*. They were the first band I saw on my first visit to CBGB, and this was their second collaboration with Brian Eno, the onetime temporary *roommate* of Steve Mass. It was another constellation with a connection to White Street and it stretched from the Bowery to Long Island City.

Chris Frantz and Tina Weymouth lived in a loft building on Forty-fourth Drive. Jerry Harrison lived upstairs and Ernie Brooks, Jerry's friend from Harvard and bandmate from The Modern Lovers, lived somewhere in the middle. Chris remembers the whole gang piling into his new Honda and "bombing across the Williamsburg Bridge headed for Mudd." There was barely any late-night traffic and a spur-of-the-moment run to White Street took about fifteen minutes. Chris parked across the street from the club and the gang from Forty-fourth Drive headed inside. *Fear of Music* was just about ready.

The Second Floor

I'd seen Talking Heads perform many times. I was a fan and they were part of Rock 'n' Roll's mid-seventies reawakening. At the Mudd Club, I was getting to know the band and followed them thru the door. I started talking to Chris but the Russian Punks surrounded me. It was after 1 A.M. and the question on everyone's mind: *When is the upstairs going to open?*

When the Mudd Club began, the second floor of 77 White was just a second floor. By late winter it had become something else and everyone wanted *up there*. Limited access immediately upped the ante.

With an ice-filled, claw-foot bathtub for a beer cooler, folding tables for a bar and a few torn vinyl booths, the Mudd's second floor was a twenty-five-hundred-square-foot dirty version of heaven. Artist and former whip-dancing go-go boy Ronnie Cutrone added a black steel cage giving the room a touch of charm, menace and art world edge that influenced the club's nondesign and salvage décor.

Andy Warhol, Alan Ginsberg and Victor Bockris, *Cocaine Cowboys* party at Mudd, 1980, by Kate Simon.

The Bathrooms

The second-floor bathrooms were equally legend and possibly the biggest draw of all. Memorable moments barely remembered took place in those strange, brightly lit rooms. Locking the door when there was one to lock, we gathered in conversation or what passed as— drinking, pissing, doing a line or waiting for the yet to occur. Time loses its frame, impossible to capture but beautiful in a cinematic Super 8 kind of way; acid-trail hazy, stoned and frozen, disappearing in the white fluorescent light.

The smaller bathroom or men's room, if labels applied, was about eight-foot square with white tiles and exposed brick, a toilet, a urinal, a sink and a mirror. There was no partition and no privacy. The door was a bifold steel contraption with a drop-lock bracer bar on the inside. It was a room built for drugs, sex and getting lost.

The ladies' room—or whatever it might've been—was more of a standard design in a public restroom kind of way. The toilets were separated by partitions that came and went with the seasons, the room itself more inviting and communal than the men's. There were mirrors on the wall, no lock on the door and most of the time, no door at all. You could freshen up, take a seat and watch the world go by.

Nick Berlin. He only looks innocent, 1979, by Bobby Grossman.

The bathrooms were modified more than once and repaired regularly during the club's history but never lost their magic. From the Kennedys to the Rolling Stones, sailors, sex workers and Sex Pistols, it seemed everyone had a lost and found moment in a Mudd Club bathroom, including me.

Phoebe and the Troubled Youth Brigade

I watched a tiara-wearing Teri Toye get up from the "throne" and wander out as Rastaman Richard "Dirty Harry" Hall wandered in. There were even what appeared to be "children" running in and out of those bathrooms, but without proof of age it was hard to be sure. Phoebe Zeeman and Ellen Kinnally ran amok, looking and playing the part of jailbait, all the while keeping Steve Mass on his toes. Phoebe's barely older sister Eloise, along with bad girl Marina Lutz, singer David Scharff, photographer Eileen Polk, musician DJ Howie Pyro and musical delinquent Nick Berlin were all part of White Street's underage troubled youth brigade. They survived the first-floor bathroom and laughed their way onto the second floor. They referred

This page: Phoebe, natural born killer, 1980, courtesy Phoebe Zeeman.
Opposite: Billy Stark, Eileen Polk, Howie Pyro, 1979. Mudd Club
portrait series, *Punks of New York* by William Coupon.

to the club's unwitting No Wave hipster contingent as *Fish Heads*, torturing some of them with early-morning crank call serenades of the "Fish Heads" song. Funny now and funny then, the *kids* were unselfconsciously radical and as deep in the Mudd as anyone.

Steve loved them all and quickly offered Phoebe and Ellen jobs. He bought them drinks and encouraged them to get fake IDs. Phoebe's mother had Steve's phone number and occasionally called, looking for the girls, checking to make sure they were okay. The word *okay*— very loosely defined.

Howie Pyro was still a Mudd Club DJ; he and Nick, along with Billy Stark and occasionally Heartbreaker Walter Lure, were mem-

Puberty Ball Memo, 1979, created by Eileen Polk/courtesy Howie Pyro.

bers of a band called The Blessed. Their twisted vision and sense of humor, along with that of the other kids, informed everything from the Rock 'n' Roll Funeral to the Puberty Ball, successfully deflating Mudd's cool intellectual bent. The pubescent coming-of-age celebration featured a giant Quaalude and Tuinal hanging from the ceiling and a squadron of post-pubescent cheerleaders on hand to fluff the crowd. A buffet set up along the sidewall was stacked with a six-foot pyramid of pimple-inducing kiddie favorites: Twinkies and Ring Dings. The Blessed performed their hits, including "Kindergarten Hard-on" and "Flagellation Rock." Fellow juvenile delinquent and Revenge girl Eileen Polk was one of the Puberty Ball masterminds and a driving force behind the event. By the end of the night the Twinkies had all been eaten.

David Scharff, another teen troublemaker, sang with The Student Teachers, whose lineup included future curator and museum director Bill Arning and Jimmy Destri's girlfriend Laura Davis. Laura and Jimmy were the second and third wheels of Bowie's nightclubbing posse.

Marina Lutz, one of the Puberty Ball cheerleaders, loved the Dead Boys, the Cramps and the Ramones. She was an eager beaver, at the club every night, and most of the time ready to help out any way she could. However, when offered big money to strap on a strap-on she drew the line (if only in pencil) but still agreed to shuttle a grocery bag full of cash from White Street to Steve's apartment on West Eighth. Someone had to handle the night deposit and who better than a teenage girl riding around in a cab at 4 A.M.?

I was still at the door when Phoebe came outside and asked if I'd seen Steve. We went inside together, ordered a couple drinks and for the moment she forgot about him.

Always one of the smartest people in the room, Phoebe Zeeman knew that "hanging out at Mudd was way more fun than working there" and never took Steve up on the job offer. My time on White Street posed the counterargument, and for a long time I had as much fun as anyone. Part of the fun was getting to know Phoebe.

TV Party

Some of those kids were in high school and some in college but Glenn O'Brien, a Georgetown grad who studied film at Columbia, was beyond all that. Born in Cleveland, Glenn started working for Warhol in

Fab 5 Freddy Brathwaite and Debbie Harry, *TV Party*, 1980, by Bobby Grossman.

1970 when Andy was looking to lose the speed freaks and "get some clean-cut college kids on the staff." In some peculiar or nonpeculiar way, he fit the bill.

I'd seen Glenn around, everywhere from CB's to Mickey's to 54. In fall 1978, someone told him to check out "Eno's club" on White Street. He went; it wasn't really Eno's club, but he kept going back. By December, not long after Mudd opened, he created *Glenn O'Brien's TV Party*, a variety talk show and entertainment hour filmed in classic black-and-white for public access cable. Unlike anything previously offered on television, the show featured a conglomeration of "celebrity" guests that doubled as the show's staff and production team. O'Brien's love of Warhol's films and the idea that "good production values weren't important and mistakes were funny" helped inform the *TV Party* aesthetic.

The regular and revolving cast seemed built around a roster of Mudd Club regulars. Cohost Chris Stein along with Debbie Harry, David Byrne, Jean-Michel Basquiat, Lisa Rosen and photographer Kate Simon all did their thing for the sake of the Party. Richard (Ricky) Sohl handled the call-in phone line with the skill of a seasoned receptionist. Bobby Grossman was the official *TV Party* photographer, Walter "Doc" Steding was the *Party* bandleader and even Steve

Mass made numerous guest appearances. Fab 5 Freddy Brathwaite's enthusiasm and resulting camerawork added to the charm, chaos and television excitement.

After taping, the *TV Party* cast and crew usually wound up at the Mudd Club, where my *Party* contribution was making sure everyone got safely inside. One of those after-show visits was Fred Brathwaite's first trip to White Street and marked the beginning of his relationship with the club. Along with actress, future "gallerist" and Mudd Club regular Patti Astor, Fred went on to help change the way we look at art from the street and art in general. As part of the notorious Fabulous 5 crew that included Lee Quinones, he realized that graffiti was ready to take on a new life. He moved sound and vision forward, guiding Hip-Hop, Rap and graffiti to a larger audience.

TV Party taped three episodes at the Mudd Club, helping to expand the show's audience and broaden its curious appeal. One of those nights Debbie Harry and the Doc Steding Orchestra thrilled the crowd with a world-premiere performance of Blondie's future hit "The Tide Is High." Still, it was hard to tell who or what, other than Mudd, drew the crowd.

***

Working the door, often six nights a week, I started to believe that proximity and association was the near equal to being *part of*. I unknowingly toyed with that belief, on and off, for years.

Whether it was a *TV Party* taping or just another evening at work, I came face to face with several hundred people a night. Between the crowd outside, the crowd at the bar and the crowd on the dance floor, I sometimes felt a connection. Eventually, though, I felt the need to hide, and the only safe place was the basement. Drugs and subterrane went hand in hand.

Over the years I'd acted out and I hid in a number of basements but this was the only one with a Mudd Club upstairs. You walked down a flight and twenty feet back from the coat check window was a wall with a door. The door had a lock and behind the door was the *other side*—the ultimate VIP room, the perfect hideaway. There was a cage filled with cases of liquor and beer that only the bartenders could steal. With enough privacy to drop your pants and pull down someone else's, or have a momentary meltdown and quick recovery, the basement was a great place to snort a few lines, smoke a joint, snap a Quaalude in half and relax.

I always had a key to the storage area door but I can't remember if it was mine or whether I got it at the bar. I'd trail past the coat check with a few people in tow and close the door behind us—an indiscreet attempt at discretion. The sound of the dance floor came through the ceiling and I could feel the beat. I could hear a muffled Bryan Ferry crooning, "Come on, come on, let's stick together..." From Robert Rauschenberg to Mick Rock to Michael Maslin, from Joni Mitchell and Bowie to Teri, Ricky, Gary and Lynette: several were my friends, the others "proximity and association."

Back upstairs the dance floor's packed. I grab a beer and dive in as the Ramones, Iggy and Motown pound the beat and rattle the brain. Ronnie and Gigi are deep in the crowd, making up new dances as they go along; Abbijane and her girl gang Heather, Jackie and Julie, spinning around in some kind of Hullabaloozified spastic seizure. The DJ's flying in the face of Disco and circling back to Rock 'n' Roll. Three-minute intervals of sound, Diana Ross' voice in the middle singing faster than I remember and the room's about ready to explode. Years of pushing-to-the-front rock concert experience paying off, I make it past the stage and into the first-floor bathroom.

A SAMO scrawl, scrubbed from the wall, is rehappening; Jean-Michel Basquiat, with a stubby blond or green Mohawk, exits, leaving another mark behind. It's so crowded that people are standing on the toilets, and one cracks under the weight. There's an inch of water on the floor but hardly anyone moves except me. It's the new reality of wear and tear, the cost of doing business—not to mention being part of the club's appeal.

The broken toilet stories wouldn't die and before long Steve's talking plumbing repairs with Glenn O'Brien on *TV Party*. Lamenting "three hundred twenty-nine dollars for nothing," he compares Mudd's exploding toilets to "something like the Manhattan Project."

Despite water on the floor my feet are dry. I cross the room and push my way past the bar, a long narrow rectangle that reaches from the door to the dance floor. Two or three bartenders in the middle are handling a crowd four deep. The DJ booth, within arm's reach of the liquor and beer, is part of the bar. The DJ: a sitting duck, his only protection a pair of headphones, a beer bottle and a cigarette. William Coupon's rogues' gallery of club denizens peers from the facing wall. Ken Compton and Boris Policeband are in position near the front door; I turn the corner and I'm back outside. Gretchen's just inside holding what's left of the door money after Steve did a cash pickup, stuffing wads of bills into his pockets. I look at Gretchen and we laugh, dip behind the door and do two blasts from a vial of coke. Louie's off tonight, Robert just took a break and Joey's somewhere inside. There's about two hundred people waiting and a few look at me like they want the real doorperson to come back. A minute later, Dan Aykroyd barrels down the stairs from the fourth floor and bulldozes thru the crowd. I step up to the chain and ask a few people, "How many?" It's after 2 A.M. when somebody screams, "Let me the fuck in!" I turn around and Gretchen's still laughing.

Before we know it, it's 4 A.M. and the fun's almost over. By 4:30 we're prowling around the bar, searching the floor for Quaaludes and hundred-dollar bills. We kick around some plastic cups, and broken bottles, pick up several empty vials and check out a few odd pieces of clothing. I come up empty-handed but Gretchen finds twenty dollars. It's cab fare and breakfast money. Tomorrow we get paid. This is the life—and I think I love it.

Colter Rule once said the first six months of Mudd were magic. He called that time "the real candy." Colter may have split, but the place was candy for quite a while.

A Boom Box and Jug Wine

Over the next several months and following few years the deed to 77 White Street bounced between Ross Bleckner and Steve Mass. The price moved up several hundred thousand since Bleckner bought the building, but the crowds kept coming, and Steve was raking in the cash.

The Mudd Club drove Ross crazy from the start and when the barely legal contraption of an elevator nearly killed him, fellow artist (and 2007 Academy Award-nominated film director) Julian Schnabel came to the rescue. Ross survived but his leg was nearly crushed and spent months in a cast. Still, he managed to paint, make it to One University Place for dinner and have a few drinks at Mudd.

Ross and his boyfriend, Ron Dorsett, offered me an easy friendship and a place to escape when I needed one. I kept an eye on the door from their front windows, caught my breath and watched the crowd. From that sixth-floor vantage point it was hard to believe that less than a year ago, in summer 1978, Ross told his friend, artist and editor Kim Hastreiter, "Something is happening on the

first floor." He told her, "They're doing something down there."
They were Steve, Diego and Anya.

Ross and Kim knew each other from Cal Arts and in '78 she was living on Lispenard Street, around the corner from 77 White. One night, months before the club opened, they decided to see what was going on and three decades later Kim remembers a large empty room with a folding table, a boom box and a few bottles of Ripple-ish jug wine. She also remembers, "There was something about the place."

We've all looked at things without realizing what we were seeing and Kim was looking at the strange beginning of something that would redefine New York nightlife. The bare-bones spirit of a boom box and jug wine was there from the start, and that spirit never left.

Waves of No and New

Maybe I had the night off or maybe I just woke up early. I left the loft and headed for the Village. *Eno is God* was spray-painted at the entrance to the Chambers Street subway station—a slightly higher-plane kind of rock idiocy than *Clapton is God* painted on the wall at West Fourth Street. Both comments made me smile but Eno hit closer to home.

It was Judy Nylon who introduced Brian Eno to Steve and Diego. He needed a place to live and Steve offered the second floor of his West Eighth Street duplex. That was only part of Eno's roundabout connection to the Mudd Club. Another part was the result of a passing friendship with Maureen McLaughlin, the first manager of the B-52's. When Eno left New York for however many months, he offered McLaughlin the keys to the apartment on West Eighth. The B's, back and forth from Athens, sorely needed a place to crash and the Steve Mass-Brian Eno pad perfectly suited that need. Steve liked Maureen, met the band, and it wasn't long before he offered them the opening night gig at Mudd. A little bit tangled web and a little bit luck— the song about a lobster sealed the deal. A few months later, that same kind of luck and tangle landed me the job at the door.

The confusion over *Eno's club*, the one Glenn O'Brien was told to check out, wasn't the club itself but the actual bar on Mudd's first floor. According to Chris Frantz, Brian Eno chose the aerial maps that were placed under the bar's plexiglass countertop. That was Eno's contribution to Mudd and a curious detail of the club's non-

Brian Eno, on the second floor, 1979, by Allan Tannenbaum.

design concept. Stories persisted that Brian created the Mudd sound system and that he was a partner in the club but they were just rumors. The countertop maps was the only story that might've been true.

Brian Eno's larger contribution was a soundtrack of the seventies. His pioneering collaborations with Roxy Music, John Cale, David Bowie and Talking Heads along with his solo work made him a hero. His cover of the 1961 Tokens hit "The Lion Sleeps Tonight" was an early evening Mudd Club favorite.

Eno produced *No New York*, the 1978 No Wave compilation album featuring Contortions, DNA, Mars, and Teenage Jesus and the Jerks. The No Wave sound was an aggressive jackhammer scream; the No Wave films of Poe, Nares, Vivienne Dick and Jim Jarmusch were equally dark, artfully demented and occasionally confrontational. The movement was short-lived but influential, challenging and curiously avant-garde. The New Wave music that followed on the heels of No and post-Punk was less renegade, having a wider range and appeal due largely to its pop characteristics and a vague definition of the genre.

Brian Eno's No Wave curatorial effort *No New York* still stands as a document. His ongoing work with such bands as Talking Heads and U2 pushed the boundaries of New Wave into next.

The Blue Tiles

I collected my paycheck once a week at Steve's Eighth Street apartment, but I never saw Eno and rarely saw him at the club. I ran into him a few times at One University Place and sat down with him and his girlfriend Alex for a drink. By that time I was burnt on Mudd and he was living in a loft on Broome Street.

The payday routine soon changed and the brown paper grocery bags filled with cash accompanied by a teenage courier changed too. The money stayed at White Street and I'd swing by the club in the afternoon. Then one day the money was gone. The safe, bolted to the floor, was missing—along with half a dozen floorboards and Wilfredo, the daytime janitor. By the next day, two new janitors were already on the job.

When Steve finally moved to a loft at Franklin and Broadway, around the corner from the club, I'd ring the doorbell, go upstairs and get paid. I remember dark blue tiles in the bathroom, empty pizza boxes in the kitchen, lots of paper garbage and not much else. The blue tiles were nice.

The only time I had a problem with the Mudd Club payroll "system" occurred during one of my mini-meltdowns. I paid myself from the door receipts and left a disbursement slip on a scrap of paper, quit my job and went home. Steve called, asked me what happened, but I couldn't really say, except possibly too much cocaine. I threw some water on my face, smoked a few joints and went back a few hours later. Steve made sure I never paid myself again.

That was the only thing he ever told me not to do and I tried to keep it that way.

Everything from the jug wine to Waves of No and New, from *Eno is God* to a missing safe and an offbeat payroll system; that was my New York in 1979. Change happened fast and the years even faster.

I remember that first season on White Street; spring was slowly closing down and the weather was getting warmer. I ditched the leather jacket and the Tony Lamas, broke out the Converse All Stars and started working the door in a sport jacket. I occasionally wore jeans even though we frowned on other people wearing them. There were a few exceptions but for the most part it was *No jeans*, except mine.

I took some of my hard-earned Mudd Club dollars and shopped for work clothes on the Lower East Side, SoHo and the Village. I found a thrift shop out near the Brooklyn Navy Yard that sold shirts with zippers instead of buttons, and vintage Western shirts for fifty cents. Back then it was still the Brooklyn my Aunt Olga referred to as *God's country*. It was still bridge-and-tunnel and it was still the Brooklyn where I was born. Back then I looked good in a shirt with a zipper and I could still wear a fifty-cent Western shirt to work.

Peep-Toes, Capes and Iowa

When the after-hours and cocaine allowed, I got home by 6 A.M., out of bed by one in the afternoon. I'd spend part of the day painting, making marks on paper: bright colors, diary entries scribbled along the edges. They happened fast, a stream of fluorescent words—no overpainting, no rewrites.

I jumped in and out of the shower and got dressed, looked in the mirror and everything seemed fine. A pinstriped shirt with broken buttons and turquoise pants from Merchant of Venice on Prince

Street in SoHo where my friend Lynne Robinson worked looked pretty sharp, at least to me. I laced up my sneakers and I was almost ready. All I had to do was roll a joint, buy some cigarettes and grab a hot dog and egg cream at Dave's. I smoked the joint walking south down Cortlandt Alley, staring at 77 White from a block away. It was early and for the moment I had plenty of time.

White Street went from empty to crazy in less than six months and working outside I got to see everything, coming and going. When Chi Chi Valenti strolled toward the door wearing peep-toe shoes, a cape and a leather motorcycle cap it was something to behold. Her hair was as close to natural blonde as a shade of white heat platinum could get. She had the alleged proof to back up the *natural* part, the nonchalance and charm to show it off. Everyone enjoyed an occasional flash.

Chi Chi was a remarkable reinvention. Born in New York City with a given name long since forgotten, she spent time in Chicago and returned to New York in the later mid-seventies. Upon arrival she dressed a few windows and bounced around on a stage or two in Times Square. A straight-talker and the real deal, Chi Chi and I connected at Mudd and became friends. Before long, we were working side by side, thru the night, and getting lost in the morning after. She *voyeured* her way thru a funny (for all the wrong reasons) 8 A.M. sexual encounter of mine, offering suggestions, encouragement and commentary throughout; by 9 we were a threesome having breakfast at a local diner. Chi Chi was the first person I heard speak the words *peep-toe* and the only person I ever met who wore a cape.

Considering my memory for clothes, drugs, drinks and faces, I have no idea what Teri Toye was wearing when we met. From the popcorn fields of Iowa (where I'm sure no one had worn a cape in years) by way of Parsons School of Design, Studio 54 and who knows where else, Teri began showing up at Mudd a month or so after I started. I'm not sure who brought her or how she landed but it was a fast friendship and before long she was hanging at my place on Murray Street.

In spring 1979, Teri was still *Terry*. Never a boy even when she was, she fooled at least half the people all the time. She could pull off the natural beauty look in a plain white T-shirt and khakis or go topless in a de la Renta skirt, a sash and a tiara. Before long she was on the front lines of Mudd, hanging at the door, sitting on the bar or hiding out in a second-floor bathroom. A true original, there was never anyone at the club or anywhere else like Teri Toye. She was a star just by being, and the first person I met from Iowa.

I never wore khakis or de la Renta but I had a handmade Mudd Club pin that someone gave me—a strange wobbly 3-D font that read MUDD. I wore it for a couple of days, pinned to the front of a stretched and torn Punk-era yellow sweater. I still have the pin but moths ate the sweater in 1982. I had also a red blinking "Andy Blinks" brooch I wore on my lapel for a few weeks but so did a lot of other insiders and regulars. One day the brooch stopped blinking and disappeared. So did Andy Blinks.

Blondie's Chris Stein liked to think that "the Mudd Club was hidden—the image of a club you'd see in films all the time." An alley, a dark street, a smoky interior; he appreciated that the club never had a logo T-shirt. The model of a certain kind of discretion, Mudd never really went public, even when it did: ads in the *Village Voice* and the *SoHo News* were just an address and phone number, the names of various bands and the occasional dose of snark. Besides, an ad didn't mean you were coming in.

Thirty-plus years later, I wish I had the T-shirt that never existed: threadbare and tattered, another memory of time gone by.

Land of a Thousand Dances

Today, the time I once had is less than plenty. Bleecker Street seems another lifetime and Long Island a distant past. Still, I remember them with barely a fade. I remember too the night in 1975 when "Jesus died for somebody's sins but not mine." That night was permanently burned into my brain.

So much of the time was reignited by her words and music but Patti Smith never set foot inside the Mudd Club. Her version of "Gloria" caused eruptions on the dance floor and "Land: Horses/Land of a Thousand Dances/La Mer (De)" was an incantatory wall of sound. I can only imagine what *live* at the Mudd Club would've been like.

Patti's guitarist, the songwriter, producer, historian and journalist Lenny Kaye, remembers, "It wasn't that unusual to stay out till dawn" and that "Mudd was about hanging out late." Lenny loved the music the DJs played and knew that when it came to the White Street sound, "You didn't have to adhere—the further afoot it went, the better." He liked to say the Mudd Club was his kind of joint. *Further afoot* certainly had its appeal.

Richard "DNV" Sohl (so named by Lenny Kaye, who thought the star keyboard player resembled Tadzio, the beautiful boy in Visconti's *Death in Venice*) was at the club nearly every night. Patti's loyal assistant and sometime supporting musician Andi "Midge" Ostrowe wasn't far behind. I stayed close to them all, closer than just "proximity and association." Friends for life.

Jane Friedman, a fellow nightlife traveler, came by as often as anyone. She was a founding partner of the Wartoke Concern, a publicity and talent development "operation" instrumental in shaping everything from the Woodstock Festival, the Mercer Arts Center and Patti's early career. Despite time, place and degrees of separation, there's a direct connection to Mudd.

Jane often arrived with Frank Zappa or John Cale, hung out at the bar, and talked to Steve Mass about music and whatever else was *happening*. She loved the club and was one of the first to say, "the place felt like home and that was important to us. It's why we were always there." From Max's to CBGB's to White Street, "we lived in those places; that's why they were special." Despite my not always spiritual take on things, we could both agree, "those places had a soul."

I thought Jane was a sweetheart, offering me a bit of comfort amid chaos. As Patti mentioned on the back cover of *Horses*, Jane was the woman "who knew."

John Cale, no stranger to White Street, is someone else "who knew." A founding member of The Velvet Underground, he's a musical genius and one of Rock 'n' Roll's great collaborators. He worked with everyone from The Stooges and the Modern Lovers to avant-garde pioneers like John Cage and La Monte Young. He produced the album *Horses*.

John performed at Mudd with Chris Spedding and occasionally joined Nico onstage for a few songs. He liked hanging at the bar with Steve Mass, disappearing and reappearing several times a night. An oddly accessible, smart and funny guy, John Cale was a hero fueled by New York City and the night. That viola on the first Velvet Underground album—there's nothing like it; hearing it from the White Street stage, countering Nico's moans, chants and harmonium flourishes, sent a dark and eerie chill.

***

Whether we were painting, making films or standing at the door of 77 White we informed one another. Working on White Street, I became friendly and, in some cases, friends, with people I'd seen around—

Ronnie Cutrone and John Cale, second floor Mudd, 1979, by Kate Simon.

with the names I knew and the voices I heard. Whatever our previous connection might have been, it was now the Mudd Club door—a connection both clear and unclear.

Rubber and Leather

By the time I arrived on White Street, my soon-to-be friends Claudia Summers and Marcus Leatherdale were already inside while I was still figuring out the lay of the land: who was who and what I really wanted.

Dressed in black, beautifully severe and just a little bit vulnerable, Claudia was a struggling musician with an eye for trouble. A San Francisco Punk transplant, she arrived in New York a few months before Mudd started happening and by 1979, Claudia had begun playing keyboards with Walter Steding and The Dragon People. Hanging out, making music and getting high, she was hiding something and searching for something else. I felt a connection and still do.

My friendship with Marcus was different. He was a young photographer from Canada—handsome, boyish and easygoing, with an iconic sense of style. He met Claudia in San Francisco; they reconnected

Marcus Leatherdale and Claudia Summers, colluding on the second floor, 1979, by Marcia Resnick.

in New York and got married at City Hall. Robert Mapplethorpe, a close friend of the newlyweds and Marcus' constant companion, presented the bride with a rubber garter belt as a wedding gift (who knows what he gave Marcus). Rubber and leather remained in her future. Their union was an open marriage and still is.

When I began to get lost in the insanity—the death drugs and kinky sex—Claudia already had one foot in. Marcus, prone to a lesser dose of drugs but a higher-profile kink, seemed to better manage the madness. Their friendship helped me survive and more than three decades later the story continues, each in our way still figuring things out.

The Mudd Club was a mixed bag. Lenny Kaye used the words "further afoot" with regard to the music but those words say it all. An art bar, a dance hall, a pickup joint and drug den, all on its own terms; Mudd cast a wide net and rarely threw anything back. An incredible incubator for talent, I believed there was a reason why the people inside were there. I believed too that we all had some sort of résumé and credentials necessary to get us thru the door. In the words of Rebecca Christensen, we "brought something to the party" and to that end we found a connection. Our diversity created a unique convergence—of cultures, cliques and individuals—and for the most part everyone got along. Steve's management skills and problem-solving tactics were whim-driven, straightforward or occasionally convoluted, but whatever they were, he got the party started and kept it going. For nearly two years I held the chain *and* the key.

The club echoed the spirit of a city on the verge, whether a changing time or a nervous breakdown. They existed in parallel, one being possible only because of the other. Freedom still ruled the street as well as the dance floor; no one realized *impossible* was lurking around the corner.

Diplomacy and Pot Stirring

Convergence and cultural diversity aside, paranoia often had a hand in the mix; Steve's on-again, off-again affair with Reggae and Rasta, uptown celebs and *bridge-and-tunnel* was hard to keep up with. Instant door policy changes often were initiated to rid the club of any perceived threat or scourge. Sometimes the innocent got caught, lost or exiled in the shuffle. Cocaine dealers occasionally got a pass while heroin dealers were mostly street or dirty boutique, though rules rarely applied. The policy changes were at times reasonable, other times arbitrary and occasionally funny. Easy targets—fatties, longhairs and the like—always fair game.

Roots Reggae band Steel Pulse, and their eventual landmark gig at Mudd, meant disorder and negotiation at the door accompanied by great music, giant spliffs and smoke-filled bathrooms. Steve, however, seemed to believe that anyone with dreads was selling pot (White Street's naïve nod to racial profiling), and such friends as musician Richard "Dirty Harry" Hall and Tier 3's Manny L'Amour were always getting tangled up in the nuance of door policy. Finding it difficult to look them in the eye and talk shit, I generally ignored Steve's instructions regarding their admission. Keeping my fingers crossed, I played diplomat and dumb at the same time, but that's not how it started.

When Steve and I first discussed my job he told me he didn't want David Bowie or Mick Jagger *types* getting out of limos and coming inside. It sounded like crap and I said okay but when the real deals started showing up things changed fast.

I made an effort to get on the same page with Steve and occasionally I'd get there first. He could be reticent and evasive until you read between the lines, his suggestions and instructions always creative and designed to stir the pot. Whether they worked or not wasn't the point.

Original Modern Lovers bassist and poet Ernie Brooks felt that "exclusivity of any kind was terrible but if you were going to have a door policy, the Mudd did it right. That's what made the Mudd Club different." By then Ernie was playing bass with The Necessaries and kept his hair long and curly. He wore jeans and lived in Long Island City but never had a problem at the door.

Steve's instigating and "pot" stirring, combined with my respectful disregard and diplomacy skills, made for good policy. The only *real* problem was figuring out what to do about the Hells Angels. Our club-to-club relationship kept getting edgier and there had been several uncomfortable incidents. Keeping the Angels outside or getting them to leave once they got in was only part of the challenge. There was no relating to, only dealing with, and the breaking point was just months away.

Free Meal Manifesto

Regardless of door policies, drugs were ever-present; a lot of people—including me—were doing as much and as many as we could get our hands on. In spring '79 I was a pot-smoking coke user. I liked to drink and I liked fooling around with a line or two of heroin. I thought that was pretty normal—and for many of us hanging out or staying out till 6 A.M., it was.

At Mudd, cocaine was everywhere. Heroin was out of the closet and somewhat acceptable. Quaaludes were a hot item and bathroom fixtures like Linda Ludes or the Russian Punks had as many as anyone wanted. Between those and the other "tips" I received, my pockets were always full and nothing went to waste. My appetite for excess remained healthy; for everything else, it depended on the offer.

I kept painting and doing some good work but did little else to avoid temptation. I couldn't tell the difference between opportunity and distraction, drugs becoming the fuel and my eventual undoing. Silence might've been the *no* that greeted people I wasn't letting into the club but I said *yes* to just about everything else—including a free meal.

Working at Mudd just a short time, I joined Pat Wadsley and a half-dozen others for a free lunch with Bryan Ferry and his girl-

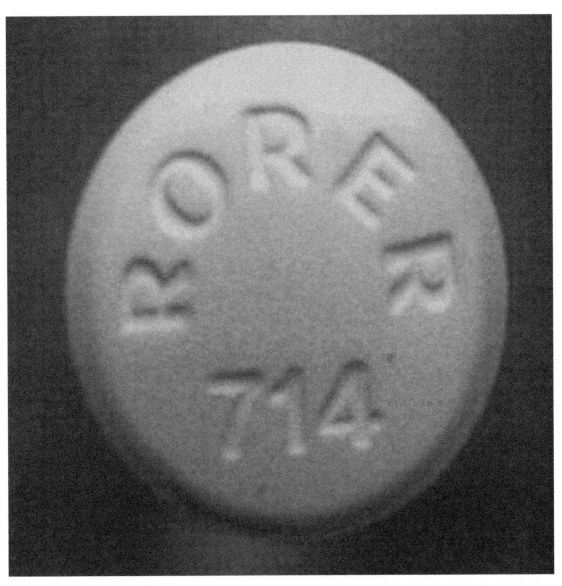

Quaalude, RORER 714, real, 1979, courtesy Richard Boch.

friend Barbara Allen (the well-connected party girl socialite) in a suite at the Carlyle Hotel. It happened because I was in the right place at the right time and I said *yes* at the right moment. It was the same way with my job at Mudd—the same with a lot of things.

I arrived at the Carlyle wearing a monogrammed Brooks Brothers shirt, a black leather motorcycle jacket and a red leather tie. When I got upstairs and walked in, Bryan told me he liked the tie. The next night he bounded onstage at the Palladium for the New York stop on Roxy Music's *Manifesto* tour wearing a red leather suit. It seemed either one or both of us was on to something.

When the show was over I grabbed a cab and headed for White Street. My ears were ringing and I could still hear Ferry wailing,

"In every dream home a heartache…" I got to Mudd and DJ Danny Heaps was playing the single "Trash" from *Manifesto*. I went back outside and told Joey Kelly where I'd been. I was a Roxy fan and felt like a kid. That was on March 29, 1979 and I was one week on the job. Everything still felt new.

***

By now, summer was slowly approaching. The Murray Street loft's *not far from the Mudd Club* location fast became popular and I started doing a lot of entertaining. On May 21, 1979, I hosted a birthday party for my boyfriend and roommate Gary Kanner. Like me, Gary was a child of suburbia and grew up in Great Neck, Long Island, just a few miles from New Hyde Park.

Gary landed in New York in the fall of '77, hung out at Hurrah and got a job at Cinemabilia, the movie, book and memorabilia store in the Village. In 1978, he found his way to The Ballroom where I was working. Before long Gary was living at Murray Street. The love between us came and went; drug-fueled camaraderie, ambivalence and animosity ensued. In between all that we shared our lives and celebrated numerous birthdays.

The twenty-first was a Monday and I had the night off. Gary and I focused on getting high, blowing out candles and trying to eat birthday cake. The previous evening, Louie Chaban inquired politely if he could bring his then boyfriend, the poet, gadfly and Warhol associate Rene Ricard to the party; I soon came to understand why someone would ask. Rene's sparkling but razor-sharp wit, encyclopedic knowledge and ability to expound on any subject were well known. Any response or reaction perceived by him to be incorrect often turned things loud and ugly. Louie knew that better than anyone. I'd yet to learn.

Richard Sohl, Anita Sarko, genteel pleasure-seeker and art connoisseur Clarissa Dalrymple and our friend Solveig Lamberg arrived early, leaving plenty of time to celebrate and make it to Mudd by 2 or 3 A.M. Glenn McDermott, his girlfriend Debbie, and fellow Mudd employee Jay Siano came by around midnight, shared a bit of coke and headed for White Street. Old friends, new acquaintances and a few people we'd never seen before strolled in and joined the party. We served a little food, a lot of liquor and what seemed like a ton of drugs. People brought flowers, champagne and more cocaine. Everyone survived, the flowers lasted for days and some people stayed all night. Ricky Sohl stayed until the next morning. Robert and Joey worked the door at Mudd and made it thru the night without me.

Despite the near certainty of volatility, Rene behaved.

Rock 'n' Roll Star

The following evening, the Patti Smith Group headed into a two-night stand at the Palladium on Fourteenth Street (the band's fourth album, *Wave*, was released a week earlier). Before the show I ran into music guru, rock legend and Mudd Club regular Danny Fields at the old Luchow's Restaurant next door. I split after a few drinks, headed thru the Palladium's Thirteenth Street entrance, sat on the floor backstage and smoked cigarettes with Ricky before the band went on. Robert Mapplethorpe and Marcus Leatherdale, all black leather and serious, nodded as they breezed past on the way to see *Madam* before she hit the stage. Fifteen minutes later, Ricky stood up, grabbed his Sharp mini-radio-television combo and drifted toward the keyboards. I smiled, stepped out into the orchestra and stole a seat up front. Patti ran onstage trailing a giant American flag, Ricky turned on his TV and the band opened with The Byrds' "So You Want to Be a Rock 'n' Roll Star."

I split after an hour and got to Canal Street with enough time to grab a hot dog and an egg cream at Dave's. I walked down Broadway and turned onto White Street. I stuffed the last bite in my mouth and picked a shred of sauerkraut off my shirt.

Patti played again the next night. I had to work but Lynne Robinson and Gary used my name at the back door. The following night the band did CBGB; I squeezed my way in and out and made it back to Mudd before I was missed. That was New York City, May 1979. The hot dogs at midnight were still hot and most people knew that an egg cream had nothing to do with an egg. White Street was still a wild time ride and the Mudd Club, a different crazy every night. Despite the bumps, bruises and too much cocaine, I loved my job, and at times I really did fit in. All I had to do was keep painting and get some sleep.

Must Attend

Two weeks later, 6 P.M. The early days of June were behaving like summer and daylight wasn't turning off till 9. I stuffed some money in my pocket and Gary and I headed uptown to Madison Books: Rene Ricard was holding court and signing copies of his first book of poetry, a thin volume with a Tiffany Blue cover published by the Dia Foundation. An early-evening, under-the-radar event, it was a *must attend* for a small but discerning cross section of New Yorkers. Gerard Malanga (*the* assistant to Andy Warhol from 1963–1970), who worked for Dia at the time, had edited the collection of poems and cohosted the evening. Louie Chaban was there, and one of us had to be at White Street by 11. Teri Toye arrived with Victor Hugo, the window dresser, Warhol instigator and Halston companion. Wearing a football jersey, a pair of Maud Frizon heels and no pants, Teri easily dazzled the room. Richard Sohl, just back from another round of endless touring with the Patti Smith Group, spoke quietly and in code about his infatuation with *downtown*. I knew what he meant but had no idea what anyone else might've known. Minutes later when Warhol arrived the evening officially qualified as a minor event.

I said hello, good-bye, and split after Rene spent a moment signing a copy of *Rene Ricard*, the new book of poetry. Inside was a hand-drawn Cocteau-like *Ricard* with a personal inscription. I thought it was beautiful and still do.

The night isn't even half over and everyone else is sticking around. I have to shift gears and get to work. Outside I hail a cab on Madison; the driver heads south on Fifth. It feels like it's going to be an easy night but you never know. Anything can happen between midnight and 5.

I arrive at 77 White and Ross Bleckner walks out the front door as I walk in. Steve's at the bar either talking with DJ David or just talking; it's hard to tell. The house lights are still on and David's digging through a stack of 45s looking for a few things to start with. Steve's looking a little uneasy, as though he can't decide whether he wants to hear "Betty Lou's Got a New Pair of Shoes" or the Village People. My "easy night" prediction is already falling apart.

Then the lights go down and DJ David has a headphone to his ear. Bowie and Eno's "Moss Garden," an ambient piece from *Heroes*, trickles out of the speakers and drifts around the room. Bartenders Greg and Elizabeth come up from the basement carrying a few bottles and get behind the bar. Greg's already hyped and Elizabeth looks trapped behind clenched teeth and her own negative energy. Luckily, she gets buried in the mix.

A minute later I step outside, Robert steps out of a cab, Joey strolls around the corner and Gretchen appears out of nowhere. The crowd waits and it's almost happening when I duck back inside and move halfway down the stairs. I snort up and lick whatever's left in the paper fold in my back pocket. Back outside a few people start looking better and Robert starts sending them in. Gretchen smiles, collects their three-dollar cover charge, and Kraftwerk's "Trans Europe Express" slowly pushes the night forward. Now we're happening.

At 5 A.M. I walked home. I slept, woke up and left the house by early afternoon. I bought a sport jacket in a thrift store on West Fourth Street and smoked a joint in Washington Square Park. I started thinking, gave up and walked down West Broadway toward Murray Street; I passed White Street, kept walking, went upstairs and rolled another joint. It was just over three months ago when Steve Mass called, looking for a new doorman. I'm not sure if it was luck or fate but I was home and answered the phone. I had no idea what I was getting into. Heading into my first Mudd Club summer, I just kept showing up and made the job mine.

Tina L'Hotsky, Mudd morning after, 1979, by Alan Kleinberg.

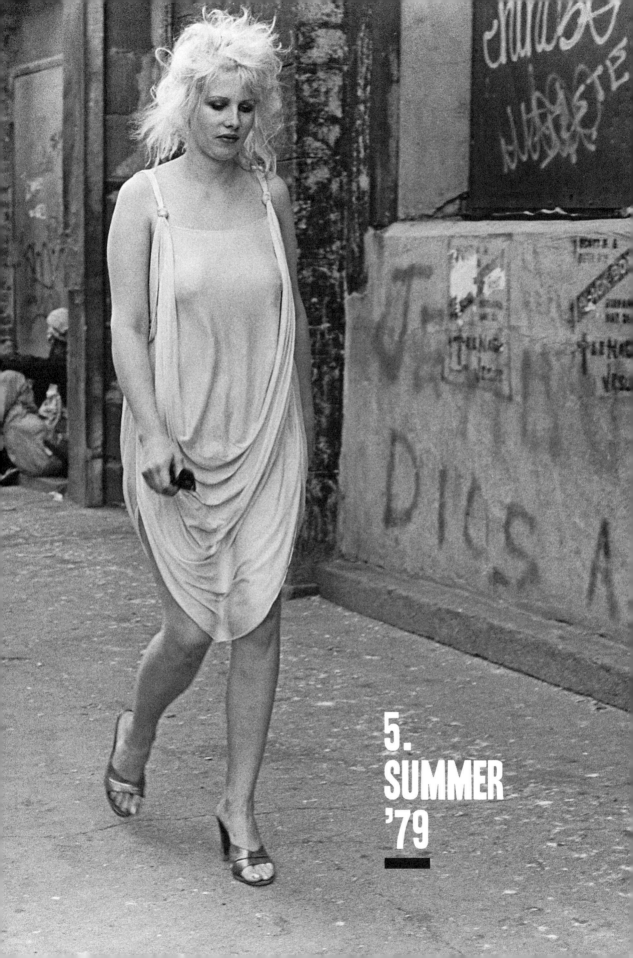

5.
SUMMER
'79

By now mid-June and summer not quite official, the weather turned warm and the air conditioning was working. I stood outside facing the crowd, sucking down a Heineken, trying to keep cool. It was still early but the bar was busy and the dance floor was full. I felt like I knew half the people inside. The other half was what paid the bills.

Below Canal Street was still an underground oasis when the Mudd Club opened. Betsy Sussler, the future publisher of *Bomb* Magazine, and Lindzee Smith were already living in the neighborhood. Actress Rosemary Hochschild and director Michael Oblowitz were my neighbors and lived above the Murray Street aquarium store. Filmmaker Bette Gordon remembers birds singing outside her open window. There was an actual beach just west of the World Trade Center and not a hint of the suburbanization to come. By 6 A.M., the sun was shining and the air was pretending fresh. Most of us were just getting home.

***

Staring at the crowd, I really was judge and jury, subject to bribes, tampering and influence. If you looked at me sideways I'd look back and wonder (almost out loud), *what the fuck?* To this day, my ability to snap and decide remains both asset and liability.

I stood at the door of the Mudd Club wearing a pair of orange painter's pants that I bought at Canal Jeans when it was still on Canal Street. I wore a Hawaiian shirt with a tropical fish pattern and a pair of white Converse sneakers that only stayed white for a minute. The shirt had a few holes but no one cared or noticed.

My Marlboro box was next to my drink on the step of the unused door behind me. Everything I needed was in that box except for what was left in my pocket. If I ran out of cigarettes, I'd grub a Winston from the discriminating but generous accompanist Richard Sohl, an old-school Camel from iconically cool John Lurie, or a Gauloise from neo No Wave White Street beauty Lisa Rosen. Everybody smoked and cigarettes were still cheap.

I must have been busy bumming or smoking when I overlooked a journalist from the Queens College newspaper. He didn't like waiting—or maybe I didn't like him—and didn't get in. The paper's mention of the club was brief but managed to squeeze in a cheap shot about the guy at the door in the orange pants. I read it twice and liked that he singled me out. If he'd worn orange pants or at least introduced himself, he might have made it inside.

Controversy surrounding my summer wardrobe wasn't the only thing going on. The Murray Street loft soon was doubling as a morning hot spot and occasional crash pad, depending on the liquor, the drugs and the company. The 7 A.M. energy was slow-burn electric; the music was loud. Again, I thought this was normal.

Another of my roommates was Wayne Bernauer, a friend from New Hyde Park Memorial High School. We shared the Bleecker Street apartment in '76 and moved downtown in '77. Wayne loved Rock 'n' Roll, CBGB's and wandering around the West Village—the only problem was his day job. By the end of '78 he was already getting buried by the late-night/early-morning shuffle and by summer of '79 I was bringing the Mudd Club home.

Wayne might have liked the access my job provided but after a while the upside-down schedule got to be too much. I was spending most of my time with Gary, and Wayne and I started drifting apart. When Teri Toye crash-landed and became a semi-permanent member of the household all bets were off. Wayne stuck around just long enough to appreciate some of the craziness and noise that a stoned and stupefied Grace Slick referred to as "morning maniac music"—the difference being, that was Woodstock 1969. Our morning mania was *killing* a near-innocent bystander who had to be at work by 9 A.M.

Combat Love Party invitation (reverse), 1979, courtesy Marina Lutz.

Wayne couldn't keep smiling and moved a hundred blocks north to the Upper West Side. He came back once, stayed for a few weeks, but that was it. It was my loss and still is.

Love

The Mudd Club also had a few changes going on. The façade of 77 White, previously a nondescript noncolor, was repainted green camouflage and draped with a monument-sized American flag. It was Wednesday, June 20, 1979, and we were getting ready for a night of Combat Love.

A fierce sense of patriotism was running rampant on White Street, *service before self* and Mudd Wanted You. Though my own sense of duty was muted at best, Steve Mass couldn't control himself. Appearing on *Glenn O'Brien's TV Party*, he noted his original intent of offering employees of nearby government offices a place to come, relax and

THE JUNIOR WACS AND WAVES
ASSOCIATION OF
THE MUDD CLUB

in commemoration of D Day
cordially invite you to attend a full dress

WAR GAMES

COMBAT LOVE PARTY

WEDNESDAY, JUNE 20
at 2350 hours (11:30 P.M.)

The Military Party Committee consisting of Legs, Arturo, Tina and
Dr. Mudd invite all M.P.'s, Wacs, Grunts, Storm Toopers, Generals,
Padres, Protestors, Peasants, Geisha Girls, Nazi Dykes, and U.S.O.
Chorus Girls to participate. (Costume mandatory)

The SCHRAPNEL BAND will stir your patriotic blood and there will be
plenty of K RATIONS for revellers. Everyone is invited to lay a wreath
at the memorial altar for the "DUKE" and use the JANE FONDA protest
doll for target practice.

Opposite: War Games, Combat Love Party, 1979, by Allan Tannenbaum.
Above: Combat Love Party Invitation, 1979, courtesy Marina Lutz.

unwind. That idea sounded exciting enough, but Combat Love quickly took flag-waving, service and civic-mindedness to a whole new level.

Louie and I stood watch as men and women in uniform arrived at the door. Standing shoulder to shoulder with other young Americans, they were hungry for glory, and looking for a drink. Victor Bockris remained in position on the first floor while helmet-wearing Debbie Harry, walkie-talkie in hand, discussed offensive strategy with Steve. War correspondent and photojournalist Kate Simon arrived out of uniform, wearing jeans and a striped boat neck pullover, passing thru the lines undetected. She approached the door and requested permission to enter.

Ten minutes later I walked inside. I headed for the second floor, looked up and saw *Nuke 'em till they glow* along with a Hiroshima-like blast emblazoned on the stairwell wall. I paused, took a deep breath and started rethinking everything I once believed. A shrine dedicated to the recently departed John Wayne was surrounded by people bidding farewell to a hero. A Jane Fonda protest doll, set up for target practice, received more than "her" fair share of attention. Security was tight, frequencies were scrambled and the Mudd Club was ready. It was a great time to be alive and feel good about America—a good time to feel some *Combat Love*.

When Debi Mazar, actress and former Mudd employee, reminded me, "So much of what we felt back then was love," I smiled, not quite sure if this was what she meant.

Brands of Cool

By the end of June, the summer stopped fooling around. It was getting hotter by the day and the crowd outside was getting restless. Euro-ish South American transplant Rudolf Piper surely felt the heat dressed in a studded dog collar, white dinner jacket and snug black tee. Pointy shoes, wraparound shades and slicked-back hair completed whatever No Wave, New Wave or *non wave* look he was aiming for. I just opened the chain and said nothing, remembering I was the one who wore the orange pants.

Rudolf was friendly and polite but distant, "Euro" in a strange but German kind of way. He greeted the door with an oddly accented "Hello" and paused a moment to flirt with Gretchen. The girls loved the whole Rudolf thing but from my middle-distance vantage point it

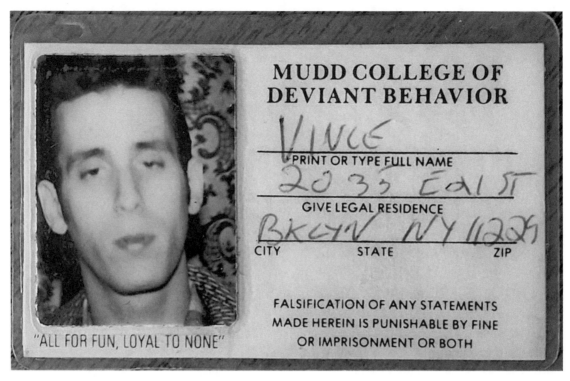

Vince, Mudd Club ID, 1980, courtesy Vince.

didn't translate. Whether it was his off-brand of cool or strange sense of fashion, I wasn't sure; the only thing I was certain about was that his style, peculiar magnetism and determined eye on New York's nightlife left Steve Mass feeling a bit cold. I always took care of Rudolf but it wasn't until much later that we exchanged more than a few words.

A minute later, Rudolf disappears and Gretchen is back to playing cashier and drinking vodka. It's busy and Louie's inside, lost on the dance floor or in the bathroom—I'm alone, staring at a crowd that's gotten larger over the last hour. Gretchen's trying to keep track of the money and the doorway's jammed. When I ask what's going on she reminds me, once they get past the chain they still have to get past her. My response: it's difficult to make change when you're snorting a line of coke, sipping a *vodka rocks* and smoking a cigarette. She laughs; I smile and grab my beer. Right now it's still early, I'm still on duty, and Vince Grupi is headed toward the door.

Vince is a good-looking Italian kid from out in Sheepshead Bay. He shows up every night, well-dressed in Rockabilly gear or a slick, forties-style suit. He drives a '72 Buick convertible, LeSabre option.

I open the chain, Vince says, "Hey Rich" (an outer boroughs version of my name) and heads inside. I check to see who else is coming my way when Larry Kaplan appears out of nowhere. He's a Bay Ridge greaser, and like Vince, drives a Buick; some nights he rides a motorcycle.

An hour later when I wander upstairs, Larry is at the bar. Vince is in the bathroom taking a piss and Cookie Mueller is standing at the toilet next to him. Her dress is hiked up and she's pissing too. I smile because I've seen it all before. Vince smiles as well, figuring any girl who can piss standing up is okay by him.

By 2 A.M. Vince Grupi is onstage introducing Buzz and The Flyers, a Rockabilly band that plays the clubs and hangs out at Mudd. Larry Kaplan is on the dance floor and Cookie's still upstairs. By 5 A.M. I'm out the door.

Thirty years later I told those guys, "I never used the word *greaser* because I thought it might be an insult." Larry explained, "It was about rebellion and style," not to mention hair.

Funny how I missed that one.

I might've been out of the loop on *greaser* but missed very little when it came to French. When I heard the name Edwige, it sounded *very*. Then I heard she had arrived from Paris and that Jedd Garet, the modern-day surrealist painter, was throwing a small party at his loft to mark the occasion. Having been invited, Marcus Leatherdale and I stopped by.

Style to spare, short blonde hair and a healthy spirit of rebellion, Edwige Belmore was a *Façade* and *Interview* magazine cover girl with an interesting résumé and a fascinating name. She modeled for Gaultier and Mugler and was photographed by Helmut Newton and Pierre et Gilles. Her first trip to New York happened after meeting Andy Warhol in Paris. She was both artist and muse and Andy crowned her "Queen of the Punks" (whatever that meant). Her *greaser* period came much later.

Most New Yorkers had no idea, but in Paris, Edwige was a big part of the scene. She left her job at the door of Le Palace to work at Les Bains Douche, the club of the moment, and considering what I was up to at the Mudd Club, I thought it was time we officially met. When she arrived at the party I wasn't disappointed.

Edwige responded to *cool* and was struck by the sense of community centered on White Street. She "loved the way people like John Lurie and Chi Chi Valenti looked" and the way they carried it off. Years later, I told her, "So did I."

"You're so interested in all this history," she responded.

"It's important."

She smiled.

Forever fierce and fearless, Edwige offered singer and underground film star Adele Bertei a hand when she noticed a "big guy and a little girl fighting it out on the Mudd Club dance floor." She tapped Adele on the shoulder, asked "Can I help?" and jumped right in.

Steve Mass liked Edwige and gave her three hundred dollars to buy a '62 Fender Telecaster. Ever the art patron, Steve had the money and Edwige, a beautiful woman with a French accent, wanted to make music. Sometimes that's all it took and sometimes it took a lot more. Decades later, Edwige is the first to say, "The Mudd Club, it's one of my roots." That's when I look across the table and think *mine too*; I was just twenty-five years old when the club opened, and today was far away.

Then memory takes me back and I wind up on White Street; I'm staring at the crowd and she's a hard one to miss.

Oh good, he's at the door. That's how Colette feels when she sees me because she knows she'll get right in. Looking like a Punk Bo Peep dressed in white ruffles and fluff, she's part of the attraction and energy that brings people to the club. She got a little weird with me when I first started at Mudd but it was a miscommunication, a one-time glitch. Since then she's been a sweetheart. When she tells me a bit about herself I try to hang on and listen. Some of it I still remember.

Colette left Tunis and headed for Nice; in 1969, she arrived in New York. Still a *kid,* she gravitated toward the city's art and music scene, hanging out at Max's Kansas City. She began creating a simple series of "Street Works" around 1970, both signaling and echoing the outlaw spirit of graffiti. Her *Real Dream* installation famously appeared at the Clocktower on Leonard Street in 1975, two blocks from the Mudd Club door.

I open the chain thinking *Colette* but remind myself that *Justine* is her new persona: the *Beautiful Dreamer* album by Justine and The Victorian Punks, the latest chapter. The distinction sometimes confuses me but I'm way too busy to think about it.

Sarcasm and Misfits

It's a Saturday, June 1979, not even midnight and already more than a hundred people are milling around outside. People arrive by 11:30 thinking that it betters their chances of getting in. I tend to think the opposite. Busy this early means a scary night ahead.

A few regulars—Roxanne, Boy Adrian, Boris and Hal—slide in along the front of the building. They're easy, and they know the chain's going to open. John the Greek, a polite kid who lives on Great Jones, comes by every night, stands off to the side and waits barely a minute. Kim Hastreiter with Branca, her *SoHo News* associate, squeeze in behind him. I step down and grab Betsey Johnson as she gets out of a cab, point to a few people in the street and they follow us in. The crowd in front looks restless and I don't like it, so I run inside, get Betsey a drink and throw down a Rémy before I head back out. Two hundred people are now in front of me and fewer than fifty are coming in.

There's a guy at the chain that keeps asking questions and if he'd just shut up he might have a chance. I finally tell his party of four, "Not right now," and he comes back with the classic line, "Studio 54 always lets us in." I easily respond, "So go there, it's a real graveyard." The foursome leaves and probably heads for Xenon. A couple standing close by smiles and a few minutes later I let them in.

Sarcasm gets me in trouble but the unavoidable *in here versus out there* vibe fortunately stops short of creating a mob mentality. People get anxious but rarely physical. Peacefully impatient is hard enough; I need a break.

Tonight I'm working with Robert Molnar. I turn around, tell him I'll be right back and head for the upstairs bathroom. One of the Russians offers me a line of coke and I tell him to give me a few more. Ronnie Shades, the missing link between Belushi and Aykroyd's Jake and Elwood Blues, is in the corner with Leisa Stroud. He steps over and offers me a sniff off the tiniest coke spoon I've ever seen. I walk downstairs, take a spin on the dance floor with Abbijane and lose myself in a Motown mash-up. Ten minutes later, I hear Abbi yell, "Hey, snap out of it!" and head back to the door.

I send in two guys from the Misfits and Robert rolls his eyes. Between their elaborate "hawks" and the spikes and studs on their gear I can't imagine getting much closer than mildly curious. Maybe with enough alcohol and cocaine I'd change my mind, but probably not. The whole package is just too *Halloween*.

I let in a cute young couple, a few cute boys and a few cute girls. The door's wide open and DJ David's cranking up the Sex Pistols' "Holidays in the Sun," I step inside and feel the dance floor moving. It's a busy night. I've got everything under control.

A Line of Heroin, Thinking It Was Cocaine

Some people I saw all the time but had no idea who they were. I saw them waiting in the crowd and I saw them inside the club. I'd see them at Dave's or Crisco's or on the street. They'd say hello and I'd say hello. There were other people I'd see once and never see again. Ghosts and one-night stands, no-names and tourists—they paid to get in or maybe not, then they were gone.

The '70s going down for the count, parts of the city still lawless frontiers: cowboys and Indians, cops and robbers, good guys and bad. Times Square, Alphabet City and the West Side piers offered a self-indulgent feast set against a backdrop of structural decay; all of it dangerous, but for many, hard to resist. There was plenty of "something for everyone" but never enough. I kept going until I found more. That was my problem.

Below Canal was different; a nether region, more void than specific. Walking the streets was safe haven and home turf, mine and anyone else's who showed up at Mudd—or lived in the neighborhood. I identified with feeling far away and found comfort in the desolate nine blocks south of White.

Walking into the club, I'd step into a "surround" of nearly anything goes, a home very different from the one I once knew. I wondered what it was about passing thru the doors that left its mark: Was it something you brought with you or something that happened when you got there? Was it the music and the dance floor or the quick comfort of whomever you met, hung with and fucked till noon? Was it alcohol and Quaaludes or did you snort a line of heroin, thinking it was cocaine?

I looked around and everywhere was talent to spare and talent wasted. The club gave it room to breathe and Steve Mass allowed it to happen. I felt the energy and heard the dance floor screaming. I could never tell if the second floor was ready to collapse or explode. Always excited, never scared, I felt the same way wandering those downtown streets, not knowing what might happen. I was a former kid from the boroughs and burbs, an artist from the neighborhood and a Mudd Club doorman. I was still young, and there was still time. I wanted to paint. I wanted to say what I had to say and I didn't want to mess it up. Then midnight to five happened and I kept getting lost in the middle.

Cookie

During the course of any given night, someone always saved me. New friends or old, they distracted me from the insanity and protected me from myself. All I had to do was survive the distraction and protection.

Cookie Mueller, the writer, John Waters film star and small-time drug dealer, was a new friend. With tattooed fingers, an arm full of bangles and way too much eyeliner, she was *the* supergood bad girl and a beautiful distraction. Between the rebel spirit and a heart of gold, Cookie was a one and only.

I felt close to that spirit but wanted closer. Standing together on the front steps, we made plans to pierce my ear at her apartment on Bleecker near Jones Street. I gave her a kiss and she headed inside. She turned around and said, "See you later, hon." I was smiling. It was still early.

Two days later, accompanied by Richard Sohl and a bottle of Rémy Martin, I arrived at Cookie's. A few drinks, a few joints, we iced my ear and lined up a cork and a needle.

I closed my eyes.

Ricky laughed.

Cookie said, "Hold still."

The *Ouch!* moment came and went.

A quick swab of something, a little more ice and she slipped a gold *X*-shaped stud thru my earlobe. We smoked one more joint, said thanks and left the Rémy behind. The years passed, I still have the hole and I still think about Cookie.

Ricky and I walk across Bleecker and head for One University Place where Ron Beckner is tending bar. He's been working with Mickey Ruskin for years and even shared his SoHo apartment with Max's Kansas City's tough and tiny gatekeeper, Dorothy Dean. I've

Cookie Mueller, 1979, by Bobby Grossman.

only gotten to know Ron over the last few months and he just started hanging out on White Street.

Artist Stephen Mueller is the curator of the One University jukebox and he's busy loading his latest selection of Punk, New Wave and old guard. He and Ron seem equally unimpressed by a Cookie Mueller ear piercing but overly impressed by the new Raincoats single. Bored after one Bloody Mary, Ricky and I walk outside to smoke a joint with Alan Midgette, the actor and Warhol doppelgänger. We're sitting across the street on a broken bench in Washington Square, working our way thru a second joint when Gary shows up. Ricky wants to go back inside for another round but I say, "Bye, see you later," and hop the R train around the corner. It's 6 P.M. and I need to paint a little, eat a little and get myself ready for work. It's already been a long day and I have to be at the Mudd Club by 11. By 7 A.M., I want to be passed out in my own bed. Where Gary passes out is up to him.

Not Quite Coke

The following night Solveig stopped by the loft for dinner. Tall, blonde and beautiful, maybe thirty years old, she's got a new car, a very rich boyfriend and a nice apartment on East Fifty-seventh. Pat Wadsley introduced us and we connected over common interests and bad habits. She walked in, stuffed a bottle of Stoli in the freezer and made herself at home. I ran over to Petrosino's on Duane Street, a neighborhood fish market a few doors west of Barnabas Rex. Gary made salad, I made garlic bread and Solveig helped steam a bag of mussels in beer. When we finished dinner and lit a cigarette, the reality of no cocaine set in. I'd find some at the Mudd Club but that was still three hours away. The psycho dealer on Charlton Street always had great coke but he wasn't around. The musician Kieran Liscoe, a nice guy, sold severely stepped-on coke—less than ideal—but he was home and he answered the phone. Solveig had the car, so we made a run to the west twenties, just north of the Flatiron.

The area was a dead zone, and calling the neighborhood nondescript would be overly descriptive. Liscoe's building was dark, the elevator just a metal box with a glass "porthole" in the door. His loft was long and narrow, a dreary affair with a herd of cockroaches grazing on the countertops of a dirty kitchen. An old-school combination safe in the corner of a closet was home to a few ounces of seedy pot, a modest stash of counterfeit Quaaludes and a bag of white powder pretending to be coke. We each picked up a gram and Solveig dropped me off at Mudd. Two hours later, she showed up with Gary and spilled whatever not-quite-coke was left on the bathroom floor. They stood at the bar looking sad and ordered more Stoli. They both drank for free.

As a team, the three of us were trouble. Separately, it was hard to tell which one of us was worse.

Music and Weed, Ray Guns and Snorkels

The nights were unpredictable—fun and trouble the double edge. A home-cooked meal turning cocaine desperate, we hunted down that shitty gram of stepped-on blow. Finding the humor only went so far. I needed to take a step back and lose myself in a bag of pot.

A few days later, my friend Monica Schofield arrived in town and stayed at the loft. We knew each other from the University of Connecticut School of Fine Arts and we shared a love of music and weed. I had a night off; we rolled half a dozen joints and headed to White Street to see Mary Wells.

Fifteen years earlier Mary opened shows for the Beatles. Now she was a bygone legend doing a lounge act and trying for a comeback. Looking either older or larger than I expected, her voice still had a sweet ring, and her blue sequin dress the kind of sparkle curiously appreciated at Mudd. Four R&B session players were moving the sound with more than enough power to deliver the hits and cut thru the dance floor haze. I was happy smoking a joint and revisiting *American Bandstand* but for Monica it wasn't enough. Thirty minutes later she went back to the loft.

When we were in school I thought of Monica as an artist, a party girl and a friend; crazy about each other was our connection. She showed up in New York, didn't get what was happening at Mudd and didn't get what was happening with me. She left the next day and we lost touch for the next thirty years. To her the Mudd Club was just, "Oh, that place." For me, I'll always remember Mary Wells singing "My Guy."

I said good-bye to Monica at Port Authority. Later that day I met up with Ray, a good-looking guy in a suburban kind of way. He was hanging at a loft on Prince Street and I was stopping by to visit a friend of Gary's. We never once discussed Mary Wells or the Mudd Club but instead talked about a *connection* that he wanted to turn me on to.

Gary's friend Charlie lived in the SoHo loft with a girl named Carrie. Gary had a thing for Charlie, and Ray had a thing for Carrie. She was blonde and beautiful and had her own thing going on with a much older, legendary Hollywood superproducer but still found time to come up with the name "Raygun" Ray. I just tried to keep track of who was doing what with whom.

When Carrie, Ray, Charlie and Gary finally took a break, they headed for the Mudd Club Beach Party. It was a rainy Sunday night and Carrie dressed appropriately in a bikini, heels and a trench coat. They hung out at the bar, had a few drinks and she flashed the crowd. The following evening her parents arrived in town and couldn't wait to see what all the fuss was about. They showed up in flippers and snorkeling gear, a day late but still taking the beach party theme full fetish.

Today I give Carrie a hug whenever I see her. She and Ray are still friends but Charlie's gone. The beach party, the trench coat, the flippers and snorkels—just another night on White.

Back outside I was working alone. The crowd was inside and I was left drifting, remembering. Arriving in the city I felt that buzz and excitement of being in New York but wanted more. Standing a few feet from the CBGB stage or lost in the back room of a West Side bar, I was always searching. I was trying to connect, but when I tried too hard the bottom fell out, that feeling a *part of something*, never more than almost. I was hoping this time was different.

Sitting on the chain, rocking back and forth, it was a rare moment of *comfortable alone* that couldn't last. The Beach Party might've been winding down but New York in the late seventies was a cultural explosion existing in a pre-AIDS, pre-Giuliani, pre-Reagan world. Less than three years after I arrived, small apartments and empty commercial lofts were still available for a few hundred dollars a month and anyone could live in Manhattan. Bohemia still existed, and people were clinging to at least some part of a soon to be lost New York. We ran around the Mudd Club as though it were high school—albeit more permissive than the one I knew. Survival was cheap and the big casualty numbers were still more than half a decade away. In 1979, it seemed none of us saw it coming, though someone surely must have—someone always did.

I had little fear and even less guilt. If either one got to me, I did a few lines of coke, lit a joint and flirted with a bag of heroin. If anyone asked, I was doing fine. Mistakes were made but *fuckups* could be fixed with a little sleep, a few dollars, a shot of penicillin and a night on White Street. Even though I was working at Mudd, painting was what I did—I was young, and that's what I believed.

***

A near-constant roar punctuated by horns and sirens, voices and cries; the city had its own sound and so did White Street. The sound of empty bottles crashing thru a chute behind the Mudd Club bar was familiar reassurance and rarely a distraction. Buried in a DJ mix of "Pop Muzik" and Pistols, the bottles had to go somewhere. After a while I stopped noticing.

Alexa, Debbie and Sama all worked at Mudd and did everything from serving drinks to picking up bottles and glasses. They did it with little thanks and even less glory—the only payoff an occasional trip to the bathroom, elevator or basement.

Debbie worked her shift wearing a nurse's uniform, giving her a touch of porn allure in a demented kind of way. Alexa was the daughter of Pop Art scholar Sam Hunter—an interesting art world pedigree, somehow lost in the artcentric world of Mudd. She went on to assist Gretchen counting covers and handling money, work that was followed by a brief stint outside, working the chain. Immortalized in a *See no evil, Hear no evil, Speak no evil* photo taken with Steve Mass at the upstairs bar, the girls look happy and Steve looks like Steve.

Alexa finally left after negotiations broke down during a wage dispute with Steve. Sama left Mudd for no other reason than it was time. Nurse Debbie hung on to her job, if not her mind, and stuck it out a bit longer.

Three decades and a fast-forward later I still see The Nurse serving drinks. I see Alexa running around carrying that bus-tub filled with empties, forever amazed that her glamorous side remained intact. I remember Sama walking out that door after she quit. I thought she was going to Dave's for a hot dog but she never came back.

Management

Empty bottles weren't the only things crashing and Glenn McDermott's management days were quickly winding down. From my fly-on-the-wall perspective, I saw it coming. Maybe he thought he owned the place and a preoccupation with cocaine might've added to the delusion, but who was I to say?

Never really part of Mudd's creative core, Glenn was mostly behind the scenes though certainly part of the mix. His girlfriend Debbie worked in the office at Reno Sweeney, the famous West Village cabaret, and sold coke on the side. She did some business at home, some at Reno's and some at Mudd. She was generous and the coke was good but it wasn't cheap.

DJ David, Gary and Solveig—our party girl partner in crime—were all friends and we hung out at Glenn and Debbie's. We drank and drugged together. We shared a few meals. They were good times, fast coming to a close: Steve Mass saw what was and wasn't happening and the writing was on the dirty bathroom walls.

When Steve hired me, Glenn appeared to be in charge of something. It was *his* idea to shuffle me from the door to the bar to the upstairs bar until Steve sent me back outside. Then one busy Friday night, less than a year after he helped open the Mudd Club, Glenn McDermott's White Street run stopped running.

I stood at my post watching Joey Kelly, Jay Siano and DJ Danny Heaps follow Glenn straight out the door. "Really, you're leaving?" was all I could say as Mudd management Phase One came to an end. Minutes later, Steve stepped outside and told me that Glenn, along with his friends, his brother, and miscellaneous associates, were no longer allowed in the club. I didn't know what Glenn's "departure" was about; I just knew it would never happen to me.

Working outside kept me in the clear, one step removed from the bullshit. I was a good employee—I showed up, did my job and behaved within the far-reaching boundaries of Mudd Club behavior. Most importantly, I never handled the money and for the moment it seemed that no one cared about the number of Rémys or Heinekens I was drinking. Trips to the bathroom or the basement were part of the job. My only responsibility: to be sure *the right people* got in.

Chi Chi showed up just after, and we started talking. I told her something just went down but wasn't sure what. I pointed to a few people and she opened the chain, handling it like a pro. She helped put the night's clusterfuck of a plank-walk into perspective. We started talking about hair color, platinum blond specifically. We followed up with a shoe fetish discussion involving those infamous peep-toes and one oddly accented Mudd Club regular who loved them. Finally, she looked at me and said, "Darling, you need a drink," went inside, got me one and disappeared. I worked the rest of the night alone, maintaining a fair share of grace under pressure. Louie and Robert would be back tomorrow but for the moment, ego and cocaine, cigarettes and beer got me thru. People asked me where Joey was. No one asked after anyone else.

Employees came and went but for the moment nothing about the Mudd aesthetic changed. A parade of creeps took Glenn's place and ripped off the club as they reattempted to manage the unmanageable. The worst of the bunch: an old man named Jim Connelly who drove a beat-up limo and talked a mile of shit to Steve or anyone willing to listen. Connelly assumed the role of "security chief"; I just tried to smile and do my job.

Looking the Other Way

Despite all the changes the neighborhood was still a tangle of old warehouses, factories and illegal living spaces without regard for building or fire codes. The Mudd Club and 77 White were no different, and the occasional visit from the New York City Fire Department meant stall them at the front door, run inside and check the back door. They'd come in, walk through and flash their lights. If you had a fireman fantasy it was fun, but in the end it was all business. They did their job, made their statement and ten minutes later got back in their big red fire engine.

The New York City Police Department was less disruptive. They'd call me over to their car and ask, "Is *he* inside?" but they never bothered me, and kept a friendly eye on the club. I had no idea what the deal was (with either Fire or Police), though knowing Steve and considering what went on inside, I assumed the arrangement was beneficial to all parties. Sometimes cops stopped by for a drink with their wives and girlfriends, some would moonlight at the Mudd Club door. The police were easygoing and no-nonsense. Whether parked in the alley or working off-duty at the door, NYPD was the best security we had.

I'm not sure who was looking the other way when fifteen-year-olds were hanging at the bar. New York's drinking age was eighteen and underage drinking a nonissue that never appeared to concern anyone, including me; sixteen-year-olds showed up at the door and drunken sixteen-year-olds left a few hours later. Phoebe Zeeman, that notorious underage Mudd Club regular, looked like a kid and drank for free; maybe we just pretended she was older. Whether she went home to her parents or back to her own apartment, had break-fast at Dave's or headed straight to first period homeroom, I never bothered to ask. Either way, *no one* ever checked for proof of age.

Years later, the actress and singer Eszter Balint told me she was fourteen when I let her into Mudd. With a straight face I responded, "I thought you were fifteen." By the time she was eighteen, she was one of the stars of Jim Jarmusch's *Stranger Than Paradise* alongside Lounge Lizard founder John Lurie and musician-actor Richard Edson. A few years earlier, they were all hanging out on White Street.

Today that's difficult to process, but Mudd existed in a time of self-destructive naïveté. Fueled by a bit of chaos and the last shred of a sixties dream, there was hunger for excess that was never satisfied. Our behavior was often more than reckless, our political incorrectness without apology. There was a freedom and magic that time allowed, until it didn't. Fifteen, twenty or thirty years old, we planned on staying young, and continued to believe anything was possible. Today "young" has become mind over matter but the *possibilities*, a challenge. The costs have gotten higher; the effort requires more effort.

Lost Pants, Visuals and Voyeurs

The last days of June 1979, there's a NYPD blue-and-white parked in the alley and I'm working the door with a Heineken in my hand. When Richard Sohl arrives from the Ninth Circle on West Tenth Street, we step inside, order a cocktail and head downstairs. I have some coke that I dump on my fist but Ricky just watches. We talk, I light a joint and he wonders out loud, "Where's Midge?" (a.k.a. Andi Ostrowe).

I look him in the eye.

"She lost her pants again, she's upstairs looking for them."

Ricky needs more information.

"What was she doing?"

I try not to laugh. "Probably something dirty."

The fact is, Andi hasn't even arrived. We both crack up, knowing the rumor has at least some possibility of truth—for any one of us.

Minutes later, I hand Ricky half a Linda Ludes bootleg lude and we walk back to the bar. I order him another vodka tonic before I step outside. It's hot but not crazy hot and the crowd's still small—hard to tell where the night's headed. It's early, the cops drive off and one of the cabbies tells me he'll be back for me later. He's got a lookalike brother who also drives a cab and I never know which one I'm talking to; but they're polite, good-looking and fuckable in a way Rudolf liked to call "sexy bridge-and-tunnel." They know where I live and if I pass out in the back of their cab, they'll be sure to get me home. Besides, I enjoy sex with visitors from other boroughs; it feels almost taboo.

By now it seems late but it's barely 2 A.M.; the club is busy and the neighborhood crowd is trickling in and out. I'd seen Eric Goode around and figured he lived nearby so when he and his friend Shawn Hausman show up I let them in.

Eric had been back and forth from San Francisco, hung out on the Lower East Side and liked going to Studio 54. He'd been in and around Parsons School of Design, where he met fellow Mudd Club alumnus, *It* girl and budding supermodel Teri Toye. Like almost everyone, Eric had no money, was interested in the art scene and fit right in. Shawn was his business partner but the business was still in the dream stage. They shared a loft at 49 Walker Street, around the corner from Mudd, and started hanging out on White.

Eric was already on his way to becoming a self-made and self-proclaimed "club connoisseur." He thought of himself as a "visual guy and voyeur" and appreciated the potential of the Mudd Club's "dark, empty box of a room." We both knew it was the people inside who made it happen but Eric knew *the box* was important too; for him, right off, "the Mudd Club felt like the real thing."

Taking it all in, drinking beer and watching the dance floor, Eric and Shawn saw something happening and knew it could be more. My vision was more shortsighted, minute-length intervals in need of instant gratification. I had only vague ideas and no plans. I was working for a paycheck while my dreams and ambition sat on a back burner, waiting for me to turn up the heat. I needed to reexamine and refocus my own idea of *more* but it would have to wait. The door was getting busy.

Cookie and Sharon arrive, a minute later Clarissa Dalrymple and Cramps guitarist Bryan Gregory. A week earlier, Clarissa showed up with Robert Mapplethorpe and the previous night she was here with Francine Hunter. Clarissa, like the Mudd Club, casts a wide net.

Viva (Superstar) appears out of nowhere. Her ex-husband, film-maker Michel Auder, is already inside. Artists Joseph Kosuth and Sarah Charlesworth climb out of a cab as actress Patti Astor slips thru the crowd. John Holmstrom's already at the chain while Jayne County and future seamstress to the stars Maria Del Greco try squeezing in behind him. Dylan McDermott comes around front and stands next to me on the steps. People are piling in and either something big just emptied out or the air conditioning at One University stopped working. It's the kind of night that feels like *everyone* is here; the kind of night I feel a part of, finally.

Last Tango

I walk home alone to a day of not quite sleep and dirty dreams. Eighteen hours, I'm back again and the crowd appears familiar but somewhat sedated. The street's quiet and Cortlandt Alley smells like piss and garbage, looking darker than usual; by 2 A.M. no one's asking for drinks or falling out the door after too many. I barely finish the thought when John Spacely, a former office supply sales-man and *Punk Magazine* publisher, corners me, leans in close and slurs, "Steve lets me drink for free but I can't find him." English translation: *Can you get me a drink?*

I like Spacely and always let him in. At least once a week security throws him out. He's the poster boy for the walking wounded or worse and sometimes it's hard to take. One eye's covered with a patch—lost to a tranny swinging a chain—and the other one's glazed over. I wonder how he keeps going, not sure that *I* could or even would.

Now Spacely's hanging onto my shoulder and asking for two drinks. He hasn't fought with anyone or gotten crazy with me so I buy him a beer and move on. The bar's crowded and I push my way thru but no one seems to mind. Steve's hiding out at the far end talking to Holmstrom and staring at a crowded dance floor. He's telling John he could fit another thirty people in the place if he stripped the walls down to the brick.

I thought for a second, realizing it didn't matter how many people we packed into the place——I got along with almost everyone. No matter how wasted people were, only one person *inside* the club, other than Gary, ever got in my face. It was a fellow employee and it happened late in 1980 when the road was getting rough and I was getting lost along the way. Outside the club was a different story: punches, threats, name-calling and bottles flying thru the air. I ducked or disappeared, did another line, had another drink. If I freaked and lost my mind, I'd find it the next day. I survived and showed up but not everybody would be so lucky.

A beautiful guy and six-string genius, he gave a shit and didn't at the same time. Johnny Thunders' guitar was still on fire but his flame was starting to fade. He wasn't the only one.

Last Tango in Paris star Maria Schneider, famously butter-fucked in the movie by Marlon Brando, shot up——and fucked up——in a Mudd Club bathroom. Moments later, she staggered toward the bar, fell over and got back up. She tried to stand. I steered her closer to a booth but she had no interest in sitting. I didn't think anything was wrong; she was just a little high on heroin. In my mind, she was a movie star hiding out on the second floor. I lit a cigarette and walked away. That's when still beautiful supermodel Gia Carangi and girlfriend Sandy Linter wandered past. I didn't know them at all but offered a smile, barely got one back and made my way downstairs. The girls were headed for the bathroom.

There was no "writing on the wall" and any warning shot went unnoticed. When the drugs ran out you went and got more. If some*thing* got in the way, you stepped around it or pushed it aside; if some*one* got in the way, you either said *excuse me* or told them to fuck off. No one thought about consequences. No one, including me, thought there were any.

Spacely drifted by again but didn't see me. Roxanne came over, I bought her a drink and we went back to the second floor. Punk power couple Gyda Gash and Dead Boy Cheetah Chrome passing us and nearly out, on the way down. Jackie Curtis stood halfway up the stairs trying to figure out which way to go. Everyone was on a mission. Roxanne and I got in the elevator and disappeared.

Supremes A' Go-Go

Saturday, July 7, and the big holiday came and went. I avoided the midtown Macy's display and the fireworks downtown were just fire-cracker noise. Other than that, I have no other real or imagined memory of Independence Day, 1979. After nearly four months at Mudd, I feel it's where I'm supposed to be. I'm working a job that came out of nowhere and those springtime days seem long ago. I'm fueled by a hot dog from Dave's Luncheonette, a half-dozen drinks and as many lines of coke. I'm prepared as I can be. My shirt's unbuttoned, unzipped or torn, depending on what I reached for in the closet or picked up off the floor. I'm at the door and the air conditioning's still working. Everything and everybody's cool.

There's maybe a hundred people waiting outside when Diana Ross blows past me—the only person I ever let duck under the chain on her own. It's one fluid motion, a full-speed reverse limbo and she does it beautifully. Studio 54 graduate and future Continental and Milk Bar owner Scotty Taylor, hanging at the door, looks over and says, "Diana Ross." I say, "Yeah" and step inside to check it out.

She's already dancing with her friend and only a few people know what's going on. The dance floor practically in heat, Diana's in the middle and the room can't spin any faster. I just stare, stay in the Mudd moment, and never once think of my 1966 *Supremes A' Go-Go* album. Thirty minutes pass in a wave of sweat, Rock 'n' Roll and a heavy beat until the DJ goes Motown, the Supremes start singing and Diana makes her way to the door. Columnist Michael Musto's at the bar wondering, *what just happened*, *why did the DJ do that?* Nobody knows but Diana's gone.

The moments come and go when my memory takes a jump. It's 1967 and I'm buying 45s for sixty-nine cents. Diana Ross is still making hits and Mary and Flo are still singing along until Blondie's "One Way or Another" picks up speed, starts bouncing around the room and snaps me out of it.

Back outside, Scotty's disappeared and the crowd's gotten larg-er. I ask several people, "How many?" and open the chain. Another cab pulls up and a tall kid with dark wavy hair makes his way thru the crowd. He's the one I've been waiting for.

Edward

Edward is either from Long Island or the Upper East Side, maybe both. He's seventeen, beautiful and still in high school. He has a vial of cocaine and a laid-back attitude and I have a joint that Dirty Harry just gave me. We step inside, go downstairs and get lost. It's a routine but with him it's different—we just never have enough time.

Leaning against the basement wall, I look at Edward and remember things about myself from a decade earlier. Thinking about him now makes me remember then. I *was* that teenage kid, looking for something and wanting more than I could handle. I do another line and Edward smiles, says nothing. Ten minutes later we pull ourselves together, head upstairs and he's gone.

Back outside I get hit with a blast of hot thick air. The street smells like street, the temperature's probably eighty-five degrees and the bottle of beer I just picked up is warm after a couple of sips. I put it down on the step behind me, light a cigarette and think about Edward—for a few brief moments forgetting everything else. Then someone calls my name. The chain is in my hand. The crowd is still waiting. Those basement moments still a part of me.

There are some people I'll never forget. Some I barely remember and others I can't even see the memory of. I never knew their names or where they came from. I never saw them leave. They were ghosts of New York nightlife, specific to the Mudd Club, White Street and Cortlandt Alley. Some were real and some I might have just imagined. Edward was real—and all these years past I still wonder. I smile, close my eyes and still feel my back against that basement wall. I'm still waiting for Edward.

***

I light another cigarette and suck down another beer. Jerry Nolan, the drummer for the notorious on-again, off-again Heartbreakers, gets out of a cab and makes his way to the door. Walter Lure, Billy Rath and Johnny Thunders round out a wrecking crew that can tear a place apart if Johnny feels like showing off and the other guys feel like playing along. I saw it happen at the Village Gate in August '77.

Jerry says hi but hardly knows me; he seems a polite guy, considering his history and résumé. Platform heels, drugs and a set of pink drums, he and Johnny left the broken New York Dolls behind in 1975. Four years later, the Heartbreakers are hanging by a thread.

Walter Lure plays guitar and looks better in a polka dot shirt than anyone I know. He's the good-natured funnyman and fills in the lead and rhythm around Johnny's loose ends. When he celebrated his last Happy Birthday at Mudd the cake was decorated with hypodermic needles. Someone had a very dry sense of humor.

Ten years earlier, Walter and I attended Saint Mary's High School in Manhasset, Long Island, a Catholic school run by the Marist Brothers. Walter was a senior as I was arriving, and Catholic clergy crime was still in the closet. Luckily my parents wised up after freshman year and got me the hell out of there. I discovered the Walter Lure connection at the Mudd Club.

Johnny Thunders is already upstairs. He's charming, lovable and impossible, a natural born killer on guitar. As a group, the Heartbreakers are iconic—a dangerous, drugged-out, sexy dirty image backed up by a workingman's version of everything that's Rock 'n' Roll. I liked almost everything about them, though songs like "Too Much Junkie Business" never got me past an all-too-obvious self-conscious roar. The band's history: some great music but more legend than anything else.

Dreamy Babble to Silent Drift

Even without a slogan or a theme song I was getting more and more drug-hungry. I wasn't sure if I could be me without getting high or if I wanted to be someone else. I was feeling anxious and it was difficult to tell if the summer was moving fast or slow. Then the phone rang.

Monday, July 9, less than a week after the Independence Day fireworks that happened somewhere, I hooked up with Raygun Ray. We made plans to purchase an ounce of cocaine, complete with an extra gram or two of regret—that feeling when the drugs are gone, the money's spent and nothing's changed. It was the connection Ray told me about a few weeks ago: they have the best coke, he said.

We hop on the train and head for Central Park. Blondie's headlining the Dr Pepper Festival at Wollman Rink, and Nick Lowe and Dave Edmunds' band Rockpile is opening the show. It's warm and sunny and my Mudd credentials get us thru the back gate.

Blondie's riding high on the whole *Parallel Lines* "Heart of Glass" insanity. They step out onstage, throw down the hits and the crowd eats it up. Chris and Debbie *get it on* and close the show with a choice cover of the T. Rex classic "Bang a Gong." Ray and I try and hang out for a few minutes afterward but eighteen hundred cocaine dollars is weighing heavy in our pockets. We cab it over to Midtown East, Ray does the deal and we arrive at Murray Street after what feels like a three-hour hour later. When he finally dumps the bag on the table it's hard to describe.

An ounce of cocaine looks big and small at the same time, it's a sexy drug—a come-on and a setup. We take some out and line it up. It's got a mother-of-pearl shine: flaky, beautiful and a little scary. We weigh it, divide it and cut half of it with whatever you use to cut coke. Then we blow our brains and profits out the window.

We have beer and pot to take the edge off and I have a few crumbling Quaaludes in a pocket somewhere. Six bottles of Dos Equis and a couple of grams disappear fast. I'm staring at Ray and he's staring at the coke. The conversation goes from dreamy babble to a near-silent drift. I take the blade, set up two more monster lines and lean into the mirror. The coke I can have but Ray I can't and even the endless lines of blow won't change that. Hours pass without a word. Brian Eno's *Taking Tiger Mountain* spins by in the background two or three times. Ray eventually splits with his share and I float away on the frozen. Night and day pass by in gray-out blur. I have to be at the Mudd Club in a few hours, unload a few stepped-on grams and get my money back. I'll need a few drinks before the regret kicks in.

I leave Murray Street sometime after 10, order a vanilla egg cream at Dave's (it's about as much "food" as I can handle) and walk over to White. The club's empty and the lights are on. The ceiling's a black painted tangle of ductwork, wires and pipes; the walls are gray and there's a trash barrel in the middle of the dance floor. I feel like lying down next to it and waiting for the music to lift me up or move me to the side of the room. I finish the egg cream and sit on the basement stairs instead.

Ten minutes later I'm at the bar staring into a room that Ernie Brooks described as dominated by void. People gave the void shape; sound and vision, combined with a tough door policy, gave it identity. Eight months after the club's official opening, the crowd, the white light noise and the void were in sync.

Moving thru summer of '79 we were busy every night and the old maxim that the city emptied out during July and August held no truth when it came to White Street. By 2 A.M. the dance floor was packed, the second floor was buzzing and people were still waiting to come in. I was working hard; I still believed my job was important but I wanted more than a doorman identity. I kept telling myself, and anyone who'd listen, that I was making beautiful paintings. With the exception of a fucked-up relationship, too many drugs, a touch of anxiety and the occasional nosebleed, I was happy. While I was busy with all of that, Steve was making plans for the Mudd Club's future. I assumed, without thought, those plans included me.

Anyone Could Go to Xenon

Saturday night, the phone at the loft happened to be plugged in when Steve Mass called. He was low-talking but less hesitant than usual.

"Why don't you wear a necktie tonight, let's try getting some of that Xenon crowd in here."

My eyeballs did the talking and rolled.

I knew I was hearing correctly and at this point nothing surprised me.

The only speak I could muster, "Okay, I will."

Xenon was the Howard Stein and Peppo Vanini default outpost for unnaturally tan Europeans, moneyed tourists and junior executives between the ages of nineteen and seventy. Located on West Forty-third Street, the club prided itself on being not much more than a lower-wattage competitor for the slowly fading Studio 54. The only difference: just about anyone could go to Xenon. If Steve thought we should or could bait that crowd with a necktie, who was I to disagree? It was the weekend and I figured what the hell.

The choices at my immediate disposal were the typical skinny, Punk and New Wave retro styles. I had a few in black, one in silver leather and the red leather tie Bryan Ferry took a liking to back in March. I tried a few on, jumped on the midtown Disco train and opted for the silver. Paired with my turquoise pants and a pale yellow sport jacket it was perfect in a ridiculous kind of way. I weighed about one hundred forty pounds and was thin enough to wear what my friend, the restrained but ever stylish Wayne Hawkins, called "circus wear." I thought it was a good look.

The lure of silver leather must have worked. By 1 A.M. the place was a madhouse and by 2 the crowd outside stretched halfway across the street. By 4 A.M. my shirt was gone, eaten by the mob or lost during the course of the night. The silver tie was around my bare neck and the jacket was torn. The necktie became my badge of courage; the missing shirt and damaged jacket, a hallmark of success. My friend Lynne came to the rescue and took the jacket home for repair.

When the sun came up I got in a cab and headed for Crisco's. The tie was in my pocket, and—whether mine or someone else's—I'm pretty sure I was wearing a shirt.

Cleveland, New York City and Cheap Dreams

Sunday morning I made it home, crashed noontime and woke at 6 P.M. I dreamed of Cleveland or maybe not. I'd been there twice but didn't stay long; maybe it was me, or maybe it was Cleveland's fault.

When Rocket From the Tombs left Ohio in 1976, they landed on the Bowery and became the Dead Boys. Pere Ubu, the progressive underground garage band, stayed behind, though bassist Tim Wright moved to the East Village, joined Arto Lindsay's band DNA and hung out at Mudd. Cheetah Chrome and Stiv Bators were already at the bar or hanging out on the second floor. In 1979, a lot of Cleveland was still headed for New York, and despite the Ohioans' progressive sense of fashion, none wore a silver leather necktie (or asked to borrow mine).

Fellow students at the Cleveland Institute of Art, Cynthia Sley and Barbara Klar arrived in May and found a place at the Arlington Hotel, a semi-dive on West Twenty-fifth Street; it's where they met their neighbor, Judy Nylon.

Everyone was somehow connected to White Street whether they knew it or not and before long Cynthia started noticing guitarist Pat Place and fellow Cleveland native Laura Kennedy wandering the East Village. Her musical taste led her to a Contortions gig on Bleecker Street and instinct, word of mouth and a love of music pointed her in the direction of the Mudd Club. I'd seen them around and when they showed up I thought, *Oh, them.*

By midsummer, I was letting Cynthia and Barbara in the door for free; soon they became willing and curious enough to participate in one of Nylon's performance pieces at the club. Surviving *that*

MONDAY, MAY 5th 10P.M.
EAST VILLAGE EYE BENEFIT·MUDD CLUB
BUSH TETRAS

Bush Tetras at Mudd, East Village Eye Benefit 1980/81, courtesy Lisa Genet.

marked the end of Cynthia's stage fright and the beginning of a career in show business.

After the performance Cynthia headed upstairs and approached John Cale, one of her musical heroes. In a deep voice, slurred by a night at Mudd, John commented, "You looked so fetching up there onstage." It was an interesting come-on that left Cynthia somewhere between amused, curious and appalled. Given John's charm and dry wit she opted for amused and ran off looking for Judy and Barbara. I walked over and bought John another drink.

Cynthia soon joined Pat Place, Laura Kennedy and Dee Pop as a member of Bush Tetras. In March 1980 they would draw a line in the sand with "Too Many Creeps," their first single released on 99 Records.

The funky, newer than No Wave anthem was a wink and sneer rolled into one. Pat wrote "Creeps" when she was working at Bleecker Street Cinema; Cynthia added a verse and creeps everywhere never recovered.

By summer 1980 the band got onstage at Mudd and I left the door to come inside and dance. Destiny, fate and a little luck brought us all together—thirty-five years later my friendship with the band lives on.

Between the Arlington Hotel and getting into Mudd for free, everyone lived *on the cheap*. The subway fare was maybe fifty cents and six people could get into a Checker Cab, chip in a dollar each and go anywhere. People went out every night.

Writer, author and former One University Place employee Linda Yablonsky, another friend and associate of Bush Tetras, recalls how "no money made everyone more inventive. Taking the same drugs, listening to the same music and hanging out in the same clubs, we were social and creative at the same time." New York City was a cheap date and allowed for almost anything.

Judy Nylon still likes to remind me, "We all lived out of each other's pockets." I remind her that even empty pockets occasionally have something to offer.

Creepy Enough

On July 18, 1979, the Midtown West world of Disco and a car full of Upper East Siders were on a collision course with White Street. Victor Hugo's theatrical debut was happening at Mudd, and despite the wreckage that spilled out of two double-parked limousines no injuries were reported.

Human Nature Is Made of Snobberies Like These was intended as a two-night affair but after the first night a second was hardly needed. The real show on that hot summer evening was the audience. Nurse Debbie served preshow cocktails on the second floor, and Gary (never one to shy away from rubbing elbows with even dubious fame) shuttled the attending VIPs downstairs in the infamous Mudd Club elevator. When showtime approached, Studio 54's co-owner Steve Rubell, Halston and McCarthy-era lawyer Roy Cohn were front and center. Despite all the nonsense and pretense, their appearance registered only mild amusement and a few turned heads.

Rubell was sweating and his eyes were lidded. Halston was stiff, mumbling in a cigarette cocaine whisper. Cohn was creepy by reputation

Halston, Roy Cohn and Steve Rubell, more cocktails please.
The Victor Hugo event at Mudd, 1979, by Allan Tannenbaum.

alone, but live he was even creepier. Flanked by Halston confidant D.D. Ryan and Studio 54 doorman Mark Benecke, they were alternately animated, frozen and comatose—ready for more cocktails, Quaaludes and cocaine along with a defibrillator and a sleep apnea device.

The show went on as scheduled and its saving grace was Walter Steding's electric violin, an always revelatory accompaniment. Teri Toye, sliding up and down the naked, bound and full-frontal beauty of sometime model Scott Daley, was a highlight. Benjamin Liu a.k.a. Ming Vauze added a touch of charm while Victor and Nan Dugan wandered around the stage doing something but not much.

I never got the whole Victor Hugo thing and the Mudd Club performance didn't help. On looks alone, Teri was the star, and Scott became a larger part of the White Street story without knowing it. A handful of telling photos by *SoHo Weekly News* photographer Allan Tannenbaum seem all that's left of an oddly remembered evening while the show itself signaled a slippery slope for Mudd Club entertainment. The end of Studio 54 was slowly approaching and White Street's connection or similarity was never more than Quaaludes, basement blowjobs and cocaine.

Scrawled Walls and the Beautiful Scream

The uptown versus downtown thing was boring at best. I crossed Twenty-third occasionally but other than an afternoon at MoMA, a movie at the Ziegfeld or a trip to Max's or Hurrah, I was happy staying south of Fourteenth, and happiest at Mudd.

Diego helped Steve orchestrate the chaos and Anya offered the encouragement of a smart in-your-face banshee cheerleader. With scattershot intent far different from the eventual outcome they opened the doors. The dark dirty fire that ignited Punk had already turned to a No Wave reactive dissonance. Ready to rage on White Street, the beat was feral, the sound tended violent but the scream was beautiful.

By '79 SAMO speak was still scrawled on the walls of downtown but Jean-Michel's blond Mohawk was either growing out or turning green. The Little Hollywood filmmakers of East Third were hanging at 77 White and No Wave's noirish bark and bite found a place to drink for free. Everybody was up to something and it was happening with a sense of community and collaboration. The shift from past to present, meditative to knee-jerk was radical, and the Mudd Club became *the* container for a new, loosely defined aesthetic. It was only a matter of time before it needed more space.

A semi-functional basement area, a minor redo of the second floor and a future third-floor expansion were all possibilities. As it stood, the club already offered a huge takeaway with every conceivable statement, overstatement or understatement on display. Art and music were still collaborating and moving forward while fashion was absorbing, processing and repackaging anything and everything it could. Diego Cortez looked at the "white, white, white—people, walls and wine" of the art world and knew something had to change; a head-on crash with what was happening in the clubs and on the street was the way to go. Punk was the force music had to reckon with and graffiti was a force ready to fire both barrels at the art world. Blondie and *TV Party*, along with Jean-Michel, Fred Brathwaite and soon Keith Haring, were just some of the visionaries and voices on the front lines. White Street stood ready.

Mudd's intellectual edge, mixed with a dose of political incorrectness and irony, made the club fertile ground—"needed and correct," as Judy Nylon dubbed it. From CBGB to Max's, Hurrah to the newly opened Tier 3, the new aesthetic—the intellect and the *anti*—were coming together. *Putting the bloat that Rock 'n' Roll had become out of its misery and into its grave* was the sentiment expressed by Punks like Anya and Richard Hell, among others. It was a radically necessary extreme, whether coming from the Ramones, Patti Smith, DNA or Teenage Jesus and the Jerks.

Saying hello or not as it strolled or staggered past me at the door, I stood where high culture and low came together. I watched it collide and squeezed thru the mess, tripped over it in the bathrooms and on the dance floor. I kept showing up for work and working in my studio. I was opening the chain and handing out those free drinks, trying to be more than just a voice in the crowd. Wanting to be part of what was happening, I came to slowly appreciate that I already was. Standing at the door of the Mudd Club I watched the world change and tried to hold on.

When I spoke to Diego he told me, "Art is made for the long haul." I thought about it and realized some of us are made for it as well. Along the way we passed thru White Street—and moved forward.

That Was Fashion

Timeless and part of the "long haul," a leather motorcycle jacket was something of a uniform. A torn T-shirt on a pretty kid from the East Village was easy, and thrift shop suits on Danny Rosen or John Lurie were classic menswear. Chi Chi's black leather corset, Wendy Whitelaw's full-on glamour and Boy Adrian's androgyny were sexy beautiful. Klaus Nomi's pointed shoulders and small-waisted futurism was a best of the moment but in turn spawned a worst-of-the-eighties exaggerated form. Animal X presented savage designs on the first floor and hung out upstairs with a baby in her arms. Natasha's Revenge Vampsuits were already a hit on the high-society, "rock idiot" and hooker circuits while her spandex gear led the way as one of the first collections to show at Mudd. The dead-end dark basement look of No Wave and the *in your face* of Punk were already being co-opted, branded and sold. Teri Toye's designer dresses from Neiman Marcus, worn with *I don't give a shit* attitude, was the backhanded *fuck off* that kept things interesting. Betsey Johnson turned it around, put a smile on fashion and made it big business. Art and music converged at the Mudd Club. Fashion hung out there and so did the kids who loved it.

SoHo Designers show, no comment, 1979, by Allan Tannenbaum.

In It Together

I had mixed feelings about fashion but either love or fear was too strong a word. Sometimes I figured it out and looked sharp but most of the time I looked like any other skinny guy dressed in jeans, thrift shop odds and ends and occasionally curious choices. The only difference, I was at the door and everyone else was on the other side of the chain. Forced to judge, I avoided the word *fabulous* and often had no comment other than a roll of the eyes. Clothes alone didn't always matter—who was wearing them did.

Debi Mazar was a kid from Queens, a saxophone player and a fashion-forward fifteen-year-old. She was hanging out at the Mudd Club dressed in a porkpie hat and a man-tailored suit, and somewhere between the drinking, dancing and radical new aesthetic, she saw what was happening. I asked Debi what made Mudd different and she told me, "So much of what was going on was propelled by love. We looked out for one another because we were all in it together." That sentiment kept us connected, and still does.

Vicki Pedersen, the writer, sometime actress and former full-time party girl, liked to say she was "checking in at the *office* every night." All these years later, she still feels "the bond between people that *lived* at the Mudd Club."

Fred Brathwaite found his way to White Street by way of *Glenn O'Brien's TV Party* and never stopped coming. The first time he showed up at the door *without* Glenn or the *Party* entourage, he heard me ask, "Fred, how many?" Grateful to see me and hear his name, he realized, "Oh shit, I'm getting in!" Decades later, I'm touched when Fred retells the story, not just because he remembers but because the memory's based on what he calls "being part of it."

I've talked to so many people and asked them all, "What was *it?*" Writer, musician and underground star Adele Bertei calls it *family.* Debi remembers the love and Vicki calls it a bond. Jane Friedman was one of the first to call it home and Fred talks about being part of *it.* Whatever *it* was or is, the connection has lasted all these years.

***

Tuesday, July 24, and I'm back at work after a night off. The Mudd Club is presenting Justine's Deadly Feminine line of clothing, the fashion show that Colette (a.k.a. Justine) has been telling me about for the last few weeks. The clothes are being sold at Fiorucci on Fifty-ninth Street, hanging in the same window where Colette slept as part of a 1978 installation. Tonight it's a full-scale White Street production but I'm feeling more like a spectator, sitting on the steps, not sure of what I'm watching.

There's an antique roadster parked in front of the club and a dozen of whom Justine considers "the best girls at Mudd" climbing all over it. It's a great photo op and a wild time until Tina L'Hotsky's heel goes thru the roadster's fold-down windscreen. Tina's shoe suffers little damage but the car is fucked and I'm left trying to spin the chaos into a three-dollar event for anyone willing to pay. Despite my confusion and the broken glass, the show must go on.

Just past midnight, I walk inside and the place is packed full of girls wearing Justine's ruched fabric creations. Charlie Yoder, the very tall artist and Rauschenberg associate, is dressed as King Kong and he's carrying Justine through the club.

It's a *gorilla-guerrilla* moment, a lot more than just a fashion show.

Colette knew, "Something like this couldn't happen anywhere else; the Mudd Club obviously had magic." I knew it too, and so did Charlie and "Justine."

Colette, in the doorway, 1979, by Rose Hartman.

I snapped out of the Deadly Feminine confusion when the sweaty Gorilla asked me for a drink. I told the bar to give him whatever he wanted.

Close to the Fire

The summer was heading toward August and I was at the club nearly every night. The door was open and the sound of Mudd was pouring onto the street. Halfway around the world the Ayatollah Khomeini of Iran was banning music, comparing it to opium. I often made the same comparison but saw no reason for a ban.

Saturday, July 28, 1979, and I still remember watching her arrive. She was wearing a gray sweatshirt and got out of an old black limo that had seen better days; a remarkable woman, who looked as if she'd seen those days too. A tragedy that screamed Russian roulette and teen suicide had buried her in personal drama and a tabloid mess. I opened the chain and asked how she was—she shook her head and went inside. I have no idea why, but I followed.

Anita Pallenberg, the Rolling Stones muse, Keith Richards companion and long-ago girlfriend of Brian Jones, was a force of nature in her own right. One of the great beauties of the sixties, her influence on fashion was huge and her influence on the Stones legendary. Smart, funny, brutally honest and a little bit scary, she could've done anything.

Anita wasn't like anyone I'd known before or since. She knew Brando and Kubrick and I was a kid from Long Island. Her Euro-, Rasta-, beatspeak was offhanded and conspiratorial whether she was talking to you or just talking. She'd been close to the fire so long that when you leaned in you could feel the heat. Following her thru the front door became a habit and hanging out with her was something I wanted to do. Getting lost with Anita was easy; getting hooked was easy too.

I leaned in close and tried to hear every word. I lit a cigarette and did another line. We were downstairs at the Mudd Club—a long way from *High Tide and Green Grass* and a long time since coveting those red wide-wale cords.

Blue Mud Facial Masque

I was attracted to badass and trouble, thinking they'd give me an identity or at least a bit of cred. When I sold some blond hash in high school I thought that would do the same. Instead, people only cared about the hash and wondered if I could get more. Now when anyone wondered *who's the badass*, they usually meant the person next to me.

Whether I was lost in the basement or drifting around the second floor, the Mudd Club offered everything from close encounters to close calls, sex and drugs being part of both. Artists and writers, musicians and dope dealers had their own kind of appeal—often related to bad reputation as much as good personality. Young, attractive and fuckable was an obvious plus, stoned and kinky was better. Even the occasional art patron turned up at the bar or in the bathroom. If one of them came by the loft and bought a painting, I was happy. If they liked to get high it was another plus.

I met Brent Ward when he showed up at the door dressed in a suit and tie. He was an audiovisual designer whose reach included a job for filmmaker Derek Jarman, the interior of a skateboard shop in San Francisco, and the staging for a one-off performance by the band Tuxedomoon. We wandered around together near the bathrooms on the second floor and wound up at Murray Street as the sun came up. He sat on the couch doodling away on a scrap paper—a thumbnail version of one of my paintings. He bought the piece a week later, and in 1980, headed home to Australia. Today that painting is alive and well, living Down Under.

I told two other guys from the club to stop by sometime. Like Brent, fuckable wasn't in the cards but selling a painting probably was. A few nights later, they called from the pay phone on the corner of Broadway and Murray; I rode down in the elevator and brought them upstairs.

Teri and Gary were getting ready for a night out and Teri was in the middle of her beauty regimen. Covered in a blue mud facial masque, she walked into the kitchen and startled my guests. When the screams finally died down we lit up a joint, went into the studio and one of the guys bought a pink painting on paper for a few hundred dollars. We smoked another joint, snorted some coke and they left. I spent the money on dinner, more cocaine and breakfast at Dave's. At some point, we all wound up at the Mudd Club.

Underground U.S.A.

The following night is like most weekdays: more than half the people are regulars and less than half of them are paying to come in. I'm outside working and filmmaker Eric Mitchell's inside shooting the dance floor scene for his movie *Underground U.S.A.* He also plays the hustler to Patti Astor's No Wave Norma Desmond. A single red gel gets the light just right and the handheld camera captures the herky-jerky of Patti and Eric's mating dance.

After appearing in a number of films, including those of Amos Poe and James Nares, Eric is the No Wave director of the moment— and I'm thrilled to be included in the movie. I play myself doing the door and exchange a single line of dialogue with Rene Ricard's character, Kenneth. The soundtrack and ambient noise of the crowd outside nearly bury the line when Kenneth and Patti Astor's character, Vicki, breeze past me. The moment's all too brief. My big break winds up small, but Eric generously gives me a credit for my fifteen seconds onscreen.

The Mudd Club lives large in *Underground U.S.A.* and Eric rounds out the cast with Cookie Mueller, Jackie Curtis, Taylor Mead and Teri Toye. With a nod to Warhol's *Heat*, it's *Sunset Boulevard* in a downtown loft and Patti plays a drug- and booze-addled actress that time passed by. The sets are familiar, the dialogue is over the top and the delivery is priceless. Teri Toye steals every scene she's in and the moments shot in the Mudd bathroom play like real time. It truly is a movie within a movie, with White Street playing a midnight-to-5 reality show. In my mind nearly every cast member is a star.

The Mudd Club, a star in its own right, was the heart of the scene: *Underground U.S.A.* is one example of why. Since the phone call four months ago I'd been in the middle of that scene, only flinching once or twice. I never looked back and the possibility of an over-the-edge crash and burn still seemed a long shot. I liked where I was standing but I had to figure a way to make a next move forward. Then I heard my name called out and saw fifty people waiting to come in.

Of its time yet signaling ahead, the Mudd Club is held in collective memory. Midnight to noon was our day and somewhere between 4 and 11 P.M. we'd catch our breath and start over. Once in a while it all got caught on film.

Patti Astor with Tina L'Hotsky, white heat, blonde on blonde, 1980, by Nick Taylor.

Chinese Rocks and the Electric Circus

August 6, 1979, and I've recovered from the disappointment of a buried line of dialogue. I start the day with a shower, a cigarette and a joint, turn on the news and get lost in the turmoil of Afghanistan. Two minutes later I'm being told Nicaragua is asking the United States for yet more foreign aid but it's difficult to grasp; I'm unsure of who or what Sandinistas are or why I should even care. Thinking about it for more than a minute doesn't help, so I split for Central Park to see the Ramones.

I catch the double R at City Hall and take it to Sixtieth Street, walk several blocks and pass thru the backstage gate just as the band hits the stage. My timing's perfect and Phoebe Zeeman and Ellen Kinnally are already jammed into the crowd up front, somehow jumping up and down. They see me and wave, I push closer and the Ramones pour it on. A minute later, I'm jumping up and down too, along with five thousand other people; Afghanistan and Nicaragua, a million miles away.

When the show's over I take the train to Canal and Broadway and arrive at work early. I can still hear the roar of Johnny's guitar and can see Dee Dee slamming the shit out of his bass on "Chinese Rocks." Phoebe and Ellen show up around midnight; they've stopped jumping up and down and they're trying to find Steve. I'm at the door checking the crowd for familiar faces, or at least someone interesting.

Meeting different people every night, nothing's slowing down and everyone in the city who goes out after midnight is going out. White Street's busy, nearly a hundred outside, and three or four limos parked in the street. I look around and spot Jerry Brandt getting out of a cab.

Jerry's got old-school charm, his eyes and ears open and a finger on the pulse. That's why he's here. Starting out at the William Morris Agency more than fifteen years ago, Jerry wound up working with Sam Cooke, Sonny and Cher and the Rolling Stones. In 1967, he opened the Electric Circus, the legendary psychedelic dance club on St. Mark's Place. I was fourteen at the time but even then I wanted in. The Circus connection is still what grabs me.

Happy to see me at the door, Jerry shakes my hand, pats me on the back and steps inside. I need a break and make a run for the upstairs bathroom.

A Real Good Time Together

Saturday, August 11, my ears are still ringing from Ramones mania when Gary and I cab it up to Central Park. The Patti Smith Group is playing the Wollman Rink for what's shaping up to be one of their last New York City performances. When the band steps onstage Patti comes charging out, and somewhere between "We're Gonna Have a Real Good Time Together" and "My Generation," the last several years, beginning with *Horses*, come flooding back. I feel like I remember every minute.

After the show Ricky Sohl and Lynette rescue us from the crush at the stage and pull us into the mobile home dressing room. It's cool outside, it's starting to rain and I'm wearing my leather motorcycle jacket on the one summer night it's ever left the house. We sit for a minute before we hop in one of the limos and head for CBGB's where the band's doing an unannounced second show.

The ride downtown is quick and CB's is already packed. The vibe inside is heavy—the Patti Smith Group, just a month away from the end of their run. I hang around just long enough to see Ricky step away from the keyboards, pick up a bass and sing "All Along the Watchtower." I walk out the back door, run around the corner and hail a cab on Bowery. I get to White Street and there's already a big crowd outside, a small crowd inside and not much happening. I don't see anyone I know but Louie spots some friends getting out of a cab, grabs them, and disappears. Now it's just me, facing a hundred people who don't seem to mind standing around in a little bit of rain as long as they think they'll get in.

Ten minutes later Louie's still missing and the doorway's getting jammed. I'm slowing things down outside when author and playwright Gary Indiana gets out of a cab. He's with Vicki Pedersen, whom Indiana once referred to as a "Nouveau personality, studying subcultural phenomena in districts north of Canal and south of Bowery." No one could've said it better. They make it thru the crowd and ask, "Is Steve around?" I say, "Somewhere" and they head inside just as filmmaker and former high school baseball star Amos Poe steps up to the chain.

The Blank Generation and a Muddy Lens

Amos is a friend of the house and a friend of Steve's. In 1976, he and musician Ivan Kral documented *The Blank Generation* at CBGB's and Max's. Likened by one reviewer as being "filmed through a muddy lens," it's come to be what many consider the first Punk film. In 1977, Amos attended the Deauville Film Festival with fellow underground cinema stars Eric Mitchell and Patti Astor. He presented *The Blank Generation* and *Unmade Beds*, his first feature starring future Mudd Club regulars Debbie Harry, Duncan Hannah and Lynette Bean as well as Eric and Patti. When Amos finally made it back to New York he was a star with a new French girlfriend but no money. That's when a friend told him, "There's this guy named Steve Mass asking about you."

Amos tracked down Steve's phone number, called and said, "I heard you were looking for me." Steve responded, "I'd like to make a movie with you. Let's have dinner." The conversation seemed a bit sketchy but packed an offer Amos couldn't refuse—one of those Steve Mass telephone calls I eventually came to know.

Amos and Steve met, drank a lot and ate a little dinner. Between Amos' recent success and a shared dream of moviemaking, things happened fast. Conversations fueled by cocktail consumption and creative passion quickly followed, and it wasn't long before an *almost film company* was born. Needing a place to say, Amos briefly moved into Steve's Eighth Street duplex.

Steve Mass had the camera and Amos had the eye, but the result: no movies were ever made. Amos, who was always working on something, soon realized that limitless drinks made for "ideas that sounded genius but by the next day were just ideas." Knowing that "filmmakers make films," he took a temporary job at Strand Books and offered Steve a suggestion, "You'd be happier if you opened a bar."

In early 1978, Amos left Eighth Street (leaving the door open for Brian Eno) and took up residence on East Third, not far from the notorious Third Street Men's Shelter. The neighborhood was fast becoming the heart of *Little Hollywood* and home to a roster of young filmmakers, musicians and future Mudd Club alumni. His neighbors included Pere Ubu and DNA bassist Tim Wright, Jerry Nolan, Eric Mitchell and White Street's reigning conceptualist Tina L'Hotsky. Poe's late-afternoon activities included serving tea to Sid Vicious.

Richard Boch 4 a.m. Mudd Basement, 1980, by Lynette Bean Kral.

BLESSED

THURSDAY
JUNE 14th

COME
TO
THE

Puberty
Ball

SEE LIVE!

THE
BLESSED

MUDD COLLEGE OF DEVIANT BEHAVIOR

RICHARD BOCH
PRINT OR TYPE FULL NAME

9 MURRAY ST
GIVE LEGAL RESIDENCE

NYC NY 10007
CITY   STATE   ZIP

FALSIFICATION OF ANY STATEMENTS MADE HEREIN IS PUNISHABLE BY FINE OR IMPRISONMENT OR BOTH

Frontal View

2A

Clockwise from top left: Mudd Club Owner Steve Mass with Mary Lou Green, 1980, by Richard Boch; Talking Heads BBC Taping, 1979, courtesy Richard Boch; Mudd Club ID Card, 1980, courtesy Richard Boch; Michael Holman, by Rhonda Paster Corte; The Blessed/Puberty Ball, 1979, by Eileen Polk; Puberty Ball Poster, 1979, by Eileen Polk/Courtesy Howie Pyro; Nan Goldin/Mudd Second Floor, 1979, by Billy Sullivan.

MUDD COLLEGE OF
DEVIANT BEHAVIOR

PRINT OR TYPE FULL NAME

GIVE LEGAL RESIDENCE

CITY   STATE   ZIP

FALSIFICATION OF ANY STATEMENTS
MADE HEREIN IS PUNISHABLE BY FINE
OR IMPRISONMENT OR BOTH

Frontal View

MUDD COLLEGE OF
DEVIANT BEHAVIOR

PRINT OR TYPE FULL NAME

GIVE LEGAL RESIDENCE

CITY   STATE   ZIP

FALSIFICATION OF ANY STATEMENTS
MADE HEREIN IS PUNISHABLE BY FINE
OR IMPRISONMENT OR BOTH

Frontal View

Clockwise from top left: Mudd Club ID, 1980, courtesy Vicki Pedersen;
Mudd Club Staff Member Debi Mazar, by Rhonda Paster Corte; Mudd
Club ID Card Flipside, 1980, courtesy Kate Simon; Cookie Mueller/
Mudd Second Floor, 1979, by Billy Sullivan; Lisa Rosen, 1980, by
Maripol ©All Rights Reserved; Richard Sohl & Richard Boch/Montauk,
1980, by Ron Beckner; Mudd Club ID, 1980, courtesy Kate Simon.

DEDICATION

INITIATIVE

INTENSITY

PROGRESS

Dr. S.A. Mudd

Founder & beloved chairman
of the MUDD ORGANIZATION
at work in his world famous
LABORATORY FOR YOUTH.
(photo by international celebrity
photographer William Coupon)

SIGN YOUR NAME IN FULL · NOT INITIALS

MUDD COLLEGE OF
DEVIANT BEHAVIOR

L. KENNEDY
PRINT OR TYPE FULL NAME

18B 6th AVE
GIVE LEGAL RESIDENCE

NYC 100B
CITY   STATE   ZIP

FALSIFICATION OF ANY STATEMENTS
MADE HEREIN IS PUNISHABLE BY FINE
OR IMPRISONMENT OR BOTH

Frontal View

IT'S
REAL!

41st
&
7th A

UR   JAM-PACKED   FLOORS   /!!/

MES SQ.
OW, JOE

The
Ever
for I
duced

Clockwise from top
left: The Times Square
Show Flyer, 1980,
courtesy Fales Library
NYU; Laura Kennedy
Mudd Club ID, 1980;
Edo Bertoglio, Opal &
Louie Chaban/Mudd
Stairs, 1979, by Billy
Sullivan; Andi Ostrowe,
1980, by Richard Boch;
Wendy Whitelaw, 1980,
by Maripol ©All Rights
Reserved; Damita, Gary
Kanner, Victor Bockris,
1980, by Richard Boch.

ART
OF THE
FUTURE

More Than You

e work of 100 New
sts — Painting — Sc
cial Events Daily — C   Shop
Open Air Lounge
COSTS YOU NOTHING
Admission is Free
• • • • • • • • • • • • • •
Times Square Show is open
Day in JUNE. Call 391-8609
o on Weekend Events. Pro-
y Collaborati

#3   R.Bock 1980

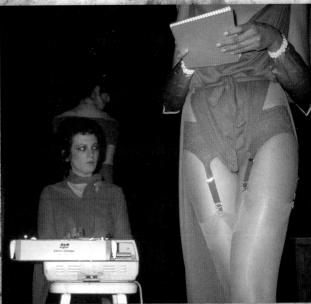

Clockwise from top left: Vicki Pedersen/Joan Crawford Mothers Day Event, 1979, by Marcia Resnick; Nan Goldin Night School at Mudd, 1979, by Billy Sullivan; Pat Ivers & Emily Armstrong, 1980, by Robin Schanzenbach; Hal Ludacer, 1979, by Eileen Polk; Eric Mitchell & Amos Poe, 1979, by Marcia Resnick; Anya Phillips & James Chance/Mudd Dance Floor, 1979, by Chris Stein.

Talking Heads BBC Taping, 1979, courtesy Richard Boch.

Clockwise from top left: Jo Shane/Colette Fashion Show, 1979, by Allan Tannenbaum; Richard DNV "Ricky" Sohl, 1980, by Bobby Grossman; Smutty Smiff, 1979, by Emily Armstrong; Richard Lloyd, 1979, by Emily Armstrong; Cheetah Chrome, 1979, by Emily Armstrong.

Clockwise from top left: Abbijane Mudd Club ID, 1980, courtesy Justin Straus; Maripol, 1980, by Maripol ©All Rights Reserved; Teri Toye & Scott Daley/Performing, 1979, by Allan Tannenbaum; Vincent Gallo, 1980, by Rhonda Paster Corte; Walter Steding/In the Cage, 1979, by Allan Tannenbaum; Edwige, 1980, by Rhonda Paster Corte; Richard Boch, Lynette Bean, Pete Farndon, 1980, courtesy Lynette Bean Kral.

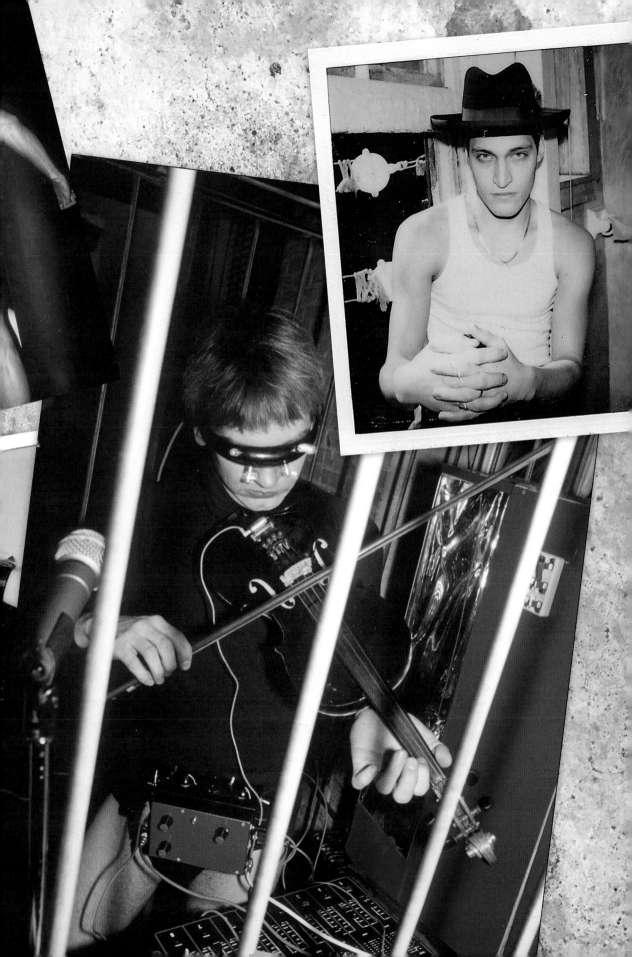

Clockwise from top left:
Richard Sohl & Bea Reilly/
Montauk, 1980, by Ron Beckner;
Gary Kanner & Richard Boch/
Mudd Basement, 1980, by
Lynette Bean Kral; Heroin
Superstore Lower East Side, by
Richard Boch; Historic, 2017,
by Richard Boch; Mudd Club
DJ David Azarch/Combat Love
Party, 1980, by Marcia Resnick.

By then I had already made my move to Murray Street. Everyone, including me, seemed anxious to do something and the next time Steve Mass ran into Amos he told him, "You won't believe this but I'm going to open a bar." It wasn't long before the new place needed a name.

Molotov Cocktail Lounge, a zany No Wave-ish designation suggested by either Cortez or Phillips, was briefly considered—the letters MCL were stenciled on the building's front window. Steve thought it might be too much; so did the State Liquor Authority.

Whether it was the blur of memory seen through that "muddy lens," or a nod to Steve's fascination with John Wilkes Booth's attending physician, Dr. Samuel Mudd, a *real* name was finally on the table. Mudd Club Lounge became the official corporate name on the liquor license and by October the Mudd Club was getting ready to happen. Five months later, I was standing out front, and the thick of it was right inside. The security gate, for security's sake, was permanently rolled down and the letters MCL were never seen again.

Like the Mudd Club, CBGB or Max's Kansas City, *The Blank Generation* speaks of time, place and future. It's the *thump, thump, thump* of Talking Heads' "Psycho Killer." The Voidoids onstage and Richard Hell spitting out a near sing-along ("I belong to the Blank Generation") lyrical slogan. Like walking thru the door of 77 White, it's an altered state; the soundtrack's out of sync, cutting loose from a 16mm dream.

That summer night in 1979, Amos walked right in. I followed him upstairs and told him about a series of monotypes I made three years earlier called "For The Blank Generation." In homage to the movie, the song and the scene, it was me wanting to fit in and be a part of that moment. Two of the deliberately soiled, flesh-colored images were written about by Jackie Brody for *Print Collectors Newsletter* and hung at the now infamous Knoedler Gallery as part of a show curated by gallerist Barbara Mathes. I was twenty-two and had just moved to the city; the show, an early stop along the road to White Street.

Today when I see Amos there's a timeline boomerang. He gives me a hug, and *then* becomes now.

Heaven

Two nights later came as a surprise, again the memory still with me. Steve let a small number of people know what was happening and I called One University Place to put the word out. Then I called Alice, to tell her and Judy Nylon, "Get down here right away." We padded the house with regulars and let in the lucky few who happened to come by.

Monday, August 13. It's 8 P.M. and the evening daylight's fading. I'm already at the door and Chris Frantz, Tina Weymouth, Jerry Harrison and David Byrne are inside. Talking Heads are getting ready to play an unannounced show at Mudd.

A crew from London is on hand to film the event for a UK Channel 4 documentary and the band is psyched. By 9 P.M., the club's half full and I'm standing near the stage with Michael Maslin. The intensity of the film company's lighting turns up the heat and the dark gray Mudd Club walls look bright white. The band opens with "The Big Country" from their second album, *More Songs About Buildings and Food*, produced by Brian Eno. They follow it with "Warning Sign" and "Love → Building on Fire." A new song called "Life During Wartime" from the just-released *Fear of Music* mentions the Mudd Club and CBGB as it barrels along on the rhythm laid down by Chris and Tina. "I ain't got time for that now" is the line that sticks while the lyrics describe a band on the run. Peanut butter also gets a mention.

I stood there smiling—trying to take it all in. Halfway through the set David Byrne started singing a song called "Heaven."

> *"Everyone is trying to get to the bar*
> *The name of the bar, the bar is called heaven*
> *The band in heaven, they play my favorite song*
> *They play it one more time, play it all night long"*

Whether he was singing about a party, a kiss or just a dream, I'll never forget how beautiful the band sounded.

The show ended by 10:30 and by midnight the band, friends of the band and club regulars started taking over the second floor. I was busy at the door but I kept running back upstairs. It was the kind of night that made me realize how much I loved New York and how much I loved the Mudd Club.

I hung out until the place was almost empty and I got home around 5 A.M. I rolled a joint, went in the studio and put a sheet of paper on the wall. I was painting. I was happy.

***

Running around in the late afternoon, working in the middle of the night and crashing midmorning—I'd been doing it for almost five months but it still felt new. Heading home at 5 or 7 or 10 A.M., the air felt different, you could almost touch it. I walked along Broadway with a lighter step. New York was hot and dirty but everything was okay; it seemed like the dead of August was the best time of the year. My twenty-sixth birthday just three weeks away and I still felt like a kid. Summer '79 felt like those long summer vacations I remembered—but disappeared too soon.

Sunday, August 19, 10 P.M. and I was looking forward to an easy night. Gerard Malanga, Cookie Mueller, Max Blagg and Taylor Mead were doing a reading on the first floor and Lounge Lizard Evan Lurie and singer Ruby Lynn Reyner were putting some music together. The club was busy by 11 but hardly anyone paid to come in. The program was an hour of literary enlightenment for the well-informed and a *What the fuck, I need another drink* for the unsuspecting. Whether you cheered and whistled, politely applauded or threw something at the stage, this was the kind of evening that gave the club its identity and the reputation for never knowing what to expect. It was White Street entertainment at its best and kept people coming back for more.

Taylor was the last to read, rummaging through pages, drifting and commenting off the cuff as only he could. When the literary portion of the evening ended, I took a break and went upstairs. The second floor felt private, cozier and clubbier than usual—the drugs and bad behavior practically part of the décor. It's where Mitch Ryder of Detroit, Bryan Ferry of Roxy Music and writer and director Paul Schrader landed when they stopped by for a drink. For guitarist Chris Spedding, David Bowie and Anita Pallenberg, it was a dirty living room with broken furniture and a bar. Michael Musto called it "incestuous," a place where "the outcasts were on the inside." I just called it the upstairs, and a few of those outcasts I called my friends.

Energy

Among those friends and acquaintances I'm still amazed at what we could do. We lived our own version of luxury in tenement walk-ups, raw commercial space and bombed-out ruins of Alphabet City. The bathtub was rusted and cracked, the hot plate was on the living room floor and there was no lock on the building's front door. The neighborhood, whether south of Canal Street or the far East Village, might have been dilapidated but it was our home.

Times were lean, and even New York City was struggling. We *appropriated* food, clothing, liquor and drugs, and occasionally did the same to make art, but we all lived within striking distance of White Street. The creative energy downtown continued to explode and the Mudd Club was the 4 A.M. ground zero. I often pushed that limit till 5 and beyond, regardless of what I was searching for. A cab ride to nowhere or a walk home to Murray moved the morning toward noon. Before the crash or after *awake*—what wound up on the walls of my studio was the response to both nighttime morning mayhem and reentry into Earth's atmosphere. Oftentimes it was beautiful, other times a mess.

I ask Linda Yablonsky, "What was different then, what allowed us to be who we were?"

She offers that one word, "Energy."

She mentions *then* being "a much bigger stew with more ingredients, places like Club 57, Tier 3 and Mudd tied all the strands together, all the DNA. Life today is more fractured."

Listening to Linda or walking the streets, I come to realize a sense of community diminished. More often than not we show up somewhere, offer a hello, engage in conversation and go our separate ways. Today, there's no longer a *next stop* Mudd Club, or what Linda calls a "catalyst."

Survival

Between those lean times and moments of truth, living just blocks away from White Street had its advantages and perils. Returning to Murray Street, whether at 5 A.M. or high noon: survival sometimes meant just getting home.

The nine blocks between Murray and Mudd seemed safe and manageable, the possibility of danger rarely considered. With a degree of purpose it took less than ten minutes to walk to work. I headed up Broadway, right on Franklin Street, turned left down Cortlandt Alley and never had a problem. Then one night I heard a woman screaming and everything changed. She was beaten, raped and slashed just steps away from her own front door, less than a hundred yards from the Mudd Club.

My neighbors, Suellen Epstein and artist Jim Biederman, had just left dinner at Meryl Streep and Don Gummer's loft on Broadway, around the corner from 77 White. Don brought them down to the street in the elevator, I turned onto Franklin and everything happened at the same time. The attacker started running, Jim gave chase and Don rushed back upstairs to call the police. Neighbors heard the screams and started yelling out the windows. I ran down Cortlandt Alley and gave the two cops parked outside Mudd a vague description. The woman barely survived but thanks to everyone who got involved the rapist was caught. The two cops stopped by later and told me the guy had been "taken care of and dealt with." It seemed a bit *old school* even then, but considering the crime, a tough call to make.

In view of the comings and goings of an endless party on White Street, a neighbor's near-death encounter with a violent predator was a harsh dose of reality. The city was dark and often deserted below Canal: a wrong turn at the wrong time and anything could happen.

I stood outside that night and kept watch. At 4 A.M., I disappeared upstairs and when I left the street was empty. I lit a cigarette and walked home. It felt as though everyone, including the neighborhood, had lost something. I wasn't worried about myself but I was worried about the city.

***

Mid- to late-'70s New York was the one I really knew. The one my parents showed me as a kid, and the one I wandered as a teenager, was a tease: the big show started when I landed on Bleecker in 1976. Crime was high but the rent was cheap, and in 1979, we were still four years away from big money moving in and changing things forever. Ed Koch was in his second year as mayor but would seem to have little power keeping rents low or getting a handle on crime. No matter how often he was elected that never changed. Artist and musician Walter Steding agrees: the pivotal year was 1983. That's when developers started *stealing* the city away from young artists—when finding a cheap place to live became a full-time job. I took a gamble when I left Bleecker and got lucky.

In the seventies, money followed art; surely the real estate money did. In the eighties and nineties, SoHo and Tribeca, along with the East Village, the Lower East Side and, eventually, far west Chelsea got eaten alive. For years Max's Kansas City founder and One University Chinese Chance owner Mickey Ruskin saw it coming and stayed one step ahead. When it came to opening up a new joint he was an artist, *divining* his way to the next hot-spot watering hole. Sadly, after more than two decades, he couldn't hang on to that gift. The year was 1983.

Today the neighborhood I moved to in 1977, the onetime creative universe just blocks from Mudd, is nearly culture-free. In its place, a mountain of money and a malled-out urban-burb built on the backs of artists who came before. Over thirty-five years ago, I grabbed a piece when I had the chance. I wound up with a loft on Murray Street, found my way to White Street, and hung on.

Now summer's beginning to darken. By 11 P.M., I'm back at the door; two hours later, the rest of the world shows up.

I look at the crowd and realize Steve was right—it feels like I know everybody. I start asking, "How many?" and start sending people in. By 1 A.M., it's somewhere between a cocktail party and a Molotov cocktail. By 2 A.M., it's magic.

Richard Boch, chain, cigarette, long tweed coat, 1979, by Alan Kleinberg.

6.
THE
LONG
TWEED
COAT

Mid-September 1979. My twenty-sixth birthday or what I remembered of it was two weeks past. The nights were cool until the summer came back Indian and the biggest problem I was facing was what to wear.

My almost semi-permanent roommate Teri Toye was hanging out with Scott Daley and both were hanging out at Mudd. They appeared together in the Victor Hugo show back in July and were still occasionally appearing together on the old fold-out sofa bed at Murray Street. I was just trying to mind my own business and solve my fall wardrobe dilemma when Teri and Scott got off the sofa and came to the rescue.

By way of a hand-me-down from six-foot-four Scott, I came into possession of the tweed overcoat. Large enough to fit over a motorcycle jacket, it was warm enough to take me into December. The summer of 1979 was almost over and I was ready.

On a cold September night, before the calendar officially turned fall, I made my move. Motivated by weather more than style, I worked the door in the new-to-me long tweed coat. When designer and fashion muse Abbijane saw me she screamed, "You've officially started the fall season!" I smiled, knowing my *unfashioned* fashion sense had just been validated.

Besides the leather jacket, I wore everything from pajamas to a denim vest and a quilted velvet-collared Yves St. Laurent jacket underneath the coat. It became my uniform and was about as fashion-forward or backward as I'd get. The MC jacket was from the West Village Leather Man; the PJs and the vest were thrift. Where the St. Laurent came from will forever remain a Mudd Club mystery.

Within a few days of Abbijane's scream I was the guy in the long coat, an identity with a shade more sophistication than last season's "guy in the orange pants." Glenn O'Brien, an enduring barometer of style and taste, remembers me as "wearing some kind of proper overcoat and never getting hysterical even when the situation warranted it." As for my state of mind and demeanor, Alanna Heiss (a neighborhood regular who founded the nearby Clocktower Gallery in 1972 and MoMA's PS1 in '76) recalls me being "good-looking and relatively sane, an unusual combination then and now." I remember the coat more than my relative sanity and credit the warmth it provided for any perceived sense of calm.

Low-Slung Weapon

Then suddenly the warm weather's back and I'm rushing around. I throw on an old blue jean jacket with a pink-and-black Levi and the Rockats button on the pocket flap and head out the door; I'm meeting Pat Wadsley at Mickey's for dinner. We quickly finish a meal of fried zucchini spears and one-dollar-fifty-cent-per-shrimp shrimp cocktail and walk seven blocks to the Thirteenth Street backstage entrance of the Palladium. The security guy knows me and we go right in.

It's September 20, 9:30 P.M., and The Clash are ready to go on. The band's DJ, Barry "Scratchy" Meyers, is making scratchy sounds as Pat and I step into the orchestra. We wander around, steal two seats about ten rows from the stage, and the lights go down. The entire place stands up and The Clash hit the stage running. "I'm So Bored with the USA" sounds like an explosion.

Three guitars and a drummer start firing songs into the crowd. Mick Jones lets loose a blast of rhythm on his Gibson Les Paul as Joe Strummer spits out the *word*. Paul Simonon breaks a wide-legged stance and leaps toward the edge of the stage, swinging and shaking his bass guitar like a low-slung weapon. Topper Headon pounds the beat and powers it all forward. Pat's hypnotized and I'm yelling so loud I'll need a couple of brandies to get my voice back. By the second song, the Palladium's out of control and a dozen songs later it's hard to pull myself away. I have to be at White Street by 11 but I'll be back here tomorrow night for more.

London Calling

Punk started out in New York, and London fired back an angrier, more politicized voice. Whether you ascribed to the politics or were only looking to get pounded by the beat, The Clash were ferocious. Ninety minutes later, my ears were still ringing.

I told David Azarch about the show, asked for a Jack Daniels to soothe my throat and tried to remember the first time I met Joe Strummer. It was either at One University or at Mudd and he showed up with Kate Simon. I already knew Clash DJ Barry Meyers, who was hanging out in both places.

Joe started calling Barry *Scratchy* after the '78 tour and the name stuck. By 1979, Scratchy was coming to Mudd whenever he was in town. There was none of that *What are you doing here?* vibe, like the one that greeted the band on their visit to Studio 54. The Mudd Club was different—I was at the door.

Friday night, September 21, I returned to the Palladium. I found a seat up close on the left side of the orchestra and the band roared thru "Safe European Home" and "Complete Control." A new song, "London Calling," nearly caused a riot and everything seemed louder and more frantic than the night before.

With the room practically on fire, Paul Simonon smashed his Fender Precision bass on the stage. It was a wild *fuck it* moment of frustration and mayhem that no one saw coming. Feedback was screaming, the Palladium went crazy and photographer Pennie Smith captured the moment. The photo became the cover of the band's next album—one of Rock 'n' Roll's great images. I was glad I stuck around.

"London Calling" rattled my brain for the next few hours and I was upstairs when one of the security guys told me, "Your *friends* are at the door." Never knowing what that meant, coming from someone who didn't know me at all, I checked it out. Paul Simonon and another guy were sitting on the steps outside, looking for free beer and some late-night *strange*. I said, "Hey, yeah. Come on in," and that was it. Having witnessed a moment that went down in history, by 4 A.M. any large talk felt pointless. The smashed pieces of a Fender bass were somewhere else, the night came full circle, and a new Rock 'n' Roll hero was shambling thru the hazy morning wreckage of the second floor. When I left the club at 5 A.M. the streetlights were still bright and a few yellow cabs still sat near the curb. I walked home, the opening chords of "London Calling" still crashing in my head.

The Baptist and the Hook

Saturday afternoon I worked on a new painting. I gave The Clash a rest and listened to Chris Spedding's *Hurt* two or three times. I left Murray Street early, went to One University, had a beer and some baked macaroni and left in a cab. I always got to White Street on time even though there was no one to tell me *You're late*. The original crew was gone and all the door staff, except for me, was new.

Colter returned from Europe, heard a rumor that "the Mob" or "the Angels" were doing security and stayed away. Gretchen was willingly abducted by a psychotic coke dealer and lived with him on Charlton

Street. Joey Kelly left with Glenn during the summer management upheaval and Louie went on a long break and never came back. Robert Molnar's Mudd Club career ended right there at the door—suddenly and without warning—during the middle of a shift. Depending on where you were standing and which way the fists were flying, his last night was one either to remember or forget.

I'd just given up trying to negotiate when security saw what was coming. Seconds later, Robert caught a punch in the face thrown by a Hells Angel named John the Baptist. When another Angel with a hook for a hand started swinging, the situation went from zero to chaos in seconds. Luckily for us, the hook got snagged in the front door and Robert and I escaped out the back. We ran down Cortlandt Alley to Franklin Street, jumped in a cab on Broadway and headed for Beekman Downtown Hospital. Robert's nose was busted, blood was everywhere and I stayed in Emergency just long enough to catch my breath and offer some sympathy, encouragement and moral support.

When I got back to the club the crowd was still outside; the Angels were inside, drinking at the downstairs bar. John the Baptist was a big, good-looking biker, a fighter and the real deal; the Hook was a man of few words with an edgier hook-for-a-hand way about him. They both seemed okay once they stopped punching and swinging and the three of us headed for the third-floor office.

Baptist John had a bag of coke in his jacket and a hunting knife strapped to his belt. We sat on a table, he stacked the end of the blade with piles of white powder while I smiled and said thanks. We shared a few beers and ten minutes later we all shook hands and hooks. They went back to the first-floor bar and I went back to the door. Robert left the emergency room, went home and never returned.

There was no reality check, just another fine line between fun and trouble. I just turned twenty-six—I was working, having a good time and making new friends. Why *wouldn't* I snort coke off the end of a weapon held to my face by a biker named after a cousin of Jesus Christ?

Robert got hurt, caught in the crossfire. I went home, smoked two or three joints and was back at the door the next night. Nothing changed and the only thing missing was a police report. A week later, Steve Mass held his ground and reached a peaceful accord with Hells Angels president Sandy Alexander. A little respect and a lot of free drinks went a long way. A standing invitation to Sandy and his wife sealed the deal. I just smiled and said, "Come on in." They seemed nice enough.

Notable New Hire

Chi Chi Valenti was by then hanging out at Mudd, getting acquainted and making herself at home. She seemed *more* than nice enough and her charm seduced everyone, including Steve Mass. The second floor still needed an "admissions director" and Chi Chi had a certain something that made her perfect to rule the stairway. She was the Mudd Club's first notable new hire in a long time and well positioned for her eventual role as The Empress of New York City Nightlife.

Chi Chi and I worked as a team and quickly became friends. We "read" nearly everyone, blew some off and wrestled with others. We found fun in the bathrooms, excitement on the second floor and trouble in the hours before and after work. We understood each other stone cold sober and when our eyeballs were rolling around in the back in our heads. I introduced her to everyone I knew, barely knew or didn't know at all and she returned the favor. Thank God she was there.

The rest of the new crew—with the exception of Aldo, whose hiring was still a few months off—were just a bunch of low-rent, not quite thugs from New Jersey. With the old man Jim Connelly in charge, security meant punch first, ask questions later and carry a concealed weapon for good measure. Their idea of culture and celebrity was *The Exorcist* actress Linda Blair, Tiny Tim, and Jay and the Americans; also, anyone who lacked irony and charm.

The big Tiny thing was already well past its fifteen minutes of tiptoe tulip fame; the sullen, demon-possessed child of Satan was closing in on her own expiration date. I sent Tiny in for free but made devil girl pay. Neither Jay nor any of the Americans ever showed up.

I stayed outside and did my job. Tiny Tim didn't stay long and left without saying good-bye. Child star Linda Blair came and went; her inevitable drug dealing and cocaine possession rap pleaded to a lesser charge. By then her career had turned into a pop culture footnote headed for the low-budget horror bin—the same receptacle where Jim Connelly and his crew belonged.

I never could figure out how that old man sold Steve his idea of security.

The Grief We All Felt

Considering my peculiar status at the door and the people I was hoping to meet, I tried to become better informed with the world beyond pop culture. I started buying the *New York Post* and noticed Rosalynn Carter was already campaigning hard for Jimmy's reelection bid, shaking hands everywhere except the Mudd Club. I wasn't surprised to hear that a cloud of doubt lingered over nuclear power given the recent Three Mile Island accident or that the United States and the Soviet Union continued to bicker over who had the bigger dick. Meanwhile, the cause of Elvis Presley's death—coming two years after the fact—was officially described as drug-related (as opposed to heart-related). The pathologist's report made note of 5,300 tablets, various downers and stimulants prescribed during a seven-month period. That number appeared to rival even Linda Ludes' recent Quaalude sales figures during the first and second quarters of the current fiscal year (I did the math and figured it out).

Sunday, September 23, 1979. Taking that knowledge in hand and to heart, I watched a Rock 'n' Roll Funeral procession slowly make its way up White Street. The long black funeral cars Patti Smith once visualized when she spoke of death and loss pulled up out front and everyone in attendance was duly grief-stricken. Dead rock stars were celebrated and memorialized—a few even hanging out on the second floor.

As a gesture of respect for those we loved, I dressed appropriately in black Fiorucci cords, the black Tony Lamas with red piping up the side, my black leather motorcycle jacket and a tie. I wore a red-and-white polka dot shirt with a button-down collar and a Heartbreakers provenance. Despite that bit of dotted flash, reaction to polka dots and leather was muted on that serious Sunday in '79. The combination hardly stood in the way of grief.

The suitably Goth "Reverend" Willoughby Sharp officiated over a solemn service on the first floor as troubled young rock star Nicholas Petti, a.k.a. Nick Berlin of The Blessed, rested peacefully inside an open coffin. When poet Taylor Mead closed the lid, sat on top and began eulogizing, young Nick spent a fearful forgotten hour trapped inside. He survived the ordeal and went to wreak havoc on the second floor while Gary Indiana, Jackie Curtis and Viva Superstar delivered the final eulogies. Taylor aimed for the bar and I headed back outside.

Funeral Etiquette

by the late Amy Vanderbilt

Funeral Etiquette, Rock 'n' Roll Funeral Ball, 1979, courtesy Amy Vanderbilt and Howie Pyro.

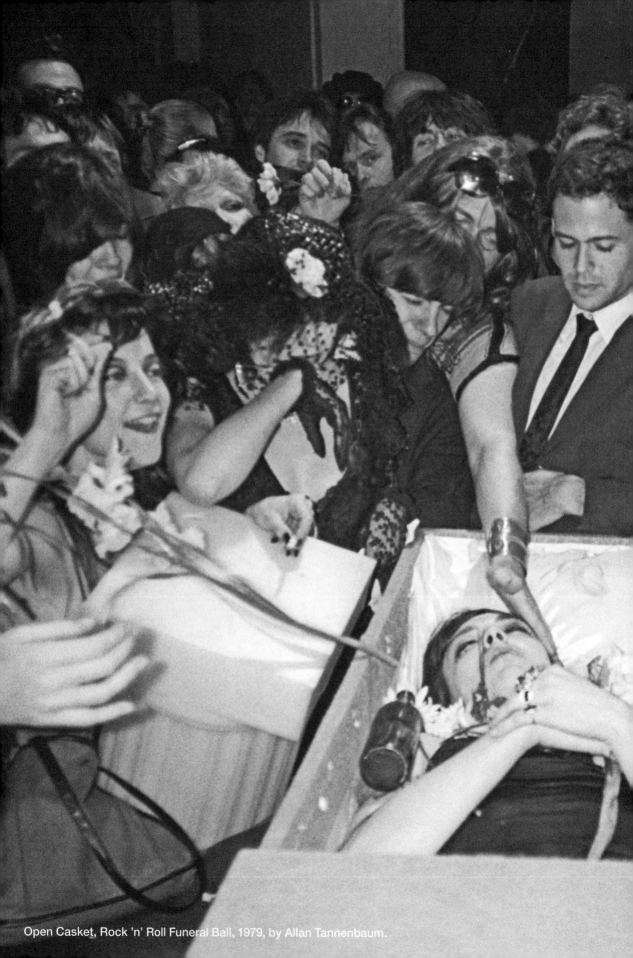

Open Casket, Rock 'n' Roll Funeral Ball, 1979, by Allan Tannenbaum.

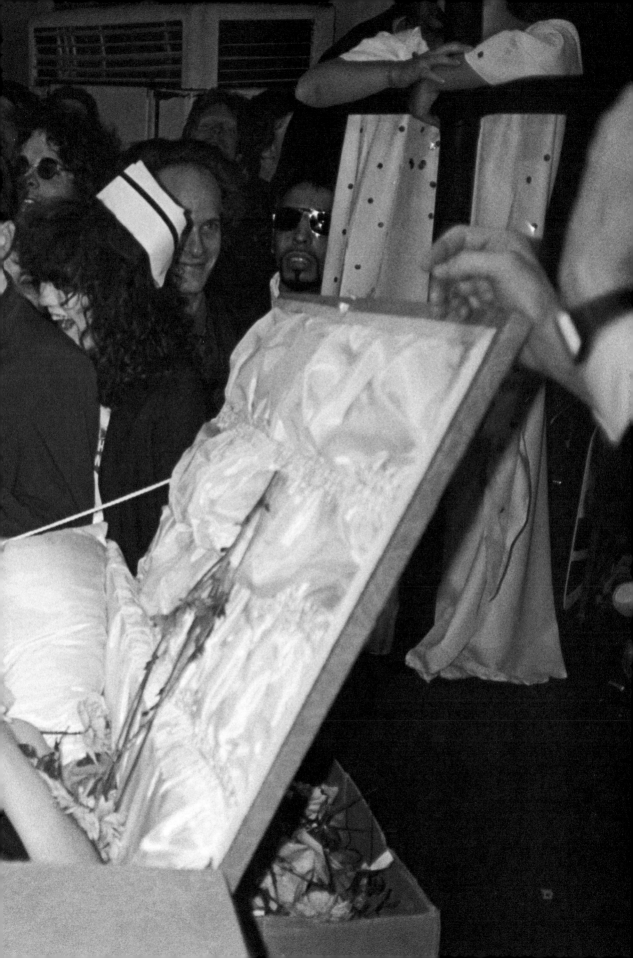

The evening carried on and the Mudd Club paid tribute with words
and music, serious and surreal tableaux. Artist Brien Coleman chan-
neled Mama Cass, working the second floor with a tray of tiny ham
sandwiches while mourners choked back toast points and tears. A
wounded Janis Joplin, as envisioned by the constantly sobbing Mer-
cedes, was nearly gone, surrounded by a loaf of Wonder Bread, a
fifth of Southern Comfort and the spent, dirty syringes that became
her undoing. Howie Pyro, doing his best Keith Moon, was tucked into
bed with a bottle of whiskey and ample sedation, enough to end anyone's pain and suffering. Tina L'Hotsky's all too real memory of

Left to right: Rock 'n' Roll Funeral Ball, 1979: Janis Joplin in repose,
Jim Morrison shrine, leather pants with snake, both by Marcia Resnick.

Jim Morrison was a pair of leather pants with a snake slithering
out the fly. Mudd vixen Vicki Pedersen knelt nearby, anguished and
inconsolable, remembering the bygone days of Jimi Hendrix.

The ghost of Sid Vicious was still in the room, sadness over his
not-too-distant passing fresh in our minds. I walked downstairs
and Jackie Curtis was weeping his way through another rendition of
"Loving You." I reached for a beer, washed down a Quaalude and went
outside just as Elvis was leaving the building. Some cried like
rain and some a single tear, but we all got the chance to say those
final good-byes that had eluded us for so long.

You are invited to attend a

ROCK AND ROLL FUNERAL BALL

Sunday September Twenty-third & Monday September Twenty-fourth, Nineteen Hundred and Seventy-Nine at ten thirty p.m. at the MUDD CLUB, Seventy-Seven White Street.

The event will be conducted in a spirit of reverence and celebration for the youthful rock and roll songbirds who died whether on land, sea, in the air, or in hotel rooms, their veins bursting with song for the fans they loved so dearly.

Appropriate costume for men and women should consist of apparel or accessories known to have been worn by the particular heroine or hero whose passing you are mourning. An alternative for bereaved women would be black chiffon veils, and black stockings; and for men dark business suits with black shoes and socks, and black ties with white shirts. Children should wear quiet colors or white.

Those wishing to be present for the official dedication of the Rock and Roll Shrines should arrive on Sunday between four and six in the afternoon. Placement of candles and flowers is permitted at the foot of the shrines. The shrines were created to include most races, colors and creeds and will pay hommage to Mark Bolan, Cass Elliott, Jimi Hendrix, Brian Jones, Janis Joplin, Paul McCartney, Jim Morrison, Elvis Presley, and Sid Vicious. Eulogies will be delivered by Reverend Gary Indiana, Honorable Taylor Meade, Doctor Jackie Curtis and Dame Viva.

The services and celebration will be impressive and elevating. As an expression of worship for the fallen rock and roll heroes it will find a response in the hearts and souls of men and women everywhere. The event will be videotaped with broadcast quality equipment by a respected American Corporation for distribution coast to coast.

Those wishing to participate in the funeral cortege or who wish to act as pall bearers, paid mourners or as the embalmed living dead should call Mr. Martin at PL8-2000.

By invitation only
ADMIT TWO
$5 Per Person

Clockwise from opposite page: Rock 'n' Roll Funeral Ball, 1979: Mama Cass with sandwiches, by Allan Tannenbaum; Rock 'n' Roll Funeral Ball invitation, 1979, courtesy Howie Pyro. Jackie Curtis, Live and *Life*, Mudd, 1979, by Bobby Grossman.

Sunday night was finally winding down.

The Dead Rock Stars—Rock 'n' Roll Funeral Ball was a landmark event—a *one-off* that wouldn't or couldn't happen again. The shrines on the second floor became a semi-permanent installation, influencing the New York club scene and leading the way for more offbeat, do-it-yourself theme night installations.

Swan Lake

Monday night was different. Anita Sarko was the DJ and by 1 A.M. everyone's grief seemed to have passed. Anita played music we loved, that we never heard before and, in some cases, would never hear again. She'd cue up wild-eyed favorites: PiL's "Swan Lake" and Lou Reed's live version of "Sweet Jane," then turn things around with Scott Walker's "The Plague," a 1967 B-side rarity. At closing time she'd occasionally crash the dance floor and clear the dregs with "The Lost Sheep" by Adrian Munsey, His Sheep, Wind and Orchestra. Whichever way she played it—and no matter how much she bitched about this and that—Anita took the smart stuff out for a spin.

There were nights after work when Gary and I left White Street with Anita and hung out at her place for hours, listening to music, talking and getting high. She lived on Jones Street in Greenwich Village; Jimmy Destri from Blondie lived upstairs and Billy Idol lived across the street. We'd split at 8 or 9 A.M. and step outside into the sunshine morning. We'd walk two blocks and grab a cab on Seventh Avenue South. I'd tell the driver, "West Broadway and Murray Street please, two below Chambers," and for some truly unknown reason the words *two below Chambers* always cracked us up.

If we were able to sleep, 10 A.M. seemed a reasonable hour to get in bed. Cocaine and Quaaludes seemed like reasonable drugs and a six of Dos Equis seemed a reasonable nightcap at nine in the morning. Running full speed ahead, it took me years to figure out the meaning of the word *reasonable*.

Avant-Garde

The rest of the week turned into a busy, beautiful mess. Club regulars poured thru the door and tourists kept showing up for a *one night only*. Most of them waited without getting inside and some went from muttering to name-calling to bidding me an angry farewell. I got caught up in the moment after getting hit with a "Fuck you asshole!" and a cup full of soda. I stepped into the crowd, punched someone in the side of the head and security broke it up after I got in a couple more shots. Back at the door, I took a swig of beer, lit a cigarette and felt like shit. Ten minutes later, I settled down and let more people in. When I took a break, I headed for the bathroom but avoided looking in the mirror.

I got called a lot of things but there were only a handful of people, other than the Mulberry Street crowd, who ever called me *Richie*. The only one who could pull it off wearing a rhinestone-studded NYC baseball cap and walk in for free was Sylvia Miles.

Whether it was the Mudd Club, back uptown to Studio 54 or a barely remembered opening night, Sylvia was either there or headed that way. She was a member of the Actors Studio, and in with the crowd at Max's Kansas City. She knew how to steal a scene from Jon Voight in *Midnight Cowboy*, telling movie audiences she was "one hell of a gorgeous chick." She could steal a scene at the Mudd Club just by showing up. I've always loved Sylvia and liked how comfortable she was being herself. She'd step thru the door, check things out and grab a spot at the downstairs bar. She'd make her way upstairs, when and if she felt like it.

Sylvia was smart—remembered everything and everyone—and never missed a party or a beat. She likes to say, "I wasn't fringe, I was avant-garde," and it's hard to argue with that. Her association with Warhol, along with her work with Joe Dallesandro and director Paul Morrissey, was only part of the story. Her willingness to take chances, inhabiting the wildest characters while chafing and rubbing against any and all available grain, made her a legend. Fearless, funny and the first to remind people she was *twice nominated* for an Academy Award, Sylvia Miles was part of the Mudd Club.

Today when we speak, she calls me Richard.

Groovy

By now the fall social season was in full swing and Club 57, the East Village rumpus room, was starting to happen. Obvious and less ironic than Mudd, the new club was offbeat and kooky and people were taking notice.

Club 57 was a think tank and drunk tank, a party room and dance hall with a bar, a DJ and a small stage. Following in the footsteps and success of 1978's New Wave Vaudeville Show at Irving Plaza, 57 (originally founded by Stanley Strychacki) became the brainchild of performance artist Ann Magnuson, filmmaker and former Mudd coat checker Susan Hannaford and poet Tom Scully. Dany Johnson was the resident DJ. Located on St. Mark's Place in the basement of a Polish church (a safe haven and alleged front for immigrants escaping Communism), it was doing its best to become the *other* place to go. Klaus Nomi, Keith Haring, artist Kenny Scharf, party girl-entrepreneur Deb Parker and performance artist Wendy Wild all commuted between St. Mark's and White Street. A band called Art had roots planted in the church basement but celebrated their Carnegie Recital Hall success with a cocktail party at Mudd. Pulsallama, the all-girl percussion and cowbell group that included Jean Caffeine on drums, found a pulse and a beat at 57. Before long they found a groove, played Danceteria, the Mudd Club, and opened for The Clash.

Despite a parallel timeline with Mudd, there was one big difference and Scharf's simple recollection lays it out. "Club 57 was groovy—Mudd was cool." The club was small-scale at the beginning: Kenny remembers walking in with Keith Haring and performer Jon Sex; Ann Magnuson was behind the bar, the jukebox was playing and they all started dancing. Listening to him tell it, it sounds like a beautiful dream.

Maybe I was too wide-awake or too tired but the few times I went there I just stood around. The Club 57 sense of camaraderie, snobbery and fun may well have been unique, but I never felt comfortable; its version of pandemonium seemed less appealing than the chaotic come-on of Mudd. To me, Club 57 felt like someone else's party and I either went back to White Street or had a drink and went home. Oddly, I wasn't sure if I wanted to fit in.

Dreaming with My Eyes Open

The seventies were quickly winding down and I wasn't sure about a lot of things. The New York I'd come to, and come to love, was changing; the world was different—or maybe it had just moved on. Somewhere in the middle of that move and change, Mayor Ed Koch started freaking out about the graffiti "problem." President Jimmy Carter was already freaking about the long-shot odds of winning a second term, while self-styled "neoconservatives" of the Republican Party were hard at work constructing a Retro Frankenstein monster called Reagan. Between all that freaking out and monster-making, I'd try a line of heroin, lie down and drift. Whether asleep or a nod, dreaming with my eyes open or closed, I still had trouble figuring out what was going on and how to keep doing whatever it was I was doing.

Working at Mudd, I had a little money but not a lot. When I started out in New York I had even less. Before that, I was in school and it's hard to remember having anything to spend, except what went toward pot, beer and LSD.

Selling my car and loading a van with my records, my clothes and one or two pieces of furniture was a bittersweet end and a new beginning. My mother and father stood in the driveway of the house in New Hyde Park and asked if I thought I might be back. I loved them for that. Despite years of finger-wagging, cautions and endless questions, my parents had always given me my independence. They allowed me the dreams and daydreams that started in my room, listening to songs I still remember.

My first apartment at 167 Bleecker Street was a noisy, one-bedroom walk-up just five blocks west of CBGB's. There was a bathtub in the kitchen and a "water closet" in the back of the bedroom. The landlady was old-school New York, called me Mr. Boch and had a bad attitude. New York *was* filthy, broke and drug-infested but somewhere in that state of decay was the offer of freedom and possibility. Musician and Bush Tetras' drummer Dee Pop calls it a "time of self-expression" before "the poetry of the city was replaced by big business."

The road from Long Island to New York City was an eye-opener; the nine-block journey from Murray to White, a revelation. Standing outside the Mudd Club, the first six months flew by and I didn't blink. Then I closed my eyes and started dreaming again. Running across the street with my friends, I was seven years old. I turned around, ran back, and I was twenty-six. I woke up and heard someone mention an alligator.

That's when I blinked.

Alligator Girls

October 23, 1979. Gary Indiana's play, *Alligator Girls Go to College*, kicked off a three-night run on White Street. I only recall the first night but clearly remember the alligators.

Billed as a Mudd Club Production, the whole thing was as far out and way off Broadway as you could get; the title alone, worth the price of admission. The playbill was pure high school charm in a twice-folded, mimeograph-scented kind of way. The story revolved around two young alligator girls who lost their jobs in the circus but refused to give up. Seeking a better life thru higher education, they tried enrolling for classes at Cyrus Vance Junior College. Tina L'Hotsky and Vicki Pedersen were the stars of the show and their performances were as compelling as their namesake characters, Norma Desmond and Mildred Pierce. Marcia Resnick, Evan Lurie and Rene Ricard were billed as supporting players. The curtain was scheduled for 8 P.M. and last call at the bar was eight hours away: in between, theatre-driven mayhem.

Ten minutes into the show the audience was spellbound, speechless and drinking heavily. Following a final curtain call the cast was exhausted; the blood, sweat and greasepaint on the alligator faces of Vicki and Tina spelled triumph. The audience either headed for the bar or ran for the door. It was promising to be a long night.

While I was busy dealing with those gator girls, the band Test Pattern was playing a few blocks north at The A-Space on Broome Street. Jean-Michel Basquiat, Michael Holman, Wayne Clifford and Shannon Dawson were still figuring things out as they blasted, bleated, synthesized and percussively triangled their way toward a crazy beautiful sound. Slowly, that sound turned Gray, and the test patterns disappeared.

By midnight, The A-Space emptied out; the crowd headed for White Street and joined the alligators. The club had been officially open for nearly a year and during that time it continued making a case in point out of Judy Nylon's idea of "correct and incorrect venues."

It was obvious—77 White was home, and no matter where the *Alligator Girls* thought they were going, they received their education at Mudd.

Madame Claude's

The crowd out front often looked anxious and unpredictable while the scene on my side of the chain was taking on a life of its own. Club regulars and friends, instigators, troublemakers and even one-time visitors were "helping" and hanging out at the door. They offered me company and conversation during lulls, moral support during the chaos, and a little entertainment for anyone waiting to come in. I got an earful of almost everything and a handful of whatever was left.

Nico, the singer, onetime Velvet Underground collaborator and Warhol dark star liked hanging at the door. She was chaos, company and entertainment rolled into one, whether spooking people at the bar or closing one of her sets with a rousing harmonium-accompanied version of "Deutschland, Deutschland über alles." When she needed air, money or a diversion she'd step outside. I usually enjoyed the company and never passed judgment on her social or hospitality skills.

Standing at the door on a warm October night, the Nico attitude and effect was contagious. When another limo pulled up in front all I could say was, "Who the fuck is this?"

Jerry Brandt waved hello, accompanied by Marianne Faithfull, music mogul, star maker and Island Records founder Chris Blackwell, and Chris' girlfriend, Nathalie Delon, the ex-wife of French film star Alain Delon. They made it thru the crowd and I opened the chain.

Nico was dressed in black, standing next to me.

In a low somber voice she said, "Hello Marianne."

In the direction of Nathalie, she hissed a reminder of another lifetime. "It's okay to say hello Nathalie, I remember you from Madame Claude's."

The mention of the notorious Parisian Madame and all it alluded to was strange and strained enough; that Nico once had a child with Alain Delon was something else entirely. Time stood still for thirty seconds until it caught up with itself. Three iconic beauties of the sixties were standing in front of me. Whether by collision or convergence, they wound up on White Street.

Nico, Femme Fatale, 1979, by Ebet Roberts.

I was still holding the chain when the dust settled and the moment passed—everyone headed inside and Nico disappeared. Chris Blackwell was carrying a plain white twelve-inch record sleeve under his arm, and Marianne's legendary single "Broken English" was making one of its first public outings. The club was packed, DJ David Azarch had the honor and no one had a clue what was happening. The bass started to rumble and the opening chords of Barry Reynolds' guitar ripped thru the speakers ahead of Marianne's beautifully weathered vocal. The room took a deep breath, the dance floor went crazy, and everyone realized we were a long way from *tears gone by*. I stood near the bar and had one of those starstruck moments. I'd never seen Marianne before and this was a crazy intro. I tried to engage but could barely speak. I lit a cigarette and went back to the door.

I told Kate Simon the story and she remembered photographing Nico in 1974. She had still found her "incredibly beautiful." By '79 things were different and the persona that once attracted everyone from Fellini to Dylan, from Brian Jones to Jackson Browne, had left the building long before I entered. There was still a compelling darkness to her music but the physical beauty was on a long slow fade, and her state of mind often questionable. Less alluring was her need to find Steve, who always seemed to owe her two hundred dollars, whether she was performing or not; if he weren't around, she'd ask anyone who'd listen for twenty.

Thinking on it now, all those years ago I only saw Nico alongside me at the door. I didn't consider or care what her motives might've been—I bought her a few drinks and she never tried to hustle me out of twenty dollars.

White Street Romance

Thirty minutes later Marianne left and I was singing whatever few words of "Broken English" I could remember. The people in the street seemed unimpressed. I just smiled and opened the chain.

Stephanie Richardson came thru the crowd, said "Thanks honey," and went inside. The once or twice we talked before, she was sweet and not too weird—always a good combination. Growing up in Spokane, Washington, she had a picture of the Empire State Building hanging on her bedroom wall. In 1976, she landed in New York, rented a room in the East Fifties and found a job handing out flyers for a massage parlor. Then she went to CBGB's, saw Talking Heads and kept going back. Other than the massage parlor sequence, the dream sounded familiar.

By 1979 Stephanie found her way to White Street. I asked her about it and she said, "The Mudd Club opened me up to a whole new life. It was more of everything, and brought everyone together." It was the perfect response and I could've said the same thing.

It wasn't long before Lenny Kaye spotted Stephanie across the room. She remembers how he walked over and said something like, "You're so beautiful you look like Miss America." Lenny was the guy who knew everyone and Stephanie was just getting started. Nobody was ready to settle down but no one was going anywhere either. Beyond the memorable pickup it was the beginning of a White Street romance, and the next time I looked they were *Lenny and Stephanie*. Last time I looked, they still were.

Quadrophenia

October was busy. The weather was holding up and the long tweed coat was taking a rest. The Rod Stewart clone and the guy who claimed he was a member of Earth, Wind & Fire kept coming to the door. I made the clone pay but didn't let Fire Liar in. I pulled the old *It's a private party* routine because it was.

Tuesday, October 30 (the eve of Mudd Club's first unofficial anniversary), the Who in association with Who Films was celebrating the opening of the movie *Quadrophenia*. The premiere took place at the Eighth Street Playhouse and the party followed at 77 White. Few of the cast except maybe Sting—whom I didn't care about even then—were in attendance. Director Franc Roddam was hanging at the bar and Roger Daltrey was floating around the room talking with *SoHo News* journalist Alan Platt. John Entwistle was hanging out near the bathrooms with three professional-looking "hostesses" and behaving like John Entwistle. I was running around, just trying to behave.

By 1 A.M., the upstairs was filled with Mudd Club regulars. Everyone from Sharon D'Lugoff (the teenage daughter of legendary Village Gate owner Art D'Lugoff) and Rockats bass player Smutty Smiff to Tina L'Hotsky, party girl Roxanne Jefferies and Pat Wadsley were all rubbing elbows with the other elbows. An hour later, Sharon, "an admittedly huge Who fan," found herself cornered in the bath-

John Waters and Cookie Mueller, Quadrophenia party, 1980, by Allan Tannenbaum.

room by Entwistle and his female accomplices. With an offer made a million times in a million bathrooms around the world he invited Sharon back to his hotel for a *five-way*. Despite the Who-ness of the gesture and Sharon's love for the "Oh my Lord!" nature of the Mudd Club bathrooms, she was caught off guard and even a little grossed out. She managed to make it out of the bathroom, went back to the bar and decided to wait for the return of Keith Moon.

For those who missed their chance or might've been present but barely there, bathroom stories live large in Mudd Club history. Sharon D'Lugoff shakes her head, starts thinking and says, "Oh, to have been a fly on those walls." She remembers the Entwistle moment clearly but now worries about coming off like "such a prude." She pauses, laughs and quickly points out, "It's not like I never took anyone home from Mudd." I laugh too, thinking we all did—just not that particular *wistle*.

A Trip to Long Island

The end of October came and went, Mudd's first anniversary unacknowledged. I wore the orange pants and black leather jacket on the thirty-first but it was hard to tell if anyone was dressed up or not. Thursday and Friday were busy and Saturday night almost did me in. As much as I tried to avoid the news, the rest of the world seemed even crazier than the weekend crowd on White Street.

Chain in hand I held my ground, while former CIA director George H.W. Bush was making a first bid for the presidency with typically hateful rhetoric and a straw poll victory in Maine. Ronald Reagan didn't seem worried. Closer to home, thieves in the Bronx set a subway token booth on fire with the token clerk inside. When I started hearing about the Ku Klux Klan shooting anti-KKK demonstrators I turned off the TV. Halloween came spooky that year and I needed a break.

Sunday, November 4, 1979. I've got the night off and I'm spending it in Roslyn, Long Island, with Iggy Pop, at a club called My Father's Place. It's a rambling old dive located under the Roslyn Bridge just off Northern Boulevard, a few miles from where I grew up. Guitarist Ivan Kral's in the band, and his girlfriend, Lynette Bean, put me and several new members of the Mudd Club crew on the guest list.

My Father's Place was the best Rock 'n' Roll club on Long Island; I'd been there often and over the years I saw some great shows. The Ramones blew the place apart more than once, and Patti Smith played the club for two nights on her first tour behind *Horses*. That was early January 1976: I was up close with Wayne (my future Murray Street roommate), and my friends Louis Minghinelli and Fred Siedlecki, smoking pot and washing down white crosses with beer. The sound of Patti pounding her chest during "Break It Up" was thumping thru the PA and "Free Money" was like nothing I'd ever heard before. When the band played "Gloria" the room was shaking. When John Cale stepped onstage and picked up a bass guitar for "My Generation" the place exploded.

The world I knew changed that night. I sat around after the show talking to Richard Sohl and stayed up till the next afternoon, buzzed on speed, poetry and a three-chord revelation. Now, nearly four years later, I'm headed back to Roslyn in a rented Davel limo for a club-sized Iggyfest. We're driving east on the Long Island Expressway—the memories of tripped-out mornings and eighty-mile-an-hour teenage adventures flash by and disappear. There's a bar in the limo and we're all drinking. I have a gram of coke and so does everyone else. We get to the club and Lynette and I head backstage; we find Ivan in the dressing room and the three of us go out to the car. Ten minutes later, the band opens with "Real Cool Time" from the first Stooges album recorded in 1969. Iggy's a powerhouse; his voice—a baritone cry—is deep, sexy and beautiful. He closes the show with the Johnny Mercer-Harold Arlen gem, "One for My Baby." It's a nice surprise and he nails it. The band comes back with a wailing, slow grind version of "No Fun." Then it's over.

After the show, I run into some people from the Mudd Club who follow and photograph Iggy. Twenty minutes later, Lynette and I say good night, join the others in the car and head for the city. When we get to White Street it's only 1:30, last call still half a night away.

The trip to Long Island left me with a sense of longing and loss; the friends who drifted away or disappeared were just a part of it. In three short years a connection to the place I once called home was gone. Things were different now, but I wondered if that might happen again. I walked over to the bar and put my arm around Lynette.

A love of Iggy Pop and a few grams of coke helped break a little ice with the new Mudd Club employees but the camaraderie didn't last more than a day or two. They came off like straights, descended from some generic hospitality trade school, with a newly acquired taste for cocaine in order to adapt to their environment. Our only real connection was based on me doing the door, and them pouring the drinks. Impossible to like everybody, those first impressions were hard to shake. That went both ways.

I Liked All of Them

A year earlier, in the fall of 1978, when the Mudd Club was just getting off the ground, Levi Dexter, Smutty Smiff and Dibbs Preston landed in New York. They'd never heard of White Street and I was still working on West Broadway. Levi, who looked about fifteen, was busy channeling Elvis circa '55. Smutty, a pretty boy covered with tattoos, was pounding and plucking an upright bass. Dibbs was the blond kid playing guitar, and photographer and Heartbreakers "handler" Leee Black Childers was their mentor and manager. Levi and the Rockats was the name of the band and they arrived from England in advance of their first U.S. shows—opening for the Cramps. They had something going on and I liked them right off.

Max's, November 10, 1978. The place was packed and the room was buzzing. A sad-looking Sid Vicious, accompanied by a girl named Michelle, grabbed two seats at our table but all I could do was say "Hey." I was with friends waiting for the Rockats, Sid looked like he was waiting for the world to end and his "date" seemed like she was just along for the ride. Ninety days later, Sid was gone.

The Cramps were the headliners that night but the crowd was ready and waiting for Levi and the Rockats. When they finished their first song, Trixie Revenge a.k.a. Plunger Girl screamed, "You're so cute!" because they were. The band had a familiar sound, with an attitude filtered thru Punk. Levi sang and danced up a storm, Smutty stood on the side of his upright bass and Dibbs' guitar ripped right thru the middle. The audience ate it up.

A year later, as I passed thru Cortlandt Alley, I heard that familiar sound again. I walked into the Mudd Club and smiled wide when I saw Levi and the Rockats doing a sound check. Leee Childers looked at me, laughed and said, "Hello darling." The boys gave a nod—happy to see that I was working the door.

Today Smutty remembers the scene on White Street having its own stars, superstars and happenings. You could dance or just hang out, get drunk, get high, get laid and come back for more. People were painting and writing, making music, making movies and taking pictures. They were doing it at midnight and still doing it at four or five in the morning. Smutty knew, "Mudd was the place to go because everybody was up to something."

Pravda

Whether it was midnight or five in the morning, at home or at the Mudd Club, no one was talking about communism or reading the newspaper that spoke its voice.

In early November, a club called Pravda, several blocks north on Crosby Street, was getting ready to try and become a New York nightlife legend. Rudolf Piper and Jim Fouratt, the activist, club manager and impresario, fronted the operation. Ron Lusker, a silent partner, owned the building and was doing the construction. Rico Espinet, the future stage manager of the original Danceteria and the next version of Peppermint Lounge, was brought in to do finishing work, while Bruno Schmidt assisted Rudolf with the club's fast-forward design. Pravda had location, word of mouth and the destiny of a huge opening night. With a great sound system, multiple DJs and a performance space it would be the perfect place for art, music and fashion. The exclusive vibe and minimalist décor (thanks mostly to Rudolf) was going to give New Yorkers another place to go.

The progress reports I was hearing said the new club was almost ready. The buzz had everyone excited but was making Steve Mass a little crazy. In a fit of cold-war paranoia and a bit of spite, he decided to clamp down on any chance of industrial espionage. Steve told me he didn't want any of those *Pravda people* getting into Mudd and I did my best to comply.

November 8, 1979, was the big night. I was working the door at Mudd and everyone else was milling about Crosby Street, waiting for something to happen. The Pravda opening party, honoring both *WET* magazine and Fiorucci, was jammed—and about to become legend for all the wrong reasons. By midnight, a few Mudd Club regulars, unable to squeeze into the new place, showed up on White Street; their only report, "Very crowded."

An hour or two later, something did happen and the crowd from Crosby came pouring down Cortlandt Alley, headed for Mudd. Pravda's opening night had unexpectedly turned into a closing night party and the following night the club was gone. Angry neighbors, the police and fire departments, along with wheels and palms never properly greased, brought down New York's Pravda, yet the legend lived on.

At 3 A.M., there was still a big crowd on White Street. I let in nearly everyone who showed up and the bar was busy giving away lots of free drinks. Mudd held onto its groove, kept its cool and was still the place to go. Steve Mass had worried for nothing.

The *Pravda* founded in 1912, St. Petersburg, Russia, stopped the presses in 1991 after eighty years of operation, twelve years after its Crosby Street namesake had a one-night stand.

***

The long tweed coat and a few dusty Quaaludes rediscovered in the pockets helped keep me warm on those cool November nights. I'd wash one down with a Rémy and get ready for the 1 A.M. rush. By 2 A.M., I was working hard but playing it loose, taking a break with anyone willing to play; 3 A.M. and my better judgment was already somewhere else. I'd occasionally sell out cheap and wind up slumming with everything from a '79 vintage variation on Dog the Bounty Hunter to a coked-up dentist or a passed-out Punk. The tweed coat kept me safe but certain memories run chills up my spine. Some nights my dream job turned nightmare.

Tonight's a different kind of dream. I'm facing off with a gaggle of high school boys from the Upper East Side, telling me they're on Andy Warhol's list. They're cute in that empty, pretty, prep school kind of way but they're not my type and I'm unmoved. Andy's not in the club and there's no way to tell when or if he's coming. He stops by occasionally, and when he does he works without a list.

I smile, stop just short of rolling my eyes, and tell whoever's working with me to please explain to the boys that it's five dollars each to come in. I step away, head upstairs and pound on the steel bathroom door. Artist Nathan Slate Joseph, a former Lower Manhattan Ocean Club manager, bartender and ex-boyfriend of Ocean Club waitress-turned-actress Ellen Barkin, exits with two blonde Swedish girls (bathroom habitués). Cookie Mueller's still at the mirror checking her makeup, and Russian Eddie's lighting a joint. I relock the door, turn around and get lost with a Marlboro, a Heineken and a dime. The Warhol fanboys manage to get in and everything works out fine. Andy's nowhere to be seen.

Concept, Felt, Animal Fat

When I finally made it back to the door Willoughby Sharp and a fedora-wearing friend were getting out of a cab. They headed straight thru the crowd, said hello and stepped inside. A conceptual artist, video pioneer and cofounder of *Avalanche* magazine, Willoughby was a legend in the art world and a regular at the Mudd Club. Two months earlier, the same "Reverend" Willoughby led a procession of mourners up White Street for the Dead Rock Stars party. He was also the curator of the Guggenheim's 1979 Joseph Beuys retrospective. The show opened on November 2, Beuys was still in New York and Willoughby brought him to White Street.

I had no idea who it was going in. It was late, I was busy and I saw Willoughby all the time. Then the thirty-second delay ended, I snapped out of it and realized Joseph Beuys, the artist of coyotes and concept, felt, animal fat, politics and performance, was inside the Mudd Club. I left the door, looked around and found them at the downstairs bar. I'd never said much more than hello to Willoughby but I had no idea where Steve was, so I walked over, introduced myself to Beuys and made sure the bar was taking care of them. Other than offering them a Quaalude it was the best I could do.

Joseph Beuys was a strange-looking guy—kind of old but kind of young with a serious stare and half a crazy smile. Though he helped transform my idea of art by moving it outside of itself, he seemed far removed from anywhere I'd been. I realize now he was part of the Mudd Club before he even stepped inside.

When Beuys left I opened the chain and said "Good night," he turned around and said, "Thank you." Starstruck once again, I went to the Guggenheim the next day. I looked at art and all it could be.

An hour later, I squeeze in alongside the bar. DJ David aims low with his own high concept and cues up the LP version of "Rock Lobster" at 45 rpm. The B-52's start spinning out of control and the dance floor plays along.

I look around remembering what it was like before I started working here—when you could still see a bit of floor between the people. I push my way forward and spot Abbijane, Julie Glantz and Lynette. DJ David moves from lobsters to Motown and Diana starts singing about a world that's "empty without you babe." Lynette grabs me and we start dancing. We're jammed together in the middle of the room, Diana's still singing but the world seems far from empty.

Baker

I leave Friday night's never-empty world of art stars and lobsters behind. Saturday's even busier and Steve wants to keep traffic light on the second floor. David Bowie's in a booth with Blondie's Jimmy Destri and Sassoon's creative director Mary Lou Green is sitting nearby with her friend, the Academy Award-nominated *Fat City* actress Susan Tyrrell. Cookie Mueller's a few feet away, engaged in conversation with Tom Baker the actor, Jim Morrison best friend and star of Warhol's *I a Man*. I walk by and Tom gives me a bear hug and a "Hey, hey Richie." Cookie gives me a kiss and a "Hi hon."

Other than Sylvia Miles, Tom's one of the select few who calls me Richie and gets away with it. Besides being a really sweet guy (despite calling me by a diminutive), Baker knows a curious strain of *everyone*. He introduced me to Ronee Blakely at the Lone Star Café after she blew the place away with a cover of Dylan's "Just Like a Woman." A few weeks later, I rode around in a cab with Baker, a few Wildings and a Getty for a wasted, dawn-breaking tour of the after-hours circuit. I survived the ride and made it home by 10 A.M.

By now it's getting late, and Joey Arias and Klaus Nomi are still upstairs saying good night. Mary Lou Green walks over and asks if they're sure they're ready to leave without meeting David. It's a simple introduction that leads to Klaus and Joey's star turn with David Bowie on *Saturday Night Live*.

I walk by on my way downstairs looking for a different kind of introduction. By 4 A.M. the first floor's winding down and the second floor's either ascending or descending into what Nathan Joseph calls "a scene out of *Satyricon*." Cinematic and sexy, it's another dirty dream, a late night lost and found. For Nathan, those nights on White Street existed in "a moment of the moment. It was anarchy, political without politics and freedom of everything." Without thinking too much, it sounds about right.

I'm ready to split but I make time for one more round. Mary Lou and Susan are headed for the door when Baker walks over, squeezes the back of my neck hard and says good night. Two hours disappear and by 7 A.M. I'm at The Nursery adding another drink to a Quaalude, a joint and a speedball combo. I've been trying to get the balance right for a while but it seems almost impossible.

Several people shake their heads, vaguely disapproving of my behavior and appetite, but only Anita Sarko and Abbijane speak up. It'll be a while before I start to listen and by then I'll be saying a sad good-bye to so many friends—Tom Baker among them.

Better or Worse

I survived that endless Saturday; Sunday and Monday disappeared. Back at work Tuesday, I was happy to see Anita at the turntables. I tried getting used to the new crew at the door but they kept changing. I started feeling outnumbered, even a bit creeped out. Luckily I had DJ David, Anita and Chi Chi to lean on.

A little guy named Little John was the new Mudd Club manager but he had no idea what the place was about. Peggy Doyle, who owned a joint around the corner on Franklin Street, recommended him, and for whatever reason, Steve listened. John had a wife who was always staggering around and falling over while he was busy snorting coke, ordering liquor and "counting" Steve's money. She was a pain in the ass and I paid as little attention to him as possible.

Other than DJ David, Greg the bartender was the last holdout from the original crew. He was a much nicer guy than Little John but shared the latter's questionable taste in women. When he met a girl named Briana at the club, they fucked around for about five minutes, did some coke and got married. Greg was in love but three days later she was back to picking up guys at the bar, getting high in the bathroom and making out in the alley. He kept busy pouring drinks and freaking out. The honeymoon was over.

I tried to mind my business but sometimes it was easier to stare at someone else's shit than look at my own. Life on Murray Street and my relationship with Gary was challenging at best. Drug-fueled and codependent, it was a constant stream of drama and deceit that caused scene after scene at Mudd, One University Place and at home. Fists occasionally flying and drinks being thrown, "fuck you," "I hate you" and "I'll kill you" were all part of our disconnected connection. I think we cared for each other, possibly even loved each other; but it was so out of control that even a diversionary basement interlude, a midmorning hookup or a pile of cocaine offered little distraction or relief. Too much alcohol made things worse. Sometimes heroin made things better.

Crazy Person with a Gun

In spite of the drama, I still loved my job. I even tried to be patient with a new security guy named Clay—a hothead psycho who liked to throw punches and carry a loaded weapon. My only thought: *Oh shit, now we have a fucking crazy person with a gun working here,* and I was right.

Clay had only been at the club a few weeks when he busted into an upstairs bathroom and punched Lounge Lizard John Lurie in the face. Leisa Stroud and Wendy Whitelaw were on either side of John and drugs were somewhere in the middle. John lost a tooth, Leisa was furious and everyone else was shocked. The scene created a Muddcentric *cause célèbre*, put a black mark on the club's reputation and temporarily damaged John Lurie's relationship with Steve Mass. Given my frequent trips to the bathroom I was an eyewitness and later deposed by a lawyer representing John. I was in a tough situation but I told them what I saw. It wasn't long after that I realized there was an even darker side to White Street than bootleg Quaaludes, heroin and bad relationships.

The drugs and the people who loved them still hung out in the bathrooms and Clay stuck around for another month. He fucked a few girls in the basement but luckily his gun never went off. Then, finally, he disappeared. After numerous fittings and adjustments, John and his new tooth returned to White Street. I kept working the door and Lurie got his saxophone to sing again. Steve handed out free drinks and paid some dental bills.

Maneuverings

Reality did and does occasionally suck and by the late fall of 1979 all I had to do was figure out how to keep going. The mirrors lying on my kitchen table and hanging on my bathroom wall were showing me more than just flashes of crazy. The occasional speedball had me pointed in the direction of a brick wall that wasn't there a year ago. Painting and not painting was another part of what was happening. The Mudd Club was the rest.

My reality was knowledge that doing the door was never an exact science: it was a sociological mash-up, part politics and part schmooze that required a thick skin, a lot of drugs and at least one person you could trust. When Louie, Joey and Robert left, Chi Chi became that person. I was impressed by her looks and charm, and she was impressed by my patience and tact. She was a smart woman who even likened a few of my moves to the reconciliation policies and diplomatic maneuverings of Bishop Desmond Tutu. I'm not sure how *Bishop Des* would've felt about the comparison but I took it as a compliment.

The door was about being a realist—friends and regulars always came first. As for everyone else, some had to pay to come in, some didn't and some couldn't come in at all. It was all gut feeling and going with your first impression—the once-over once. A second chance, usually a mistake. Sometimes it worked out; sometimes it didn't, but that's life.

Ford to City: Drop Dead

New York City, along with the rest of the world, was having an equally *that's life* kind of year. A tugboat strike (seemingly the last thing anyone was worried about) left barges stranded in the river and garbage piled up in the streets. Crime was out of control and the newly founded Guardian Angels were running around, sometimes helping and sometimes not. Etan Patz, the six-year-old from Prince Street who disappeared back in May, was still missing and the posters were still everywhere. Former U.S. Congressman and Democratic leader Ed Koch, an open-minded guy except when it came to graffiti and his own sexual identity, was already two years into a twelve-year run as the city's mayor. Everyone else was trying to get out from under the financial crisis of the mid-seventies and live down the infamous *Daily News* headline, FORD TO CITY: DROP DEAD.

Far and near, the seizure of the American Embassy in Tehran fucked everything up and brought down Jimmy Carter. The Shah of Iran, seeking exile and upset by Mexico's rebuff, continued to look for a new home. Margaret Thatcher became England's prime minister, forming a not-so-curious bond with soul mate Ronald Reagan. Moving south, then farther east, the Sandinistas liberated Nicaragua, and China instituted the *one child per family* rule. In the biggest name change since Muhammad Ali, Rhodesia became Zimbabwe. It sounded better; or so I thought.

For those who had the time, Norman Mailer's *The Executioner's Song*, a thousand pages about Gary Gilmore and a firing squad, won a Pulitzer. Closer to home and more culturally relevant, *The Warriors*, a gang war saga directed by Walter Hill, developed a cult following. The art scene in SoHo was thriving while filmmakers from the New Cinema on St. Mark's, and East Third Street's Little Hollywood, were hanging out at Mudd. Alphabet City was still dangerous—a war zone—both inhabited and visited by a large number of the White Street contingent. There was a lot going on and that was just the half of it, or less.

Primal Scream

That's life continued to be—though I tried to avoid complacency and boredom. Mudd kept me busy while my personal life left me chasing after drugs and sex. My studio work continued but my painting often reflected a scattered focus. Moving forward only meant days passing, turning pages on a calendar.

Looking back, I can still get lost; other times, it's possible to grab hold of a moment and clearly describe it. Sharon D'Lugoff even remembers what she was thinking after that Mudd Club bathroom encounter but cutting thru the fog isn't always so easy. Glenn O'Brien claims his "memories are sort of spotty regarding the Mudd Club—they've all sort of blended into one." He continues, "Maybe primal scream therapy would help get them back?"

For me, I've tried screaming and sitting quietly, waiting to see what shakes out or which tongues start speaking. I'm not sure either works.

The *anything could happen* world of Mudd was pretty blurry then; how could it be different now? Trying to line things up with a mark in time is even more difficult.

Glenn thinks he remembers my "long-suffering, remarkably patient and polite tenure" at the door. (I'm not sure about all that, but his memory is kind.) He recalls Steve Mass "running the club like an art project" but at the same time "doing a lot that was counterintuitive." He refers to Steve as "The Master of Irony," a grand title and a perfect fit.

Alice's

Another bit of irony is remembering the blur and beauty of a White Street night, but losing some of the friends who were there. Alice Himelstein drifted in and out of the blur, part of the beauty of my long twenty-one-month night.

We started the evening smoking pot and drinking vodka. We wound up eating spaghetti, salad and garlic bread at Alice's 2 West Sixty-seventh Street apartment. The view across Central Park from the ninth-floor duplex was a New York City dream; the scene inside, a sort of VIP annex to the Mudd Club. Dinnertime, party time and crash-pad luxury, there were *regulars* hanging out, others just passing thru.

The faces around the table were often familiar. They were at Mudd the night before and I'd be seeing them again later on. Judy Nylon and Mary Lou Green, Little Debi Mazar, Lynette Bean, Gary Kanner and Ricky Sohl were part of the crew at 2 West. A revolving cast of British rockers and downtown Punks, friends from Toronto and itinerant *strange* added to the mix; Cheetah and Gyda, Johnny Thunders and Chrissie Hynde—a who's who from who knows where—rifling the medicine cabinets, taking a nap or just hiding out.

I was usually the first to leave and someone always shared the cab. I'd get to White Street just as DJ David was getting ready. Before the club filled up I'd make a slow trip across the room and let the sound wash over me. It was midnight, the stars were out and Wilson Pickett stopped waiting. An hour later, Iggy Pop was singing about his "lust for life" and the music, dance floor and DJ were one.

David

I met DJ David Azarch at the Mudd Club. He was a skinny Rock 'n' Roll kid with a modified moptop and a great record collection. We became friends early on, hung out and got in trouble together. If or when we got caught, Abbijane would read us the riot act. David just smiled and kept cuing up the Motown. I stood there while she wagged her finger in my face. Then she'd grab me and we'd dance.

A year after the club opened, DJ David was as much a star as anyone; for him the Mudd Club became "a real education for a boy from Washington Heights." He played the big and not-so-big hits and the dance floor went wild: he felt that "the room told him what to play." When he cued up Roxy Music's "Street Life" you could feel it in your gut and the beat took you away. He'd play a song you never heard before and bring it back home with something you heard a thousand times. David could take that old song and hand it back to you for a first-time experience. You'd hear it and start to dance.

Tonight David Bowie's in the house and DJ David is kicking off an early morning set of Mott the Hoople and Iggy Pop—no real *Bowie* Bowie, just a little *Idiot* "Funtime" instead. The dance floor is crowded, security's watching the door and Chi Chi's watching the stairs. I'm on my way to the basement, a bottle of beer in each hand with my friend Edward right behind.

It was *once in a lifetime* every night. We ran wild on White Street because we could; *allowed* is the word I keep coming back to. With a vision wider than his reach, Steve Mass opened the doors, "allowing" everything and anything to happen.

Walking thru those doors, I came inside when David cued up "Pop Muzik" by M, a one-off hit from behind-the-scenes pop music veteran Robin Scott. The DJ booth at Mudd was *the* launchpad for new music and the dance floor was the acid test. Like "Lust for Life," "Sex Machine" and "Take Me to the River," "Pop Muzik" became a song people identify as part of the Mudd Club soundtrack. When it landed on the turntable, heads started bobbing. People hit the dance floor and everybody was talking about "Pop Muzik." Today it's just a memory, not much of a song.

Bless Its Pointed Little Head

Ten minutes later and back outside I do a double take twice. Jack Casady, the legendary bass player for Jefferson Airplane and Hot Tuna, is in front of me on the other side of the chain. I grew up with those early Airplane albums and for me there was nothing like them. I listened on the way up and on the way back down from the tripped-out Orange Sunshine adventures of high school and college. The front cover of *Volunteers* cracked me up and the sound on *Bless Its Pointed Little Head* blew me away. I heard them play it live a few times and felt the rumble—body and mind. The Airplane crashed in the summer of '72 and Tuna's on hiatus, but Casady's in town with his new band SVT.

Brian Marnell was SVT's singer, songwriter and guitarist, a great talent and a beautiful guy. He hung out at the loft on Murray Street more than once and loved the Mudd Club as much as anyone. Then one night I looked at Brian sitting in a booth upstairs and saw what I often felt but couldn't see in myself—trouble, and the uneasy feeling of almost fitting in, but not. Biding his time and getting high, he wasn't sure of what he wanted, or what was next. Marnell thought the Mudd Club was the greatest place and found something bordering on comfort in a booth or a bathroom on the second floor. A sweet guy, the desperation neatly tucked away; I knew what it was like and I went looking for that same comfort. Some nights I found it on White Street, some nights I found it with my friends. Not sure Brian ever did. I'm wishing he were still around.

A "Hey, Jack" across the chain was the beginning of Casady and SVT's relationship with the Mudd Club. We went inside, I got him a drink and he asked me if I had any coke. I introduced him to Steve, told the bar "Take care of him," and we headed for the bathroom. Five minutes later, Jack returned to the bar and I went outside. A couple nights later, Jack was back and I was running around—upstairs and down—still searching for my own version of comfort.

Trustworthy and Reliable

Not everyone who showed up at the door was an easy choice, or as much fun as a Rock 'n' Roll hero. Darwinism and natural selection aside, a small degree of tolerance was a big part of the job. Publicists and managers accompanied by terrible bands with a sense of entitlement were one thing; celebs with big egos and a bag of coke they rarely shared were another. Tourists who read about the club in *People* or *New York* Magazine tried White Street first before they tried someplace else. If anyone offered a bribe, generosity was key.

The Mudd Club was the toughest door in the city and for some strange reason I knew what I was doing. Calling it *my job* sounds funny (at least to me) and despite my own bullshit, confusion and frustration, it felt like the best job in New York. The training was nonexistent—it was watch, look, listen, and then do whatever you want. I can still hear Louie saying, "I'll be right back" before he headed inside. Thirty minutes later, he was still missing and I was learning fast. That's pretty much how it went.

Steve Mass hired me because he thought I knew everyone. Years later, when I ran into Mudd manager Glenn McDermott he said, "You were meant to be there," and I guess I was. I showed up, tried to fit in and never missed a night. No one second-guessed us, and after Louie left, there was no one second-guessing me. I said, "Hi, how many?" and decided whether or not to open the chain. After any number of drinks, not to mention the occasional speedball, I was still breathing, standing and working hard. I was a trustworthy, reliable employee and whether it was Mudd Club destiny or mine, it all worked out and I lived to tell.

Today the word *speedball* doesn't even sound like a real word.

The Lamest Song

Real or unreal. I was staring into the street, trying to focus, when a former classmate from New Hyde Park Memorial arrived with The Knack. She appeared shocked to see me and the only thing she could say was, "Richard?" Her name was either Margaret or Maria and she may have been the band's publicist, handler or babysitter. I wanted to let her in for free and buy her a drink but in this case I just couldn't do it—The Knack being responsible for "My Sharona," 1979's lamest song. There was no warm and fuzzy reunion; instead it was "Five dollars each please, pay inside." They paid, went in, hung out for a while and left. I never saw Maria again and The Knack never came back, musically or to the Mudd Club.

Scott Severin was standing outside that night, watching it all go down. He remembers me pointing him out in the crowd and telling security, "Let that kid in." Scott was mostly a weekender until he left home in Canarsie and found a place in the East Village. After that, he started coming around all the time and the White Street experience turned into a rite of passage for another kid from Brooklyn.

If we liked you and you didn't annoy us, if you were cute, had drugs or any combination thereof, sooner or later you came in for free. I liked Scott, he never annoyed me and he was sort of cute in a snotty kid kind of way. I have no idea if he had any drugs but we always let him in.

Thirty years after the fact, Scott told me I shouldn't ever have let The Knack in, even for five dollars each. There's no second-guessing at this point but he's probably right. It's funny the things we remember. "My Sharona" I'll try to forget.

Russians Are Coming

I still remember going to an upstate drive-in when I was twelve, where my biggest problem was not enough popcorn. The movie was *The Russians Are Coming The Russians Are Coming*, a 1966 submarine-comes-aground-in-New England comedy. The thing I remember most is the title.

Twenty-three years later, the Russians came back. They left Queens Village, landed on White Street and stepped up to the door of the Mudd Club. No submarine or popcorn was involved.

Mia and Lenny, Eddie and his sister Bella, Julie, Misha and a couple of others were half Punk-half Punk poseur, and none wanted to pay. Mia was a beauty and worked in a downtown peep show. The blond Russian guy in black leather looked to be straight out of gay porn. Some were junkies, one or two sold coke and all of them played To Pay or Not to Pay at the door.

"Oh come on Richie, I never pay."

"Oh come on Richie, why do I have to pay?"

"Oh come on Richie, please? I have no money."

That's how the nightly volley started. If I tried to ignore them, they'd wear me down and give me some coke or a Quaalude. There was no diplomacy, no negotiation, just a real-time waste of time. I usually gave up and let them in.

Turkey Dinner

Far back as I remember there was always some real-time happiness when it came to the holidays. My family got together and my grandmother made at least six apple pies, including a small one for me. I'd run around and play with my cousin Johnny until it was time to eat or go home.

Thanksgiving, 1979. Gary and I made plans to have dinner at my Aunt Olga's house in Gerritsen Beach, Brooklyn. I was working at Mudd that evening but didn't have to be there until 11 P.M. My parents showed up before heading off to Florida and a few aunts and uncles came in from Long Island. I'd been at the Mudd Club till 5 A.M. that morning and was still a mess when we arrived. Gary wasn't much better but his glasses hid some of the damage. Cocktail hour was a welcome relief.

We sat down to dinner and the turkey was perfect but at one point the word *fuck* slipped out of my mouth. My mother looked across the table and gave me a stare. The *out all night with no sleep* caused her concern enough; the four-letter language only made things worse. Uncle Johnny was already loaded on a half-dozen bottles of beer and his girlfriend Edna was chain-smoking Kents and drunk on Scotch. My father just shook his head and kept eating. The rest of the table heard nothing, saw nothing and talked right over the F word.

After dinner my aunt pulled me aside in the kitchen. A world traveler who'd seen it all, rubbed elbows with Castro in '59 Cuba and rode a jeep across the Serengeti in '62 thought hearing *fuck* at Thanksgiving was a problem. My mother, Rose, who'd spent ten years working for J. Edgar Hoover's nearly all-male FBI, followed by a stint at a Park Avenue law firm, also had seen and heard it all. My father, Armand, once stationed in the South Pacific and later a civilian with U.S. Department of the Navy, didn't care and just wanted us to stop. On that note, I gave up and said, "I'm sorry."

After coffee and a heavy dose of Aunt Olga's Blitz Torte for dessert, my father and Uncle Andy drove us back to the Kings Highway subway station. We caught the D train, headed home and smoked a joint when we got there. I thought about my cousin Johnny who was killed in Vietnam a dozen years earlier and wondered what he would've been like had he survived. I thought about how small my family was, started feeling sad and rolled another joint. We cabbed it to One University to check out the holiday spread that Mickey put out for the regulars. I ordered a drink, tried not to say the word *fuck* and made it to White Street by 11.

My appearance and behavior made my parents suspicious and Thanksgiving 1979 marked the beginning of the "I'm not sure what you're on, but you're on something" period of our relationship. It was almost a decade before that changed.

SoHo

By 5 A.M., Thanksgiving was yesterday gone. I was beat and the idea of anything turkey made me gag. I needed fresh air and opted for the easy nine-block walk to Murray Street. I left the crowd, the bathrooms and some of the drugs behind. A stroll down Broadway, one or two cigarettes and a bottle of beer—the night was already day, the day already tomorrow.

While I was sleeping, just getting up or just getting into bed, the daylight hours several blocks north told a different story. SoHo was home to the New York gallery scene and nearly all the major players, contenders and spectators saw the new wave coming. Mary Boone might've been drifting in and out of Mudd in the middle of the night but by the following day she was up and running her namesake gallery on the ground floor of 420 West Broadway. The Leo Castelli, Sonnabend and Emmerich Galleries were upstairs at the same address, and Holly Solomon Gallery was a block away. OK Harris was across the street, a few doors south of the DIA Foundation's permanent installation of Walter De Maria's *The Broken Kilometer*. Tony Shafrazi, the *Guernica* vandal and former art advisor to the Shah of Iran, was showing up at Mudd nearly every night—his first New York gallery a few blocks north of SoHo, his Mercer Street location still a few years away.

By the time the Mudd Club opened in 1978, Julian Schnabel had fully transitioned from working in Mickey Ruskin's kitchens to making wax paintings and paintings out of broken plates. By October '79, the plate paintings were hanging at Mary Boone and Julian was hanging out on White. He'd stop by and have a drink, walk upstairs and visit his friend Ross Bleckner; on the way in or out he could be all charm or not but was always nice to me. He offered to come by my studio and take a look at my work but I dropped the ball and never followed up. It still bugs me to think about it and makes me realize I was chasing drugs and wasting time with greater passion than looking for a way forward. Opportunity was close at hand but possibility was slipping thru my fingers.

Ross Bleckner was another chance not taken. I had every occasion to talk about my work and ask about his, but again figured proximity and association were all I needed. He had his studio at 77 White and he lived there while I was downstairs nearly seven nights a week. In retrospect, his discipline was remarkable where mine was lacking.

Along with Julian, Barbara Kruger, David Salle and One University "jukebox curator" Stephen Mueller, Ross helped round out Mary Boone's stable of artists. In their 2 A.M. downtime they were hanging upstairs in Ross' loft or rounding out the crowd at the Mudd Club bar.

Artist Jeff Koons, another White Street regular, worked at MoMA. He wore a suit and tie, a smile on his face and was headed for a zillion-dollar pop, porn and puppy mill payoff. Keith Haring was soon running around with a pocketful of Magic Markers, stopping by Mudd and hanging out at Club 57. Jean-Michel Basquiat was slowly phasing out the SAMO graffiti and adding his tag to works on paper. His Xerox pieces were already hanging at The A-Space on Broome while he was dancing at the Mudd Club and getting ready to make history.

It was a new age and a changing of the guard. The front door of 77 White was the ultimate vantage point. Lined up at the bar, hanging in the bathrooms or drifting from floor to floor, future stars and A-list names ran around inside. Whether the Mudd Club was anchored in the art world or the art world dropped anchor at Mudd, it was hard to tell. Despite the missed opportunities, I thought I was doing my best to pay attention and stay on top of things. I was painting, showing up and trying not to fall behind. During the spring, summer and fall of 1979 I was still hanging on tight. Then winter started closing in.

Ponytail Guy

Sunday, December 9, I'm sitting with Chi Chi in a back booth near the kitchen door at One University Place. It's our night off and we both order club steaks. After dinner I leave for thirty minutes to pick something up from the psycho coke dealer at 2 Charlton Street. I cab it back to Mickey's and a minute later we're out the door. Iggy's playing at Hurrah on Sixty-second and Broadway; he's allegedly going on in half an hour.

There's a crowd outside when we arrive but we keep walking. Haoui Montaug's doing the door; he gives us a kiss and sends us in. Squeezing our way toward the bar, the place is packed solid but there's no sign of the band. Someone says it's going to be another thirty minutes before they hit the stage. A guy with a long blond ponytail who follows Anita Pallenberg around comes over, starts giving me shit about the Mudd Club and wants to know why I make him pay to get in. I've already got a steak dinner, several drinks and more than a few lines of coke under my belt so I tell him, "Go fuck yourself, you can forget about coming in at all." He tries to backpedal but things get louder and he wants to know why I'm giving him a hard time. We're both behaving badly and I'm featuring my own little version of a public meltdown. Hurrah staff steps in and lets Chi Chi and me hang out in a back hallway until showtime.

Cigarettes, more cocaine, a couple drinks and forty minutes later, Iggy's finally onstage. It's the same band I saw in November featuring Ivan Kral, Glen Matlock of the Sex Pistols and Brian James of The Damned. The show's great, Iggy's going wild but I feel like I'm starting to crack up. I ignore the warning signs and do more coke.

A week later, I let Ponytail Guy back into Mudd for the five-dollar cover. Three days after that, Steve tells me not to let him in anymore.

Peterbilt and Pendleton

I've been feeling better since my broken psychotic episode at Hurrah. Christmas will be here soon and 1980 is just around the corner. *Go fuck yourself* remains a part of my verbal communication but I'm trying to manage its use and abuse, especially around the holidays.

Weatherwise the nights are getting colder, I'm outside often working alone, and the long tweed coat's doing its best to keep me warm. I've got a head of thick wavy hair tucked under a Peterbilt Trucks cap and Pendleton tartan scarf around my neck. The corduroy jeans, denim vest and Fair Isle sweater say *Who cares?* about fashion.

I step inside to warm up but one of the security guys is sitting on the radiator collecting the money. Steve's at the bar with Danny Fields, Arturo Vega's watching Anita Sarko spin records and Little Danny just walked upstairs.

Danny Fields often stops by White Street after starting out at CBGB or the Ninth Circle. He's the ultimate music biz insider: an influential journalist, band manager and publicist. By 1979, he's already legend, and his connection to everyone from the Doors and Nico to The Stooges, MC5, Lou Reed and the Ramones stretches all the way from Max's back room to *16 Magazine* and the *SoHo Weekly News*. Little Danny is a kid from Boston—a good-looking roadie and Ramones mascot who likes to fool around, fuck around and hang at Mudd whenever he can.

Arturo Vega is the Ramones' artistic director, created their iconic logo and has been with them from the beginning. He's back home on a night off, torturing DJ Anita and trying to get her to play "Pop Muzik." When she's tells him she just played it he reminds her, "It was fifteen minutes ago."

Anita sees me, looks over and rolls her eyes. I smile, give Arturo a hug and buy him a drink. We walk away talking, Anita cues up the Sex Pistols and we all try to forget about "Pop Muzik" for at least a half-hour. Back outside the only people waiting are the same ones who were waiting when I left. The security guy looks at me and shrugs so I turn around and go upstairs looking for Little Danny.

The second floor's full and Nurse Debbie is busy serving drinks to some very sick patients. I move toward the back of the room and spot August Darnell, formerly of Dr. Buzzard's Original Savannah Band and currently leader of Kid Creole and the Coconuts. He's coming out of the bathroom with two women in tow who may or may not be *coconuts*. I take a quick look around, give up on Little Danny and go back to the door.

There's only about twenty people outside and two walk over to ask me if I'm still letting people in. I tell them "No" just as Andy Warhol and Benjamin Liu a.k.a. Ming Vauze get out of a cab. I open the chain, say "Hi," and Andy whisper-speaks, "Oh hi, how's your cute boyfriend?" My answer, "He's inside somewhere." The two people I said no to look at me and ask, "How come they're getting in?"

Ignoring the question, I light a cigarette and think about the new coat someone just gave me. It's like armor, heavier and darker than the one I have on, and by January I'll probably need it. Maybe by then, I'll even catch some sleep.

Boys Keep Swinging

I make it home before daybreak. I crash and the week flies by. Saturday, December 15, I'm getting ready for work around the same time David Bowie, Klaus Nomi and Joey Arias are getting ready for their appearance on *Saturday Night Live*.

The performance turns into a big deal, with Klaus and Joey singing backup and more on "Man Who Sold the World," "TVC 15" and "Boys Keep Swinging." Jimmy Destri is sitting in on keyboards and a large pink poodle with a small closed circuit TV in its mouth adds a bit of cute and scary to the *SNL* stage. Bowie's vocal comes through loud and clear, Joey and Klaus cut through the mix and they all rise above the peripheral poodle insanity. Wearing a Da-

daesque Tristan Tzara-inspired tuxedo for the first song, David turns into a marionette with a Bowie head for "Boys Keep Swinging." Going for something less dramatic but equally striking, they all wear pencil skirts cut below the knee for "TVC 15." It's high culture and low—another constellation that came together on the second floor of Mudd.

Lizzy, Richard and Boris

From Greenwich Village to Bowery, from St. Mark's to Mudd, whether it was Dylan's twang and phrase, Patti Smith's poetry or Richard Hell's lyrical howl, the power of the word kept the song moving forward. When Bowie's accessible sophistication became a counterpoint to No Wave's scream and cry, walls continued to tumble.

It was 1978 when Lizzy Mercier Descloux, a Punk Parisienne, recorded the popular EP *Rosa Yemen* featuring the song "Herpes Simplex." By 1979, she was living in New York and recording her first solo album, *Press Colour*, released by ZE Records, the company founded by entrepreneur industrialist Michael Zilkha and Lizzy's partner, Michel Estaban. ZE was also home to New York No Wave favorites The Contortions and Lydia Lunch as well as Kid Creole and the Coconuts. Before long Mercier was appearing at the Mudd Club.

Lizzy's White Street performance was an introduction of sorts. On the heels of the *Rosa Yemen* disc and the influence of an earlier connection to Smith and Hell, she took the inspiration in a new direction. Steve Mass presented it at Mudd, and the famously hard-to-read Mudd Club crowd was enthusiastic. The Worldbeat sound, Punk attitude and wild cover of "Fire" by The Crazy World of Arthur Brown pulled me off the door and onto the floor. It was one of those nights that came out of nowhere.

Only a few months earlier, that *high concept, nonconcept* Mass credo of allowing and presenting anything and everything opened the door for Richard Hell (minus the Voidoids) to offer some of his lesser-known work at Mudd. Following a reading of "Unrequited Narcissism" and "Confessions of a Polymorphic Soul," the Punk originator noted, "I should be a real preacher and give a real fucking sermon every Sunday."

Taking the high-nonconcept of allowing and presenting one step further, Steve scheduled another performance by Boris Policeband.

Boris Policeband, 1979. Mudd Club portrait series, *Punks of New York* by William Coupon.

Under a single white spot on a darkened stage, Boris began with his electric violin and police band radio amped to the max. The sound was stunning, cathartic, and cleared the room. Beyond art, genius or any sense of acquired taste, Policeband was a No Wave assault, a total White Street experience.

At least half the entertainment at Mudd was the unseen getting seen and the unheard finally getting heard. Steve gave everyone a chance to present sound, vision and ideas that otherwise would've been lost. It kept the club out of any potential rut, opting for risk rather than surefire success. Even established performers and

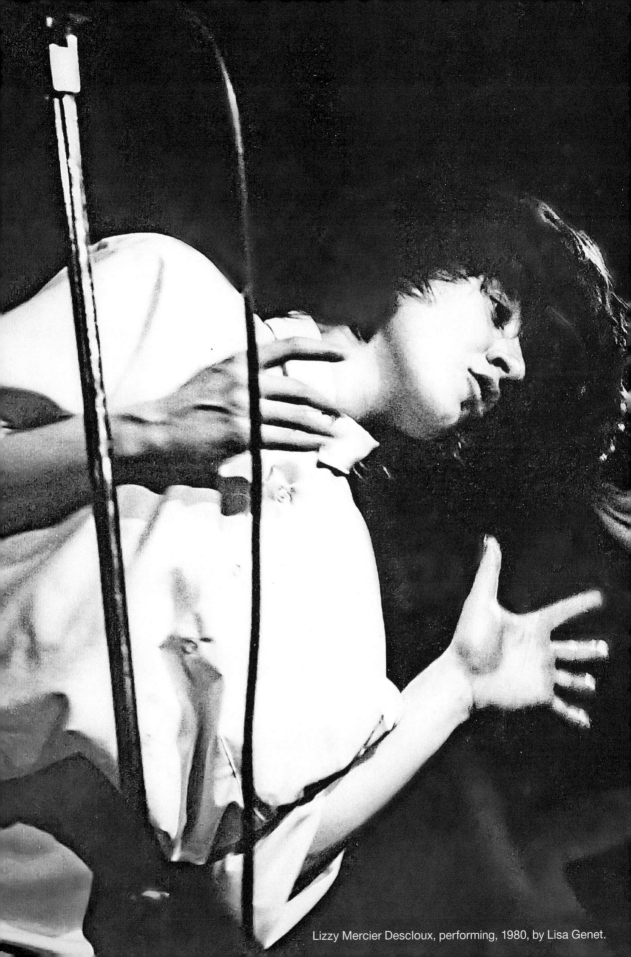

Lizzy Mercier Descloux, performing, 1980, by Lisa Genet.

familiar faces were presented in such a way that anything might happen—and often did. When composer Philip Glass took the White Street detour, bypassing Lincoln Center, he lulled a crowd that came to drink and dance. Lydia Lunch stormed the stage and unleashed a furious barrage of spoken word—to an unnerving, heckling silence. Always stoned but usually polite Johnny Thunders ducked when Spacely jumped onstage and threw a few wild drunken punches; then Johnny let loose with his guitar, swinging a Gibson Les Paul Junior and connecting with Spacely's head. The audience cheered. Performance and art were still social adventure.

As Judy Nylon deftly put it, "Mudd was the correct venue at a time that so many places weren't."

Goodwill

Unlike Mudd Club entertainment, selling a million drinks at the bar and getting people to pay at the door was the commercial arm of the operation. Giving away what seemed to be half as many drinks as we sold was a near necessity that spurred creativity and fostered goodwill. It was the White Street way of giving back to the community, Steve being the occasionally reluctant but always generous host.

As Legs McNeil, editor, author, instigator and Punk, succinctly put it, "I could drink for free, people put coke under my nose and I could get laid." Obviously, I felt the same way.

***

We're closing in on late-night crazy. Steve is at the DJ booth saying something to Anita that she's doing her best to ignore. Legs walks past, though I can't remember seeing him arrive. I order a drink for myself, and step outside. Downtown party girl, DJ and onetime asymmetrical hairstyle model Delphine Blue is waiting impatiently at the chain. Lori and Joe Barbaria get out of a cab and squeeze their way toward the door; Lori's brother Robbie, a cute kid in red leather jeans, is already inside. Morgan Entrekin, a blond, preppy-ish Mudd regular, crosses the street and moves thru the crowd. His hair's a bit shaggy like mine and he's wearing jeans; regardless, the chain opens easily.

I step back and watch Richard Lloyd from Television rush thru the door looking for Anita Pallenberg. He finds her and they leave in a flurry of vocal and animated distress. Taylor Mead floats by with a wave and a mumble about money and the crowd but can't decide if he wants to come in. Michael Shrieve, the Santana "drum machine" and youngest performer to play Woodstock, arrives with several friends. He's still got a head full of curls and looks younger than he did in 1969. When the door opens, Hal Ludacer steps outside, pokes me with his finger and wants to know if I've seen Adele Bertei. I tell him, "I think I have, but it might have been last night."

Ramones fan and future nightlife wizard Steve Lewis stops for a minute, then walks inside and takes a shot at charming Chi Chi into an upstairs *pass*. Humbled by repeated rebuffs, he finally breaks through with the offer of a single red rose. After that, there's no stopping him. Years later, Lewis commented, "The only mistake Richard ever made at the door of Mudd was letting me in." I can honestly admit I did make a few but Steve Lewis was never one of them.

I step inside, replacing streetside fray with smoke and music. Kate Simon's across the room with Steve Mass, talking about life and what it all means. I walk over as Steve's walking away and offer Kate a Rastaman spliff that Manny L'Amour just gave me. She laughs out loud and we head upstairs. Five minutes later, I'm back outside. Even though it's mid-December, it's not too cold, and strangers, friends and anonymous curiosities continue to arrive well after 2 A.M.

In a momentary lull, photographer Allan Tannenbaum gets a picture of me in my new overcoat. I smile for the camera just as Andi Ostrowe runs out the door, throws up in the alley and falls into the back seat of a cab. Teri Toye and Richard Sohl are still floating around or "sleeping" somewhere inside. I reach for my drink as Jean-Michel Basquiat tumbles out the door laughing. He turns around, grins and lets a smile say good night.

When Dylan McDermott arrives after a shift at his family's bar on West Fourth, he hangs around for a couple of minutes keeping me company. He's good at it in an effortless way—eighteen, handsome and likable with a *seen a lot for so young* look in his eyes. I'm easy, he's untouchable and I send him in for free.

The door opens; people in and out. It's Dave's Luncheonette, breakfast for dinner and the slow-go morning rush of Canal Street. The night's over and it's still dark outside. I walk home alone.

I've got to put some fresh paper up on the studio wall. I've got to paint. I've still got to figure out what's happening.

The Pink Loft

Asleep by 10 A.M., when I wake up it's my own version of tomorrow. I grab a bite at One University, walk over to Bleecker and pick up a small bag of groceries. I'll stash them in the coatroom at Mudd and bring them home later. Still feeling burnt, I'm hoping it's going to be another *work and then home* kind of night. A minute later, I run into Betsey Johnson, the designer and scenemaker who lives in a big pink loft on Church Street about two blocks from the club. We share a cab, she bypasses home and we arrive together on White Street. I get her a drink, run downstairs with the juice, bananas and Pepperidge Farm cookies and head back outside to work. The autopilot's already on.

After a while, I'm back inside and talking to Betsey. It's over six years since she moved into the pink loft and nearly a year since she showed the first namesake Betsey Johnson Collection on White Street. It was January and I was still just a customer. Photographers Dustin Pittman and Allan Tannenbaum were on hand taking pictures, capturing the chaos. The catwalk that night: a wobbly lineup of folding tables extending from the stage and held in place by the crowd, several rolls of duct tape and a little luck. The clothes were stripes and neon; the models wore everything from Juicy Fruit boxes to Comet Cleanser cans on their heads. Betsey still laughs about the accessories, calling them "Pop Art, tongue in cheek" and without pause continues, "It was the best kind of fashion show I could ever do. Sexy and Rock 'n' Roll."

The bar's getting crowded and Betsey wanders toward the dance floor. I grab another beer before going back to the door. Inside for good around 4 A.M., the handsome and popular Frankie DeCurtis takes a photo of me in the basement. My teeth are clenched, I guess I'm smiling but I can't tell if the picture makes me look really good or really bad. I pick up the bananas, juice and cookies and jump in a cab. I really need some sleep.

Betsey Johnson and model, preparing for the show, 1979,
by Dustin Pittman.

Elvis

The seventies were slowly getting ready for 1980 and the holidays were less than two weeks away. Gary and I carried home a ten-foot balsam fir from the Farm and Garden Nursery located on the future site of the Roxy (Tribeca Grand) Hotel. Chi Chi came over after work and the three of us tinseled the tree; I got up on a ladder and stuck the star on top. I climbed down and crashed.

Twelve hours later, I woke up, went into the studio and started slicing up scraps of paper. I made about thirty handmade Christmas cards out of everything from brown paper bags and painted envelopes filled with tinsel to swatches of acid green fun-fur tied with a red ribbon bow. All I could say was "Merry 1979."

The message slowly changed to "Peace and Love," the years turned into a life and the mailing list kept getting longer. Along the way, part of it got lost, part of it got erased, and part of it's just gone. Like an old address book with pages missing and names crossed out—people I knew, barely knew or never knew at all. A few names from Christmas '79 are still on the list. People I love, survivors like me.

I ask friends who or what they remember. I think of now and then. Then is where we came from, a decades-old dream when everybody was young and lived at the Mudd Club. Photographer Henny Garfunkel called it "the days of struggling without a struggle." Most of us made it through.

I worked the Mudd Club door on Christmas Eve. Jeff Koons stopped by and slipped me an annual membership for MoMA as a holiday thank-you. He was working at the museum and surely "purchased" the gift at a substantial discount. Danny Fields arrived and gave me an actual old-school Christmas card with a much appreciated fifty-dollar bill tucked inside. Everybody else gave me a Quaalude, a joint or some coke. There was no snow that night and the temperature was in the forties. Christmas Day was even warmer. I called my parents. I roasted a turkey. I listened to Elvis sing about the holidays. The eighties were just a week away.

Gold Krylon Spray

New Year's Eve was like any other night at the Mudd Club with a couple of extras thrown in. There were free bottles of fake champagne, noisemakers for extra noise and party hats just because. The stairway to the second floor was painted gold, thanks to Gennaro Palermo, his boyfriend, Costa Pappas, and two dozen cans of gold Krylon spray. By 11:30 the club was already filling up but the paint wouldn't dry and it started rubbing off on everything. The stairs got slippery and the gold dust haze was a holiday huffer's delight. The giant hourglass on the side of the stage was almost empty and 1979 was nearly over.

The temperature outside dropped down into the thirties and a chill in the air kept me on my toes. The crowd in the street was happy and everyone who came in got a heavy dose of fake champagne. I started out with my own private stash of Veuve Clicquot that I drank from the bottle at midnight. It was very 1980.

By 1 A.M. I moved on to brandy, beer and a gram of coke. When things started getting a little too festive I shoved a cut straw into a dime bag of dope to take the edge off. The eighties were just a few hours old and my midnight buzz of drunk and happy was on the verge of becoming a half-frozen speedball drift. For the moment I stopped worrying about my behavior.

When my friends Sara Heidt and *New Yorker* cartoonist Michael Maslin arrived it was time to leave the door and offer them some bottles of the free not-quite-Champagne. Bubbles in hand, Sara disappeared onto the dance floor while Michael and I headed for the basement with photographer Mick Rock. Except for my twenty-dollar bottle of Veuve, it felt like *just another night at Mudd*.

Well into post-midnight morning, Marilyn, the Mudd Club's official chanteuse, stepped onstage. Wearing a tight green dress, green painted lips and green-tipped platinum hair, Marilyn sang the shit (or something like it) out of her "hit" single "Sex Means Nothing When You're Dead." As only a cadaverous white girl could, she put a new spin on sex, death, and holiday entertainment.
According to what Marilyn called "an exclusive agreement with Steve Mass," she was paid two hundred fifty dollars a show. For New Year's Eve, she might've gotten two seventy-five. When it was finally over the DJ cued up the Sex Pistols' "Pretty Vacant" and Marilyn's performance disappeared into the gold Krylon haze.

Marilyn, "Sex Means Nothing When You're Dead," 1980, by Nick Taylor.

I stepped back and looked across the bar. I walked upstairs and squeezed into the bathroom. It was close to 4 A.M. and the unhinged craziness of the Mudd Club was a beautiful thing. The new year was bound to be interesting, the old decade having left me in a sentimental mood. I found my way out of the bathroom and woke up on my way downstairs. Thinking about sex and drugs and getting high, I was lost in the same soft-core dream turned hard that started when I was a teenager. Within a few short years I crossed the line; and now, January 1, 1980, I stopped thinking. I looked around and stepped outside to get some air.

The eighties were here. The seventies were really over. Happy New Year!

Glenn O'Brien's *TV Party* at Mudd.
Charm, chaos and television excitement, 1980, by Bob Gruen.

I'm not sure what got me so desperate. Maybe it was too much cocaine and not enough sex or maybe I had it backward. I ran around all morning in the cold chasing two bags of heroin while my dirty white Converse high tops went from wet to frozen. Avenue B and Fourth Street, I found a cab. Ten minutes later I was home; five minutes later I was warm. I worked in my studio for the rest of the day and never went to sleep.

By 9 P.M. I was buying a forty-five-dollar half-gram of coke from the psycho dealer on Charlton Street. He only sold grams or larger but was doing me a favor. An hour later I was staring at a plate of food I couldn't eat; 11 P.M., I was on White Street. I was wearing motorcycle boots and my feet were dry but cold.

Tired but wide awake and getting busy, I spotted Wendy as she got out of a cab. She offered the usual "Hi Sweetie," gave me a kiss, and I sent her inside.

Wendy Whitelaw was seventeen when she arrived in New York. She started doing makeup, landed at Studio 54 on opening night and wound up "painting" the faces that appeared on more than seventy-five covers of *Harper's Bazaar*, *Elle* and nearly every variation of *Vogue*. Dark hair, pale skin and red, red lips—Wendy Whitelaw was beautiful, and she was good at what she did. She remembers how "It happened fast, it all fell into place."

Before long, Wendy hooked up with Glenn O'Brien and Maripol, the Polaroid-snapping artist, future Madonna stylist and *provocateur occasionelle*. Then she headed for White Street where Robert Molnar pointed her out and introduced us. I wanted to know who she was, and Robert wanted to make sure I'd always let her in.

Tonight she strolled into the upstairs bathroom, looked in the mirror and reached for a lipstick. The only color to choose was "Cherries in the Snow," created by Revlon and released in 1953. Deep red with barely a hint of pink, it was glamour, retro and Punk all at once; by 1980, Wendy Whitelaw had girls at the Mudd Club and women all over town wearing "Cherries." Lip-printed on my cheek and smudged on the collars of John Lurie, Danny Rosen and Ken Compton, it was Wendy's signature, a *kiss me come-on* that went with everything.

Ten minutes later I'm still outside, bundled in the heavy wool overcoat, sipping a double Rémy from a plastic cup. It's snowing but the wind's just blowing it around. Chi Chi's minding the stairway wrapped in red fox, keeping warm regardless of what she is or isn't wearing underneath. I light a cigarette and finish the brandy.

Deadpan Was Alive

I think it was January, maybe two weeks into a new decade; the weather warmed up and for the moment I forgot about overcoats, fur coats and red lipstick. I was outside wearing a motorcycle jacket, slowly drifting back from a post-seventies hangover. It was hard to say if anything or everything had changed.

Minding a small well-behaved crowd at the door, I watched Glenn O'Brien park his Toyota Corolla across the street. The club was open early, people were already inside and Glenn was set to tape one of the Mudd Club episodes of *TV Party*. No one, except *Party* orchestra leader Walter Steding, was ready.

The cast, crew and *TV Party* guests were pretty much one and the same: whether the night's cavalcade included Debbie Harry and Chris Stein, Basquiat, Bowie, a Bride of Funkenstein or rap pioneer Li'l Rodney C didn't seem to matter. The dance floor was filling up, Walter's electric violin was starting to speak and by 11 P.M. the camera was on. Thanks to the show's wide-ranging appeal and my deft handling of the door, Glenn had a room filled with what he liked to call the "weird mix" of people he came to expect at Mudd—a back-handed but genuine compliment.

The panel discussed issues and nonissues of the day while the audience stood spellbound in the glare of quasi-celebrity. Deadpan was alive and Glenn O'Brien's "cocktail party that could be a political party" was happening.

The night's episode closed to a smattering of applause and Glenn graciously thanked everyone, including the audience. I asked for a beer and went back outside. Everybody else headed upstairs. That's when it happened.

Unstoppable

Over a dozen black-and-white photographs were hanging on the walls of the second floor. They were portraits, some candid, and they included almost everyone on *TV Party*. The photographer was Bobby Grossman.

A familiar face at Warhol's Factory and a regular at CBGB's, Bobby had come to know nearly everyone, including Steve Mass. When the Mudd Club opened he showed up on White Street. Steve eventually offered him the opportunity to show his photographs, giving him money for plexiglass to protect the images but warning there could be no guarantee the photos would survive. Bobby wanted to do it anyway, hoping it would become a permanent installation.

The pictures were hung in time for the *TV Party* taping and everything seemed fine. The show ended, the second floor was packed, Bobby's photographs looked great and the *plexi* was doing its job. The only problem: an unstoppable Teri Toye.

It's hard to remember, and harder to describe. It happened fast, in plain sight, in a crowded room. Teri grabbed three photos off the wall, including a shot of Richard DNV Sohl, and disappeared, leaving a trail of cracked plexiglass behind. Everyone else kept drinking.

TV Party was always enlightening and entertaining no matter where it was taped. Add a bit of post-*Party* vandalism, a dash of true crime and a beautiful woman with a big dick, and it was Mudd Club magic.

Nightly Swarm

Midwinter, strange weather—cold one night, fifty degrees the next. My new oversized overcoat is working overtime trying to adapt. My priorities continue to seem out of whack and my better judgment seems to have flown south. Meanwhile, the country's better judgment (or lack of any at all, depending on what side of right wing you were on) has moved Ronald Reagan that much closer to a White House run. Like the freakish weather, it's difficult to predict how things will go but given the political climate, I'm cynical at best. From the back pages to the front, the Soviet Union and Afghanistan continue to be a problem while the storm over immigration and border security along with the increasing burden of student loans seems to only get worse. Even from the relative safety of detachment, with a drink in one hand, the chain in the other, I still wonder how and when it will end.

Though I'm handling the door like a pro, fitting in remains the occasional challenge. I take pride in some of my paintings but moving forward leaves me at a loss. Feeling comfortable is more closely related to drugs than people with whom I'm close. The new overcoat tries to help as best it can.

Facing a nightly swarm of strangers, I've started calling people I barely know my friends and drifting from those who really know me. It's become harder to think straight leaning over a mirror with a razor blade in one hand and a straw in the other.

The Red Sea Routine

My Friday night crash turns into a broken late-morning dream. Saturday and Sunday go sliding by. I'm off on Monday and Tuesday is hardly there. By the middle of the week, I'm standing in front of that not-quite-mob of so-called strangers, looking for anyone who meets the *I know them, I like them, they look interesting* criteria. I'm about ready to give up when photographer Marcia Resnick appears out of nowhere. She's got on her leather jacket and black hat with a pair of black Wayfarers to keep the moon out of her eyes. When she moves toward the chain the crowd does what Marcia refers to as "the Red Sea routine." Maybe it's the way she walks or simply mind over matter, but the few who make it happen I count on one hand.

Marcia Resnick frolicking on the second floor, 1979, courtesy Marcia Resnick.

Marcia studied at Cal Arts, Cooper Union and New York University. Like me, she was born in Brooklyn, she knows *everyone*, and we've been running around together on and off since I started working on White Street. She'd just moved into a loft at the west end of Canal Street far enough out of range, but still within striking distance. Marcia loves to hang out, says the camera makes her feel "less guilty" about it. Even behind a pair of shades, her *eye* sees everything.

From the front steps of 77 White I saw everything too. I ran around before and after hours but never felt guilty about hanging out. I felt bad about other stuff and might've gotten chills when I looked in the mirror, but that only happened after too much coke, an ugly confrontation or some reckless, anonymous fuck. Except for a few blackouts and black hole nods, the coast was still pretty clear. I wanted to believe that almost everything was working, though finding the right amount of the right drugs combined with the correct number of drinks still baffled me. That constant desire for late-night/early-morning sex made me feel awkward and obvious. The heavy wool coat could only do so much.

Aunt Olga and the Top-shelf Martini

The worlds of art, music, film and fashion continued to converge and collide on White Street, with no sign of slowing down. Even my Aunt Olga heard what was going on from all the way out in Gerritsen Beach and wasn't going to miss the chance to see what was happening. She told me, "I'm looking forward to a free Beefeater martini" and kept threatening to show up at Mudd. I told her, "We only have Tanqueray" but she didn't care.

Olga was sixty-five and her friend Katy was seventy but that wasn't a problem either. Living in Brooklyn their whole lives, they weren't much afraid of anything. They hopped on the D train at Kings Highway, changed to the double R, got off at Canal and walked the two blocks to White Street. When they arrived at the door the crowd did the "Red Sea routine."

Olga was impressed by the mob outside but thought the location was shabby. She thought the place was interesting, crowded and loud but couldn't help telling me, "It's not the way we danced when we were young." She drank a few martinis, met Steve and hobnobbed (her word) with the Punks, the No Wave and the New Wave. On my advice she avoided using the bathroom. An hour later, I put them in a cab and warned the driver what he was in for.

Just after 1 A.M. but it felt like the night had already peaked. Aunt Olga mixing it up at the Mudd Club, surely a metaphor for something.

Find Me Later

Taylor Mead, nearly a decade younger than Olga, is almost as worldly. A poet and one of the original Warhol Superstars, he's wandering around in the middle of the street, scratching his head, looking over at the door but not really connecting. It's a distraction on a busy night and I don't like it.

With a combination of duty, kindness and impatience I open the chain and step into the crowd. I hear, "Richard, Richard" but look straight ahead and move toward Taylor. A few probably wonder what's with the old guy in the street, but if I don't reel him in he'll be floating around out there all night.

I grab Taylor and spot Peter O from the *SoHo News*, Ernie Brooks from The Necessaries, and Tim Wright, the bass player from DNA.

Taylor Mead getting excited, 1980, by Marcia Resnick.

Patti Astor, the downtown film star and future graffiti galler-
ist-connoisseur, exits a cab, seizes the moment and follows us to
the door. The crowd's big and people wearing heavy coats make it
seem even bigger but the Red Sea does its thing and the six of us
keep walking. I turn and ask a good-looking clean-cut kid standing in the crowd, "Who you with?" He says "No one" and I say "Come
on." Security opens the chain and we all step inside. I try and get
everyone a drink but Taylor, a self-proclaimed trust fund baby,
wanders toward the dance floor and Patti's already on her way upstairs. Tim's disappeared and so have Peter and Ernie.

I look around, spot the good-looking clean-cut kid and we head
for the second floor. I bang on the steel door of the men's room,
say it's me, and it opens. Roxanne's inside with someone I've never seen but must have let in. I'm already bored with the *kid* so I
bite into a Quaalude, stick half in his mouth and tell him, "Find
me later." I walk through the second floor, hear Alice Himelstein
laughing and squeeze into a booth with her and Mary Lou Green. Alice looks at me, laughs some more and leaves me thinking, *well OK*.
Jo Shane, Vicki Pedersen and Millie David are sitting nearby with
art world muse Edit DeAk's boyfriend, John Savas. He's wearing a
wig from one of the Fourteenth Street wiggeries that specialize in

Dynel creations so the girls start calling him Johnny Dynel. The name sticks, and he likes it. He adds a second *L* and makes Dynell his real last name.

By now it's getting late, I'm downstairs and DJ David's hungry. He cues up the eleven-minute version of James Brown's "Sex Machine" and makes a hot dog run to Dave's. It's a smooth move, timed perfectly, and he's back in time to change the record.

Back outside, the door's the same as I left it twenty minutes ago except there's no Taylor Mead to rescue. The clean-cut kid I found in the crowd and lost in the bathroom steps outside to talk to me but doesn't have much to say. He's got two more Quaaludes in his hand, gives me one and wants to know what I'm doing later. The ludes say *RORER 714* and look like the real thing so I snap one in half and chase it with a beer. I tell the kid, "Don't leave, have another drink and we'll get out of here by five."

So far, it's been a stellar night.

Johnny, Edit and Chi Chi

I'm not certain I ever knew Clean-Cut's name but when I woke up he was gone. The hookup was another round of random; the sex an empty hour of noise and sweat. Promiscuity for its own sake was becoming equal to the throwaway gratification of cocaine. Both left me trying to forget but wanting more. More was becoming equal to nothing.

I made some coffee and jumped in and out of the shower. I rolled a joint and scribbled on a few sheets of paper in the studio. It was already getting dark outside—the 4 o'clock afternoon of another day. I put on an old Quicksilver album, *Happy Trails*, and tried to escape. By 8 P.M. I started getting hungry so I headed for One University Place. By 11 I was back at the door of 77 White Street. A few hours later, the newly named Johnny Dynell showed up.

I met John Savas at the Mudd Club during those pre-Dynell days. He told me he "grew up in a tiny, tiny town way, way upstate," landing in New York City in 1975. He didn't know anyone and hooked up with a roommate via the bulletin board at the School of Visual Arts. His first apartment, at Bleecker and MacDougal, was a block from where I once lived. The roommate "turned out to be a wacko" (as roommates often do).

Johnny started hanging with his neighbors who introduced him to Marie's Crisis on Grove Street, the Ninth Circle on Tenth Street and the wild "West Village world of poppers." He got a job at Food, a popular restaurant founded in 1971 by the artist Gordon Matta Clark and located at the corner of Prince and Wooster in SoHo.

In 1978, Johnny met Edit DeAk, the writer and critic, during a party at Edit's loft. He moved in with her and it wasn't long before she brought him to the Mudd Club. After that it was only a matter of time.

One year later, on a 2 A.M. nighttime stroll between White Street and Dave's Luncheonette, Johnny and Edit ran into Chi Chi Valenti and a friend. Edit knew the friend so they stopped to talk while Johnny and Chi Chi just stood there, staring at each other. He remembers the connection was "boom, click, immediately" until Chi Chi and her friend walked away. He kept staring, and Edit knew it was over for her and Johnny.

Chi Chi had a certain something, different from all the other certain somethings out there. Everyone flirted with her, Rudolf Piper *dated* her and I ran around with her after work. Steve Mass was fascinated and intimidated by Chi Chi and hired her to work at the Mudd Club. The next time Johnny saw her she was wearing the fox fur coat and standing at the foot of the stairway to the second floor. I was outside, clueless to what was going on.

A cheap Dynel wig from Fourteenth Street and a new name was just the beginning. The Broadway stroll kicked off a Mudd Club romance and the "boom, click, immediately" turned it into a lifetime together for Chi Chi and Johnny.

Unsafe Panties

Past 1 A.M., Dynell heads for the dance floor and I keep watching the crowd. I'm looking for someone a little dirtier than the clean-cut kid but it's probably still too early. I open the chain for Pat Place and Laura Kennedy instead. I say "Hi," Laura keeps walking and Pat cracks half a smile. I think we like each other. No one else outside looks interesting but they all look willing to pay. It's Saturday night, it's already crowded, and the club has to be making a lot of money.

Inside, drink tickets have become the new currency, making things easier and more complicated at once. Steve usually hands them out, always gives me a decent-sized stack and I give most away. Besides the tickets, I use the not-quite-mutual respect for the bartenders that allows my friends to drink for free. With me at the door it's an arrangement that works both ways.

Outside, the scene hasn't changed. I grab Chi Chi and we take the elevator up to Ross Bleckner's, leaving the fate of the door and second floor in the hands of the *other* people. Ross isn't home so we make ourselves comfortable, finish our drinks and have a cigarette. Fifteen minutes later, we look at each other and laugh. We better head back downstairs.

I get sidetracked at the second-floor landing but Chi Chi keeps on walking. I try and push past photographers Nan Goldin and David Armstrong but they look confused and can't figure out which way to turn. Vicki Pedersen, whom Gary calls Blanche (as in Yurka, the actress who portrayed Madame De Farge in MGM's *A Tale of Two Cities*), tries to get my attention but I just wave. I move toward the bar, where Steve is talking to Danny Fields while Danny tries to figure out what Steve's talking about. Years later, he still had no idea.

I walk toward the back, and the door of the small bathroom is open. Teri Toye is standing there in a bright green dress and a combined state of dismay and amusement after accidentally flushing two hundred dollars down the toilet. Steve gave her the money for whatever reason, and Teri apparently put it in her panties—the *unsafest* place of all. She exits and breezes past me.

Doomed *Vogue* cover girl Gia Carangi and makeup artist Sandy Linter were on the dance floor earlier, where Allan Tannenbaum snapped a few photos. Now they're just feet away smoking cigarettes, unaware of the careless flush. Gia's pioneering supermodel status still seems intact even though she's looking a bit wasted—her eyes just a dark late-night stare far removed from a bright shine cover shot or an ad for Dior. *Lesbian chic* hasn't yet been invented or applied but Gia—only nineteen—is out front well in advance. Right now she's just standing there, beautiful but not moving; I say "Hey" and Gia nods a slight smile but says nothing. I step out of the bathroom, head for the stairs and spot John Lydon leaning against the wall near the bar or the bar near the wall. He looks unhappy and I'm not even going to try.

The PiL vocalist ex-Sex Pistol was the last to arrive and still upstairs when I left. I wandered down Broadway alone and went home. I started to brush my teeth, dropped the toothbrush, it bounced off the sink and into the toilet. I stared at it for a minute and went to bed.

I woke up early, returned to the paintings started yesterday and moved them past scribble. Later I took a cab to 2 Charlton Street and spent another ninety dollars on cocaine. The purchase didn't make me feel good or bad—just a little bit lost. I left Charlton, walked two blocks and bought a new forty-nine-cent toothbrush at a deli. I jumped in a cab, headed for One University and the driver wanted to know if I was working that night. I leaned forward to see *who the fuck* was asking and realized it was Cedric, a regular Mudd Club cabbie; I told him, "Yeah, but not till later."

Maybe it was the coke or maybe it was me, but right then I had the uncomfortable feeling that my world was getting way too small. Intent on fitting in, I was pushing myself out. Fucking around, playing with heroin was asking for more trouble. Copping from Joey and Ligia, a drug-dealing couple on Bond Street (separated by two degrees from the Rolling Stones), I was late to realize that no one using, or selling, heroin gives a shit about anything except dope.

Still I pressed on, and nights later found myself in a loft on East Thirteenth Street with Claudia. Upstairs, downstairs or next door to Larry Rivers' old place, we picked up a half-gram of so-called China White. We hung out and got off with our friend Steve, the bass player for one of downtown New York's headline attractions. He was our connection for the night and another one of my future semi-permanent roommates.

I left Thirteenth Street feeling good. I didn't feel lost, though I was starting to nod. I walked to the corner, drifted off the curb and hailed a cab. I closed my eyes and heard myself say, "Broadway and White, two blocks below Canal, left side, far corner please." The high was close to perfect. I guess I was going to work.

Mutant Grift

Ten minutes later I walked into the Mudd Club, the lights were still on and Anita Sarko was digging through a box of records. I leaned on the bar, asked for a soda, and tried to steady the China White drift.

Outside only a few people were waiting but by 1:30 or 2 the place was crowded. I sat on the chain, leaning back against the front of the building and hoped the fresh air and some mindless conversation would keep me awake. When Sally Webster, one of the Mutants from San Francisco, jumped out of a cab and came running for the door I got up and let her in. Two minutes later, the driver got out looking for the girl who just *beat the fare*. It was the free ride Mutant grift and Sally pulled it off like a pro. The cabbie got burned; the excitement got me moving.

Soon after, my friend's mother came by dressed in her usual trench coat and beret and just stood there staring at me. The still "Handsome Dick" Richard Manitoba was a few feet away looking as if he weren't quite sure what was happening. He reached in his pocket, pulled out a scrap of paper and presented his version of a high school pass signed by Steve Mass: "God bless Handsome Dick Manitoba and let him in free at all times." He shrugged, I opened the chain and they went inside—my friend's mother went upstairs and Dick went down. I turned around and Chris Spedding, a man who could kill with a Gibson Flying V, was walking toward the door. He barely said hello or nodded acknowledgment but that was part of the appeal. I kept the chain open as Claudia and our friend from Thirteenth Street came in right behind him. She looked at me and tried to roll her eyes but they only rolled halfway; I tried to smile but my eyes rolled instead. The China White turned out to be the real deal.

I never even buttoned up my coat and by the time I figured out I was cold it was 4 A.M. There was an open bottle of beer in my pocket and I finished it on the way upstairs. I headed for the bathroom and found a couple lines of coke.

In the scheme of things, January was a challenge. It was the first full month of winter, the nights seemed darker and it felt kind of strange standing outside. I was getting confused and wasn't sure if my job was important, if I was important because of my job, or if any of it even mattered. I started losing sight and was struggling to get some of it back. In early 1980, I wasn't up to the *looking inward* part of my story.

Oblivion and Enlightenment

I make it home and crash on the sofa. An old black-and-white portable TV my grandmother gave me when I left for college is propped up on a trunk in the middle of the room. The trunk sits on a dirty pink rug that was clean when our friend Solveig gave it to us. Gary, a total TV freak, leaves the set on whether he's home or not. There's no remote so at five or six in the morning I wind up watching everything from test patterns with static buzz to *I Love Lucy* and the early morning news. The biggest story of the day is the American hostage crisis in Tehran. Kurt Waldheim, the UN secretary general, tries to negotiate, Jimmy Carter gets *shit on* for the way the situation is being handled, and the Russian invasion of Afghanistan only augments the tension. Despite my wide-open mind I'm selectively oblivious, but from a distance it looks like a mess. My own little world seems self-contained and peaceful by comparison. From Fourteenth Street south all the way to White Street and Murray Street, the late-night, early-morning hours offer nearly everything I need. The only side effects of this life I'm living are too many drugs and too little sleep—leaving me flying blind or cocaine frozen.

I wake up trying to work out what day it is and when I do it's nearly gone. Later, I'm back on White Street, when Peter Nolan Smith, a self-described "unknown writer," shows up. He works at Hurrah, has the night off and likes hanging out on the front steps of Mudd. He finds the White Street experience somewhere in that "middle ground between oblivion and enlightenment" but I just listen and only half agree. My time of enlightenment or any other personal Age of Reason hasn't yet arrived so I ditch Peter and step inside in search of oblivion.

Dragon People

The following night I see myself looking at a long taxi ride to the nowhere world of the barely Upper West Side. The near legendary Jim Fouratt, along with Ruth Polsky, a booking agent and music promoter (who years later was hit and killed by a taxi on Sixth Avenue), are running the show at Hurrah. The club's been featuring performances by everyone from the Patti Smith Group and Iggy Pop to the Ramones and the Sun Ra Arkestra. Walter Steding and The Dragon People are going on around 11 P.M. and I'm meeting Marcus Leatherdale at his place on Grand Street before heading uptown. Glenn O'Brien's introducing the band, Blondie's Chris Stein is joining them onstage and Marcus' wife, my friend Claudia Summers, is a keyboard-playing Dragon Person.

We arrive a few minutes before the band takes the stage, order a drink and move up front. Glenn makes the introduction and the PA system briefly crackles and pops before Walter's vocal turns into an indescribable wail. When his violin starts screaming and scratching the entire band heads into its own dark account of funky No Wave *electronica*. Andy Warhol gets nearly trampled as a good chunk of audience runs for the door. It's a wild show and I stick around long enough that my ears start ringing. I grab a cab on Broadway and tell the driver to wake me up at White Street.

***

It didn't matter who was spinning or what was playing—unless it was a Pat Boone record or some other grenade Anita Sarko occasionally hurled onto the dance floor. For the moment, it was X-Ray Spex and Poly Styrene was screaming over the beat while Johnny Dynell stood in the booth taking DJ lessons from Anita. Steve Mass was watching and offered him a job on the spot. Johnny said yes and figured he'd "just do it, to do it." I thought it was a good decision.

The "Love to Love You Baby" era was a half-decade past and the glory days of Studio 54 were already winding down. We were in the thick of post-Punk when Johnny Dynell bravely took Disco retro before it had a chance to go there on its own—a bold move but not without its Disco-hating detractors.

His first night was a Saturday and his set list walked a line between inspired and dangerous. He played Michael Jackson at his own risk and got harassed by a few freaked-out Punk-loving White Street denizens. He knew James Brown was safer but he didn't care. Dressed in Jordache jeans and a tight-fitting tank top, he gave us "Disco as a concept." He called Blondie's "Atomic" "the last Disco record" and when he played it the crowd roared. Johnny Dynell was spinning the dance floor in a new direction but he's still quick to point out, "David Azarch and Anita Sarko were the soundtrack of the Mudd Club." Johnny just gave it a kick in the ass.

Marianne and Fried Chicken

While the dance floor spins, the place is buzzing. Word gets out that Marianne Faithfull is set to play the Mudd Club in February and appear on *Saturday Night Live* the night before. It's a big deal and everyone's talking about it, but no one has any idea what a live Marianne performance might be like. The only clue is *Broken English* and if songs and sounds on that record are any indication, we're in for a great night.

In addition to Marianne's upcoming event, Michael Holman's busy working behind the scenes with Steve Mass putting together a Soul Night at Mudd. Originally planned for Club 57, budget limitations couldn't accommodate Michael's vision of what was becoming a grand-scale event. That's when Steve stepped in with the big money, a bigger space, and enough guarded enthusiasm to make everything from décor, entertainment and fried chicken a reality.

Taking Pictures

Trying to keep my excitement over Marianne and soul food on a back burner, I start sending people in two or three at a time. I'm moving around, hoping to keep warm and wondering if there's anything else going on that I need to know about. The small but anxious crowd looks cold and I'm doing my best to get them in quickly. My friend Allan and his camera are off to the side keeping me company.

Allan Tannenbaum is a self-taught, "picked up a camera as a kid" kind of guy and he's still teaching himself. He took his first Rock 'n' Roll photo of Jimi Hendrix in 1968 while living in San Francisco. In 1972 he settled into a loft just blocks from where we're standing. *SoHo Weekly News* publisher Michael Goldstein hired him in 1974 when the going rate was five dollars a picture; by late 1978, Allan heard about "the new Punk club on White Street." He figured it would be "another place to take pictures," stopped by and found a lot more. Now he's outside in the cold, waiting for the next shot.

Ten minutes pass, Rastaman "Dirty Harry" arrives and hands me a spliff. I give whoever's still waiting a quick glance and leave Allan and his camera outside. I move toward the bar, DJ David cues up Roxy Music's "Love Is the Drug" and the sound of an engine kicks it off. A few seconds later, Bryan Ferry starts singing. I grab Alice

Bush Tetras. Pat Place and Cynthia Sley, 1980, by Lisa Genet.

and we head upstairs, sit in a booth and fire up the Dirty Harry special. Another ten minutes pass, she's laughing nonstop and I'm trying to get back outside. When I finally make it out the door Allan snaps a picture; I look at the crowd and start laughing.

Hanging Out at the Door

Just about anyone going out in New York City wound up standing in front of the Mudd Club—even in the cold. Photographer and CBGB doorperson Roberta Bayley (she shot the iconic cover of the Ramones' first album) always thought, "the scene outside was the best part." She's also first to admit she "was never really a Mudd Club person," though it's difficult to say what that means.

Ten minutes hanging with me at the door, Roberta watched the White Street version of "who pays and who doesn't." An hour inside and she'd be ready to leave. Sixteen years later, in the summer of 1996, we walked in to the Sex Pistols' Filthy Lucre Reunion Tour at Roseland together. For me it was a first; for Roberta, who hopped on the bus for a stop along the Pistols' ill-fated 1978 American tour, it was full circle.

***

It never mattered if the crowd outside was big or small. From where I was standing the Mudd Club was always the heart of the scene. Max's and CB's were already landmark institutions and Studio 54 still had its moments. No one I knew had any idea what went on at Xenon nor was interested in finding out. Hurrah drew a crowd depending on the popularity of whoever was playing, and Club 57 offered events with clever names, throwback themes and lots of cocktails. The latter sounded familiar, but for the most part I stayed below Canal.

Tier 3 on West Broadway was as different as it was essential. Just blocks away from Mudd, the place was a small-scale multilevel dive with an often raucous next-wave Rock 'n' Roll vibe. Hilary Jaeger, who began working as the club's manager around the time I started on White Street, was booking great bands like the Slits, Madness, and The Raybeats. The newly formed Bush Tetras were getting ready for their first show at Tier 3 on February 4, 1980. Three months later they were playing the Mudd Club. People were back and forth between both places depending on the night's lineup, where they could get in, and if they could drink for free.

By now it must be 1 A.M. and the twenty people standing outside an hour ago just turned into a crowd. I'm clearheaded but cold, puffing on a cigarette and focused on taking care of the regulars, the neighborhood and any marginally polite celebrities and freaks who might show up. If you look good and seem interesting, fuckable or all three, you'll probably get in as well. If you behave like an asshole, based on what the general consensus considers that to be, you can forget it.

An hour passes and I'm mid-conversation with a woman I've never seen before who doesn't want to pay and she's asking for *Richard*—as if I'm someone else and he's somewhere inside. I let Aldo bat the ball back and forth while I open the chain for "angelic" Punk icon Damita Richter and Victor Bockris. It's after 2 A.M., both are wearing dark glasses and the only thing they want to know: "Is Steve around?" I tell them "Maybe" because it's the short and honest answer. Director and photographer Edo Bertoglio and girlfriend Maripol follow them inside while the chain is still open. He says "Hello" and she keeps talking to no one in particular, possibly asking the same question about Steve. I offer her the same *Maybe*. An hour later, they're all still on the second floor where Maripol is connecting with friends, faces and acquaintances, though most of her actual Polaroiding takes place back at her loft. Some of the instant images are beautiful, some are funny, and some are just used film, but together they paint an artful, interesting and sometimes messy picture of a golden time.

Talking Dirty

The night's almost over and I'm moving around without thinking. The dance floor's crashing and I'm talking to a bouncer from a place called the Funhouse. He wants to "get high" with me after work and he's already talking dirty a half-inch from my face. I tell him to meet me upstairs for one more drink—and one last trip to the bathroom. Twenty minutes later, we're at Murray Street, fucked up and fucking our brains out. Sometimes it helps and other times I don't feel a thing.

I passed out around ten and woke up at noon. Funhouse was gone and Gary never came home. I threw some water on my face, made coffee and lit a cigarette. I licked the mirror that was still sitting on the kitchen table. I was looking forward to Soul Night and excited about Marianne Faithfull. I thought about starting some new paintings. Then Yoyo called.

Xs, Os and Pure Mania

I met Yoyo Friedrich at the Mudd Club. He's got a connection with a gallery in Germany called Gestalt Reform that's mounting a show of billboards in Frankfurt. Yoyo's part of the show, our friend Charlie Yoder (last seen in a gorilla suit at the Justine-Colette fashion event) is included, and I've been asked to participate. It's a big deal for me—another *big break*.

Working hard, I set up the project and map out a grid for a scaled-down model of the billboard. The final piece is an eight- by twelve-foot series of hieroglyph-like *X*s and *O*s, outlined in black, painted in pink and blue and set against a yellow ground. Every night I head straight home from White Street, put on a record and paint. Lynette Bean and Frankie DeCurtis stop by and take photos of me working on a ladder, dressed in a white paper jumpsuit. We smoke pot, drink some beer, turn up the music and take more pictures.

After two weeks, the billboard is finished. I get off the ladder, light a joint and put on the Vibrators' *Pure Mania*. When I look at the painting the pink and blue glyphs start dancing. I start dancing too, experiencing a sense of joy that I often dismiss.

In spite of everything—or maybe because of it—the work's a success and ships to Frankfurt on time. I feel good, like I'm working hard and really doing something. I've already started a few smaller editions of the *X*s and *O*s but right now I have to clean up and jump in the shower. I need to eat and get to the Mudd Club by 11. It's 9 P.M. and Chinatown's the easy answer.

Chow Something and the Heroin Craze

Gary just got home and he's hungry too. By 10, we're sitting downstairs at Wo Hop on Mott Street, waiting for soup, two egg rolls and a shrimp chow something. The food's cheap, the hot mustard's hot, and they use whatever tea is left in the teapots to wipe down the tables. It's crowded but the service is quick. When the food arrives we eat fast and leave.

Ready for work and almost smiling, I'm thinking about the billboard. I think about Yoyo, Charlie, Frankie and Lynette—the Mudd Club was our home turf, common ground. From Murray Street to Frankfurt, 77 White and beyond, it all lined up with the Walter Steding Constellation Theory; a beautiful light with boundaries undefined. Then I think about Wo Hop, two dollars eighty-five cents for that *shrimp chow something*. I think about Gary and me as we head up Mott Street, walking our way back from Chinatown.

The next morning, alone with a bag of dope, I think about a breaking point years before the break finally came. Defined or not, I think about the zero boundaries when it came to living with Gary. We were constantly stoned, always looking for the next high and fucking around all over downtown. We'd disappear for a day and a night and meet up at One University or Mudd.

In 1976, when I arrived in New York, my drinking was already out of bounds but cocaine was barely in the picture. Heroin was just a curious drug with an odd appeal used by other people I hardly knew. I was intent on making art, fascinated with the Punk scene centered on CB's and Max's, and obsessed with easy, casual and often kinky sex. Two years later I met Gary, and cocaine brought us together. When heroin moved in, we made speedballs with the leftovers. I wasn't a daily user but it didn't take me long to discover heroin's appeal, and for a while it made things easier: the job, fitting in and being *part of*, all benefiting from a quick fix. Then I started to become one of those *other* people; and slowly, I began to disappear. I thought I was just getting high but I was losing sight of what I really wanted.

When *New York* magazine mentioned a "heroin craze" at the Mudd Club they were late to the party. No regrets—but I was there on time.

***

264

MUDD CLUB NEWSLETTER

DR MUDD TAKES MEASURES AGAINST ANTI-SOCIAL BEHAVIOR

On a routine inspection of the Mudd Club premesis Dr. Mudd recently discovered two patrons of the club engaged in an act of intercourse inside a toilet stall. With characteristic discretion Dr. Mudd did not interrupt the couple as they perched dangerously on top of the toilet seat. Instead, Dr. Mudd consulted his I.S.C. product guide and immediately formulated a plan for the staff which would enable them to rapidly confront and solve this

particularly pressing problem. This involves the use of the CCC Security Blanket, which according to the manufacturer can completely immobilize an offender without inflicting physical harm. The device emits a high intensity burst of light which causes disorientation and quickly causes the perpetrators to initiate withdrawl. The weapon has been effectively used on airplane hijackers.

AL22 Security Blanket

DR. MUDD INTRODUCES SIMPLIFIED SOBRIETY TEST INTO MUDD CLUB:

In a mood of deep concern over teen alcohol abuse Dr. Mudd has implemented a test geared to the typical Mudd Club client. The test involves simply requesting that the individual write their name, address, and phone number on a 3 X 5 card. To the

left is a sample test in which the examined individual failed in 4 basic categories: (a) Required more than 3 minutes to complete the card; (b) Could not keep the lines of the address parallel; (c) Forgot that they had written their name on the top of the card repeating it again at the bottom; (d) Did not know zip code. The advantage of this test is that results can be analyzed on the spot with no scientific equipment and the decision to terminate the individual can be made immediately.

DR. MUDD SKEPTICAL OVER FAITH HEALING WITNESSED AT ROCK CONCERT:

In the incident in question fabulous Freddie Schneider of the B-52's lost his voice at the end of his first set in a recent Mudd Club appearance. Gargling and throat lozenges as well as physical threats were employed to bring Freddie's voice back. A teen idol, Mr. B. happened to be next to the stage and according to some when their eyes met an incredible surge of power returned to Freddie's throat restoring his voice to its full octave range. Observers said they saw a ray of light from Mr. B.'s eyes which beamed at Freddie causing the "miraculous" change. With his characteristically healthy scientific skepticism Dr. Mudd offered a more plausible explanation. Noting that the stage had been placed three feet higher than the B-52's previous concert, Dr. Mudd saw the voice loss as a kind of behavioral recall related to Freddie's known fear of heights, a kind of acrophobic speechlessness. Once Freddie stepped back from the stage and was not looking down, the fear dissipated and Freddie's voice returned to normal.

DR. MUDD SETS ASIDE SPACE FOR STUDY OF TYPICAL TEENAGER:

The special laboratory will have a normal teen environment where the creature can be observed 24 hours per day. Typically the walls will be poster covered, and piles of decal tee shirts, high sugar content snacks and acne lotions will be in evidence. Dr. Mudd is seeking a typical Queens teenager for this lab study. The teen should originate from a large apartment complex, should weigh about 170 pounds, have mild acne and attend 6 rock concerts per month. The teen room will have remote viewing to reduce self consciousness in lab subjects. (more in next newsletter)

Newsletter featuring notes on antisocial behavior, sobriety testing and faith healing, 1979, courtesy Richard Boch.

Trying to be bad—drugs and drinking were part of that ambition. Some places I could misbehave and get away with it, other places not. Tuesday, January 29, 1980, I was hanging at One University and the smart move would've been to stay there. Instead, I left with Marcia Resnick, walked over to Reno Sweeney on West Thirteenth but didn't make it through the show. We got tossed out after heckling Robby Benson during his performance.

I was the guilty one and Marcia got caught in the middle. Her only crime: listening to Robby sing and play guitar. I got stupid, things got ugly, and there was no excuse. I got what I deserved.

Two hours later, I was working at Mudd, trying to shake off my embarrassing behavior. Ross Bleckner had been in the audience at Reno's and gave me a puzzled look when he spotted me at the door. He smiled but couldn't help asking, "What was all that about?" I wasn't smiling and didn't have an answer. The next day I went back to Reno Sweeney and apologized to the staff.

That was the last I heard of Robby Benson and the last he heard of me. He never came to the Mudd Club but if he had, I probably would have let him in—for five dollars.

Ex Dragon Debs

From that point on I tried to stick with entertainment that I understood. Sometimes that meant music, sometimes sex and sometimes drugs, but usually all three. Then I heard what Lisa and Judy were up to and it seemed to make sense that a neo-girl group would find a home on White Street.

Between fashion icon Lisa Rosen, designer Mary Lemley and Sophie VDT, they had style to spare. Judy Nylon had Snatch (her Eno-produced musical collaboration with singer Patti Palladin) under her belt and fit right in. Screenwriter Wesley Strick provided the simple keyboard accompaniment long before a successful Hollywood career came calling. Together they were the Ex Dragon Debs.

Judy and Lisa were the brains of the operation and Mary Lemley had a hand in the costumes. Painted paper dresses and purple Afro wigs, cut and trimmed *Eraserhead*-style, were just part of the look: matching tutus and ruffs pulled it all together. The only piece missing was a full-on Phil Spector Wall of Sound.

Judy Nylon and transient tattoos, 1979,
by Lisa Genet.

Lisa remembered that "a lot of thought and no money" went into the costumes for what was "possibly the world's worst pop group." What she probably forgot was that once someone put on a tutu and a purple wig, good or bad didn't matter. Standing in front of the Mudd Club stage, I gave up trying to wrap my head around the girls' version of song, choosing instead to get lost in the spectacle of White Street entertainment.

Edit DeAk (who, along with Walter Robinson, cofounded the mid-seventies publication *Art-Rite*) shot some Super 8 footage of the Ex Dragon Debs' Mudd Club performance. Her sharp eye but unsteady hand created a unique bit of camerawork that Judy described as "an unusual puffball effect." It was the only live-action document of the Debs, and sadly it's lost forever.

Steve Mass paid the girls with a case of champagne that arrived in a gray plastic garbage pail filled with melting ice. It was one of those backstage moments wrapped in showbiz tradition that had Mudd stamped all over it. Judy Nylon left for Europe shortly after and fifteen-year-old Eszter Balint, the Hungarian actress who'd been hanging at Mudd since she was fourteen, filled the void. A few months later, the Ex Dragon Debs played their final show at the Squat Theater.

Judy still travels back and forth from Europe, and Eszter, the daughter of Squat Theater cofounder Stephan Balint, still sings. Artist Walter Robinson, Edit DeAk's onetime publishing partner, became Lisa Rosen's second husband. Lisa's as beautiful as ever but decided to forgo a career in popular music. Despite my continued friendship with Judy and Lisa, all I remember of the night's performance is a flash of purple fluff.

Squatting

Besides playing host to the Ex Dragon Debs' swan song, the Squat Theater was an important underground venue and cultural center. Founded by members of the seminal avant-garde Squat Theater Group, its resident squatter was Nico, and the Sun Ra Arkestra was practically the house band. I spent many early evenings there listening to everyone from Lenny Kaye, John Cale and James Chance to Johnny Thunders, DNA and John Lurie and the Lounge Lizards. A one-time-only Cheetah Chrome and Nico guitar-harmonium duet was a Squat-inspired stroke of genius: Mudd-like in its *anything goes* bravado; it was hard to forget.

The place was a strange, dark and interesting stop on what seemed an endless run thru the New York night. More like an opium den than some happening place with lots of people running around—whatever it was or wasn't—Squat had its moment.

Paella with Wavy Gravy

Nights later, there was plenty of food but no opium at a small dinner party in an old Art Deco ballroom on East Eleventh Street. David Azarch showed up with Abbijane, I arrived with Lynette Bean, and Jerry Brandt was our host for the evening. The eclectic group of guests included Rob Halford of Judas Priest (who inexplicably played the Mudd Club shortly before I began doing the door), Cheryl Rixon, the 1979 *Penthouse* Pet of the Year (and Halford's beard), and Wavy Gravy, whom I mistakenly identified as a children's party clown. It was quite the mix and Jerry was our only connection. We sat around a table in the middle of the dance floor feasting on a large platter of paella from the ballroom's kitchen.

Wavy (the Woodstock Festival MC) was an old friend of Jerry's; the *who*, *why* or *what the fuck?* presence of Halford and Rixon was curious at best. The point of the evening was Jerry's presentation of what soon would become The Ritz: a dance floor, a bar and a wraparound balcony, a few of the best DJs in town and a brilliant one-note formula presenting some of the biggest names in music. The Ritz wanted to be the next big thing in New York nightlife and we were there to see how we might fit in.

While Jerry gave us the tour my mind was racing, living in an outcome that was years away and brief at best. I wanted to get outside to talk to David, though I knew it wasn't time to make a change or even think about leaving White Street. We could do anything we wanted to at Mudd and get away with it. A change of venue might mean we'd have to behave.

I think Jerry would've loved having us. I looked at David and I think we were tempted for a minute. Then I shook my head and looked away. It was barely 1980, the Mudd Club was our home and we weren't going anywhere.

As soon as dinner and the tour were over, Lynette and I walked the few short blocks to One University. Mickey was in his spot on the brass rail near the entrance to the dining room wearing his favorite pink sweater with holes at both elbows. Nathan Joseph was next to him, and John Stravinsky, the grandson of Igor, was behind the bar. We headed for the bathroom, and then the back room, to see who was playing Asteroids and Space Invaders. Ronnie Cutrone and Gigi Williams were standing on a chair cheering Richard Sohl, who was going for a new high score personal best. Teri Toye was either sitting on top of or next to Andi Ostrowe, who was either asleep or passed out. It wasn't even 1 A.M. as we settled into that little backroom pocket of New York City. It was my night off and way too early for White Street.

One U was always the crazy cafeteria clubhouse. Places like Squat and even The Ritz—just slices of life, moving parts of the old and new decade.

Mudd Club was the bridge between then and now.

Donuts

Ricky's hooked on Asteroids and he's back at One University the following afternoon; I'm back at work the next night. I've got a small joint in my Marlboro box but I haven't snorted heroin in days. I leave the loft, walk to Broadway and Canal, and pick up an egg cream. Holman, Basquiat, Wayne Clifford and Vincent Gallo are sitting at the counter drinking coffee and smoking cigarettes. A downtown version of a junior Rat Pack, they carry themselves with a loose swagger that's a little Sinatra, a little Sammy Davis, a little cool and a little crazy. Together with Danny Rosen, Boris Policeband and Ken Compton, they float back and forth between White Street and Dave's Luncheonette.

I pass the counter and say "Hey, see you later." I walk to work and the night disappears.

Closing time and Michael Holman's still upstairs with Steve. They're figuring things out for the Soul party that's happening on the third Sunday in February. I'm still downstairs, the lights are up and I'm sitting on the bar trying to figure out who or what I'm waiting for. Danny Rosen, Jean-Michel and Vicki Pedersen are headed out the door and wind up winding down at Dave's for another round of cigarettes, coffee and grease. Ten minutes after they walk in, the donut delivery arrives: set on the counter in a gray cardboard box, fresh crullers and jellies just a few feet from the door. It's an easy grab and a minute later the "kids" and the donuts are gone.

Vicki's calling the shots and the boys are in over their heads. To her the donut heist is just a "crime of opportunity" but for Danny and Jean it's a quick-start, carbed-up sugar rush breakfast. Back on White Street, the Mudd Club's empty and I'm still sitting on the bar.

Should Have Gone Home

I'm not hungry and not about to start stealing donuts so I grab a cab and head for The Nursery instead. There's a garbage truck roaring outside and the warm stench breaks thru the cold morning air. Inside, the dead-end thrill of getting frisked for a weapon is about as much excitement as I can handle. Mudd Club alumnus Joey Kelly is hanging out and Johnny Thunders is shuffling around at a forty-five-degree lean looking for anything he can find. Nursery girl Krystie Keller walks by and disappears up the stairs. Hours earlier, Iggy was bouncing around the Mudd Club and now he's spending his downtime here; I offer up a "Hello, James" and keep walking. There are Hells Angels at the bar whom I know by name but they have no idea who I am—that's a good thing and I keep it that way. On the stairs to the second floor I run into Anita Pallenberg, who's just asked Krystie if she's a boy or a girl; now she's asking me if there's anywhere to go after this. I light her cigarette and tell her the only place left to go is hell or home. Neither of us laughs.

Somewhere between there and nowhere Rockets Redglare, the actor, bouncer and former Sid Vicious bodyguard, walks over and starts telling me a story. He's a really big guy with really bad teeth; he likes to talk but I'm afraid of getting trapped. The other problem, Steve Mass doesn't like Rockets and doesn't want him in the Mudd Club. I have little patience at this hour, and thirty seconds into a potentially long-winded report of how I shouldn't worry because he's got my back, I start to drift, say thanks and move on.

The Nursery's crowded and the scene is murky. There's always someone around I let into Mudd five hours earlier who'll give me some coke that's been stepped on within an inch of its life. A guy selling bags of street dope with the Doctor Nova stamp of approval seems like a scam but at 7 A.M. I buy one anyway.

The morning starts to fade, the air feels thick and the place looks darker than when I arrived. I try and find someone to talk to but I can barely speak. Sex seems out of the question but it somehow never is. By 8, I'm standing in the dark smoking a cigarette and holding an empty plastic cup, my head spinning, my body refusing to crash. I have to get out of here but it's hard to move.

The cold night turned cold winter morning. I'd left the Mudd Club around 5 A.M. and should have gone home after work. It was February 1980 and I was twenty-six years old—long before I realized there's no such thing as *should have*.

Marianne

Friday night I took a break from the after-hours crawl and did the same on Saturday. I went home after work and slept as best I could. Sunday afternoon I woke up early. When the phone started ringing I unplugged it without answering, took a long shower and got ready. Before I knew it, it was time to leave.

I walked up Broadway to Franklin Street and cut thru Cortlandt Alley. I turned onto White Street, stepped onto the loading dock and went inside. Sound check was happening and the band was tearing into "Broken English." There were a dozen people standing around but the singer was nowhere in sight.

Sunday, February 10, 1980, was a big night at the Mudd Club. Marianne Faithfull, the ultimate Rock 'n' Roll legend, muse and wild card, was scheduled to sing at 1 A.M. The scene on the street was sure to be as crazy as the one inside, and everyone from high society to rock's idiot fringe gave up trying to contain the drool of curiosity. The previous night's performance on *Saturday Night Live* was both revelation and disaster as Marianne's barely audible vocal struggled to hang on to the key, the chord and the beat. The brilliant material she wrote with guitarist Barry Reynolds, buried beneath a spectacle of crash and burn.

Marianne needed a rematch and White Street was the place. Anticipation was running high but the crapshoot was uncertain at best.

DJ David was at the turntables, the bar staff stood ready and the cover charge was an unheard-of ten dollars. Steve pulled me aside

Marianne Faithfull, onstage at Mudd, 1980, by Bob Gruen.

Anita Pallenberg, fully loaded. Mudd Club staircase, 1980, by Allan Tannenbaum.

before he disappeared and said, "Everyone has to pay." I smiled but the pressure was on.

There were more than two hundred people in the street before the doors even opened. I stepped outside around 10:30, looking forward to the chance of telling a number of freeloaders, "Ten dollars please." I apologized, made sad faces and did my best with the *Everyone Has to Pay* routine. Cookie arrived and whispered, "Hon, I can pay if I have to." She didn't have to, but I loved that she offered. Not everyone was that nice.

I kept smiling and kept the crowd moving. I was lucky I didn't have to deal with a Paul Simon type or anyone else asking, "Do you know who I am?" The only brief back-and-forth came and went with *who gives a shit* '70s supermodel Cheryl Tiegs. She'd never been to Mudd, couldn't understand why she had to pay and threatened to leave. She wouldn't stop pouting, and her date finally paid the ten.

By midnight, we had a full house. By showtime, we squeezed in nearly every person south of Fourteenth Street who was out on a Sunday night. I went inside before the show started, grabbed a beer and a double brandy and pushed my way up front. The dance floor was packed so tight it was scary and the club was as crowded as I'd ever seen it. Coming on the heels of the December '79 headline, WHO CONCERT DISASTER in Cincinnati, we were lucky to avoid a stampede. That's where our luck ended.

When Marianne stepped onstage the place went wild, but two seconds later I knew we were in trouble. Her hands were Day-Glo pink and matched the streaked color of her hair (a do-it-yourself dye job without rubber gloves). She was wearing a crazy blue jumpsuit that was half astronaut, half sanitation worker. As fucked up as everyone else was, Marianne (wrecked on cocaine or maybe procaine) was past the frozen blur, into the beyond. She grabbed the mike stand, leaned against the pillar at the edge of the stage and tried to hang on. When she opened her mouth, not much came out. The band carried on but "Broken English" was broken and two songs later, Marianne was gone.

After the show, the third floor of 77 White became the *second* second floor of the Mudd Club. Anita Pallenberg and Marianne sat together receiving well-wishers and admirers while everyone else stood around trying to figure out what just happened. Teri Toye sat in a corner doing God knows what with Richard Sohl while I parked myself on a couch nearby. I watched photographers Berry Berenson and Allan Tannenbaum wander around capturing what became truly lost moments, until Teri started laughing at the open fly on Berry's corduroys. That was my cue to head back outside.

The night was long and about as Mudd Club as it gets. Like drugs in the bathroom or a barely remembered moment on the dance floor, the music and the chaos, the wreckage and the high, all came together. Marianne Faithfull was a mess, but undiminished and undeterred. Her vocal delivery and the performances that followed eventually caught up with the inspired greatness of the material. Her comeback became her career and time was still on her side.

DJ Anita Sarko remembered being introduced to Marianne by the other Anita and gushing like a fan. It was part of the Pallenberg plan to cheer up Marianne after her memorable—albeit for all the wrong reasons—performance. I remember watching Marianne leave White Street in a limo but it was long before the club emptied out. An hour later I walked home alone. I had a full week ahead of me and next Sunday night was sure to be another wild one.

The Soul Party

Marianne seemed a strange source of inspiration but proved to be just that. Her performance became a survivor's touchstone—and White Street, the path forward. I spent the following days hanging out in my studio, working on several new paintings and doing my best to avoid heroin and cocaine. Each night I was happy to be standing at the Mudd Club door, even in the cold.

Michael Holman was inspired by an equally strange source. His neighbor, a schoolteacher with a unique sense of interior design, was channeling his inner pimp: just inside his apartment, a fur-lined, spade-shaped doorway curtained with strands of hanging plastic beads. Michael was "so turned on" he knew what he had to do—and after weeks of planning, there was only one place he could do it.

Michael's vision was far out, right on, and perfect for the Mudd Club. Steve Mass loved his idea and came up a budget of ten thousand dollars. A "pimped out" reality of fur coats and round fur-covered beds, a ghetto beauty shop and a fried chicken buffet was finally going to happen. The Soul party was less than a week away.

Gennaro Palermo and Costa Pappas signed on to build the props and lay out the décor based on Michael's specifications. Design-

Richard Boch and Chi Chi Valenti,
Soul Night, 1980, by Allan Tannenbaum.

er Millie David trekked to the wilds of Brooklyn hunting for old-school salon chairs and Turbinator-style hairdryers. Other than a few hundred orders of fried chicken, the only thing left to consider was the entertainment—and it had to be the real thing. Two names were at the top of the list but there wasn't a lot of time.

Holman dreamed of the Ohio Players taking the stage but the "Love Rollercoaster" was out of service and looked like it might be a while before it made another comeback. Steve wanted Clarence Carter, the blind Soul singer whose hits included "Patches," "Making Love (At the Dark End of the Street)" and "Back Door Santa"—and to everyone's surprise, Clarence wanted the job. The pieces were falling into place, Michael was nailing down the details and Soul Night was taking on a life of its own.

Sunday, February 17, 1980, and it's freezing outside. Never one to costume other than pajamas, I'm wearing my heavy overcoat, the tartan scarf and a pair of BOY London leather pants—an accidental hand-me-down from Blondie's Jimmy Destri. It's early, the club isn't open yet and I'm keeping warm up on the second floor. Gennaro and Costa are in the "Soul bedroom" fussing with a fake fur bedspread on the round king-sized bed. They take a last quick look and add final touches to the gold-veined mirrors, the gold TV and gold telephone. No detail is too small and Millie David's busy making sure the "Beauty Shop" is up and running. The white courier van Holman's been driving makes a run to One Hundred Twenty-fifth Street and brings back fried chicken, cornbread, collard greens and sweet potato pie. The *uptown* waitresses Steve hired are wearing little white aprons and seem to know their way around Down Home cooking but have no idea what they've gotten themselves into.

It's almost time to open the doors when Gennaro walks past me to the elevator. He's wearing a hairnet and he's got a nickel in his ear. Debi Mazar, dressed like schoolgirl trouble and looking younger than her fifteen years, is right behind him. No one's sure if she's supposed to be working and neither is she, so for the moment Debi's sticking close to Gennaro. I make a quick grab at some chicken, stuff a piece of cornbread in my pocket, walk downstairs and step outside. Chi Chi exits a cab in her fur coat, wearing a chain-link headband and a pair of peep-toe heels. I can't tell if there's anything under the coat. She runs inside and takes her position at the foot of the stairs while I toss a few chicken bones into the alley. The suitably soulful crowd standing out front looks anxious, so I take a bite of cornbread and open the chain.

Soul Night aftermath. Giorgio Gomelsky, making his move, 1980, by Ebet Roberts.

Michael Holman is ready at the turntables; he knows better than anyone, "Soul Night is about the music." When he cues up "It's My Thing," Marva Whitney starts sockin' it to us every which way she can.

The place is jam-packed and everyone's cast in a black-light pimpadelic haze. The walls are lined with Day-Glo velveteen posters featuring Kama Sutra pleasure positions played out in giant Afroed silhouettes. Michael goes it one better, dips into some down and dirty George Clinton and everyone gets in deep. "Red Hot Mama" and "Alice in My Fantasies" from Funkadelic's *Standing On the Verge of Getting It On* release a wild dance floor orgasm.

Minutes later, I'm walking thru the room and Jo Shane grabs me. The Ohio Players' "Skin Tight" comes blasting out of the speakers and we're both lost in the mix. Soul Night is happening, the crowd's eating it up and Steve Mass is at the bar near the DJ booth taking it all in. Dressed in a printed silk shirt and a pair of self-belted polyester flares, he's ditched the faux fur pimp hat and opted for a pair of Ray-Bans instead. I come off the dance floor and move toward the bar. Steve says something but I keep walking. There's still a big crowd outside and Clarence Carter's going on in fifteen minutes. I've got to work fast.

Nearly 2 A.M. and the club's going full tilt. No one moves or takes notice until the music stops and the monitor lets loose a blast of feedback. Clarence is onstage and I'm wondering if he can see or even feel what's going on. He strums his guitar and says "Hello." The mike picks it up and the PA system sends it back, loud. Clarence is ready but I'm not sure if anyone else is. I'm smiling half a laugh, thinking, *Patches, we're depending on you, son.*

By 3 A.M., Clarence is gone, the door's on autopilot and we're letting in just about anyone. I make my way upstairs and pick up a beer at the bar; I step into the ladies' room and see at least six girls in front of one cracked mirror putting on too much makeup. Someone gives me a kiss, hands me a Quaalude and says "Thanks." I stash the lude and split.

I spot my friend Solveig with trumpeter Randy Brecker looking out the window at some uniformed cops coming in the front door. They think it's a raid and get queasy until I explain, "those cops come in all the time—they like to be part of what's happening." I turn, walk over to the Soul Bedroom and lie down on the round king-sized bed. Chi Chi's already there, rolling around in the fluff with two soul sisters, when Allan Tannenbaum begins to snap pictures. Minutes later, I'm up, looking for more fried chicken.

Soul Night turned into a live-action party scene straight out of a Pam Grier blaxploitation flick. It was installation art. Site-specific, made for Mudd and a dreamworld away from the work of Kienholz or Grooms. It was White Street 1980.

At 4 A.M. the party was still going strong. I picked up my brandy and swallowed the Quaalude. Gennaro oozed by, high on sweet potato pie. He still had the nickel in his ear.

Huckleberry Finn

Ten minutes later I'm downstairs looking at an empty stage. Two of the velveteen Day-Glo posters along the wall are gone, two others torn. I walk out the door as Soul Night turns into Monday morning.

By 9 A.M. I'm ready to crash. The loft's quiet and Gary's missing in action. I wake up late afternoon, walk to Morgan's market at the corner of Reade and Hudson and buy three or four bottles of Perrier. The bubbles help burp away the fried chicken and a quick shower helps wash away whatever's left of Soul Night's morning after. I call Solveig to see what's up but she's already made plans to see Randy play at a club called Seventh Avenue South. I call Lynette and we decide to meet at One University around midnight. I make a couple more calls, unplug the phone and start working on three new X and O drawings. They're charcoal, paint and enamel on paper, rough around the edges, thirty-eight by fifty inches and a lot smaller than the billboard. I paint for several hours, roll a joint, put John Cale's *Fear* on the turntable and take another shower. We finally have a real tile bathroom with a real door—remodeled by Jackie and Sandy, two carpenter dykes from New Jersey I met at Mudd.

I get out of a cab at One University around midnight, order a drink and look around to see who's doing what, with whom. I say hi to photographer Michael Halsband, crack a smile at Betsy Sussler and land in a booth with Rebecca Christensen, downtown's go-to girl. We're both drinking Jack Daniels and I'm still on the first one when Ricky walks in with Teri. Lynette shows up a moment later and by 2 A.M., even on my night off, I'm ready for White Street.

Outside, a cabby we know is parked at the curb. It's Cedric Baker, an artist and former Pratt student who works the club scene and rarely takes a ride above Twenty-third. He's gotten to know his own version of *everyone*, and driving a cab gives him some "insight into the heartbeat of what's going on." That's what brought him to the Mudd Club. Whenever he has time I let him in for free.

Without a word, Cedric knows where we're headed. Lynette and I settle in, stretch out and smoke a joint in the Checker's wide-open backseat space. Ten minutes later, he lets us out in front of 77 White but the street's deserted and no one's at the door. We go inside to find the dance floor half full and the bar half empty. The second floor's quiet, hardly anyone around. The bartender's missing so I fish a tepid beer from the watery tub and look around. James Nares is in a booth with Adele Bertei, DJ Johnny Dynell, and Ross Bleckner's boyfriend, Ron Dorsett. When Ron gets up, he looks in the mirror on the wall behind the bar; James offers, "If you like it, we'll get it for you."

Minutes later, with a smooth move, fast enough to rival the infamous Dave's Donut Heist, the mirror is gone. The gang disappears in a flash of penny-ante criminal mischief and makes a run for Ross and Ron's place on the sixth floor. Ten minutes later and the only thing James remembers before "floating down the river on a raft like Huckleberry Finn" was passing around a suspicious joint. High on crime, angel-dusted and nowhere else to go, they were Trouble looking for Fun on a cold winter night.

I saw nothing, heard nothing and said nothing about the mirror. I pulled another beer from the tub and went downstairs looking for Lynette. Monday turned Tuesday, February was sliding toward March and daylight was still running late. Walking home alone, I left a quiet Mudd Club morning behind.

The Wedding

I lost track running between Murray Street, One University and Mudd. February was a long short month and March daylight rarely seen. Nighttime Broadway was still cold; White Street felt the same. Spring was making an effort, and I kept waiting for winter to say good-bye.

Sunday, March 16, 1980, I have to be at work by 11 P.M. Smutty Smiff and Gail Higgins, the Heartbreakers associate and co-manager, are getting married in the late afternoon.

The previous night, Smutty's stag party was a rough one. I worked the door and tried to keep a safe distance while a crew of twenty-year-old Rockabilly boys, a gaggle of female fans (including L'Hotsky and Pedersen) and some *not quite* cougars all splashed around in a sea of limitless alcohol on the second floor of the Mudd Club. Factor in a steel cage, the bathrooms and Smutty's lost and found memory of getting "blind shit-faced drunk" and it was everything a young bachelor could ask for.

The aftermath and morning after found people passed out upstairs, some waking up in Cortlandt Alley and others headed for a 7 or 8 A.M. one-night stand. I managed to make it home but never went to sleep. A number of celebrants including the groom were listed MIA until they were rounded up, hosed off and put back together in time for the ceremony.

The big event took place at Ashley's, a restaurant on East Fifty-second Street. Gary and I hailed a cab at the corner of Murray and asked the driver to go straight up Sixth Avenue and across Twenty-third. The driver decided to head across Canal Street instead and got caught in traffic. When he made the left into Little Italy I asked him, "Where the fuck are you going?" He stopped for the light at Mulberry and Broome, we tried to get out but he wanted his money. When the cabbie grabbed my jacket, I took a swing and cut my arm on the partition in the cab. The Broome Street boys of Little Italy were hanging on the corner, watching it go down. They pulled the driver out the cab, threw a dozen punches in the direction of his head and shoved him back in the car. They looked at me and asked, "Richie, you okay?"

Those guys were a handful when they came around White Street and carried on like junior wiseguys. They were ballbusters but I was happy to have them on my side. One of them hailed us another cab and we walked into Ashley's at the same time Smutty arrived, smiling and fully recovered. The faces inside were all Max's and Mudd Club refugees, and I knew nearly everyone in the room. When Gail appeared she looked beautiful and Smutty looked almost as pretty. The ceremony was a quickie and before you knew it they were man and wife.

A minute and two drinks later, I'm headed for the bathroom with Marcia Resnick, the official wedding photographer. She snaps pictures of me leaning against a tile wall with a cocktail in my hand and a fresh battle scar on my forearm from the cab fight. The shots capture *time and place, drugs and bathrooms* and one of the photos becomes a personal favorite.

I stay behind and freshen up while Marcia makes her way thru the room taking pictures. She gets a shot of Gail and Smutty that's headed for the cover of next week's *SoHo Weekly News*.

I grab a quick something to eat and it's time to leave. I kiss the newlyweds good night and tell everyone else, "See you later." I stop by One University on the way downtown, check out the crowd and try to find a couple lines of coke. I hear a screech from across the room and see that it's Rene Ricard, screaming at two oversized Romaine lettuce leaves used to garnish the seafood special. He calms down, places the lettuce on the floor and continues eating. At this point, the Mudd Club seems like a sane choice.

Richard Boch and Pete Farndon, friends, 1980, by Lynette Bean Kral.

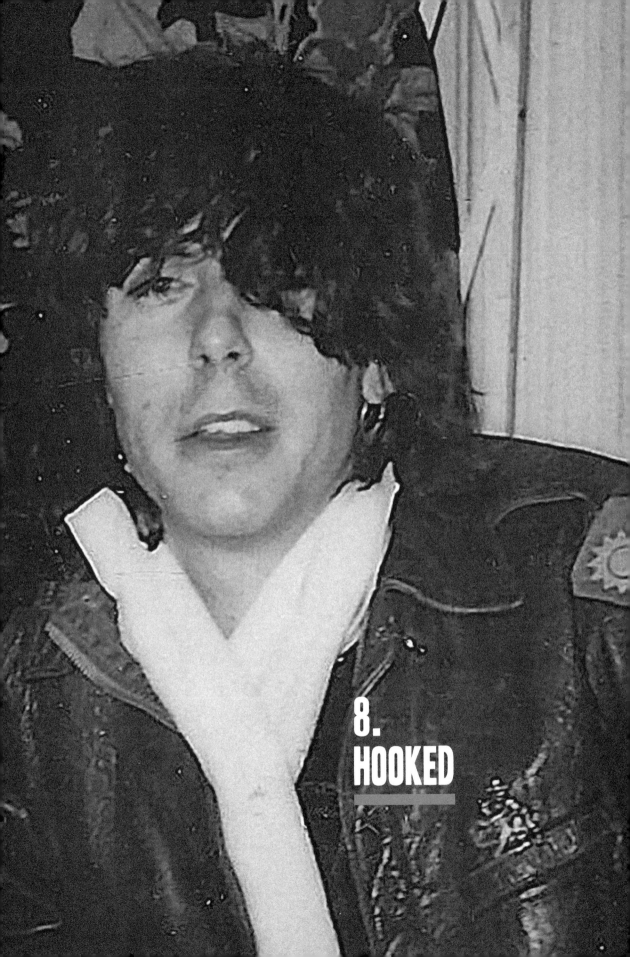

8.
HOOKED

It's late and I'm standing inside when Johnny Thunders blows thru
the door with Chrissie Hynde. She's got on the same red leather motorcycle jacket she's wearing on the cover of the Pretenders' first
album. It looks authentic, a little rough around the edges, and so
does she.

They just left Max's where they must have had a good time because it's hard to tell if either of them knows or cares where
they've landed. They head for the downstairs bar, then wander upstairs, and stumble back down. Fifteen minutes and they're outside
getting a cab. It's a quick visit, short and sweet, and no one gets
in any trouble.

The security guys are used to Johnny's brand of slurred and rag-
ged charm but Chrissie's *get out of my fucking way* attitude is harder to swallow. I don't care either way. I like her voice, I like the
red leather jacket and I want to see the band.

The Pretenders were in town for a few East Coast gigs before heading off on a six-week tour. New York City would have to wait. DJ David was already playing the self-titled debut album, and "Brass in Pocket" and "Mystery Achievement" were dance floor favorites. "Precious," Chrissie's up-tempo, in-your-face Cleveland dream, came fully loaded with the unforgettable "Fuck off." The band's first single, "Stop Your Sobbing," had a B-side called "The Wait," a song Kate Simon describes as "fucking brilliant." That's a lot of fuck for one album.

The sound was big; Pete Farndon's bass and Martin Chambers' drums were the bedrock and the beat. When Jim Honeyman-Scott's guitar let loose and Chrissie started singing, there was nothing like it. I still hadn't heard the Pretenders live, but I already knew.

I think I know it all but still don't see what's coming. I've got a few dime bags of dope tucked down the side of my Marlboro box and I'm headed for Lynette's on Bank Street in the West Village. Her roommate is away; the roommate's pet monkey isn't home. Ivan Kral, Lynette's longtime on again-off again boyfriend, has been on the road forever, but Herman, their longhaired cat, is still there. I like Herman but my allergies don't, and my eyes turn bloodshot whenever I walk into the apartment. Fortunately, it's nothing a few lines of dope won't fix.

It's early evening and there's no plan; we smoke a joint when I arrive but I keep quiet about the dimes. Lynette's got a friend coming over and he's already on the way. She spins positive, tells me I'll love him but I have no idea.

The doorbell rings and a minute later, Pete Farndon of the Pretenders walks in. I recognize him from the album cover and Lynette introduces us. It's completely different from the previous night's encounter with Chrissie at the club, and in no time the three of us are getting on like old friends. Pete's open, easygoing and beautiful, and he comes off a real gentleman. I respond to all of it and I'm hooked. It's the beginning of a friendship that lasts a little over three years.

Lynette grabs her Polaroid and shoots some photos of Pete and me wearing motorcycle jackets.

She lights up a joint but Pete isn't into it.

I take out the dope and ask Lynette, "Is it cool?"

Pete looks at me. "What did you just say?"

Lynette tells him. He laughs out loud. We all get high and the three of us walk over to One University Place.

The cold air feels good as we cut across Washington Square. We walk in and Mickey Ruskin's in his usual spot, perched on the brass rail at the end of the bar, sipping a shot of Sauza Conmemorativo. I introduce Pete to Mickey and order drinks. Mickey keeps sipping his Sauza while the three of us slip into the men's room to finish up the last dime bag. Pete's smiling, I'm leaning against the wall and Lynette's laughing. I'm not sure if it's the dope or the fact that we're crammed into a bathroom stall together but there's already a connection. It's a *we three*, *just us* moment and nobody else is in on it. A round or two of Space Invaders in the back room seals the deal, and we hang for one more drink before we split. Mickey makes a point of saying good night, and Pete can see why we love the place. We jump in a cab outside, and tell the driver "Broadway and White Street, two below Canal, left side far corner."

Fast friends, three short years. I still look at those Polaroids. Sometimes I cry.

Serious and Ridiculous

Good memories or bad, some we hold on to and some we lose—it's never our choice. Now it's 4 A.M. again. The Mudd Club's almost empty and my newest friend, found and gone. Ten minutes later I'm home alone, looking in the mirror, saying good night.

By two in the afternoon I'm up, out the door and on my way to visit Andi. She's reinvented herself as part of the Electric Lady Studio staff, having replaced manager Dory Hamilton, who retired to become Mrs. Allen Lanier. I got to know Dory at Mudd and she's a sweetheart—blonde, beautiful, a great smile and addicted to Rock 'n' Roll. Allen is a founding member of Blue Öyster Cult, a brilliant musician, and one of those people who knows everyone. We become friends, connected by Mudd, music and our eventual (if somewhat demented) love affair with late-night Mary Tyler Moore. It's the Walter Steding Constellation Theory in spades.

When Andi finishes work we head for Midtown to buy a Polaroid SX-70. We land at Thirty-second Street Camera where the girls behind the counter know me from the club. I sort of recognize them but I'm not quite sure (Saturday night bridge-and-tunnel brunettes all look the same). We chat for a minute, I buy the camera and we're all set. The girls keep talking and give me two extra packs of free film

Teri Toye and Ronnie Cutrone, peace pipe soliloquy, *TV Party*, 1980, by Bobby Grossman.

because I always let them into the club. I say thanks—but they'll still have to pay.

Andi and I cab it down to Murray and call Richard Sohl. We take Polaroids of each other looking both serious and ridiculous. By 10 P.M., we're in the back room of One University taking shots of Space Invaders, Asteroids and Joseph Kosuth's neon wall sculpture. We kill a pack of film in a few minutes and move into the dining room; we haven't eaten all day and we're both hungry. Melvone, our waitress, tells us the kitchen's backed up and suggests a bowl of Navy Bean soup but both of us are a bit unsure about a bowl of beans. Melvone's black and beautiful, a London transplant with an accent that somehow suits the words *Navy Bean*. It's hard to say no.

Ricky Sohl eventually arrives with Teri Toye just as Lincoln Scott, the dreadlocked dining room manager, slowly wanders past our table. Ricky heads straight for the back with a pocket full of quarters, intent on playing Space Invaders. Teri squeezes into our booth intent on ordering a Kamikaze. Andi and I split a bowl of soup, head back to Murray Street and roll a few joints. "The soup of the day is Navy Bean," spoken with a *Melvonian* accent, becomes our new laugh line.

By 3 A.M., we all show up at the Mudd Club. By 6 or 7 A.M., with a little luck, a line of dope and a half a Quaalude, I'll be asleep.

The Polaroid camera's the first new toy I've had in a while. For whatever reason, I rarely take it to the Mudd Club.

Andy, Gerard and Marcel

Thursday, March 20, 1980, officially one year on the job. The anniversary goes by unnoticed and unrecorded by me, my Polaroid or anyone else. I'm at the door smiling and opening the chain while Steve's busy throwing a thirty-seventh birthday celebration for poet, photographer and filmmaker Gerard Malanga. The invitation reads ABOVE THE MUDD CLUB and the party's taking place on the mysterious *third floor*. It's the same floor where I'd bring Robert Rauschenberg to meet Steve, where I snorted coke off the end of a hunting knife with the Hells Angels and where Marianne partied after her performance went up in flames. It's the private reserve of late-night adventure and the occasional freak-show sexual encounter. There's even a rack of old wedding gowns just in case someone's fetish impulse runs amok.

Besides a third-floor birthday party at Mudd, Gerard's own history is woven into the creative fabric of the avant-garde: the path that led him to White Street, as wild as it gets.

In the early '60s Gerard assisted Andy Warhol with nearly all of his large silkscreen paintings. He also appeared in many of his early films. It was some of Warhol's seminal work—masterpieces that for me defined and redefined art.

Gerard danced in leather pants and cracked a whip in Warhol's Exploding Plastic Inevitable presentation of The Velvet Underground. He continued to write, take photographs and make films of his own. Gerard met everyone, witnessed and participated in everything.

In the fall of '63, he and Andy traveled to Los Angeles for a show of Warhol's *Silver Elvis* paintings at the Ferus Gallery. At that same moment, the Pasadena Art Museum was presenting the first retrospective of Marcel Duchamp's career.

By way of fate and coincidence, Andy and Gerard met Duchamp at an outdoor café, a block from the Pasadena museum. Marcel was sitting alone eating a sandwich when Gerard and Andy approached.

Acting like teenagers who could barely contain themselves, Gerard remembers the experience leaving them "giddy and starstruck."

Every art concept and idea from the Beats to Rauschenberg, from Warhol and Pop to Punk, No Wave and graffiti bore the mark of Marcel Duchamp. The Mudd Club in some strange way was the ultimate readymade, the empty space that became something more, something else. Dark, playful and Dada in spirit, 77 White felt the hand of Duchamp if only by osmosis. Gerard Malanga shook that hand, and then ours.

Officially Gray

The spirit of Dada continues to transcend and the band Test Pattern is now officially called Gray. They're part of the new guard informed by everything and everyone from the streets of downtown to Duchamp and Pollack, Miles Davis and John Cage.

Saturday, March 22, two nights after Gerard's birthday party. Gray are doing a show at CBGB's, opening for DNA and I'm working the door on White Street. Either way we're both dealing with a tough crowd.

***

Standing outside, I thought my days on White would keep going on and that New York City would always stay the same. I thought I was ready for almost anything.

I was wrong, and what came next was bound to happen.

Jim Connelly, the odd sixty-year-old retired former something from New Jersey, was supposed to be in charge of Mudd security but he turned out to be a bad joke. He never liked me, the feeling was mutual, and somewhere between "Get out of my way" and "Fuck you" his fist landed in my face. I knew immediately—and he found out thirty minutes later—the moment he threw that punch he became a former Mudd Club employee.

Teen party girl Ellen Kinnally was standing next to me; Tina L'Hotsky was on her way down the stairs. In a show of solidarity, they took me to Steve's loft around the corner. We rang the bell and Steve buzzed us in to the *wild bachelor pad world of Doctor Mudd*.

Andy Warhol, with camera and camera-ready, Mudd 1980, by Kate Simon.

My nose had already stopped bleeding, my teeth all present and accounted for. I was pissed, the girls were yelling at Steve and he was already on the phone. He hung up and told us to wait twenty minutes before we returned. "Security" had less than ten minutes to pack up and leave.

Tina and Ellen came to my rescue, Steve took care of the situation, and several drinks took care of me. At last, the posse from New Jersey was gone and thirty minutes later, wounded but happy, I was working the door alone.

Staring down Cortlandt Alley I start thinking about the phone call that came out of nowhere and the now familiar voice that said, "Pat tells me you know everyone." I still don't—but I'm still here.

Fab 5 Freddy Brathwaite, The *Times Square Show*, 1980, by Bobby Grossman.

9.
BIRDS
AND
FLOWERS

Winter might be over but I'm still wearing the heavy coat. It's cold and it's Saturday night, the end of March 1980; Chi Chi and I are both outside and Aldo's working security. From the corner of my eye I catch a glimpse of a big blonde woman who used to work at the club. Built like a pro wrestler, with the soon-to-be-apparent arm and aim of a major league pitcher, she disappears in the crowd. A minute later, a dead pigeon comes flying at me, catches me off guard and hits me hard in the shoulder. I've never been hit with a dead bird before and nearly lose my balance. I have no idea how to react and standing in front of two hundred people doesn't help. Someone in the crowd points as the big blonde jumps in a car and drives away. It's like a scene from a rickety black-and-white newsreel, and for me the moment is a total *What the fuck?*

I look at Chi Chi, head inside and walk up the stairs. A few people know what's happened and follow me. I'm worried my overcoat's messed up and the idea of a dead pigeon makes me feel sick. I pass thru the second floor without looking at anyone, kick the metal door of the bathroom and go inside.

I'm a few drinks and half a gram past banging my head on the wall and just short of coming undone. I feel around in my pockets for a Quaalude, bite one in half and snort up two lines of coke from David the Dentist. Russian Eddie lights my cigarette and shoves another blast under my nose. Phoebe Zeeman looks at me and flicks a feather off my shoulder. They all mean well but I'm not feeling it. I still can't believe it: I've been hit with a dead bird.

Ten minutes later, Phoebe comes back with Ellen Kinnally to check how I'm doing. I've pulled it together enough to ask for a double Rémy. I want sympathy too—just don't touch me.

I throw down the brandy in one cough-inducing gulp and head downstairs. Outside everything looks gray. The pigeon's gone but the crowd's still waiting, relieved to see me but not sure what to expect. I'm pretty out of it and won't look at anyone. Chi Chi looks at me, shakes her head and laughs just a little. I grab the chain and we slowly start letting everyone in. Phoebe comes outside and tells me to come back upstairs. It's freezing and she's wearing a sleeveless cocktail dress and go-go boots. I eat the other half Quaalude and let in the last of the stragglers. I follow Phoebe upstairs. I'm not sure if I'm feeling better or not feeling anything at all. I'm not sure it matters.

Wilted Carnation

The following night starts out like any other. Streetlit on the outside, empty inside, it's the Mudd Club waiting to go another round. There's one cab and only two people waiting. It's a dark-alley, soft-focus blur right out of a Hopper painting, the address still years away, if ever, from becoming a desirable location. I'm at the door smoking the short end of a spliff less than twenty-four hours after getting hit by a dead pigeon. My pride's wounded, my coat slightly soiled.

Around midnight, two girls bring me a flower. It's a wilted carnation, likely nabbed from a coffee shop vase. It's sweet, the thought that counts, and it almost makes me feel okay. I fold up the stem and wear it sticking out of my pocket. It gets me through the night. Thank God it's Sunday.

At 4 A.M., I walk to Murray Street. I just want to lie on the floor and stare at the ceiling. The only things I want near me are cigarettes and dope. I'll close the shutters, put on Roxy Music's *Siren* and drift away. I'll get up when it's dark again. I'll take a shower, look in the mirror and try to smile.

Boggs

A day later I'm pulling myself together. I manage to distance myself from the bird debacle and appear on *Midday Live* with Bill Boggs. One of the show's producers, a semi-regular at Mudd, had asked me, DJ David, and other so-called nightlife personalities to appear and talk about the club scene. It was a good example of bad daytime television.

Coming from Boggs the word *scene* sounded more hollow than usual. He made things worse by presenting us as a bunch of weirdos running around in the middle of the night. I said very little, the others said a bit more and Bill did most of the talking. The show taped in the late afternoon and aired the following day.

I went to work that night, went home and stayed up till noon to watch *Midday Live*—a show that was *live* yesterday. The picture looked grainy on the small black-and-white TV and the segment was a nonstarter for my on-air career. Solveig, always the supportive friend, watched from her place and called up laughing, telling me it was great. Bill Boggs never visited the Mudd Club and I wasn't interviewed on television again for nearly ten years.

There was a time when my ego would've gone wild, even over a *Midday Live* appearance. Now, between the drugs and a pigeon, I'm off balance. I'm hoping warmer weather and springtime will make a difference.

I crash and wake up around 9 P.M. Dinner is two hot dogs with onions and sauerkraut from Dave's—the last bite swallowed on the front steps of Mudd. Aldo's already outside, I'm as ready as I'm going to be, and the first people to arrive say they saw me on TV. I let them in but they have to pay five dollars.

I'm still cruising along on the hot dogs when John Waters, the American trash master, writer and film director, steps out of a cab. He's friendly and polite and there's a lot about Mudd that's in sync with his humor and proud sense of perversion; for him, no doubt, a well-aimed dead bird would be a standing ovation.

Chiclets and Dos Equis

When a limo pulls up and Anita Pallenberg gets out I forget about everything else. She's wearing a white hat, white jacket and a single earring covered with diamonds. It's large, either Winston or Van Cleef, the mate probably long since missing. She mumbles something and we both walk in. Teri Toye comes over, starts whispering in Anita's earringless ear and the conversation looks about as close to *real* girl talk as these two can get. I feel left out and return to the door.

Hours later, sitting on a bench in the basement with Anita and Lynette, I'm relaxing with the help of a low-dose lude. The early departures are picking up their coats at the checkroom but nobody bothers or comes near us. Mona and Lisa, a mother-daughter team who live nearby on Duane Street, are working the coat check and Mona's sixteen-year-old son, Steven, is sitting six feet away, making out with Teri. Lynette's talking fast and laughing, and Anita's been digging around in her bag for what seems like ten minutes. I light a joint, pass it to Lynette, and everything seems as it should be. Near closing time, the basement's become a waiting room with everything happening and hiding in plain sight. Anita, still digging deep down in her bag, eventually finds what she's looking for. I'm still wondering *what,* until she turns and hands me a thin yellow box.

"You want a Chiclet?"

It's tempting, though the Chiclets look like they've been hanging out since *Barbarella* days or at best The Rolling Stones' American Tour 1972. Thinking twice, and despite the possibility of a vintage provenance, I decline.

Without much more to say I disappear thru the storage area, take the elevator to the second floor, pick up a beer at the bar, and head back down the front stairs. It's after 4 A.M. Aldo's still watching the door but there's no one outside except the people leaving. John Lydon just slipped in for an early morning visit and maybe thirty people are left upstairs. Lydon's wearing a red suit and he's hard to miss.

I wind up sliding into a booth with Damita Richter. She's all dark innocence with an angel face, a full-color cowgirl pinup tattoo on her forearm and two crooked barrettes in her chopped-up hair. She looks about twelve going on twenty. I get up and grab two beers at the bar; I make a quick reach for one more and the bartender gives me a dirty look. I want to say *fuck you* but hold back,

Damita with cowgirl tattoo, 1980, by Ebet Roberts.

saving it for another night. Damita and I head for the door, hand a beer off to Lydon and hop in a cab. Five minutes later, we're buying a six-pack of Dos Equis and a pack of Marlboros at the deli on Church Street. We hang out at 9 Murray, playing records and lying on the living room floor with the TV on. It's dark outside and the shutters are closed tight. Damita crashes at my place for the next few days and disappears for the next few weeks. It seems kind of sad, makes me feel kind of lucky.

I survive another morning of beer and cigarettes for breakfast. I catch some sleep and paint for a few hours. The weeks seem more and more like one long night and it's beginning to feel as though I've been staring down Cortlandt Alley forever. At times I can't even tell if I'm stoned, whether the drugs are even working. The joyful swirl of Jack Daniels and LSD is nearly a decade past, a joint or cigarette now just a prop. Cocaine's become the paralytic, jaw-clenching mindfuck; Quaaludes are a sleepwalk minus the dream. Alcohol's the free and easy default while heroin smoothes all rough edges. I'm not sure if I'm confused or lost but happiness is becoming hard to measure. I avoid trying, roll another joint, and keep showing up.

Another nighttime day and the crowd out front looks the same; at least the weather's improving. The metal steps seem softer underfoot and the chain feels lighter in my hand. The up and down feelings come and go. Maybe spring is really here.

***

Sometime before last call, Nancy Miller and her dog Turu stepped outside for a walk. She and her roommate, Andrew Earl, shared the fifth floor directly below Ross Bleckner and regularly offered me safe haven. While Nancy fearlessly navigated the perils of living above Mudd, Andrew seemed indifferent, only occasionally coming downstairs for a drink. Either way, it had to have been a challenge.

Today Nancy's forever amused by the *lived upstairs from Mudd Club* experience. Funny but difficult to imagine—the miracle being she survived. Ross, however, had no hesitation telling me he "hated it."

Shöx Lumania

March was slowly becoming April. The weather kept getting warmer and I kept trying to figure out what to wear. When Stephanie Richardson walked into the club and spotted a guy wearing a general's uniform and a crazy hat she felt inspired and did what she had to do.

The guy in the uniform was Lari Shöx, and he'd just started a band called Shöx Lumania. Stephanie told him she'd "love to see it" and Lari told her, "See it? You can be in it." With Lari on vocals and Stephanie reimagining "Yoko at her worst," their sound could peel paint off the walls and get people dancing at the same time. Between the synthesizers, no guitars and composer Man Parrish's music, the Lumanians and their crazy headgear were a hit.

The band played all over town, but for Stephanie, "A show at the Mudd Club was like playing for a roomful of friends—it was home." That sentiment never got old.

Some weeks later, I stood by the bar and watched Shöx Lumania onstage. I moved onto the dance floor and couldn't stop laughing at the odd apparatus-like stagewear attached to Stephanie's head. Abbijane came up behind me, gave me a shove and we started dancing. That's when Diane showed up looking for Lynette.

Number One

I met the artist Diane Dupuis at Mudd. Adventurous to a fault, she picked up *Punk Magazine* issue #1 in January 1976 and entered the trivia contest on the back cover. Despite high hopes, Diane needed more than a contest win to keep things going so she searched the *Village Voice* classifieds for work. She dialed a number cold and, oddly enough, *Punk Magazine* answered. Diane mentioned her participation in the trivia contest along with the fact that she was a girl, both of which appealed to cofounder John Holmstrom. She won the contest, got the job and established a brief but brave tenure at *Punk*.

In 1978, she left for London, hooked up with Lynette Bean and ran around chasing British rockers—and occasionally, the music. In December '79 she returned to New York, walked thru the doors of the Mudd Club and headed for the dance floor. When springtime rolled around she was still dancing and by some miracle or just plain luck, so was I.

***

Whether we were connected by the dance floor, the music we loved or the bands we chased around, the Lene Lovich show on White Street was a night that brought everyone together. A quick stop on a mini-tour in support of her second album, *Flex*, the set list included some of the material I loved from *Stateless*.

The Mudd Club, with its loose schedule of live music, was the perfect venue for a band with a night off. A small poster in the entryway went up two or three days before the show and word of mouth did the rest. I called my friends Alex Rozum and Phyllis Teitelman and told them to come by. They were big fans of Lene, and Phyllis was a big fan of crazy on White Street.

I arrived after the sound check and only knew Lene from the records. The dressing room was set up on the *off limits* third floor and the band showed up just before midnight. Lene and Les Chappell, her partner and lead guitarist, arrived a short time later. They were more freak than beautiful—all business, no smiles and barely acknowledged anyone. I took them upstairs and they didn't say a word. I rolled my eyes for my own benefit, walked back down and went outside. Something told me, this was going to be good.

The small but unnecessary guest list was a scribble of music-biz types and downtown rock writers; the rest of the crowd was a strange brew of Lovich fans and club regulars. Steve was outside "helping" and I was grabbing the people I knew when Solveig arrived, adding a touch of glamour to the evening. We stepped inside, she ordered a Stoli rocks and both of us disappeared into the basement. Ten minutes later the band was onstage. Lene was singing "Bird Song."

Solveig and I were still downstairs when the band finished "Say When." The strange beat of "Lucky Number" started coming through the floor and Lene's bizarre vocal acrobatics brought us back upstairs. I looked at Solveig, said "Let's go" as we cut our way into the wall-to-wall wave of bobbing heads.

By midset, Lene was spinning around in front of the microphone. Her yelps, bleats and bird noises were flying around the room and her bugged-out eyeballs, swinging pigtails and braided buns were all just part of the show. Who knows what she was like at home—but if you came to see her live, this was what you were here for.

After half a dozen songs, I had to get back to the door. The band's cover of the Tommy James classic "I Think We're Alone Now" was the kick I needed to ditch Solveig, squeeze past the bar and head outside. The street was all but deserted except for the cabbies. Alone without the crowd felt good and Lene and Les must have felt the same way; when the show was over they were gone.

After 3 A.M., but it feels early. "Lucky Number" is still bouncing around in my head. The first floor's crowded though danceable, and I just made out with someone but have no idea who. Outside, only two sad-looking people are hanging around—three, if you count the person passed out on the hood of a taxi. I ask the driver, "What gives?" and he tells me the guy's waiting for his friend. I duck back inside to put my skills to better use and by 6 A.M. daylight I was home, working in my studio. Thursday came and went without notice and by the weekend I was ready for whatever it had to offer.

***

Friday is one of those nights where nothing and everything is going on. The place is crowded by midnight and Sylvia Miles is at the bar chatting with Steve. A fast talker with a self-described "elephantine" memory, she refers to Steve as *Stephen*. I can't imagine the topic or depth of their conversation.

Marcia Resnick drifts past me and I tag along. We turn the corner and start walking upstairs. Howie Pyro and Siouxsie Sioux are steps ahead of us and Hal Ludacer and Russian Mia stand in a cloud of smoke on the landing.

Billy Idol comes out of the second floor and offers a "Hey mate."

I give him a "Hey" back. "You want a drink?"

The slurred response: "Sure."

It doesn't take much. Everybody's easy. Bryan Ferry is upstairs hanging out with Henry Edwards, the failed screenwriter partially responsible for the painful 1978 film version of *Sgt. Pepper's Lonely Hearts Club Band*. Bryan's wearing a suit and looks like what you expect Bryan Ferry to look like. I walk over, introduce myself and remind him that we met at the Carlyle Hotel just over a year ago. He's polite but it's doubtful he has any memory of the encounter.

Ferry's a huge star and both his solo work and Roxy Music can tear up the dance floor—his cover of Wilbert Harrison's 1962 single "Let's Stick Together" blows the place apart. His presence causes a bit of a buzz on the second floor but everyone's either too cool or too stoned to make a fuss. He never sits down and just seems to loiter a bit with a drink in his hand near one of the booths. Oddly enough, *he* fits right in.

On the other end of what's happening is the kid selling Tuinals in the bathroom. It's like high school all over again, except for the bar filled with drunken artists, rock stars and Mudd Club regulars. The kid looks bridge-and-tunnel, Queens, maybe, or even New Hyde Park, but nobody knows him and he's too sketchy, even for a teenage drug dealer. I'm not the one who let him in so I head downstairs and ask security to toss him. It's a pretty good night for a Friday.

There's a crowd six deep standing around the front steps. Delphine Blue comes around the side and I open the chain. She's already dreaming about a possible job at the new place on East Eleventh. A minute later, Mary Lou Green gets out of a cab with "Little" Debi Mazar and asks if I've seen Steve. I step inside for a soda and John Cale comes over, asking the same question. I tell him yes, about an hour ago, talking with Sylvia Miles; he counters with a rude but funny non sequitur. Everybody's asking but Steve is nowhere to be seen. I'm not finding what I'm looking for either, so I ditch the soda, order a drink and go back out.

Dylan McDermott's walking down White Street, headed toward the door. He'll hang and talk but never asks for a drink. He walks in at the same moment French Chris, stoned, beautiful and hard to resist (right down to the lure of a prison tattoo), shamelessly asks if I'll get him a Martell. I tell him we have Rémy or Hennessey.

Soon-to-be-legendary vocalist Dolette McDonald arrives, offers to pay for a group of friends, and drops a wad of cash on the steps. I reach down and hand it back to her but she's confused as to where it came from. I tell her, "it's YOURS" and send them in for free. Finally, Lynette arrives with Peter Davies, the one- or two-time Iggy tour manager. The three of us walk upstairs and head straight for the bar. The drinks are on the house and Peter leaves the bartender five dollars, a surprisingly good tip.

The three of us get ready to make a move when Anita P. pulls me aside. She's with a young man I've never seen before and wants to know where Steve is. It's starting to feel more like two days than two hours since *Stephen* and Sylvia were at the bar. Anita and her new friend leave without getting an answer.

At last the coast is clear and Peter and Lynette walk with me to the elevator. I tug on the cable and we go for a ride. Five minutes and half a gram later, I drop them off and take the elevator down to the basement. I sit alone for a minute, collect myself and catch my breath. I dump another pile of coke on my fist and just stare at it. A moment later, I'm asking for a drink at the first-floor bar, trying hard to speak thru a frozen smile. DJ David's got the whole room spinning and Abbijane's dancing with her childhood friend, Julie Glantz. Red Head Heather, Diane Dupuis and Jackie Shapiro, a cute uptown delinquent, are all awhirl, caught up in some sort of neo-Twist gyration. There's a bit of open floor around them, and when anyone gets too close Abbi's hand goes up with a *stop right there* palm to the face. It's a classic move and when I look over at David we both start laughing. Giving up on any attempt to speak, I move onto the floor and dive in.

I survive the dance—and another night at the door. Home before the morning rush, I finish the last lines of coke and wonder why I can't sleep. Sometimes I wonder what the fuck I'm doing; other times I tell myself, "I'm fine." There are still moments when I see myself becoming a good painter. Maybe what I'm doing—whether it's the Mudd Club or the drugs—is just a phase; twenty-six, running with a fast crowd in the fast lane and dodging bullets. Too much coke, then three or four drinks to avoid a tooth-grinding freeze that even a bag of Poison or Doctor Nova can't melt away. Then there's the shifting reality of standing on the steps of 77 White, facing an anonymous crowd—and feeling or not feeling alone.

Word's Out

One night the following week, I look over at Steve. He's not talking but keeps asking me if I've heard anything. I tell him the only thing I've heard is, "it's happening."

Word's out that Jerry Brandt's new club on East Eleventh Street is opening in May. From what I can tell it'll be a place to go first, before Mudd, to see a band, then head for White Street around 1 or 2 A.M. It's what everyone does anyway.

The next *word*, DJ Justin Strauss is leaving Mudd for East Eleventh but I have no idea if it's true. Abbijane's his best friend so she must know, and if she knows, DJ David knows. I like Justin and I'll miss him, but I'll see him at the new place.

I'm ready to head outside when David cues up Elvis Costello's "Watching the Detectives." It's loud and heavy and the floor's shaking. I turn around and start dancing.

Justin might be leaving—but the dance floor at Mudd is unstoppable.

The Colombians

For better and for worse, I was unstoppable too. When I met the Colombians on the second floor of the club, things quickly went beyond anywhere I'd been before. Friday night was turning Saturday and it was still dark when we departed White Street. I believed I knew what I was getting myself into.

We arrived at the loft, I put on some music, and the three of us finished off an eighth of an ounce of coke. I couldn't move; my mind and body disconnected.

The Colombians made themselves at home and laid their gun on the table. They decided they wanted one of my paintings and insisted we make a trade. I managed to stand up, figured out how to speak and rolled up a large painting on paper that was hanging on the wall. We took a cab to an apartment on East Seventh Street along the south side of Tompkins Square Park and made a seven o'clock swap for nearly two ounces of golf-ball-sized rocks of cocaine. We got back to Murray Street around 8 A.M. and opened a bottle of Rémy I had stashed under the sink. I spilled the bag of rocks on the kitchen table and just stood there, trying to breathe. I'd never seen anything like it.

I called Solveig and told her, "You have to get down here right away, you won't believe this." She called the garage, got in her car, came right down and couldn't believe.

A frozen dream lasting several sleepless days—and as many bottles of Rémy Martin—started to play itself out. I wanted to fuck the Colombians but they wanted to fuck Solveig: aside from the coke, a lose-lose situation. Together we wore them down and the Colombians left by early afternoon. The rocks stuck around for a few weeks. Solveig and I cleaned my studio, rehung some paintings, swept the floors and rearranged furniture. The painting that left Murray Street began a new life on East Seventh, never to be seen again.

Monkey in the Bedroom

Eight hours later, I was back at the Mudd Club. The door was busy but I could barely speak. The Colombians came by to drink and find girls who'd fuck for cocaine. Lynette showed up, came home with me after work, and we dove deeper into the frozen. We left my place around noon and cabbed it to her apartment on Bank Street. By the time we got there, my head was pounding, my nose was bleeding and there was a caged monkey in the bedroom. I was wide-eyed and crazy but the monkey was real. We smoked a joint and tried to relax but I couldn't shut my eyes. Lynette pulled the curtains on the daytime night and I drifted without sleep.

Within two or three hours, the noise in my head finally stopped. The monkey stayed in its cage and never made a sound. I could hear myself breathing.

Getting up, nearly 10 P.M., I pulled myself together. I walked from Bank Street to One University Place and sat in a booth with Patti D'Arbanville and a good-looking, blond Canadian hockey jock.

I didn't know Patti but I knew she grew up in Greenwich Village and started hanging out on Bleecker Street when she was either twelve or thirteen. She appeared in Andy Warhol's *Flesh* when she was barely legal; her film and modeling career and relationship with Cat Stevens were all part of the D'Arbanville mystique. We hung out for an hour or two and left One U after midnight. We stopped by Murray Street, sat around the kitchen table and broke out the rocks. We got thirsty and walked up Broadway to the Mudd Club. Steve was happy to meet Patti and she was happy to be back in New York. Singer-songwriter Elliott Murphy rushed over and gave her a kiss. Lynne Robinson leaned over and whispered, "Oh God, she's a fucking legend." I was just happy that my nose stopped bleeding.

The rocks were so pure and hard, I shot one across the room trying to crush it with a spoon. My friend James snorted up a pile and had to lie down on the couch, panicked and wiped out by a mini-stroke or mild heart attack. His girlfriend, Lisa, iced his neck and forehead while I lit a cigarette and did another line. An hour later, we headed for White Street.

I knew cocaine was a losing game but I kept playing. I froze more than a few brain cells, burned a million more and sold a piece of my soul along with that painting. Trapped in some sort of holding pattern, I felt like I was running in circles and still had no clue. I was writing off the wreckage as a minor scratch-and-dent, unable or too distracted to look at myself. I believed that drugs and drinking and even sex were all part of the creative process. Surrounded by visionaries fueled by excess, I ignored the bodies on the side of the road. I wanted to be happy and successful but was unwilling to make even the slightest change.

No Food in Her Braces

Assuming everything would remain the same or get better on its own, I couldn't see the possibilities of tomorrow. Blinders on, I never looked past *tonight*. I figured I'd keep working at the Mudd Club, keep painting and at some point sell my paintings for dollars instead of ounces or grams. At some point I'd tire of cocaine and get bored with heroin. I never considered that a hot dog and a subway token would ever cost more than fifty cents. I was dreaming.

Then, on April Fools' Day 1980, New York City's transit workers walked off the job and everyone quickly realized it wasn't a prank. I couldn't imagine what kind of grievance anyone would have driving a bus or working in the subway, but it seemed that some people were never happy. Living nine blocks from the Mudd Club, the dispute for me was a minor inconvenience, but the first transit strike since 1966 affected nearly everyone else. For Jackie Shapiro it was panic on the Upper East Side.

Jackie usually had her nightly routine figured out. "No food in her braces" was rule number one. Number two was to make sure she had her keys, lipstick and ten dollars tucked in a Marlboro box. Avoid using Mudd Club toilets was number three. She played it by the book until the transit strike threw everything out the window. She had to get to the Mudd Club but if she wanted to eat at Dave's, Wo Hop or the Kiev, her budget wouldn't cover a taxi.

Jackie took a few deep breaths and with careful consideration decided the only solution was to hitchhike down Second Avenue. Hoping for the best, she hooked up with her friend Karen and stuck out her thumb. In a scene right out of a *Texas Chainsaw Massacre* sequel, a freak with what Jackie called a "full coverage, religious icon dashboard" pulled over. Karen jumped in back and Jackie sat up front talking, trying to keep the "creepy vibe" in check. In what amounted to a Mudd miracle, their new friend kept the chainsaw in the trunk and drove them all the way to White Street. The strike ended April 11, its effect on club attendance minimal. Jackie survived, stuck to her budget and never missed a night.

I never knew what the transit workers were so upset about but was happy it all worked out. I never stopped to consider that New York City and the way I was living might change, and get very expensive. *Gentrify* and *yuppify* were soon to become dangerous, dirty words; Bohemia, just another body tossed to the side of the road.

Ecstatic Stigmatic

Two nights later I put away the cynicism and lost the sarcasm. The news was bad and the circumstances unbelievable. Despite a lack of detail, I kept hearing the story all night long.

On April 12, 1980, Mirielle Cervenka was killed in a car accident in Los Angeles. The accident was a freak hit-and-run. She died instantly, while the others involved were barely injured. Mirielle was the sister of Exene Cervenka, the singer from the band X; and she was married to Gordon Stevenson, formerly with Lydia Lunch's band, Teenage Jesus and the Jerks. Mirielle, an artist and No Wave pioneer, lived with Gordon near White Street and hung out at the Mudd Club. The news spread quickly; the dance floor seemed to pause for a minute.

Mirielle was in L.A. for the premiere of *Ecstatic Stigmatic*. Gordon made the film and she was the star. The movie explored themes of religious fanaticism and insanity with enough blood and *Gotharific* imagery to make it entertaining. The supporting cast, seemingly drawn from a Mudd Club pool, included voluptuous vocalist and performer Brenda Bergman and No Wave New York associate Arto Lindsay. (Mirielle and Gordon, along with artist-musician Robin Crutchfield, were all founding members of Lindsay's band DNA.)

Posters for *Ecstatic Stigmatic* covered the neighborhood and lined Cortlandt Alley. The movie's premiere went on as scheduled—April 14 in Hollywood.

I can still see Gordon and Mirielle walking up to the door; I can picture where they stood and I remember opening the chain. Then I remember hearing the awful news.

Before long Gordon returned to New York and came back to the club several times. His own death a few years later signaled a community on the verge of devastation, battling an enemy no one could comprehend. Cookie Mueller was Gordon's friend and she wrote about him. That's all I recall.

The Walter Steding Theory would consider it all part of another constellation, one that burned bright before spinning out of control. I didn't know Mirielle or Gordon well. I've never seen the entire movie.

Roommates

The loft on Murray Street was spinning too, but I managed to hang on. The nights went on for days, and the brain cells kept burning. Teri had moved uptown with Ricky Sohl and Wayne was gone nearly six months. Lynette's friend Peter Davies started crashing at the loft, unofficially taking up residence.

One night when Steve Mass was outside I introduced Peter as my new roommate.

"Everybody lives at your place," said Steve.

"Almost everybody."

Peter easily adapted to the never-ending party and the odd hours of a passed-out doze masquerading as sleep. There were no house rules, no privacy and no commitment. The arrangement lasted a month until Peter spiraled off on a downhill run, searching for a place of his own. Gary and I weren't alone for long.

Musician and Lounge Lizard Steve Piccolo left East Thirteenth Street around the same time the *other* bedroom at Murray opened up. We had a lot of the same friends, a high tolerance for crazy and shared many of the same interests. The rent, if you paid it, was cheap, and you could walk to the Mudd Club in less than ten minutes. The setup was perfect and Steve moved in. The wheel kept on spinning and nothing seemed to change: I was still working five nights a week, still running in and out of One University, still chasing something I've never been sure of.

No Jeans

Walking up Broadway on my way to work I'm able to talk to myself, ask hard questions, but only answer the ones I choose. I'm able to breathe even while smoking a cigarette. Between two roommates at home and working with a clubful of more than half strange, this is the only time I'm ever really alone. Standing outside Mudd saying *yes* or *no* is still hard work but the warm nights make things easier. My new uniform is a light-green windbreaker, some beat-up Levis and a pair of pointy, tan suede cowboy boots. My hair's getting longer and I'm wearing a paisley bandanna tied around my neck. The entire look is a retread nod to college life, yet far removed from dropping acid and catching the Dead or Hot Tuna at the Waterbury Palace.

I tell the crowd outside "No jeans" and if anyone points at me I tell them, "Mine don't count." I make some exceptions and even allow an occasional denim-clad friend in for free. If Steve asks how that person got in, I throw one of the security guys under the bus.

The exception I take responsibility for are two handsome South Americans dressed in white shirts, good shoes and tight-fitting jeans. They shake my hand with a folded-up fifty, never stop to talk and always pay the cover. I usually take a break after they arrive, unfold the bill and spend a long moment admiring the half-gram inside. It's the good stuff, flaky and golden with that mother-of-pearl shimmer: Bolivian cocaine before it's been stepped on.

I pull a straw out of my Marlboro box, do some lines and fly back up the stairs. I've become a pro when it comes to squeezing thru the crowd and I'm at the door in thirty seconds. No *excuse me*, no wasted time. If I stop for a drink, the trip takes a full minute.

Tonight I make it back outside just in time—I turn around and there he is. I'm not sure if he arrived in a cab or just came walking down White Street, but despite the pedigree and reputation, Lou Reed is easy. He steps up to the chain, I say "Hi" and he walks in. Ten minutes later, I walk inside to check on him, and he's at the bar alone. Thirty minutes later, he's gone. "Sweet Jane"—the live *Rock 'n' Roll Animal* version—always a Mudd Club favorite. Nobody cared that Lou Reed was wearing jeans.

I'm back watching the crowd when my friend Edward stumbles up to the door. He's with three others, including Frank Schroeder, an artist and Mudd regular who lives in the neighborhood. It's a party of four guys and they're a little drunk, but the fact that I like Edward works in their favor. Two go in for free, two pay.

A few minutes later, Edward's outside again, standing next to me, stoned and beautiful. It's his birthday and he might be turning eighteen. I look around, check the crowd once more, and ask a pretty girl, "How many?" She points to the pretty boy next to her and I say, "Okay." I spot longtime Mickey Ruskin employee Big Ron Beckner getting out of a cab with Linda Yablonsky, whose own *Story of Junk* is still a few years away. I send them thru and let in a dozen more people just to loosen things up.

It's getting late when Edward and I make a run for the basement. I have a little dope, we both have some coke and it takes thirty seconds to get downstairs. Edward dumps two white piles on my fist and I spill the dope on top of mine. We lean in and blast off, look at each other and float away. I have no idea if we're sitting or standing. For a minute I'm not even sure where we are.

When I finally snap out of it, we're both leaning against the basement wall sweating, and a little worse for wear. I light a cigarette, grab Edward's beer and finish it. We take the elevator to the second floor, Edward finds his friends and I slowly make my way downstairs.

I pass Siouxsie Sioux on the way but have no idea when she arrived. I loved the first record and jumped around to "Hong Kong Garden" when it was released two years ago. "Happy House" is her latest single but it hardly looks like she lives there. I say hello and smile—she doesn't and keeps walking. It's time I get back to the door.

Outside a few people call my name. It's late and if they're a little pretty and only a little drunk I'll send them in two at a time. I don't know any of them so they'll all pay.

Talk of the Town

I'm not sure how everyone managed to go out and spend money or where the money came from. New clubs were getting ready to open and White Street wasn't slowing down (even though the U.S. economy was in the toilet). Unemployment was high at nearly seven percent and a recession, deeper than anyone anticipated, was in the forecast. Conflicts in the Middle East were only part of the problem and Democrats were surely to blame for everything else. Meanwhile Republicans claimed to have better ideas (like tax cuts and pandering to the rich) but were intent on keeping those ideas secret. Their only non-secret: zombie Ron was getting ready to run—again. Affairs of the state were dire.

Given the nightmare scenario, I was employed, had a nice place to live, and despite my obsession with death drugs and random sex partners, I was healthy. Besides all that, the Pretenders were finishing up their first U.S. tour—ten dates, big cities—and Pete Farndon periodically would call from the road. Last I heard, they were in St. Louis, had time off, and were headed this way.

The band's show on Saturday, May 3, at New York City's Palladium was their last stop, and they were staying at "The Gramercy." When Pete got to town on April 29, he had time on his hands and money in his pocket. We ate and drank at One University, hung at the Mudd Club, shopped at Fiorucci and visited Andi at Electric Lady. I had to work but didn't let the Pretenders get in the way of my job; I tried to make them part of it.

When Saturday rolled around I met up with Pete and went to the sound check at 3 P.M. I hadn't heard the band live until that moment but it was something worth waiting for: the Pretenders' sound was big and loud, and Chrissie's voice was her own. They tore it up for thirty minutes, the band went back to the hotel and I went home to rest. The Necessaries, with Ernie Brooks and Jesse Chamberlain, were opening the show at 8, but I wasn't sure I could get there that early. I arrived with Pete around 9.

The Pretenders opened slow and heavy with "Space Invader," an instrumental written by Farndon. From there they barreled into "The Wait" and followed up with a set that included a cover of Ray Davies' "I Go to Sleep" and a beautiful new song called "Talk of the Town."

I went backstage when the show was over, said *see you later*, and cabbed it to White Street. Chrissie went off to Kate Simon's and the boys showed up at the Mudd Club late. The next day they were gone.

Pete Farndon was a sweet guy and we had a strange connection: trust was part of it, drugs another. It's always been hard to figure what makes a friend.

The Original Danceteria

Even *standing* at the door I was always running, and after fourteen months on the job it was full speed ahead. The Mudd Club was on a different run and never had to compete with anything except itself. Steve might've seen things differently.

By the end of April 1980, nearly six months after the momentary clusterfuck that was Pravda, word was out that Jim Fouratt and Rudolf Piper were ready to open a place called Danceteria. By the first week of May, that rumor became fact, adding to the already Ritz-induced paranoia that was driving Steve crazy.

Danceteria would be a weekend-mostly affair, opening late and staying open. Bands might play at 2 or 4 A.M., still onstage when the sun came up. For Jim, the fearless revolutionary who stood his ground at Stonewall, it was a semi-logical next move. For Rudolf, it was a big-time second shot. Together they were ready to pull off a huge illegal club operation, extending into the after-hours and serving liquor without a license.

Jim Fouratt was already lining up a unique roster of local and regional bands along with new faces from the West Coast and Europe. Mudd Club regular Haoui Montaug, who worked with Jim at Hurrah, was set to do the door. My friend Iolo Carew, whom I met at Sunny's Mac-Dougal Street pot and subway slug emporium, was hired as a manager, with Sean Cassette and DJ Mark Kamins switch-hitting on the turntables. Future art stars Keith Haring and David Wojnarowicz rounded out the crew of busboys, bartenders and checkroom attendants.

Rudolf was the master of design: contributing the visual details and cleaning up the edges, adding the polka dots and a bit of finesse. His uncanny sex appeal and oddly accented charm was set to do the rest.

For the past week Steve appeared more than anxious, and I was outside listening to every bit of news. Danceteria was almost ready and summer 1980 was little more than a month away. Jim kept showing up on White Street but I hadn't seen Rudolf for a while. I was holding my own at the door but tension was building and something had to give.

That's when Steve pulled me aside and told me Jim Fouratt was no longer allowed inside the Mudd Club. He might have mentioned Rudolf too but by that time my head was spinning and my eyes glazed over. I'm not sure if it was paranoia or spite, whether Mudd secrets and ideas were at risk or not; I did as I was told—and as usual, tried to play both sides.

Going one-on-one with Jim, delivering a "You can't come in," threw me off and I was clearly rattled. It was no flying dead bird to the shoulder, but it *was* a crack in the armor.

Fouratt may have been sympathetic but I felt like shit. After he left, I picked up my beer, went downstairs and did more cocaine. At closing time, I hooked up with the Funhouse bouncer and stayed out till noon. I slept, went back to work and let almost everyone in. Danceteria's opening was less than a week away and I was sure I'd never see the inside. In the meantime, White Street was doing its best to keep everyone guessing.

What You Is

Thursday, May 8, promises to be wild even by Mudd Club standards. The joint's filling up and Jane Friedman's hanging with me on the front steps. About two dozen people are waiting and I'm working alone, letting in a few at a time. A cab pulls up, Tina L'Hotsky gets out with Willoughby Sharp; Gary gets out of another cab with Mary Lou Green. Lynette arrives alone, starts talking, loses her train of thought and goes in. Steve sticks his head out the door, looks around at no one in particular and doesn't say a word. I look at Jane; we both smile. A minute later, I step inside, use the phone in the entryway and call Alice. Judy Nylon answers and I tell her to come down early. A minute later, two bridge-and-tunnel kids walk up to the chain, ask what's happening and I tell them Frank Zappa's going on around 1 A.M. They look at each other, then back at me and say, "No, really?" They're a little nerdy but kind of cute so I send them in. They'll either get eaten alive or be back tomorrow night for more. It's early and I'm already having fun.

Frank Zappa always loved coming to the Mudd Club. At the Nova Convention held at Irving Plaza in December 1978, he read "The Talking Asshole" from William Burroughs' *Naked Lunch*. He was a hit. The after-party at Mudd gave Frank his introduction and connection to White Street.

I always loved opening the chain and saying, "Hi Frank," and he liked hanging out at the DJ booth end of the bar, taking it all in. He wrote a song called "Mudd Club" that appeared on his 1981 release *You Are What You Is*. The club had the same free-for-all vibe and orchestral chaos that I picked up in his music and for a while "Mudd Club" was a staple of his live show. When he was asked about Mudd he responded, "It's funny, I don't know whether the place is happening or not, but I like it and I wanted to play there."

An hour later, the band's onstage. Zappa's guitar is singing a song called "Chunga's Revenge" and the sound pulls me inside. It's one of those moments so good it makes you laugh.

Frank finished his set around 2 A.M. Jerry Brandt breezed in, handed me an invitation to the opening of The Ritz on East Eleventh Street, looked around for Steve and left a minute later. The big party's Tuesday, May 13, just five days away, and the club officially opens the following night. I'll be working on White Street but I'll try and stop by.

Late-Night Outpost

I was still lost in Zappaland when Danceteria opened Friday, May 9, along an anonymous stretch of West Thirty-seventh Street between Seventh and Eighth Avenues. I worked at the Mudd Club till 4:30 and grabbed a cab to midtown. Despite being bookended by Madison Square Garden and Times Square, the Garment District at night was even darker and more desolate than White Street. While Danceteria wasn't much to look at from the outside, inside was different. There appeared to be a lot going on but like any other packed opening night it was hard to tell. I wandered upstairs, sat down on an old sofa and started watching TV.

Ahead-of-the-curve video artists and pioneers Pat Ivers and Emily Armstrong used a $300 budget to set up a one-night Video Lounge installation on the club's mezzanine. Two or three thrift-shop coffee tables and couches, along with several old television consoles to house the video monitors (they used plexiglass on top to keep the monitors safe from cocaine residue and spilled drinks), and it was ready. Poet and writer Max Blagg, tending the Video Lounge bar, was the final, perfect touch. The popular spot outlived the one-night installation and remained open indefinitely; Pat and Emily's videos featuring performances by everyone from the Dead Boys to Iggy Pop and the Cramps became a document of the time.

Over the course of a few short months, everyone from R.E.M. to Tito Puente, Jayne County, Sun Ra and Suicide graced the stage. The Video Lounge became the future. The basement dance floor: dark, sweaty and lost in time.

Danceteria was the latest semi-outlaw, totally illegal, all-night nightclub, and for one summer in the city, was a perfect after-Mudd outpost. I kept going back and despite Steve's anti-Danceteria edict, I never had a problem getting in. For me, it became somewhere else to run to—another place to try and find what eluded me. I just needed to try harder, find a path forward and find comfort identifying as *me*.

The Ritz

Danceteria's Video Lounge recalled a do-it-yourself ethos at work. From the early days of the Ramones and *Punk Magazine* to a Rock 'n' Roll Funeral at the Mudd Club, everything started out as a crazy dream, and in a sense remained just that. When I moved into a loft on Murray Street with no kitchen, no shower and no hot water, I took that crazy DIY spirit to heart.

Photographer Bob Gruen recalls how "monetary gain was never part of the equation" at least within the creative walls of downtown. Danceteria might have stretched the neighborhood boundaries but it was all the same. People were making music and art, film and fashion because it was what they loved to do—and usually fun (even for those No Wave warriors). Gruen remembers how "five or ten bucks in your pocket meant you had money"—and not every endeavor had dollar signs attached. It's a reflection of Judy Nylon's idea that "we lived out of each other's pockets" and we often lived well. Even Diego said, when it came to White Street, "it was never about the money," and it's true; the Mudd Club opened with little to no regard for commercial success. Then the bills rolled in, free drinks were handed out freely and cocaine became a work-related expense.

When the eighties arrived money began speaking with a louder voice and there was no way to turn down the volume. The Ritz never had a connection to *do-it-yourself* but for a time managed to find a degree of balance on the cusp of *monetary gain* and a love of music for its own sake. Jerry Brandt ran a tight ship and, to his credit, never forgot where he came from.

The soon-to-be former Mudd Club DJ Justin Strauss was ready to start spinning at The Ritz. He'd never forget White Street but with three turntables and a DJ booth the size of a small apartment, this new move was sure to be a great gig. Justin's a star but can't do it alone, and radio DJ Delphine Blue already has a hungry eye on those turntables.

Opening night, there's a mob outside on East Eleventh. A blonde named Beverly is doing the door; she knows me and I go right in. The New Orleans band Li'l Queenie & the Percolators offers an understated start to what soon becomes a mind-blowing roster of talent. Chuck Berry, U2, PiL and Kraftwerk, along with Tina Turner's legendary comeback show, are just some of the names and events that eventually headline The Ritz. The challenge is getting people to stick around after.

The Ritz gave New York what it wanted and needed, and became an institution for nearly a decade. In 1980 it was the place to go before the Mudd Club and a great venue to see a band. I had a lot of fun at The Ritz but it just didn't feel like home. When the show was over I never stuck around.

Gennaro

Part of *feeling like home* means sometimes running away. Timing is everything and I was getting burned around the edges just as Gennaro Palermo was getting comfortable at the door. He'd been working with me during the busy hours and occasionally filling in on my nights off. The rest of his time was spent on the dance floor and in the bathrooms. Gennaro knew many of the club people but had no clue about the neighborhood, the artists or the Rock 'n' Roll crowd, a minor catch offset by ample style, quick wit and a language all his own. The best part about Gennaro is that he wasn't some dubious referral or employment agency drone. If he could pull off wearing a hairnet with a nickel in his ear on Soul Night, he could definitely handle the door. Between Chi Chi and Gennaro, Aldo on security and Debi Mazar standing at the ready, we were in pretty good shape. It looked as though I might even wind up with a regular five-night schedule.

Almost Civilized

By mid-May, days were getting longer and nights just kept on going. If I made it into bed by 7 or 8, I was trying to get out of it by noon. I was sleeping less, painting more and getting high in the studio. Wandering around the East Village and the Lower East

Gennaro Palermo and Millie David, Mudd Club basement, 1980, by Nick Taylor

Side, I found what I wanted in a ground-floor shag-carpeted room near Houston: a hole in a wood-paneled wall that took your money and spit out dime bags of heroin. It was quick, easy and almost civilized compared to the bombed-out no-man's-land cinder blocks of the far-east Alphabets. I'd cab it back to Murray Street and have the afternoon to paint and get high. It was simple and I had it all figured out.

I was moving forward.

I started working on some new paintings, still playing around with a version of the tic-tac-toe imagery I used for the billboard in Frankfurt. Lincoln Scott, the manager at One University, came over one morning after Mudd, and the following day, Mickey Ruskin told me he wanted to come by and have a look.

Several days later Mickey arrived at Murray Street with Lincoln and Michael Arlen, part of his inner circle of friends, cronies or henchmen. The back of Lincoln's head was the *face* of Chinese Chance, and appeared on the One University posters and T-shirts. Arlen hung out at One U every night and occasionally stopped by Mudd. I knew both of them but I didn't really know them at all.

Someone grabbed a mirror off the wall and laid out lines. I leaned in, nose down. Mickey walked into the studio, stood in front of three paintings, looked over at me and said he liked them. He pointed, said, "This one" and offered me a tab of fifteen hundred dollars. I told him it meant a lot to me and it did.

Back at the kitchen table, we all did one more *nose down* on the mirror. They split and I put on *Marquee Moon*, painted for a while, and crashed.

By early evening, I'm sitting across the street from One University. I'm smoking a joint with Gary and Ricky Sohl on the grassy knoll at the northeast corner of Washington Square Park. It's the same north side of the same park where a stranger once said to me, "Hey sonny boy, want to buy some pot?" More than a decade later, here I am again.

Hanging out in the park, there's a sense of freedom that still exists in New York City, and still exists in me. Riding the music—Punk and post-Punk all the way back to sixties Rock 'n' Roll. Art and poetry; it's the writing on the trains, buildings and bathroom walls. Sex and drugs—it's what we learned and what we didn't. There's no guilt, little caution and a lot of questions. Some I'm not ready to ask and some I can't answer.

***

The following afternoon Ricky and I stop by Electric Lady Studios to harass Andi. She's sitting at the front desk dreaming of writing and recording a song about our obsession with the video games in the backroom of Chinese Chance. She asks what we're doing and I tell her, "Looking for trouble."

I head for the bathroom and do a line of dope. Andi walks in and does half a line. Ricky appears and wants to know what we're doing but by now there isn't any left. I look him in the eye and blame Andi.

Back home, I nod off.

Around 9 P.M., I plug the phone back in and it rings. It's Gretchen, and she's coming to town for Gary's birthday, which is a week away, Wednesday, May 21, at our place. She's bringing a friend and wants to stay at the loft. I tell her okay, fine, talk later and bye.

Arriving at work, I make a quick run for the basement, stop by the coatroom and hear about the upcoming nuptials of Lisa the coat check girl and a bartender named Gary. She's eighteen and lives in the neighborhood; he's at least ten years older. Her parents are horrified and think she's nuts but book the reception at the Mudd Club anyway. I think we're all nuts and run back upstairs.

I'm smiling as I head outside and start thinking about the birthday party. I've already told Steve and Mickey, Ricky and Andi. Teri's back in Iowa for a spring popcorn festival and won't be able to attend. Cookie and Sharon, Ross, Lynette and Alice are definitely coming. Anita and Anita, Marcus, Claudia, Rosemary and Michael all know about it. That's about ten percent of *everybody* and exponentially equals a few hundred people. Steve definitely will come by to see who shows up and who doesn't. I'm telling people there'll be liquor and drugs and that they should bring more. I'll have a case of champagne and cases of beer to get things started. The psycho dealer from Charlton Street's a pain in the ass but we'll need cocaine so I'll have to invite him too. I'm kind of possessive about the Mudd Club door but I'm letting go and taking the night off. Party planning's tough but I've still got a week to figure it out.

Hard to Miss

It's an easy night and DJ Anita's just made a clean, screaming segue from Buzzcocks to Stranglers to Sex Pistols, and "Holidays in the Sun" comes blaring out of the PA. Thirty minutes later I'm in a booth on the second floor, sucking down Heinekens with Lauren Hutton. Even at this hour she's hard to miss, and the few who can still see are staring. Lauren stopped in to surprise Bob Williamson, the Svengali grifter who's been taking care of her and her career for more than a decade. At 4 A.M., she finally asks if I know what time *the old man* usually gets here. I don't have an answer but offer another Heineken. Bob's nowhere to be seen and it's not my job to tell her he's probably fucking one of the waitresses from One U.

I walk her downstairs to a cab, come back up and head for the bathroom. It's late and whoever's still hanging out looks desperate—including me.

I head home with two guys named Richard and Stephen. Each has coke but it's gone by 7; I call Sculls Angels for a cab and both are gone by 8. I might've had sex with one of them but I can't remember which. I'm wiped out and the white-light morning's pouring in. I put on *Stranded*, the third Roxy Music album, and "Song for Europe" is the most beautiful thing I've ever heard. I close the shutters and tear open the empty dime bag searching for one last line. I lay down in the living room and try to unwind. If I could stop grinding my teeth, I'd be fine.

It was long before I'd realize *fine* had little meaning.

Speedballs and Balloons

Two days before Gary's birthday and I'm running around the club telling anyone I might have missed to come by the loft on Wednesday night. I remind them there's no buzzer, to call from the pay phone on the corner.

Gary's working too, running around the dining room at One U. It's surely busy, and with all the nightly nonsense going on, no one notices a lonely manila envelope sitting on an empty banquette. When Gary finally takes it into the bathroom and checks it out he finds a thousand dollars cash, an ounce of cocaine and a half-ounce of brown heroin.

Left to his own devices, Gary may not have survived the discovery. The dubious decision to share his find with Mickey's business partner, Richard Sanders, was a blessed curse. Gary wisely stuffed the money in his pocket while Richard kept a healthy share of the treasure. He doled out half the coke and dope to Gary, offering to protect him from whoever might come looking for the goods.

It's a tangled spooky web, but we have the party funds and favors we need. Wednesday's almost here, it's time to get ready, and nothing says Happy Birthday like cake, champagne and speedballs.

The day before the party Gretchen and her friend Elizabeth arrived early. We went to the Village shopping for plates, cups, forks and balloons. We picked up the champagne and beer, packed up a cab and hauled it all back to Murray Street. The girls made spaghetti with whatever was on hand and shortly after I headed off to work.

I stood on the front steps of 77 White and thought about Gretchen. She was my friend, and when she left her job at the Mudd Club it was a mistake. Moving in with the psycho coke dealer on Charlton Street gave her a warped sense of security that came loaded with drugs, guns and money.

She tried to escape and moved into the Murray Street loft—an impermanent solution bringing mixed results. Charlton Street wouldn't let go; he paid me her rent with grams of cocaine and sucked the two of us in. When at last the nightmare was over Gretchen headed home to Springfield, Massachusetts. I hadn't seen her in a while and I was glad she made it to the city for Gary's birthday.

Getting the Candles Lit

May 21, 1980. It was up to me to get it all together and my job to pick up the cake. By early afternoon I was riding the RR to Eighth Street and walking the five blocks to Veniero's Bakery on East Eleventh. The cake was a big, brightly colored Happy Birthday model, decorated with blue and pink buttercream flowers. All I had to do was find a cab and get it home.

By 8 P.M. I'm in the shower and Gretchen's making dinner. We settle down by 10 and do a few lines of coke to hold us over; the big stash of brown Persian *tide* is high and dry for now.

The phone starts ringing at 11 and I head down in the elevator. Richard Sohl, Lynette and Solveig come up. We crack open a bottle of Mumm Cordon Rouge as an advance mini-celebration of Ricky's birthday on the twenty-sixth. The phone keeps on ringing and I keep making trips up and down. By midnight, the loft is getting crowded, the champagne's moving fast and the cocaine's moving faster. Anita Sarko shows up and hands Gary a copy of Aleister Crowley's *Diary of a Drug Fiend*, everyone's favorite read. Julie Glantz and Thunders' manager Christopher Giercke are hanging in the studio, checking out the painting with a Johnny Rotten story scrawled around the edges (two weeks later they buy it). Cookie's in the kitchen talking with Steve, and Sharon Niesp's listening and laughing out loud. Marcia Resnick just arrived, dressed to party in Ray-Bans and combat boots; she looks around and says, "So this is where everybody is." I give her a kiss and make another run downstairs to get Ross Bleckner and Mary Boone. The up and down at this point is too much so I prop open the front door and leave the elevator unlocked. It's a 1 A.M. free-for-all on Murray Street.

Back upstairs I find Linda Ludes, the Quaalude dealer, going through my drawers, looking for more drugs. If ever there's a night *more drugs* seem like overkill it's tonight; but when you're talking about someone whose nickname is Ludes, all bets are off. I ask her, "What the fuck?" and tell her to leave.

Immediately, I feel better seeing Alice Himelstein in the kitchen. She's talking to Gary and laughing that big loud laugh. Ricky comes over and we make a quick move, dipping back into the bedroom. Lynette follows us in and asks what we're doing. I reach in my pocket and pull out the Persian brown. By now everyone's up, down or somewhere in the middle.

Marisol the sculptor, whose figurative work defies any label, is wandering around in a daze, accompanied by oceanographer Cathy Drew; Marisol whispers a heavily accented but barely audible "Happy Birthday" in Gary's direction and Cathy gives him a squeeze. Linda Yablonsky and Big Ron arrive with Lincoln Scott and One U hostess Hester Laddy. The place is well past crowded when printmaker Larry Wright walks in with Charlie Yoder. Mickey's a no-show but sends his greeting via Michael Arlen.

I walk over to Jean-Michel Basquiat, who's on the sofa talking with a girl whose name I never knew. Marcus Leatherdale's on the windowsill with a guy named Todd, a good-looking downtown carpenter who's along for the ride. Claudia Summers appears out of nowhere and starts talking with Jean-Michel and the mystery girl.

People are making themselves at home in a good way (as opposed to going through my bedroom drawers). No one seems to be wanting, and everyone's still standing. Gretchen is lighting the candles and Gary's waiting to blow them out. I turn off the music and anyone who can still speak sings "Happy Birthday." Anyone who can still eat grabs a piece of cake.

I wander back across the living room, crank up Bryan Ferry's "Let's Stick Together" and the party moves quickly out of cake mode. I'm in and out of the bedroom with just about everyone and Gary's in and out of the other bedroom with everyone else. By 2 A.M., it's starting to feel like the Mudd Club second floor.

Rather than spinning out, the party slowly winds down and Steve encourages everyone to come to White Street. The birthday boy's the last to leave and splits with Lynette. I pull an open bottle of Mumm's out of the icy kitchen sink and I take a long drink. The sound of Neil Young's *On the Beach* is drifting around the room when Gretchen and I finally lie down and crash. The only question, *who'll get up to change the record?*

I Was Too Busy

The brown dope was a tipping point and I wound up doing some every day. I wasn't paying attention. I don't know if anybody was. I thought I was working hard, making an effort and moving forward. I was always a smart guy and I threw a smart party, but didn't realize what was happening.

Abbijane warned me. Anita Sarko and Ross Bleckner warned me too. I was too busy and didn't hear them. I didn't see what was coming and it would be years before I could or would.

Running out of drugs and finding, buying or asking for more was both a problem and a routine. I found myself drifting further in and out of *real*, riding an occasional wave of desperate.

Saturday, Memorial Day weekend, and Gary's stash of dope was nearly gone. I worked on White Street till 4, left Danceteria early-midmorning stretched out on the back seat of a cab. My head was spinning, my eyes were open, my mind racing. I thought about where I'd been and where I was headed. I rolled down the window, lit a cigarette, closed my eyes and saw everything.

In 1975, I was still twenty-one and there was nothing more radical than Patti Smith and the Ramones. The Contortions and Teenage Jesus came along, adding fuel and fire to the juggernaut. By 1978, Diego Cortez grokked it. He and Anya Phillips helped Steve redefine club life and for some, life itself. As graffiti began to radicalize art, the streets replaced the white walls of SoHo. People were inventing and reinventing themselves. Chi Chi Valenti would one day again reference the "*do it yourself* ethos," that point of ignition where so many of us began.

Like Mickey Ruskin before him, Steve Mass gave us the room to breathe and for a few short years, even when it skipped a beat, the Mudd Club was the heart of what was happening. I might've been unsure of myself, but I managed to land right in the middle.

Trying to look ahead and move forward, I sometimes wondered if I was just standing there holding the door, and watching it close.

Times Square

A beautiful, rough mix of *moving forward* found a temporary new home in an abandoned massage parlor at 201 West Forty-first Street and Seventh Avenue. Someone told me The Raybeats were playing but I had a feeling that was only part of it; I headed for Midtown to see for myself.

The *Times Square Show*, opening June 1, 1980, was the brainchild of sculptors Tom Otterness and John Ahearn. Organized by the Collaborative Projects group (Colab), in cooperation with Bronx-based Fashion Moda, the posters called it "Art of the Future." The art of presentation would never be the same.

Like Mudd, *Times Square* had that same kind of collective energy and do-it-yourself vibe, packed into a deliberately transient thirty-day run. Haring and Scharf, Basquiat, Brathwaite, Jenny Holzer and Kiki Smith put effort into the effort, distinguishing themselves as a cutting-edge renegade force. White Street girls Vicki Pedersen, Mary Lemley, Sophie VDT and Eszter Balint set up a Fashion Lounge with the help of Basquiat. Salvation Army clothing smeared with paint was a big part of the fashionably artistic Lounge statement, or what Pedersen calls "our ragtag chic manifesto."

Whether you were there for the art or took a wrong turn looking for "massage," all who participated were part of that *energy*:

a spirit and edge akin to Colab's independent, communicative and not-for-profit ideal. Square-foot pricing and a corporate mentality had yet to destroy the remaining studio and affordable living spaces available. We still hadn't experienced the corrosive effects of art's investment-grade appeal.

In those early days of June 1980, the sound of The Raybeats drifted thru the building, and the work of those involved painted a new and exciting picture. Like the *happening* on White Street, the *Times Square Show* became its own work of art: another new container for a creative, anarchic spirit. Within that chaos and freedom, and thanks to the forever loved but soon-to-be lost ruins of a changing city, New York was still Bohemia.

When the filmmaker Bette Gordon mentions an "open window," she recalls the opportunities that "allowed for a collaboration and overlapping of creativity." She remembers the passion of that brief, 4 A.M. *wild time* existence when "drugs fueled the work until things got out of hand."

Those moments were often dark but beautiful, inspiring and transformative—impossible to repeat. They were a statement of time and time passing. Those moments, along with Mudd and *Times Square*, were a first and last stand.

***

I can still hear The Raybeats as I wander south on Seventh Avenue. I feel the clock ticking even though my friend Larry Wright reminds me I'm still a kid. I'm twenty-six and he's thirty. It's after 9 P.M. and the sky's almost bright when I step out of the cab in front of One University. I head inside; my tic-tac-toe painting is on the right—the first thing you see when you walk in. Two hours from now I'll be on White Street.

Exene Cervenka and John Doe, X, 1980, by Eugene Merinov

10.
SUMMER
OF
LOVE
PART 2:
HEROIN,
SURF
AND
SAND

It's almost midnight and Dave's Luncheonette is filled with freaks, blue-collar weirdos and kids crashing and refueling. For half the clientele, White Street is the real destination. I grab a hot dog and run.

Summer just got started and the Mudd Club's busy seven nights a week. Gennaro's working the door on Saturday and Sunday nights and I finally have the weekends off. I just have to figure out what the hell I'm doing.

I stop by Danceteria, run around inside but never find a comfort zone. Studio 54's still happening (to a degree) and so is Max's. CBGB's seems like it always will be. Club 57 is busy doing its own version of pop culture snark minus the irony. The Ritz has the early part of the night covered but leaves me underwhelmed until the band comes on; whatever's onstage is the real and only draw. That's why White Street's different: you go to the Mudd Club to go to the Mudd Club.

Furs and Lobsters

The White Street newsletter had become a thing of the past, re-placed by ads in the *Village Voice*: a bit of editorial nonsense and a lopsided lineup of acts. Still, most nights were carried by word of mouth, and meant to be a surprise. I always enjoyed the elev-enth-hour revelation.

The weekend of June 21, 1980, I arrived at the club and a crowd was already waiting. I heard the band's name a few times but didn't know a thing about them. I only found out they were playing when I saw their poster in the doorway.

The Psychedelic Furs were just off the boat, playing their first American shows. They turned up the volume and blew the doors off the Mudd Club two nights in a row. Steve Mass was staying on top of things, kicking off the summer with a dose of Heartbreakers-style "fuck art, let's dance" enthusiasm and the crowd on White Street was ready. By midnight the place was full.

A weekend run by any band was unusual for the Mudd Club and I was sure it had something to do with Danceteria and The Ritz. When Joe Jackson played a one-night stand over a year ago, it was on a Sunday and he was touring behind a hit record. The B-52's, a *band of crazy* with a quirky hit about a lobster, opened the club six months before that.

Tonight's different and the place is packed. Bowie's in the house and by 1 A.M., *the Furs* are onstage. John Ashton's guitar snakes thru the room and Duncan Kilborn's sax starts wailing. Richard But-ler's vocal grind jumps out in front and brother Tim Butler's bass takes the whole thing for a ride. "Sister Europe" and "Imitation of Christ" are loud and raw; "India" sends the dance floor over the edge. The Psychedelic Furs and the room are in sync and the Mudd's art bar, post-Punk vibe is channeling its inner Rock 'n' Roll dive. I'm standing in front of the stage and the door seems miles away.

***

The Mudd Club's high- and lowbrow aesthetic, its irony and random political incorrectness existed on and below the surface. Hidden behind a painted camouflage façade, it was, in the words of Glenn O'Brien, "the laboratory of a generation" and everyone was part of Dr. Mudd's human experiment. The club's intellectual and semi-in-

MUDD FILMS OPEN CASTING 11/12
FIGHT FOR LIFE
(FEATURE FILM)

NOVEMBER 12, 11 PM. Mudd Films casting 8 actresses (no experience necessary) for film about legendary rock group which has fallen on hard times. The 8 women nurse them back to stardom through vegetarianism and California living.

ROLE BREAKDOWN

CAMILLA—Sparrow-like in mid-twenties.

JOANNE—Brunette, sensitive and secure.

MARY—Blond, sensitive and insecure.

BRANDY—Gets thrown down the dressing room stairs type.

LUCY—Fashionable, rich and bitchy.

GILLIAN—Wholesome, preppie type.

DAWN—Vixen, voluptuous with confidence.

SHIELA—Athletic, motherly type.

**WOMEN APPEARING FOR CASTING WILL BE ELIGIBLE FOR PRIZES INCLUDING 2 TICKETS TO:

ROLLING STONES CONCERT
Information call: 227-7832

MUDD CLUB   77 WHITE STREET

Fight for Life, open casting. Are you Brandy? 1980, courtesy Howie Pyro.

tellectual bent, along with its art world sway and *anything's allowed* attitude, kept things alive—and occasionally dangerous.

My behavior, and nearly everyone's I knew, was reckless at best; the Mudd Club, and New York City, encouraged it. If you fell down the flight of stairs from the second floor, you got up, made sure you didn't lose your cigarettes or drop a Quaalude, and headed for the bar. Sex in the bathroom or in the alley was easy: no names, no

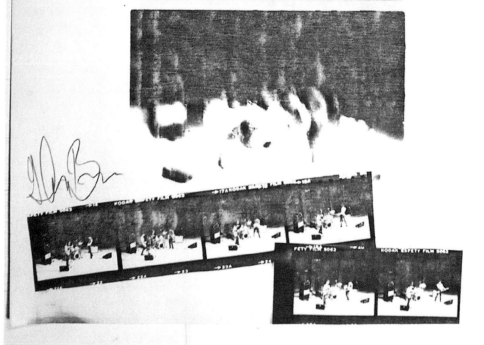

STATICATTHEM
UDDCLUBMON

28

Opposite: Glenn Branca/Static poster, Mudd Club, 1979.
Above: Glenn O'Brien with Mary Lou Green and Leisa Stroud, 1979, by Marcia Resnick.

memory and little regret. Pull up your pants, straighten out your skirt, you were ready to dance and have a good time. No one I knew had any idea what was coming.

Seeing and hearing the unexpected was less hazardous, but just as interesting. Avant-garde musician and trumpet player Jon Hassell, percussionist David Van Tieghem, guitarist Rhys Chatham, and saxophonist Dickie Landry all performed at 77 White. Philip Glass doing a 10 P.M. performance in front of leather jackets, de Menils, the *Einstein* beach crowd and Boris Policeband was a smart idea for a dance floor warm-up. They were all local talent with a connection to the neighborhood. I'd seen them around but I'd never seen any of them play.

I saw Jon Hassell having dinner at One University and introduced myself. He and Brian Eno were working together in the studio and the result was the 1980 release *Fourth World, Vol. 1: Possible Musics*. The Eno connection caught my interest and the Mudd Club was the perfect place to hear what Hassell was up to.

Wednesday, June 25, the club was only half full. By midnight, Jon Hassell took the stage. A line of China White left me dreaming and Hassell had me riding the *Enofied* sound manipulations of a trumpet.

I stood there until my elbow slid off the edge of the bar. I walked outside to get some air and the music followed me into the street.

An hour or maybe hours later, I'm facing what's left of a crowd. Losing track of time, it's like I've been standing here forever but can't pull myself away.

Johny Hit and Run

Thursday and Friday night hit me hard; the crowd wouldn't give me a break. Saturday night Gennaro was on the door and I never left Murray Street except for the half-dozen 3 A.M. nightcaps at Mudd. Late Sunday morning, by way of youth and chemistry, I fully recover. I take the D train to Brooklyn, borrow Aunt Olga's car and drive to Toms River, New Jersey. My parents are here until November and then back to Florida for the winter. I spend the day, we all get along, but as Jo Shane would say, "It's like high school all over again." Pretty much all the time now, they think I'm either *on something* or *something's going on* but can't put their finger on it. I just smile and think about growing up on Long Island when the music was too loud, a funny smell was coming from my room, and I was staying out too late. That was over ten years ago; some things never change.

After dinner, I make my way back to Brooklyn and by midnight, I'm back at Mudd on my night off. I slip thru the crowd outside, step thru the door and stop short. X from Los Angeles, one of America's great Rock 'n' Roll bands, is onstage. John Doe, Exene Cervenka, Billy Zoom and DJ Bonebrake are putting out a sound so loud and beautiful that it pulls me to the front of the dance floor. I just stand and stare.

Large freestanding crucifixes covered with plastic flowers (the work of Mirielle Cervenka) flank both sides of the stage: it's life and death, the band's playing fast and everyone's trying to hold on. John Doe's bass and the Bonebrake beat carry the sound—the Zoom guitar slices it up and makes it dance. When Exene's vocal pulls up next to John's, her voice wraps around his and they let loose. He's all skinny Rock 'n' Roll passion and she's in your face with a sonic force of words. Together it's a sweet scream that I haven't heard since the glory days of *the Airplane*. When they put "Johny Hit and Run Paulene" into overdrive it takes my breath away. Wanting to meet them, I head upstairs after the show.

Zoom was all cool, the grin flashing on and off. DJ was animated, out of breath and taking on all comers. John was sweat wet and talking to friends. I cut in, introduced myself and he responded with easy charm. Exene was different—approachable but cautious, and no wasted words; her sister Mirielle was only gone a few months and Gordon Stevenson stood nearby. I looked at Exene, said, "Thanks, it was beautiful," and walked away. Three decades later, John still knows me as *Richard from the Mudd Club*.

I arrived late that Sunday night and missed one or two songs. Maybe walking in midset was the way to go—part of that *You never know what's happening next* at the Mudd Club. I stayed till closing and left with a drumstick in my hand. DJ Bonebrake signed it with a marker, and it still stands in a pencil holder on my desk. With a few other memorable sticks keeping it company, it's a moment in time, one that I can reach out and touch.

Faded Floral Print

Monday morning I keep playing the X cover of the Doors' "Soul Kitchen." Monday night, White Street, I'm trying to sing along with the song in my head. Twelve hours later, Tuesday morning is closing in on 11 A.M. Teri's hanging out at the loft and Roxy Music is back on the turntable. We've been up all night, not ready to sleep, unable to eat. We need something to do.

I'm wearing a Secret Rocker T-shirt, Converse sneakers and a pair of red cotton pants, the same clothes I wore to work night before. Teri's wearing her own version of yesterday: Maud Frizon heels and a royal blue cocktail dress, her blonde hair pulled into a tiny bun at the top of her head. With black Ray-Bans it's an impressive look and together we're trouble looking for trouble. Cabbing it to Second Avenue and Houston, we walk to the corner near the gas station on First Street. I duck into an entryway on the ground floor, shove forty dollars through a hole in the wall, and four dime bags of heroin come back at me. Nearly noon, we head over to One University for a few Bloody Marys. Big Ron is tending bar, surprised but happy to see us.

Two minutes later I'm in the men's room, Teri's in the ladies' and Ron's just laughing. Back at the bar we order drinks, give Ron a taste of a dime and grab a cab to Murray Street; we go upstairs and get lost. By midnight, I'm on the front steps of the Mudd Club, thinking about two things: I have to make another trip to First and Houston, and I need to get out of town for a few days. First Street's the easy part; as for the getaway, Big Ron has a brilliant idea.

Ron had heard about a place in Montauk; he called and booked two rooms for the weekend. It sounded too good to be true and I had no idea what to expect. Saturday I worked until 5 A.M., and by 7 we were on the Long Island Railroad. Three-and-a-half hours later, I was wiping sand off the faded floral print contact paper covering the top of an old dresser. I was looking out a window across Old Montauk Highway. I could see the waves and hear the ocean. It was beautiful, a home I never knew until then. I laid out two lines of dope, grabbed a towel, and walked downstairs. Ron's brilliant idea was called "Bea's Surf and Sand."

Dogs

The weekend getaway lasted just thirty-six hours but left me feeling like I'd lived there forever. Leaving Montauk Sunday night, I was already planning my return. Monday, back at work, kissing and hugging people I barely knew and sending most of them in for free. I looked around before I took a break and spotted my friends Bruce Crocker and Michael Maslin. They'd hang out across the street, wait for me to *give 'em a sign* and make their way thru the crowd. They knew me well enough that the idea of me working the door at Mudd cracked them up. I'm not sure I kissed either one hello.

Bruce was a very young 1980 "Mad Man" working for an agency on Madison. He played drums, guitar and sang in a garage band when he was twelve but his music career, admittedly, "peaked in the eighth grade." He'd seen Hendrix, Cream and Moby Grape at Woolsey Hall in New Haven when he was a kid and thought he was ready for anything.

Michael, whose work I collected and admired, was the only published cartoonist I knew, his drawings regularly appearing in *The New Yorker*. He never played the drums or sang in a band but grew up loving Dylan, the Beatles and the Stones. I turned him on to CBGB, he cheered Patti and Television, and kept an open mind.

Stepping thru the door, they headed into the Mudd Club on a night when *anything is possible* was in full force. It didn't mat-

Thor. Spinal Tap before Spinal Tap, 1980, by Ebet Roberts.

ter if you'd seen it all or not. This was different—and no one was ready for Thor.

A Prince Valiant haircut and pumped-up muscles: black leather boots, wrist cuffs and peekaboo lace-up pants. The music was a heavy metal variety of Vancouver descent—blowing up hot water bottles with lung power alone, the explosive but not very special effect. A cluster of fans carrying Thor's album, *Keep the Dogs Away*, along with a midset call for "Dogs, Dogs, Dogs," brought on the anxiously awaited title cut. Several audience members barked their approval.

Thor was Spinal Tap before Spinal Tap, ahead of his time and beyond even the archness of Mudd Club irony. I'm not sure how or why he wound up on White Street but things tend to happen for reasons we seldom understand. By 3 A.M., I was upstairs with Michael and Bruce. Thor had left the building.

***

Early summer 1980. Heroin by now was the sometimes Happy Hour choice, and everyone I knew was fucking around with it. Working on White Street Monday through Friday, I wandered Rivington, Norfolk and Chrystie Streets in the afternoon looking for Doctor Nova or one of his friends.

Running around night and day became a series of loose ends. I was somehow functioning, painting a little and smiling most of the time. I'm not sure if I thought anything was wrong. I'm not sure what I thought.

Teri was back and forth from Iowa and living at Richard Sohl's West Eighty-fifth Street apartment. They were showing up together at the club every night. Andi's song "Chinese Chance," about video game addiction and the goings-on in the back room of Mickey's, was almost ready to tell the story. The song about Mudd had yet to be written.

We were all getting a little crazy, but just how crazy was the question. Lounging around in underpants for Executive Board Meetings (EBMs) at Andi's apartment on East Thirty-first Street was the fast answer but seemed to skirt the dementia's root cause.

Ricky, Teri, Andi and I held several EBMs and Doctor Nova attended every one; boxers, briefs and panties kept us cool. We discussed plans for the summer, came up with the name "Square Point" for Andi's music company and talked about spending time in Montauk. We even talked about removing Teri from the board of directors because of her unprofessional and erratic behavior, which in light of the company was hard to imagine or describe.

Teri's response to the threat of dismissal, "Don't try it, Grandma."

My response to the board, "Ignore her."

After a few hours of back-and-forth nonsense, I'd fall into the back seat of a cab and head home. I'd wake the next afternoon usually wearing my own underpants.

Two nights after our last meeting at Andi's, I walked into One University. Gary was at the bar and Rene Ricard was at a table eating a meal that someone else was undoubtedly paying for. Always the entertainer, spewing words of sharp unsubtle cut, Rene looked over and let go, "Here comes the artist-doorman and his hustler boyfriend." I put down my jacket, picked up a chair and threw it at him. The next thing out of his mouth was a shriek, followed by a squeal, "Mickey! Mickey! He threw *a chair* at me!" Everyone else kept eating; I sat in a booth and ordered dinner.

For the moment, heroin shrouded any embarrassment and an hour later I left for work. My response to the throwaway words of an erratic, gifted poet was a sad and crazy comment on the type of behavior I assumed I could get away with. It would take time before I could look in the mirror and the truth be told.

Bing Cherries and Beefcake

Rene and I remained a friendly acquaintance; I made it through the night without throwing things at anyone else. After work I went home and passed out. When noontime arrived I took a shower, put on some clothes and stared into an empty refrigerator. A lonely cup of Dannon yogurt and a few Bing cherries was breakfast; my last Marlboro, lunch. I washed it all down with a half-bottle of flat Perrier, went out for cigarettes and worked in the studio for hours. I headed for White Street around 10:30, smoked a joint on the way, and kept my bloodshot eyes behind a pair of tortoiseshell sunglasses. I walked inside, looked over at DJ David and the lights went down. I asked for a Coca-Cola with a lot of ice, and I stepped back out. Moments later, I heard a familiar "Hey, hey Richie!" as Tom Baker stepped out of a cab and started a conversation from thirty feet away. He wanted to make sure I'd look out for his friend Joe Dallesandro, the actor, Warhol superstar and former beefcake model. I thought to my-self, *Why wouldn't I?* More than a decade past his prime, the iconic star of *Trash*, *Flesh* and *Heat* was still beautiful and he was still Little Joe; by 1980 White Street seemed the *wild side*.

Dallesandro and Baker, either directly or by degrees, informed the attitude, behavior and style of the sixties and seventies. Moving forward and thru the doors of 77 White, that style and at-titude became part of the mix, and we all took notice whether we realized or not.

Tom went inside; I lit a cigarette and reached for a beer that wasn't there. I finished my soda and cracked the watery ice be-tween my teeth. I sat down on the chain and rocked back and forth. It was quiet—just the sound of the street and twenty people wait-ing outside. I was waiting too, on Joe and anyone else who might come along.

Thirty minutes later, Alan Midgette arrived and the place was still empty. No one was dancing, the perfect setup. Alan smiled hello, headed inside and walked onto the middle of the dance floor; he stretched out his arms and started to spin. I started letting people in and the bar filled up. People started dancing and Alan kept spinning. Tom Baker was hanging out, and an hour later, I was still waiting.

Little Joe never showed.

Punk Pussy

Baker stuck around till late and I left early, just after 4 A.M. The following night I'm back outside and a few moonlighting NYC cops are working security. They're a little overwhelmed by the door but come in handy dealing with everything from nasty bridge-and-tunnel girls to drunken bachelor parties looking for *Punk pussy*.

When three suburban girls—a variety even worse than outer bor-ough bridge-and-tunnel—get shoved around in the crowd they open the chain themselves. I close the chain and tell them, "Get the fuck off the steps." One of them grabs my arm and tries to slap me and the security cop tells me to go inside. It's not even 1 A.M. and I'm already pissed off.

I head for the basement and walk into the coat check room to see what Mona and Lisa are up to. I sit on the floor in a corner and hide. I start wondering how much longer I can do this. A minute or two later, I snap out of it and head back out. The girls are gone and the security cop tells me to smile. He says my friend Dory's inside looking for me.

Made for Dancing

Allen Lanier's always on the road with Blue Öyster Cult and Dory Lanier likes hanging out on the second floor of Mudd. She's between the cage and the bar talking to Nurse Debbie. I get a big smile and warm hug as we walk toward the back of the room.

We laugh when we spot teen idol Leif Garrett sitting on a small yellow crushed velvet couch just outside the bathrooms. His hair's long, wavy and blond, he's dressed all in white, and he's got a girl sitting on his lap. He's pretty but not beautiful, about nineteen and a little old for his job. He hasn't been to jail yet, but he's already damaged. His last hit single was called "I Was Made for Dancing," but he's not. It's a Mudd Club disconnect; Garrett appears unsure what he's doing here, and I occasionally feel the same way.

Back outside, Lynette, Diane and British Punk poet John Cooper Clarke arrive. He's really skinny, with big hair and dark glasses, but in the summer of 1980 so am I. Two seconds later, Taylor Mead sidles up and asks if he can hold the chain. I tell him NO. Lynette laughs, drags me back inside and saves me.

Last Half Second Dog

I can't remember leaving White Street and I don't remember going home but a day later I'm making a midnight hot dog run to Dave's. Hal Ludacer is at the counter when I get there, staring at his coffee, smoking a cigarette. I can't tell whether he sees me or if he's coming or going—having breakfast, lunch or dinner. There's little sense of time, just the blurry continuum of endless night. I order two hot dogs with sauerkraut, onions and mustard. I wander back to Mudd in a slow drift, dreaming about Montauk.

I'm swallowing the last half of the second dog when Steve appears out of nowhere. Living around the corner at Broadway and

349

Franklin makes it easier for him to do the *now you see me now you don't*. He walks over and tells me the second floor is closing for renovations.

"Really, when?"

"Yes, soon, Sunday."

"For how long?"

"Not that long."

When I ask if I should let people know he tells me, "They'll figure it out." I roll my eyes, thinking, *That's nice*, and a minute later he's gone.

The second floor of the Mudd Club is a dump. It's part of the charm and people like it that way. I think all that Ritz balcony and multilevel Danceteria Video Lounge stuff has something to do with whatever Steve's planning and he's just trying to stay ahead of the game. Sometimes I think he forgets he's way ahead of it.

So I start telling people that the second floor is closing for a week. When I mention it to artist Jenny Holzer, whose blurbs of *Truism* cover the walls of neighborhood buildings, she doesn't seem too upset. When Rebecca Christensen arrives with onetime *crucified* conceptualist Chris Burden she introduces us but I make no mention of renovations. It's a low-key visit—no guns or Volkswagens involved—and they head straight for the bar. A minute later, an out-of-character Boris Policeband rushes the door with a woman who appears to be Louise Bourgeois (or a Bourgeois stunt double). Artists Kiki Smith and Walter Robinson stroll across the street and step up to the chain. I start mumbling something about the second floor, lose interest and follow them in. The Ramones' "Blitzkrieg Bop" comes roaring over the PA system and the dance floor is almost full. The place looks its dirty, dark and beautiful self. I make my way toward the basement but Talking Heads' "Life During Wartime" pulls me back.

This is *my* life. Tonight it feels right. Not sure how it's going to feel tomorrow.

Not Scary Beautiful

Friday night, it's early. The door, the crowd and 77 White: a small world getting smaller. Time moving slow or fast, it's hard to tell. Steve's nowhere to be seen, but I'm still wondering what a second-floor renovation could possibly look like. I forget about it and smile when Marcus Leatherdale arrives and introduces me to his friend Lisa Lyon. It's hot and she's wearing a tank top and leather pants; she's beautiful but not scary beautiful. The cop working security gives her a long slow once-over—two or three times.

Encouraged by Arnold Schwarzenegger, Lisa Lyon won the first Women's World Professional Bodybuilding Championship in 1979 and never tried again. She was an art student at UCLA, met Arnold and turned herself into a work of art. Now she's everywhere: magazines, television and running around the city with Marcus. She's got a shoot with *Playboy* coming up and there's a collaboration with Robert Mapplethorpe somewhere on the horizon. She winds up loving the Mudd Club and I love telling people, "She's the Women's World Bodybuilding Champion." It's an out-of-context credential that jumps the chain; it's borderline freak, full-on fetish and fits right in.

I look around trying to find Steve. She's someone he'll definitely want to meet.

Worlds Apart

Lisa Lyon was the highlight of a near-civilized evening but by 4 A.M. I had a hard-on for something less. In the summer of 1980, a place called Laight Street became the latest neighborhood after-hours joint with the ability to answer that call. It was a sometimes fun, sometimes desperate watering hole located at the northeast corner of Hudson and Laight, just off the entrance to the Holland Tunnel. Thrown together by former Nursery employee Pauline Darling, it was the perfect spot for anyone who didn't know when it was time to go home. I fell into that category and I fell in often.

Sturgis Nikidas, a musician and Mudd regular, was the Laight Street DJ. Krystie Keller, a Nursery denizen, journalist and writer who interviewed a variety of rock legends, Punks and Dead Boys, worked behind the bar. Just several blocks from White Street and a short walk to Murray, for a few minutes in 1980, Laight Street was perfect.

With only an hour to kill, I ditch Mudd, stop off at Laight, and come pretty close to figuring out when it's *time to go home*. Peter, Paul and Mary's hit version of "Leaving on a Jet Plane" keeps playing in my head—the only difference, I'm leaving on a 7 A.M. train and I know that Monday, I'll be back again. I bought the single when I was sixteen and still have it. It's a beautiful song.

I say good-bye to Laight Street after one beer, run home and pick up my bag. It's Saturday, 6:30 A.M., and there's no traffic, no problem finding a cab. The train leaves on time.

I spend the next three hours in a smoking car on the Long Island Railroad. I'm reading a barely used copy of the *New York Times* that someone left behind and getting high in a bathroom the size of a phone booth. The ruins of Alphabet City and the dunes of Montauk might seem worlds apart but I'm doing my best to bring them together. I've got four dimes of Black Mark and Red Star traveling with me.

I arrive at The Surf and Sand alone. I float around, ride the waves and sleep away Saturday night. Sunday disappears and it's the end of another thirty-six-hour weekend. Monday night I'm back on White Street with a dime bag still in my pocket. I have no idea how it's gotten this far but I need to make it stop. The chase, running in circles, pissing away money—I can't tell whether Montauk is a place to rest or just part of a bigger circle. A year ago, I thought the Mudd Club was the answer—and sometimes it still is; other times it's part of the run.

Monday feels like a quiet night. A chat with Steve and a walk thru the second floor tells me the renovation's happening fast. There's an enclosed DJ booth made out of either shatter- or bulletproof plexiglass and a spiral staircase winding its way to the stage. The bathtub beer cooler is still behind the bar, but the bathrooms look reinforced, and ready for the next round of *anything's allowed*. The faux Naugahyde vinyl reupholstered seating looks suitably retro and a little less dirty. The whole place looks almost new and somewhat improved, nearly identical to the old second floor of the Mudd Club. People won't even notice, they'll just be happy it's open.

With upstairs nearly ready, the only other bit of Mudd in need of a makeover is the basement. It's a concrete, plywood and sheetrock mess with a cigarette machine and a coat check. It's a fixer-upper with the three things that matter most: *location, location, location*. It's a great project for somebody.

More Than Ten Minutes

Talking with Steve Mass was an odd comfort. More an employer and associate than almost-friend, there was still a connection. Privy to *most of*, though sometimes not, Steve allowed me to be myself or die trying. I'm grateful I didn't try too hard.

The crowd outside hasn't slowed down and the regulars are having a hard time dealing without the second floor. John the Greek can't figure it out while Phoebe and Ellen keep running in circles between the bathroom and the bar. Mick Rock just keeps smiling and calling me *darling*.

On a break, I'm walking toward the dance floor when DJ David takes it up a notch and the Pretenders start pounding out "Mystery Achievement." Ronnie and Gigi start jumping up, down and sideways. I whirl around Alan Midgette-style and bump up against the DJ booth. Steve's at the bar talking to Victor Bockris, both have sunglasses on and Steve's holding a highball glass with a vodka and grapefruit that's glowing in the dark. I squeeze by, head back outside and walk over to a guy standing at the chain. He introduces himself as Nils Lofgren. I let him in and tell the door to let him thru. I'm probably the only person at Mudd, other than Lenny Kaye or Kate Simon, who knows he's played guitar with Crazy Horse and Neil Young. I even have the album *1+1* by Lofgren's band, Grin. The almost-mainstream cred is interesting and he comes off as a friendly guy. He's inside, at the bar, in the thick, and I'm introducing him to Anita Pallenberg. She's gracious but she's never heard of him.

It's late, maybe 3 A.M., when I check out the crowd one last time and pull in the faces I know. I let in one of those easy, good-looking suburban kids for free and instruct him to wait for me at the bar. I step back from the chain and I tell it like it is. "The club is full. If you've been standing here for more than ten minutes, you're not coming in."

I begin to ramble about coming back another night. I lie and tell everyone that it's early enough to go somewhere else. There's a low groan and some grumbles, but nobody moves except me. I turn around and tell security, "Nobody," knowing there'll be girls they can't resist, guys who'll slip them twenty bucks and people who'll claim to be my friends. I head in and grab two beers, along with the suburban kid with no name. We crash the bathroom on the newly reopened second floor and the kid pulls out a vial of coke. Some girls are at the mirror doing what pop culture maven, singer and self-proclaimed

Rock chick Bebe Buell calls "adjusting their glitter." I smile at a girl I let in hours ago and she gives us two Quaaludes. It's 4 A.M. when No-Name and I head for the elevator, but at this point it's just late-night/early-morning foreplay. Twenty minutes later, we're at Murray Street.

It's eighty-five degrees and there's no air conditioning at the loft. Cold beer, drugs, some frozen cans of lemonade and a strategically placed fan help cool things down but like everything else it's not enough. No-Name tells me he goes to NYU and he'll tell his friends about the place. I try not to listen, we fuck for a while and he splits around 9 A.M. I'm passed out by 10 and wake up six hours later dreaming about Bea's Surf and Sand.

Somewhere Between

The past two weeks were summer-appropriate: sex, drugs and hot dogs, let alone Rock 'n' Roll and a female bodybuilder. By midnight Friday, I'm well into my second Fourth of July at Mudd. There's a constant rumble from Chinatown and skyrockets pop and fizzle overhead.

Saturday morning, July 5, Montauk is waiting and I'm on the 7 A.M. train headed for Bea's Surf and Sand. I want to jump into a cold ocean, do a few lines, lie down, nod out and relax. If I'm still breathing at 9 P.M., I'll drink at the bar and play Loteria, a kind of Mexican bingo. It's one of my thirty-six-hour vacations and every second counts.

Midnight Sunday, I'm back at One University. Fried zucchini and several rounds of Space Invaders realign my system for the week ahead. I'll be at the Mudd Club by 2, hanging out in the new and improved, beer-cooled, cocaine-fueled second-floor inferno.

Monday, and I'm back to standing outside, already feeling anxious. Then a speedball came sliding in and the week was gone.

Saturday, July 12, I stayed in town and gave Montauk a rest. I met up with Lynette and we headed for Times Square to see Peter Gabriel play the ballroom of the Diplomat Hotel. I never cared much about Genesis (overrated and why bother); I felt the same about Gabriel but the opening act was Tom Robinson's new band, Sector 27, and I was at least curious.

Sticking to what we did best, Lynette and I connected with the band's bass player and guitarist, Jo Burt and Stevie "B" Blanchard.

We hung out together, left after three or four Gabriel songs, stopped at One U, and finally made our way to White Street. Sector 27 was scheduled to play Mudd Club the coming week and Danceteria next weekend. We gave Jo and Stevie a full-tilt Saturday night preview of what they were in for.

The gig at the Mudd Club happened late on a hot, crowded Wednesday night. Sector 27 put on a great show that included "2-4-6-8 Motorway" and the Tom Robinson Band's 1978 UK hit "Glad to Be Gay," a now forgotten liberation landmark.

When the show was over I went outside. Two weeks short of August I looked around, stared at the crowd but something felt different. Maybe it was me, or maybe somewhere between the dance floor and the front door I realized nothing lasts forever. Holding the chain, staring at the remains of a weeknight crowd, I was smiling but not sure why.

Super 8 Home Movies

Two days later, Saturday morning, I have my cigarettes, half a dozen joints, the usual four bags of dope and two hundred dollars. There's paper, paint and brushes in my bag and Big Ron's meeting me at Penn Station. We'll be on the train at 7 A.M. and by 11, I'll be on the beach.

Gary, Teri and Ricky arrive by early afternoon. I crash for an hour, get back up and work on one or two small paintings. It's 6 P.M. when we cross the Old Montauk Highway, stumble over the dunes and head for the water. The waves are huge and crashing hard. Teri drops her towel, walks into the ocean and the surf knocks her over; seconds later, the ocean tosses her back on the sand. Another wave rolls in, hits her again and we can't stop laughing. Her navy blue one-piece swimsuit's practically turned inside out. It's slapstick, a waterlogged version of Teri and Ricky dressed in pajamas tumbling down the Mudd Club stairs. She keeps trying to stand, and ends up crawling her way back to the towel.

I run for the water, dive thru a wave and come out the other side. I'm out past the break, catching my breath and still laughing. I'm treading water, looking back at my friends. It's like watching an old Kodachrome Super 8 home movie and everybody's smiling and waving. I'm feeling almost nostalgic until I look toward the horizon, start thinking about *Jaws* and swim back in. I sit on a towel and light one of Ricky's Winstons. I lie down, exhale and look up. The sky's where it should be and White Street seems a world away.

Bea Reilly

Back at the house there's a real person named Bea Reilly who owns The Surf and Sand. She thinks we're celebrities and takes care of us. She loves Teri, loves having another girl in the house, but she has no idea. Weathered, blonde and beautiful, Bea Reilly was the Angel of Summer 1980.

I light another cigarette. Bea's behind the bar and passes me a drink. I've got two short days to chill out, get my shit together and get back to the Mudd Club; one day's nearly gone. Tonight I want to toast marshmallows over the hibachi, order a pizza and have some drinks, tomorrow walk to town, come back and lie on the beach. I wind up staying Sunday night: smoking joints and walking the water's edge, swimming in the dark. I've done it all before, the ocean between Long Beach and Jones; I was seventeen, just a kid. Memories still with me, resisting the fade.

Back in the city by Monday noon and it's already ninety out. I try to paint, try to avoid, and forget about the Lower East Side. Mexican Village for dinner, a drink at One U; I'm always at the door by 11.

Approaching summer's midpoint, I'm not sure when something or anything might change. Some days I feel lucky and others, exhausted. What's the endgame, I wonder, for a doorman at Mudd? Am I an artist or just hiding out? Is Montauk a place for reflection or just a *quick fix* party at the beach?

I turn twenty-seven in September. I feel like I'm getting old and I feel like getting high.

Chubby

Wednesday morning, July 23, I got up early. I gave up trying to avoid and forget, and made a run for the Alphabets. I looked for any hole in any wall that was open and spent twenty dollars on two bags of "yellow tape." By the time I got to Mudd I was feeling better until

I noticed what was happening. I'm not sure if it was Steve's idea or someone else suggested it, but again, one of the bartenders was working as a cashier at the door.

I always thought the same hand in two tills was a dumb idea, unless you wanted to make sure your bartenders could afford an extra gram or two of cocaine. With no real accounting for cover charges other than clicking a handheld tally counter, who knows what went on? I just kept working the chain, minding my business.

It was a weird, warm and humid night and I stood outside with Brian Doyle-Murray of *Saturday Night Live*. Part of the comic relief that busted a hole in what was then late-night television, Brian and the *SNL* cast and crew added another layer to Mudd's unpredictable cool fool.

I leaned back against the set of unused doors and took a swig from my Heineken while Brian went in to get a drink. I started talking with Debbie and Conover, two party girl "models" from DC who never paid to come in. They had Quaaludes, looked good hanging out at the bar or in the bathroom, and were unaccustomed to the word *no*. (In early 1982, Conover would meet Pete Farndon in Tokyo and marry him a month later. In spring 1983 Conover and I crossed the same sad path.)

I watch Bill Murray get out of a cab, his brother Brian still at the bar. They'd been coming around since the beginning, but Brian was here all the time. I went inside, got Bill a drink, and told him a band called the Go-Go's were going on in about an hour. It was a *non*versation, and a minute later, I went back outside. A short time later Rolling Stones Records chief and Jim Carroll producer Earl McGrath arrived alone. He said he came to the Mudd Club to see the band. I guess someone had to.

I heard one of the Go-Go's played drums with the Germs. It seemed barely a factoid, and she only lasted a minute or two. The Germs lasted a couple of minutes longer, breaking up when singer Darby Crash committed suicide. Thinking about it now, the whole thing sounds like a mess.

Leaving the door for the upstairs bathroom, I run into the Go-Go girls before the show. They're busy doing a version of getting ready, and left any charm they might have had in the van. I don't care one way or the other, but first impressions are hard to shake.

Belinda Carlisle, Jane Wiedlin, Charlotte Caffey and Gina Schock had a sloppy pop sound, a bratty attitude and a pretty good beat. It worked within its limitations and seemed curiously destined for mass market. Belinda jumped around, sang and wore a rag tied around her head—half L.A. gang style, half Hattie McDaniel. The rest of the band did whatever it was they did. They came out of the same L.A. Punk scene that spawned X, but the Go-Go's were different. X was and is a great band.

I stood in the middle of the dance floor, intrigued by what I was watching. The crowd was sparse and Earl McGrath was near the wall a dozen feet away. Bill Murray was standing next to me.

I leaned over and said, "They're pretty good."

He leaned in. "Chubby."

That was enough for me. I asked the bar for a fresh Heineken, or maybe even a Budweiser at that point, and went back outside. The Go-Go's kept at it for another thirty minutes while a few regulars started to arrive. Writer Lynn Tillman stood on the steps and we talked for a while. Victor Bockris came outside and asked if Steve had left. I didn't even know he was inside until that moment, and didn't know Victor was either.

The club never filled up, and there wasn't much for me to do. I was Go-Go'd out and bored. Dave's Luncheonette by 5 A.M., I stared at a pair of fried eggs that seemed to be staring back. I sucked down a vanilla egg cream and twenty minutes later I was home. I lit up what was left of the spliff Dirty Harry had shared with me earlier. The test patterns on television were already winding down. I stared at the ceiling until I fell asleep.

By Thursday afternoon I'd already forgotten about Wednesday. The Go-Go's, gone for the moment, were playing Danceteria on the weekend. I planned on being anywhere else.

Towncraft and Western

I got up, jumped in the shower and went shopping for some five-dollar vintage sportswear on Eighth Street. I hadn't been to the Laundry Loft on Leonard Street for two weeks and didn't have anything clean enough to wear, even at night. I poked around for ten minutes until I found a gray-striped, short-sleeved Towncraft shirt for two dollars. It left me enough money to pay six bucks for a black-and-turquoise Western shirt with pearl snap buttons. I still have the gray-stripes; the cowboy shirt's long gone.

Finished shopping, I headed over to One U. Big Ron was working and I figured I'd suck down a free Bloody Mary. I thought about taking a walk to the Lower East Side to see who was open for business but decided to wait till tomorrow and buy a ten-pack bundle. I felt a little fucked up but I was fine. The Pretenders' "Stop Your Sobbing" was playing on the jukebox. I asked Ron for another Bloody Mary.

Summer Wind

Thursday was my fourth night in a row at the door and I had one more to go. Gary came out to Bea's with me on Saturday; Teri and Ricky were arriving later that day. It was sunny and over ninety degrees. Summertime—the *dead of* and *dog days*—real beach weather, I didn't want it to end.

By the first week of August, The Surf and Sand had turned into that perfect place you'll always remember. The air was fresher, the nights cooler, and it was ideal for predawn, early-morning sex with drunken townies. The sound of the ocean was perfect, and Frank Sinatra on the jukebox singing "Summer Wind" was perfect too.

At night we sat around the old horseshoe-shaped bar and played Loteria. We met the local fishermen and local *locals*: everyone from a guy we called Vodka-Water to a middle-aged drunk named Pat who said she *loved* rubbing elbows with celebrities. She thought Teri was a famous model and asked Ricky Sohl to play us a song. She wanted to know what I painted, and told me she "loved paintings of cats and clowns." We never saw her again, but for the next month Ricky walked around saying, "I love paintings of cats … and *clowns*."

Our friends Lori and Joe Barbaria, along with guitarist Thomas Trask, liked to drive over from East Hampton or Springs, wherever they landed for the summer. They'd stay for drinks and several rounds of Loteria before heading back. Teri soon brought along Stephen Sprouse, and Lynette made plans to come out and visit. Even Kate Simon made an appearance to check out the beach, dabble in the *shniz*, and see what the hell was going on. By the time Steve Mass showed up, Bea's Surf and Sand was *the* place to go. All you had to do was find it and get there.

Gray

Sunday, August 3. Michael Holman's at the Mudd Club and he's been working hard all day. When Jean-Michel walks in, Michael can see that JMB is "blown away."

Jean-Michel goes outside, drags in a wooden crate from Cortlandt Alley and tosses it onstage. He reaches up and gives a last-minute tear to the perfect *unfurl* of backdrop paper. A final brushstroke, gestural, painterly and a little offhanded: imperfect makes it perfect. Now it's Michael's turn to be blown away.

I'm back from Montauk by 10 P.M. In and out of Murray Street I grab a cab and make a pit stop at One University. By midnight, I'm on my way to White Street. Gennaro's working the door and already there's a buzz inside. The 4' × 4' plywood cubes that make up the stage are reconfigured with a middle one now missing. The discarded wooden crate from the alley sits off center, its open end facing the room. A bare bulb hanging from an overhead cord illuminates the crate's shiny metal edges and red Chinese letters. An off-kilter scaffold-like cluster, put together with oddly tangled two-by-fours, looks spare and beautiful. It's Jean-Michel and Michael's very own Ignorant Geodesic Dome, and it's waiting for something to happen.

Just after 1 A.M., Basquiat and Holman, Wayne Clifford, Nick Taylor and Vincent Gallo shuffle onstage. Jean-Michel and his Wasp synthesizer sit inside the crate. Holman's kit of industrial percussion is out of sight, deep in the void of a missing plywood cube. There's a quick blast, a rattle and a slow drift. An occasional rhythm punctuated by machine beats, blips and blasts starts moving around the room. It's industrial bebop and a rattletrap grind that's a little over the head and hard to define. I know the sound though I've never heard anything like it. At once distant and in your face, it's the sound of a strange signal calling. Gray, the neo-No Wave *rat pack* of a band, is finally playing the Mudd Club.

An instant legend, a White Street ghost; Gray played a few gigs and was gone.

Onset of Puberty

Some of the guys onstage—not to mention the bar, the bathrooms and the dance floor—looked barely old enough to drink or whatever else they were doing. Eighteen was legal but no one carried ID. That was about to change.

In summer 1980, Steve Mass set up a Mudd College of Deviant Behavior recruiting station in the basement of the club. *Initiative, Dedication, Intensity and Progress* was the official school motto. "Students" were photographed, asked to sign their full name, and issued a *universally* accepted ID card. In some cases, people checked a box indicating a sworn "Anti-vegetarian loyalty oath" while others noted their personal "Onset of puberty" date—all of it vital information. The cards were laminated on the spot and immediately used for identification.

When Television guitar hero Tom Verlaine arrived I brought him downstairs to register and sign a Mudd Club ID card. His photograph came out fine. I introduced him to designer and Ex Dragon Deb Mary Lemley and she took him upstairs to the second floor. Over the years Verlaine's guitar had taken us from past to present, leaving us with sound and song that marked the era. Working the chain and doing my job, I'd get lost and wander the days ahead. When the door swung open, the music brought me back. The nighttime air was almost cool but still felt like summer. I smiled remembering Tom Verlaine, CBGB 1976, knockin' on heaven's door, and blowing it away.

Steve Mass once again raised the bar, and set the standards high. The ID cards, tangible evidence of the life we lived and a time that disappeared. In some states, countries and border crossings they're still valid today.

***

The Mudd's second anniversary is less than three months away and the club is experiencing a revival of sorts. The regulars, celebs and quasi-celebs are still showing up, and a new Mudd Club photo ID is in everybody's pocket. The upstairs renovation has transformed the second floor into the same old second floor, and begging for drink *tickets* has replaced begging for drinks. Sex and drugs remain as popular as ever.

The front door of 77 White continues to be a tightly controlled operation. The chains are still in place and I'm still standing.

INFORMATION FOR MUDD CARD HOLDERS

Revised Benefits and Penalties under Title 8
Section II of Mudd Code MR 981.

APPLICABLE TO ALL HOLDERS OF GREEN, WHITE, INTERNATIONAL, &
PINK MUDD IDENTIFICATION CARDS ISSUED FROM JULY 4, 1980 &
CONTINUING THROUGH JULY 4, 1981. . (Said cards to be referred to herein
as GWIP cards).

Section MR 43998.2   BENEFITS
                              (designated as new)

1) Holders of all GWIP cards are to be entitled to discounts of from 10.4% to
   99.2% off ticket prices depending on the event.

2) Holders of GWIP cards will receive invitations and schedule of unadvertised
   events for WEDNESDAY, THURSDAY, AND SUNDAY SALON NIGHTS.
   (e.g. half price will apply to the David McDermott Hollywood Biblical
   Tableau and showing of the film the Long Island Four.)

Section MR 43998.3   BENEFITS
                              (designated as retained)

1) Deviant Behavior Research Assignments will continue to be given to GWIP
   card holders.

2) Where applicable GWIP cards may be used as free entry to theatres, discos
   fashion shows and Eagles concerts.

Section MR 43998.4   GWIP SECURITY CLEARANCE

1) Receipt of card through U.S. Postal service indicates completion of security
   checks on GWIP card holders and their families. No further interrogation
   of neighbors, fellow employees, or family can be initiated without
   authorization of the GWIP Security Council.

Section MR 43998.5   PENALTIES

1) Falsification of information on GWIP cards may result in forced marches.
2) A penalty of .66 cents will be assessed holders who lose their cards.
3) Mutilation or burning of GWIP cards will subject violator to 81 push-ups.

Section MR 43998.6   GWIP DISCOUNTS ON MUDD PRODUCTS

1) Any Products issued by the Mudd Organization nor or in the future can be bought
   at 20% discount by GWIP HOLDERS. Products under development for future
   marketing will include deodorants, baby food, perfume, maternity wear and
   lingere.

NOTE: Without GWIP card it will almost be impossible
for you to attend Wednesday, Thursday, Sunday
(WTS) Salon Nights.

Executive order 5674747474
Mudd Executive Council

Above: Mudd ID Card information, benefits, penalties and security clearance clarification, 1980.
Opposite: *They Eat Scum,* East Village Eye Benefit, 1980, courtesy Howie Pyro.

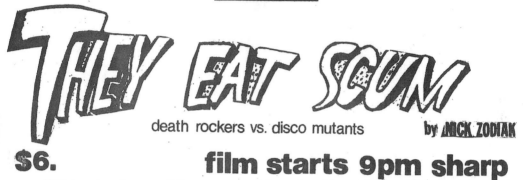

JILL KROESEN
joe hannan
darrell perry

DAVID McDERMOTT

PLUS:

THEY EAT SCUM

death rockers vs. disco mutants   by NICK ZEDD

$6.   **film starts 9pm sharp**

77 WHITE STREET   RESERVATIONS 777-6157

Chi Chi is looking as beautiful as ever, and Gennaro is speaking his own language, doing his own thing. Aldo is handling security with silent strength and patient resolve, while Debi Mazar is either watching the stairs, losing herself on the dance floor or getting trapped in one of the bathrooms. Most important: crowds keep coming, bands keep playing and people keep waiting.

August 4, I arrived at work early, looking forward to an easy Monday. The *East Village Eye*, a newly established old-school rag with cheap ads and a great sense of what was happening, was having another benefit to help keep the paper alive. Nick Zedd's film *They Eat Scum* was being shown at 9 P.M. followed by the Revelons, a band more affiliated with CBGB than Mudd. The film had an air of rabid Punk nihilism rather than No Wave deadpan noir and synced nicely with White Street's oft-preferred entertainment gone astray. Referring to himself and his like-minded collaborators (Lydia Lunch and Lung Leg to name but two) as the loosely banded Cinema of Transgression, Zedd went on to make a number of films, among them 1983's *Greek Maggot Bingo*.

Leonard Abrams, a Mudd Club regular, was the publisher of the *Eye* and Pat Wadsley, well suited for her position, was the Special Sex Editor of the Summer 1980 issue. The club was busy by 11 and the film lived up to its scum-eating title.

Ricky, Teri, Gary and Andi all showed up late and by 5 A.M. we headed off into our own versions of sleepless night. When we weren't at the Mudd Club, we continued to pass away the downtime at One University Place. Engrossed with Space Invaders and Asteroids, we owned the back room. I'd see Andi sitting on the back of a chair, watching the action until she was either overcome with excitement or the chair tipped over. I heard the *husk* in Teri's voice, cheering until she was hoarse, then running to the bar for another Kamikaze. Ricky went through a lot of quarters. We all went through a lot of drinks.

Inspired by our collective obsession, Andi wrote a song called "Chinese Chance."

"Always not knowing
Which course to choose …
Chinese Chance
Drop in a quarter
Chinese Chance
Try your luck …"

One University Place—it's where we lived for a few hours each night.

Run Through the Jungle

We're connected by where we live and the people we know—in those days, by where we drank and danced, and by the drugs we did or didn't do. The distance between zero and six degrees offers little separation and when someone got nudged we all felt the push. Every now and then people fell over; most of the time they got back up. Sometimes they didn't.

Lydia Lunch's band 8 Eyed Spy played their first New York City show to a packed house at the Mudd Club back in October '79. With a dark sound, sharp jangly edges and a heavy beat, Lydia was all screamed out after a set that included Creedence Clearwater Revival's "Run Through the Jungle." The people wanted more, Lydia said

Lydia Lunch, smiling 1980, by Lisa Genet.

no, Steve Mass stepped in and gave her a hundred-dollar bill. She stepped back up for an encore. That was ten months ago, when encores were still cheap.

The guys in 8 Eyed Spy drifted in and out of Mudd, but Lydia only came around if she had a gig. Guitarist and keyboard player Pat Irwin lived around the corner on Franklin Street, started coming around at the beginning, and even saved the B-52's on opening night. (They blew an amp and needed another; he ran home and brought one back.) Soon he was playing with Lydia, and fooling around with another band called The Raybeats. He eventually became an unofficial B-52.

Drummer Jim Sclavunos was a member of Teenage Jesus and the Jerks and another of Lydia's bands, Beirut Slump. Bassist George Scott III was a founding member of The Raybeats until he left and officially joined 8 Eyed Spy. Before that, George had been a player in the short-lived proto-Punk band Jack Ruby with violinist Boris Policeband. He'd worked with James Chance and the Contortions, James White and the Blacks, and played some with John Cale. He'd only been in town about five years.

The third of August was a busy night. While Gray played the Mudd Club, 8 Eyed Spy was playing at Hurrah, recording live tracks for what they hoped would be their self-titled album. Later that week on Wednesday, August 6, Claudia Summers walked up to me at the door and said, "You knew George, right? He OD'd yesterday."

I knew who George Scott was and I'd seen him play, but I didn't really know him. I wasn't sure if it was a push or a shove, but I felt something when Claudia told me he died. I looked around, the street was empty, and hardly anyone was waiting. I left the door and went inside to see what was going on. I asked the bar for a soda. Death came and went. 8 Eyed Spy was finished.

Persian Brown

The following night, it's heat-wave crazy. Eighty-five degrees at 3 A.M. and I've been lounging on the second floor too long. I climb over Andi, tell Ricky and Teri to move, and gently push Plasmatics bass player Chosei Funahara out of the way. I pick up my beer and head for the door but the bottle's empty by the time I get downstairs. Half a dozen cabs are idling at the curb and the night's almost over.

I've got a crumble of tinfoil with a line or two of brown Persian dope in my pocket. It's from Pierre, a heroin dealer from Marseille. My friend Kirk introduced us, and I introduced Pierre to some friends at the club. It's 1980 and introducing heroin dealers to friends still feels like the right thing to do.

Closing in on 4 A.M., I look around and walk inside. Downstairs is on a slow fade, the dance floor is down to a stagger, the barflies are headed upstairs. By 9 A.M., I'm standing in the sunshine outside Laight Street and I've lost track of the last five hours. I want to go home and sleep but sleeping is difficult. Something's getting in the way and I'm not doing anything to help. Maybe tomorrow I'll try and figure it out, try and do something different.

The summer's been up and down with a wild streak thru the middle. It's still got another month to go. Next week the French navy pulls into New York harbor. They're part of this story too.

Joni

Friday night and I've already lost track of Thursday. Standing at the door smiling, the crowd seems to smile back. We're *all* part of the story and I want to let everyone in but it's just not possible. Then a taxi pulls up and Nathan Joseph gets out, his friend Joni Mitchell right beside him. I open the chain and the three of us walk in. Thirty minutes later, Joni's onstage strumming a borrowed guitar and singing songs as only Joni Mitchell can. The dance floor stops. She blows the place away.

It was dark when I left the club with Joni, Nathan and Gary. By the time the sun came up, around 6 A.M., we already had crashed in and out of an after-hours joint a few blocks away. By 7 we're back at Joni's loft on Varick Street drinking beer, smoking cigarettes and playing pinball. It felt like the usual, but it wasn't—we were drinking Joni Mitchell's beer at her place and shooting pinball on her machines. I thought about the first time I heard that strange, affecting voice, maybe "Clouds." A decade later I felt more a connection. That voice and those songs: 1969, 1980 and forward.

Joni lit another cigarette and she and Gary kept talking. I kept playing pinball.

Jimi Hendrix Studio "B"

Saturday, August 9, 1980, and we made it home from Varick Street by 10 A.M. Later that afternoon Andi Ostrowe gathered her friends at Electric Lady Studios. It was four years to the day that she went to the Record Plant where Patti Smith was recording the song "Radio Ethiopia"—the day Andi and Patti officially met. She stuck around; Patti couldn't do without her and still can't. I couldn't either.

Andi booked Hendrix's legendary Studio B to record a cover of Pete Townshend's "Nothing Is Everything." "Chinese Chance," the pop song that took Andi about twenty minutes to write, became the A-side. The band was Richard Sohl on keyboards, Andi's cousin David Ostrowe (a.k.a. DRO) on drums, Gary Buildings on bass and Jimi Monroe on saxophone. Jay Burnett was producing. Everyone was at the ready when one of Patti's jagged and worn *REFM* (Radio Ethiopia Field Marshall) guitar picks, used in 1976 to tear up the strings on her Fender, finally arrived special-delivery from Detroit. That's when Andi picked up her guitar.

An all-star lineup of hand-clappers, including me, Gary Kanner, Pat Wadsley and the entire band, added just the right touch. Andi worked hard and the songs sounded great. I got to design the record sleeve. Now all she needed was a test pressing.

Coasting along on less than no sleep at all, I left Electric Lady with Ricky and Andi. They stopped at Mickey's for some food and I headed over to First Avenue to cop from Patrick and Melanie, a freakish but friendly couple who sold heroin to support themselves and their habit. She was tall and skinny with Sanskrit letters tattooed on her forehead; Patrick was cadaverous and burnt out. Given that, and despite the giant green iguana running around the apartment, it was still less scary than crawling thru the ruins of Alphabet City.

An hour later, I was back at One University. When I tried to leave Jesse Chamberlain pulled me aside. We got in a cab, stopped at his place a few blocks east, and ended up on White Street by 2 A.M. The Saturday crowd was backed up into the street, the temperature was stuck on a permanent ninety and the scene outside was chaos. Aldo was on security and Gennaro was on the door. From the look of it, I was glad I had the night off.

Jesse and I pushed thru the crowd, grabbed Chris Frantz and Tina Weymouth, and opened the chain. Gennaro's reaction was delayed, surprised and grateful; he was in a jam, past the point of seeing faces, and only seeing a crowd. People began calling my name and I started pointing, letting them in one or two at a time. It was my job, and in some strange way that crowd was mine too. I had to step in. I couldn't help it.

When I got inside, Talking Heads' cover of Al Green's "Take Me to the River" was bouncing around the room. Loud and heavy, the dance floor seemed caught in a slow-motion whiplash. Jesse, waiting with two Budweisers, looked at me and said, "Richard to the rescue." He shoved me toward the bar, I ordered two more, and we walked upstairs to the bathroom. It was nearly empty but for two Russian girls nodding out, trying to put on lipstick. I smiled, said hello, and locked the door. I lit a cigarette, sucked down the first beer, did a line of coke and looked over at Jesse. He handed me the second beer and we started laughing.

Locked inside that little room, leaning against those dirty walls, I was still high from the First Avenue connection. The coke and beer kept me going, and Jesse kept me talking. We were hanging out in a Mudd Club bathroom on my night off. I thought it was the right place to be.

We finished the beer and I was out of coke when one of the Russian girls tipped over. It was a nothing yet indelible moment—and it could've been me.

At some point, she got up off the floor and finished putting on her makeup. Jesse and I grabbed two more drinks and jumped in a cab. Sunday morning, almost 4 A.M., we kept going. I was tired but I couldn't stop, and it was too early to go home. I looked over at Jesse. I wanted him to say something, to tell me where he was going and what he was looking for. Maybe he was waiting for me to do the same. I wish I could ask Jesse if he remembers any of this. I wish he were still here.

Call Waiting

Being there and remembering. Today people keep saying, "The Mudd Club felt like home," but really what was it about the place? Was it the bar or the dance floor, the bathrooms or the often Punk-informed *fuck off!* door policy? The low-key, art bar, performance space vibe, mentioned in the lease-acquiring lie of 1978, surely couldn't be it. As an institute of higher learning, the Mudd College of Deviant Behavior offered a bit of everything.

Without even trying I remember it all, the cool of dirty white tile and the scrape of brick where the tile ended. The bathrooms alone were a small faraway world of comfort and distraction: a sometimes last resort, a *home* away from home.

Nine blocks south, the extra bedroom at Murray Street was twice the size of any Mudd bathroom. Darker, slightly more private, the room made its own offer of homey comfort. Even so, Lounge Lizard Steve Piccolo didn't last very long as a roommate. His brief residency was more of an extended crash with phone, bathroom and kitchen privileges. He might've thought paying rent was merely an option, our friendship loosely based on music, drugs and being there.

Laura Kennedy, the Bush Tetras' bass player, was next in line. She made it thru the revolving door and stayed long enough to establish tenure. To keep up with our busy lives we added the new *call waiting* feature to the phone, changing our number to accommodate the advanced technology. My days of unplugging-the-phone escapism were over.

A roommate who actually paid the rent, and I loved her for it; I loved how tough Laura thought she was, and I loved how she played a bass line you could feel in your gut. We were kids, twenty-two and twenty-six. We thought we knew everything that was going on and we did. Laura became my friend and partner in crime—the scene of the crime, wherever we landed.

Who Shot J.R.

I ran around with Laura and she was running around with Claudia. Gary was either running ahead or behind. The Bush Tetras were rehearsing in their East First Street studio or planning their next gig. The in-between moments were spent at the Mudd Club.

Between the bathrooms of White Street, the bedrooms of Murray and the rest of the world, summer 1980 was a busy time. I was fully aware of the United States' boycott of the Moscow Olympics but oblivious to the Great Grasshopper Plague of South Dakota. A propane-leaking tanker in the Hudson River fucked up New York City traffic and even shut down the George Washington Bridge, but it had little effect on late-night cab service and even less effect on me. Charles Manson was let out of solitary *again*, and David "Son of Sam" Berkowitz was back in court to determine his competency to do anything at all.

El Salvador was falling deeper into political turmoil while Mexico's heroin trade only added to the endless supply trafficked across the Silk Road of the Far and Middle East. The American hostages, and their three hundred days and counting of captivity in Iran, had already damaged Jimmy Carter's chance for re-election; the stalled U.S. economy killed it.

Ronald Reagan, the former B-movie star governor of California, was gearing up for his run against Carter but few people I knew gave a shit. The bigger news was the Hollywood actors' strike, jeopardizing the long-awaited answer to 1980's burning question, "Who shot J.R.?"

Back in New York, the Democrats, in need of friendly territory but not knowing which way to turn, chose Madison Square Garden as the site for their convention. Danceteria, on nearby West Thirty-seventh, became the drunken delegates' destination of choice, and for security's sake the Feds paid a visit. They ignored Danceteria's illegal hours and liquor status but discovered fire exits blocked by a stage. A quick reconfiguration followed and the club stayed open, but the episode bore the warning of things to come.

Pom-poms

The world was changing, people were adjusting and so was White Street. Hard news, pop culture, politics, gossip—what mattered was a matter of opinion. I tried to be open-minded and keep things light at the Mudd Club door, even offering a former reject a second chance.

A year earlier, when Bianca Jagger attempted a Mudd Club invasion in a two-limo caravan, Louie had turned her away (invoking Steve's *no Mick Jagger types* rule or his own freewheeling sense of doorman discretion). Tonight she arrived by cab, wearing a white pantsuit, carrying a long-stemmed red rose. Opening the chain with a welcoming hand I let her in, and ten minutes later she's six deep in the crowd. The pantsuit still looks white and she's dancing with Gary.

Shortly after, and light as a summer breeze, Teri Toye showed up at the door and slipped inside. Recently returned from a family visit to Iowa, she had new clothes, a fresh attitude, and her little sister Tami along for the ride. I'm not sure if New York was ready for two Toyes, but the sisters Toye were ready for New York—and White Street, of course, ready for anything.

It was still early, and tonight's version of *anything* was Alan Midgette getting out of a cab with what looked to be three young sailors. Wearing hats with large red pom-poms could only mean one thing: either the circus was in town or the French navy just dropped anchor.

Big Ron got to Mudd around 2 A.M. asking if Alan and the sailors had arrived. I told him, "They sure did," and together we went inside. One of the boys was at the downstairs bar, and Alan was on the dance floor, spinning. He was wearing a hat with a big red pom-pom. I looked over at Ron and started laughing.

We headed for the second-floor bathroom and passed three girls in a booth with sailor number two. Sailor number three was in the bathroom simply standing there, hard to resist, and not shy about *ready for anything.* By closing time, *Who's bringing a pom-pom home?* was the question on everyone's mind.

Half porn fantasy, half stoned reality, no matter how drunk they were we let the French navy in for free. It was an *appel du devoir*—a call to duty—and for the next week served us well.

The Ventures

The sailors were all over town, from the Wild West Forties to the East Village, from the Alphabets to One University to 77 White. Those pom-poms fit in everywhere and good times were easy to find.

Before I started at Mudd I'd never met any French sailors. The East Village and Alphabet City had long come undone and the West Forties were a lost netherworld dotted with Broadway musicals. By 1980 (aside from sailors on the loose, and me standing at the door of 77 White) not much had changed. White Street, for a second year, remained summer's midnight oasis; there were one or two red pom-poms in the crowd, and the Ventures were going on around 1 A.M.

An inspired booking and a band well past its prime, the Ventures took the stage and returned to early sixties form. When they covered the Surfaris' 1963 hit "Wipeout" (a Ventures hit in '66) the Mudd Club got hit with a wave of original Surf Punk—a sound-bite memory from a time we knew but thought we'd left behind.

I stood near the stage with future gallerist Patrick Fox and artist Robert Hawkins. I turned away and walked out front, feeling what videographer Pat Ivers likes to call "a weird time travel dislocation." Catching the vibe of a familiar past, we tried but couldn't overlook the nightmare of Nixon and Vietnam, Manson and Altamont. Now, the well-intentioned clusterfuck of Carter was paving the way for Reagan's sleepwalk of a presidency: we were ducks sitting on the cusp and someone or something was ready to take a shot. Another battle was warming to a war—this time with an invisible enemy—whose unforeseen, innumerable casualties and consequences would nearly overwhelm the survivors. We never thought we'd get caught, let alone hurt. Despite our behavior and forgetting the occasional crash, dying wasn't on our radar.

Twenty minutes later the Ventures finished with a song that sounded like another "Wipeout." I listened from outside. I was working and people were still waiting to come in.

This Is Crazy

Whether it was on the street or the dance floor, I still had the occasional feeling of being alone in a crowd. Almost everyone knew who I was, but hardly anyone really knew me. Most of the time I was okay with it but sometimes I got confused. My personal life and working at the Mudd Club had become one and the same. I needed something more; I kept on looking.

Friday night the search continued. I was back outside thinning the herd when my friends Louis and Fred arrived. We all grew up in New Hyde Park, where Louis and his sister Diane were the kids next door. They were like family, and still are.

Louis and Fred made it thru the crowd and stepped up to the chain. Lou looked at me and said, "Richard, this is crazy," and Fred just laughed. I just shrugged; they hadn't really seen crazy yet but I knew they could handle anything from a *planet shift* to whatever the off-kilter White Street universe might offer. They headed inside while I kept working; two worlds were about to collide.

My memory says cab, not limousine; they were low-key and under the radar—even more so than Louis or Fred. The crowd was focused on getting inside, oblivious to Keith Richards and Patti Hansen walking toward the door. They were on a date and coming to the Mudd Club. I guess I opened the chain but I can't remember.

They stopped for a moment and chatted while a hundred people began to stare. We went inside and I took them to the second floor. I didn't see Steve right away so I parked them at the bar near Lou and Fred. I ordered drinks, said "make yourselves at home" and wandered off. I started laughing, thinking about "Satisfaction" spinning on the turntable in Louie's basement, summer 1965. Fifteen years past, this was almost too perfect.

An hour later, I shook Keith's hand, opened the chain and said good night. Louis and Fred hung out, waiting for me to finish. Two hours later, we wound up at a neighborhood after-hours club—Patti and Keith were there, as friendly at 5 A.M. as they were at 2. I just kept thinking about all those songs we listened to when we were kids, those songs that meant everything. I smiled, did my thing and introduced Keith and Patti to Louis and Fred.

It was a *moment* but I had to run. Saturday morning—the train was leaving Penn Station at 7 A.M. and Montauk was waiting.

You Know What to Wear

I disappear for two days and show up at Mudd on Monday night. Gone by 4 A.M. and I'm back on Tuesday. White Street's busy and the crowd looks almost pretty. I run upstairs and find SVT vocalist Brian Marnell hanging out near the plexiglass DJ booth. There's a girl on each side of him. I head for the bar and start talking to Jack Casady. I'm still a diehard fan and I want to see his band, SVT, play the Mudd Club. I want to hear Casady's bass guitar shake the walls of 77 White.

Diego Cortez is on the other side of the room, opposite the doors to the stairway, and directly facing the Bay Area's psychedelic past. He's at the other end of the spectrum—No Wave or next wave—and far less distant from the post-Punk present. Alone, he's leaning against the wall and watching what is.

Diego's moved on, though he still comes down to White Street; sadly I can't say the same for Anya Phillips. She came by the night Debbie Harry taped a Gloria Vanderbilt Murjani Jeans ad in Cortlandt Alley but that's long past. Chris Stein wrote the jingle, Debbie sang, and a smoke machine fogged up the alley until the action moved inside. John Lurie was playing saxophone onstage and there was a quick last flash of Anya dancing with James Chance. Debbie faced off with the camera in the final shot, singing those immortal words, "When you know where you're goin' you know what to wear."

Back at the bar, Jack's disappeared, and Marnell's still flirting with the same two girls. I take another beer, ask Diego if he wants one and go downstairs. Outside, it's the same hundred people who always seem to be there. I let some in, light a cigarette and let in some more. Is this really what I do?

Half-Breed

I walked to Murray Street in the morning light—with sunglasses, a cigarette and a beer. I hung out at the loft and painted all day. I left for work around 10 P.M. I guess I did the same on Thursday. Friday night I showed up at the club wearing my favorite shirt: gray with black and red trim, short sleeves with a zipper down the front. It was classic Television-era stagewear, Richard Lloyd circa 1976. I loved that shirt.

I had to work Saturday as well because Gennaro was missing in action. Called Bea and said I'd be doing Montauk on Sunday and Monday—a day late but I'd be there. She said my room was always ready; two windows looking out at the ocean, the shredded remains of a curtain filtering sun and breeze. Sometimes I shared the room with Gary, other times with Ricky and his boom box. We were always playing a new cassette by Cher and her boyfriend, Les Dudek; the band was called Black Rose. They were terrible, but it was still Cher, and we figured a boom box in Montauk was the only way to play it. Then we heard the news, headed for Central Park and made the most of Saturday in the city.

Andi and Ricky offered their Patti Smith Group credentials and I offered *door at the Mudd Club*, as we passed thru the backstage gate of Wollman Rink. Black Rose, without a mention of Cher, was opening for Hall and Oates; she was just the singer, trying hard to be one of the guys.

We stood there hoping for the best, but like the record, their live sound was awful. Cher looked great in tight black cutaway spandex and leather boots but the idea that she might belt out "Half-Breed" or "Little Man" was just a dream. Black Rose was all about a boom box at the beach, but we already knew that; the only reason we went to Central Park was to see Cher.

The rest of the audience had barely a clue as they sat there waiting to hear ninety minutes of watery blue-eyed soul. Ricky and Andi had bigger fish to fry and I had to work. We left before the headliners came on. To this day I have no idea what Hall and Oates is all about.

Twenty-five, Six or Seven

Sunday morning the beach was calling and I was gone. Monday was a dream and Montauk was deserted. Tuesday I'm back, running all day, no time to stop home. Dirty jeans, a T-shirt and a new pair of Converse All Stars would have to do. I'd be the example and set the tone: dress like this and you're probably not coming in.

I hadn't done any dope in days but was feeling fine. I called Pierre in the afternoon and he planned on coming by early to see me; when he showed up at 3 A.M. I was ready for a break. DJ David was playing the Supremes' "You Keep Me Hanging On" but by then I felt more like the Vanilla Fudge version. We headed for the basement storage area and parked ourselves on a couple of cases of cleaning fluid. At least I wasn't drinking it.

Pierre handed me a small foil package with a large amount of brown heroin for the bargain price of one hundred dollars. He told me to put it away and pulled out his own stash, his own piece of foil and a straw. He lit a match and we *chased the dragon*. I've never used the expression until now.

I sat on that case of brand X not-quite Pine-Sol and Pierre went back upstairs. I thought about Bleecker Street, the people I met, and how it all began. I started this job when I was twenty-five years old. I can't remember turning twenty-six but I'm sure I was at the Mudd Club. I planned on celebrating twenty-seven in Montauk and assumed I had about two weeks to get it together. That's not how it played out.

Ten days before my birthday, the Pretenders came to town for a much-anticipated show at Wollman Rink in Central Park. Chrissie was hanging out with either Kate Simon or Judy Nylon and Judy was hanging out with Alice. Lynette, Andi and I were hanging out with Pete Farndon. The rest of the time the band was out in Flushing, Queens, for the U.S. Open. John McEnroe was going for another championship and Vitas Gerulaitis was hitting it hard, on and off the courts.

The Mudd Club and Mickey's, Montauk and the Pretenders—Marlboros, Heinekens, cocaine and heroin. The weather was beautiful and there were only a few weeks left of summer.

Lucifer, Scorpio, Anger

Just before the Pretenders showed up, Kenneth Anger arrived at the Mudd Club. His 1972 film *Lucifer Rising* was finally out in limited release, and the filmmaker and *Hollywood Babylon* author was making a scheduled "appearance." His connection to everyone from the Rolling Stones, Anita Pallenberg and Tennessee Williams to Satanist Anton LaVey and Manson associate Bobby Beausoleil was certainly colorful. Anger's influential homoerotic biker and occult film *Scorpio Rising* was a thirty-minute, dialogue-free pop music feast. *Lucifer*, on the other hand, was an aborted mash-up of Beausoleil's music with a cast that included Marianne Faithfull, Chris Jagger (Mick's brother) and Jimmy Page. On the night of Anger's appearance at Mudd, scenes from both films were projected on the walls of the first and second floor.

The Anger "show" fit right in with the Mudd Club's wide-net/wide-vision range of enlightening entertainment. Smart stuff: dirty and dangerous, funny and beautiful. For me it was the kind of weird scary shit I loved. I hung around inside and took the opportunity to get close to Mr. Anger for a few minutes. Despite his ability to channel darkness, he came off as polite, open to conversation and kind of normal. I'm not sure what I expected, and not sure if my assessment says more about him or me. I told him it was a pleasure, and I returned to the door without offering him a Quaalude, a line of cocaine or even a drink.

Central Park, Grace and Precious

My personal variation on dirty, dangerous and scary weird seemed kind of normal too. My daily routine had its own broken rhythm but I was still able to play along. Then Pretenders came to town.

Pete Farndon's hotel on West Fifty-seventh Street was close to Central Park but thirty minutes from everything else. A room at the Gramercy would've been more convenient, at least for me. By day we were shopping our way around the Village, hanging at the loft and playing Space Invaders at One University. Lynette was sticking close to Pete and by 2 A.M. they were showing up on White Street. Pete was getting psyched for the big show while I was preoccupied with heroin and anxious about everything. Pete was less anxious but equally preoccupied.

Summer 1980 was the last season of scheduled concerts at Central Park's Wollman Rink. Dr Pepper had been sponsoring the series since 1977, following in the footsteps of Rheingold and Schaefer Beer. The Pretenders' Labor Day Weekend show was a big event and the final concert at the rink. The city was busy and the Mudd Club was packed every night. Somehow I had the entire weekend off.

Saturday, August 30, is the big day. At noon I head over to the Lower East Side, to a new hole in an old wall with two one-hundred-dollar bills. I'm meeting Andi at 5 and we're meeting Pete at the hotel. I'm not sure where Lynette is but she'll find us—she's good at that.

Late afternoon and we're on our way to the Buckingham on Fifty-seventh Street, a nondescript but upscale establishment with some sort of Mormonish affiliation. There's no bar, no minibar and no booze—a condition heretofore unknown to whoever booked the tour.

Pete looks happy when Andi and I arrive, and five minutes later we're all happy. I'm lying on the bed with Andi-Midge and Pete's doing a last-minute look in the mirror. Pretenders' manager Dave Hill comes knocking and we're on our way.

Chrissie and her friend Diane are already waiting at the elevator. It's a quiet ride to the lobby until Chris wants to know, "Who's the little one?" referring to all sixty inches of Midge. It's the needed tension-breaker and a memorable moment.

Three decades later, Andi's down to fifty-nine and three-quarters inches but we still get a laugh out of that line.

Through the lobby and out the door, five of us are in the first car. Two blocks up Sixth Avenue onto Central Park Drive, the limo goes off-road and winds its way through the rocks to the backstage entrance. The place is a madhouse—sold out with another few thousand hanging outside. The cops start banging on the back door yelling, "Rolling Stones out here!"—generic cop code for a Rock 'n' Roll band.

We pile out of the car, the door opens, and from over my shoulder I hear a voice I'd know anywhere. *The voice that launched a thousand trips* is asking the stage-door question of the moment, "Is Ron Delsener here?" Andi jabs me hard with a finger and says, "Grace Slick, Grace Slick." I turn around, look at Grace, and all I can say is, "Come on." Delsener, the concert promoter who founded the festival series in 1966 with CBGB owner Hilly Kristal, is around somewhere but for the moment, it doesn't matter.

Pete and Chrissie head straight for the dressing room trailer. Jimmy and Martin are still ten minutes behind. Black leathered and greased-hair guitar slinger Chris Spedding stands at the ready. His on-and-off girlfriend and future wife, Erasers bass player Jodi Beach, is hanging out nearby. Moving on, I pass thru a mix of usual and unusual backstage suspects. John and Yoko came by to see Doug Sahm, who opened the show, but they're gone before we arrive. Vitas Gerulaitis just walked in; Alice and Judy Nylon are already down in front, cocktails in hand. I'm standing behind a stack of amps talking to Andi when Lynette comes thru the back door. Grace and her husband, Skip Johnson, are sitting on a trunk a couple of feet away but I'm at a loss for words.

Grace is someone I've always wanted to meet who's never been to White Street. Her band, Jefferson Airplane, opened my eyes and blew my eighth-grade mind back in '67. *Surrealistic Pillow* and the next four albums, a barrage unlike anything I'd heard. Now, over a decade later, we're face to face; I step over to where she's sitting but all I can come up with is, "I've been in love with you since I was thirteen years old." Grace smiles at me and says, "Thank you." I return the smile with a nervous laugh and extend an invitation to the Mudd Club. She starts talking and I start to loosen up until the crowd starts to roar. The band's almost ready.

The Pretenders hit the stage and open the show with "Precious." When Chrissie fires off the infamous, "Not me baby I'm too precious, fuck off," the place goes berserk. The band follows with a beautiful version of "Kid," "Talk of the Town" (from *Pretenders II*, released August 1981) and every song on the first album.

It's tight and loud, short and sweet—a fast and furious hour and twenty minutes. At the end of the show, Chris Spedding, armed with a Gibson Flying V, joins the band onstage and they tear the Wollman Rink apart. Second encore: "Precious" for the second time and I'm laughing out loud, yelling for more. It's one of the best shows I've ever seen.

Rodney

I know at some point we'll wind up at Mudd but for the moment I have no idea what's next. It's early, maybe 9 P.M., and everyone's decompressing in the trailer. Thirty minutes later, we split with Pete, and unwind back at the hotel. By 11, we're sitting around a front table at Dangerfield's, waiting for Rodney.

Between all the excitement and the Alphabet City nod, I never saw this one coming, and hanging out with the Pretenders has its limits, even for me. Andi and I offer our thanks, tell Pete and Lynette, "Later," and head for White Street. By the time we arrive, Saturday night's moved into Sunday morning.

Andi and I freshen up, order a drink and walk downstairs. There's a new Space Invaders in the Mudd basement waiting for us. An hour and several drinks later, I hear Lynette scream, "Oh my God! We knew we'd find you here." She's laughing her way down the stairs and

Pete's right behind her with two beers and a pocketful of quarters. By 5 A.M. we were heading in three different directions.

Hammerhead's and a Full Baggie

September 1, Monday, forty-eight hours after Central Park, we're on the Long Island Expressway driving thru the first seventeen years of my life. We pass Exit 34, New Hyde Park Road—just a mile from where I first listened to John Lennon, Keith Richards and Grace Slick. It's where I saw Dangerfield and Cher on *Ed Sullivan*. I was maybe twelve years old and that wave of information, the songs and the words, set my life in motion. *Then* became a connection to *now*, impossible without those voices.

Lynette's got a friend with an old beat-up station wagon, and he's doing the driving. I'm smoking a joint and staring out the window at the disconnected world of my spent and misspent youth. Nothing and everything seems the same.

The Pretenders are playing a Labor Day show at a club called Hammerhead's, somewhere along the south shore's mid-island sprawl. I spoke to Pete earlier and he knows he's on Long Island but he's not sure where. I tell him we're coming, we'll find him, and we'll see him later.

A barely legal left turn and we cross six lanes of Sunrise Highway traffic. Hammerhead's is located in a strip mall; the club, about the size of a small, low-ceilinged supermarket and a big change from Central Park. The band is already playing "Kid," again their second song, as Lynette and I squeeze our way onto the side of the stage. Pete looks over, shakes his head and laughs. His bass lets out a rumble and the band takes it for a ride. It's such a beautiful song.

After the show, John McEnroe, Vitas Gerulaitis and a baggie full of cocaine come backstage. Pete tosses me a beer that I actually catch, and tells me to wait. John and Vitas play it cool and the band gets busy signing albums, autographing T-shirts and posing for a photo with Mr. Hammerhead's kid. Thirty minutes later, it's time to split, and Pete rides with us in the station wagon. There's no traffic and we're flying along the expressway, windows open, headed for the city. A quick stop at the hotel and by 2 A.M. we're back at the Mudd Club, exhausted, stoned and drinking beer. Gennaro's working the door, and I have no idea what day it is.

Happy Birthday to Me

Tuesday's reality sets in and I'm back outside of 77 White with the chain in my hand; I feel good about everything but my love life, my heroin chippy and my wardrobe. At least I've been inspired to start some new paintings.

By Wednesday I'm ignoring the crowd, letting Aldo do the work. I'm dreaming about The Surf and Sand when Betsy Sussler (still a year away from *Bomb* magazine) arrives and mentions she'll be in Montauk for the weekend to work on a movie. I tell her I'll be there too, celebrating my twenty-seventh birthday.

Thursday night at the door, waiting for the night to end. My birthday is two days away and I'm trying to figure out what's happening and who's coming out. Steve Mass keeps asking me questions about Montauk, and I have a feeling he's going to be there.

I get on the train Friday morning with a pocket full of money, a pack of cigarettes and a weekend's worth of dime bags. I sit down, close my eyes and wonder if I'm young or old. I curl up in the seat, change trains in a town called Babylon and wake up in Montauk.

That evening, Lori and Joe stop by again with Thomas Trask. Their house is just fifteen minutes west of Montauk and they drove over in their Renault *Le Car*, a cute little cube of an automobile. Sitting around the bar with Gary, Ricky and Teri, we drink and play Loteria, go out on the porch and smoke pot. The air feels cool and we can hear the waves. Bea's behind the bar mixing drinks, chatting up the locals. Saving ourselves for Saturday night, none of us go off the rails or over the edge. I tell Lori, Joe and Thomas, "Come back tomorrow, for my birthday, and we'll have some cake."

Back inside I look over at Bea. She loves what's happening at The Surf and Sand and so do the rest of us. I ask her for another drink, go upstairs and smoke another joint. Looking out the window and staring at the ocean, it's only 1 A.M. but I'm ready for a good night's sleep.

Saturday morning rolls in slow and Steve Mass rings the pay phone downstairs at 10 A.M. It's hard to tell if he's up late or early. He tells me he's chartering one of those seaplanes that take off from the East River near Twenty-third Street and flying out in the afternoon with John Cale and his wife, Risé. He wants to see what we're up to and wants to be on hand for my birthday. They need two rooms for the night and Bea has to see what she can do.

MUDD CLUB SCHEDULE
SEPTEMBER 5—14

Sunday September 7,
SOFT BOYS

Monday September 8,
MODETTES

Tuesday September 9,
BAUHAUS

Wednesday September 10,
CINEMUDD FILM SERIES Begins at 9:30 PM
ANIMAL X FASHION SHOW Begins at 11:00 PM

Thursday September 11,
NO JAPS AT MY FUNERAL Video by James Nares)Begins at 9:30)
PANTHER BURNS Band begins at 11:00 PM

Friday September 12,
EX—MUDDY WATERS BAND

Sunday September 14,
BEDROOMS OF EUROPE

MUDD CLUB 77 WHITE STREET 227-7777

Schedule, 1980.

Big Ron shows up at 11 A.M. and it's already eighty degrees. The visitors' plane is set to land late afternoon, arriving at Bea's in plenty of time for the party. Ron, Ricky and Gary carry a cake back from town, and Lori, Joe and Thomas show up to help blow out the candles. Betsy Sussler and her "crew" come by after a day of moviemaking. Even the psycho coke dealer from Charlton Street makes the quick trip from East Hampton. Bea stays behind the bar, doing her Surf and Sand hospitality thing, while I run upstairs to roll more joints. When I come downstairs everyone's singing "Happy Birthday" to me.

I had hoped for a *Fudgie the Whale* ice cream cake from Carvel, but the IGA supermarket special does the trick. I'm smiling and happy, surrounded by friends, people I barely know and people I don't know at all; it's Mudd Club on the beach.

I remember swimming in the ocean that night. I don't remember sleeping but I probably did. I walked the sand in the morning, filmed a brief scene and spoke a few lines in Betsy's movie. On the way back I jumped in the waves. Sunday afternoon, everybody went to Gosman's Dock, the big seafood joint in Montauk, and Steve picked up the tab. The visitors flew back to the city; the rest of us got high and headed back to the beach. The water felt September warm and I swam past the breakers. I closed my eyes, treaded water, and the day disappeared. By 9 P.M., I was on the train. I was officially twenty-seven years old.

Taxis, Drinks and Drugs

Back on Murray Street just after midnight and Steve calls the minute I walk in. He tells me to come by the club, says he'll be up on the third floor. I have no idea what he wants.

I get out of my shorts, into my jeans, shake Montauk out of my sneakers and walk to White Street. There's a few people waiting outside and Gennaro's working the door, flirting with anyone who'll flirt back. Someone calls, "Richie, Richie," but it's not my name unless you're Tom Baker or Sylvia Miles. I keep walking.

When I get to the third floor Steve asks me what I'm doing. I assume he means tonight and not with my life, so I mention stopping at One U, seeing the Lounge Lizards at Danceteria and coming back here later. He responds with two hundred dollars in twenties, tells me to go to Danceteria, buy people drinks and to bring them back to White Street. I know what he's up to, and it sounds like a plan, but three hundred sounds better. Steve bites and I'm on my way with a wad of cash to spend on taxis, drinks and drugs.

Danceteria's crowded and the Lounge Lizards are already onstage. Jim Fouratt walks over and hands me a bottle of champagne for my birthday. I pour half of it down my throat, walk up front and pass the bottle to John Lurie. He takes a long drink, passes it back and I finish the rest. I buy a bunch of drink tickets and wander thru the club looking for coke, Quaaludes and someone to fuck around with. I'm here on assignment, doing my job and buying people drinks makes me popular.

By 2 A.M., I leave Danceteria bored, distracted and fucked up. I feel like disappearing but I can't. Six of us in a Checker headed for White Street, and the driver looks about a hundred years old. We're doing 60 mph down Broadway and I'm listening to mouth noise coming out of five people I barely know. I'd rather be home painting or passing out but ten minutes later I'm back on White Street.

Again I'm left wondering, *Is this really my job?* I keep thinking about what Steve asked me: *What are you doing?* Leaning on the bar, the Mudd Club going full tilt, I'm trying to figure out a real answer. How to paint more, work less, stop using dope and still go out every night? I still don't know. I'm still missing something. I still can't see *it*. Maybe he needs to rephrase the question.

Monday morning, walking home alone. I'm thinking about the phone call nineteen months ago: Steve Mass telling me to come see him.

Remembering those first few weeks, I thought I found myself when I landed on the steps of the Mudd Club. I met a lot of people and made my share of friends but all I really found was another place to hide out, get high and go crazy.

Now it's September 1980. The weekends in Montauk are almost over, the weather's changing and the nights are cool. My hair's the longest it's ever been and I'm working the door in jeans, a T-shirt and the green windbreaker. The long tweed coat's still buried in the back of the closet.

Monday night, 9 P.M., and the only other question is dinner. I'm hungry and I have to be at Mudd by 11.

Meltdown

The following week Lynette arrives in Montauk around 3 A.M. It's one of my last visits to Bea's Surf and Sand. We climb out the window, onto the roof, smoke some hash, and wait for the sun. I start thinking back to the summer of '75. Nights on Lido Beach smoking pot, drinking quarts of Colt 45 and running toward the ocean. Summer 1976 was Bleecker and Bowery, Television and "Venus de Milo," Talking Heads and "Psycho Killer."

John Lurie, saxophone and shadow, 1980, by Lisa Genet.

Now it's heroin on the beach and getting high in a second-floor bathroom on White Street. The summer is fading and two weeks after my birthday, Montauk's almost over.

On the last day of the last weekend all I want to do is swim in the ocean one more time. The water's calm, the waves barely slapping the sand. I keep walking till I'm neck deep, lift my feet, lie back and float. An hour later, I'm wrapped in a towel, walking back to The Surf and Sand. I get upstairs and completely melt down. I'm lying on the old blue carpeting on the floor of my room, crying. Bea's talking to me, doing her best to help, but time's running out. The train leaves for the city in an hour. She gives my hand a squeeze and goes downstairs.

I light a cigarette and try to stop shaking. I pull out a bag of Red Star dope but there's nothing left. I get on the train with the other *kids*, hide behind a pair of dark glasses, and smoke my way home in the smoking car.

Ricky tells me, "Just relax."

Teri, always the tender soul, seconds the advice with "Go to sleep, Grandma."

"Okay." I light another cigarette.

White Street, 2 A.M. There's a guest DJ upstairs and Marianne Faithfull's spitting out the words to "Why'd Ya Do It." Arto Lindsay's band DNA starts screaming from the stage downstairs. I'm drinking a beer, not sure if I should dance or bang my head against the wall. I'm at a loss, and getting high is starting to feel the same as low. I'm afraid I'm becoming one of those *other* people—giving a shit and not at the same time.

Tomorrow I'm back working the door. Maybe by then I'll feel better.

One Last Time

Later that week, Bea made a trip to the city. Nearly forty years older than the rest of us she spent most of her life in Montauk, but at heart Bea Reilly was a woman of the world. For two short summers, she was our family and our friend.

Bea stayed at Big Ron's Sullivan Street apartment, and we all went to dinner at One University Place. Ricky and Teri, Gary and Ron—no one wanted to say good-bye. We sat around till after midnight; 1 A.M., we headed for 77 White.

Standing at the bar on the first floor of the Mudd Club, Bea looked around, looked back at us, and she *got it*. We felt the same way walking into The Surf and Sand. It's a feeling that's hard to forget: of being home, but knowing you'll have to leave before it leaves you.

Thirty minutes later, we squeezed ourselves into a booth upstairs. Steve came around and handed out drink tickets, wondering why he paid for his own drinks when he stayed at Bea's. I just said thanks and Ricky was already at the bar. Teri asked him for more tickets. Bea looked happy and kept smiling.

We were all together one last time, closing down the summer of 1980.

Mudd Club, 77 White Street. Outside wanting in, 1979, by Bob Gruen.

11.
BEAUTIFUL
AND
GONE

"Out of my mind, I just can't take it anymore," Buffalo Springfield, 1966, Neil Young singing, sad and beautiful. That was over fourteen years ago, half a lifetime. Standing at the Mudd Club door, the song keeps playing in my head. Inside, DJ David Azarch throws a bitter-sweet curveball onto the dance floor. "Redondo Beach," written in 1971 and recorded in 1975, Patti Smith singing, sad and beautiful. People are dancing and I'm outside, still trying to figure out what I'm doing.

I look across the street and stare down Cortlandt Alley. I keep thinking about that phone call—the call that changed everything. The people I met on White Street—I loved almost all of them. Sometimes because of who they were, other times simply because they were there. Most remained strangers while some became friends; they made New York City, and the Mudd Club in particular, special places during an extraordinary time.

Steve called and I fell right into the job. I watched a small page of history unfold from the steps of 77 White. Despite my own insanity, weirdness and insecurity, I did my part and shook everyone's hand. If they wanted a drink, I had one too. Nearly everyone who made a mark, highbrow or low, on the dance floor or the street, stepped up to the chain. Most times, I opened it.

Drink ticket, 1980.

Neil finally stopped singing; Patti settled down and DJ David had Nancy Sinatra and her boots walking all over the dance floor. Three hours later on the second floor, I'm hanging with *SoHo News* editor Peter Occhiogrosso. We're both thirsty and need a round of Heinekens. The bartender, also named Richard, puts two bottles in front of me and asks for two drink tickets. Things quickly go down-hill from there.

I'd never used a ticket for my own drinks, and wasn't going to start at 4 A.M. upstairs at the Mudd Club. I remember Peter yelling, "Richard, don't!" as I heaved a full Rubbermaid "Roughneck" trash can across the bar. The bartender tried to catch it and wound up in the icewater melt of the bathtub beer bottle cooler. It's hard to imagine things getting worse until I started yelling *"Get the fuck out!"* The bartender left and never came back; I drank one of the two Heinekens that started it all. The second floor kept going till 5 A.M.

It was an ugly scene but it was all on me. The bartender was an idiot, but I topped it. Trying to figure out if it was too much co-caine, not enough heroin, or just an overload of ego, beer and bad attitude didn't matter; clearly, I was having problems.

When I later asked Peter about that night he recalled "some sort of incident." I remember not wanting to look in the mirror for days.

Blow

Luckily, the week happened fast. I tried to stay at the door, and if I ran around inside, I tried not to throw things at anyone. By the weekend, I worked up enough courage to look in the mirror again, and almost smile. Monday night, back outside, I was doing my job. I never got a chance to tell that bartender *I was sorry—that he was an idiot*.

September seemed a long month and slow to close. New faces were coming around and a young Hip-Hop promoter and manager, Russell Simmons, was inside talking to Steve. The club was approaching its second anniversary and entering the next phase of post-Punk cross-cultural pollination. White Street, still ahead of the curve.

Graffiti writers, break-dancers and beatboxes, rapping MCs and *scratchmaster* DJs were in the process of spawning a Rap and Hip-Hop revolution. Fab Five Freddy Brathwaite and Afrika Bambaataa, Basquiat, Haring and Futura 2000 were all there at the beginning. Debbie Harry and Chris Stein were already recording "Rapture." Kurtis Blow, a Rap avatar, Simmons collaborator and future founder of the Hip-Hop Church had a new single called "The Breaks" and was ready to make his move in a white club on White Street.

With the "Christmas Rappin'" single firmly behind him as well as a newly released album, Kurtis Blow got onstage at Mudd and the next wave came rolling in. I stood there listening to a twenty-year-old kid from the Bronx, the beat both familiar and brand new. I clapped my hands and listened while he was *rappin' about the breaks*.

The Brides

Sometimes I struggled to keep up with Dr. Mudd's inspired lineup of midweek entertainment. Working at 77 White, I had no choice, and living in New York, there was no slowing down.

Months earlier, when the Brides of Funkenstein, a George Clinton Parliament-Funkadelic spinoff, became part of that lineup, I stopped struggling and just went with it. Like the Mudd Club, P-Funk's *trickle-down effect* showed us where we came from, what was happening, and what was next. Following in the footsteps of Soul Night, the Brides added a kick to the White Street mayhem, opening a new door of musical enlightenment. Beauty and Funk became part of *anything can happen* at Mudd. Rap and Hip-Hop, Bambaataa, Brathwaite and even Blondie took note of Clinton's lead.

Dawn Silva and Lynn Mabry were the original Brides. Lynn was Sly Stone's cousin, and both she and Dawn spent time singing with Sly & the Family Stone. By the mid-seventies they were working with George Clinton. The Brides of Funkenstein officially arrived January 1978 but by 1979, they'd already left the Clinton collective. They landed on White Street in 1980.

When Dawn Silva heard they were playing a club called Mudd she wondered out loud, "What kind of place is THAT?" She walked in the door thinking, *Whoa, this is weird-looking.*

A couple of hours and a sound check later, the Mudd Club's steel security gate-stage curtain rolled up and the girls were ready. Dressed in head-to-toe Larry Legaspi and looking like Wild West divas from outer space, the Brides of Funkenstein poured it on. Dawn and Lynn's signature "one voice vocal," Rodney "Skeet" Curtis' bass, Tyrone Lampkin's beat, and Michael Hampton's guitar had the funk bouncing off the walls. They played a song off their first record, *Funk or Walk,* and another from their second album, *Never Buy Texas From A Cowboy.* They covered Talking Heads' "Once in a Lifetime" and Lene Lovich's "Lucky Number." Toward the end of the set, they burned the house down with a killer version of Funkadelic's "Standing on the Verge of Getting It On." Through it all, the great Bernie Worrell was the maestro with a groove, and his keyboards made everything fly.

The Brides closed the show with a ten-minute version of 1978's "Disco To Go." The security gate rolled down, people in front started pounding on the steel curtain, and the audience kept screaming. Steve stepped in, told the band, "They loved you" and the gate rolled back up. The encore was pure celebration, and "Disco To Go" kept going.

Post-Punk took a funky turn that night and didn't stop. By the late summer-early fall of 1980 both music and Mudd were moving in a new direction. I was still working the door but things were starting to feel different. Part of my problem was an unwillingness to change until my back was either against the wall or slamming into it. By now I was getting close.

Thirty years later, I asked Bernie Worrell (a Funkadelic founder and major mover when it came to Talking Heads' early eighties sound) about the Mudd Club. He'd never been there until the night he played with the Brides, but he still remembered a "great show at a crowded little place downtown."

He loved the way audience and performer felt a sense of camaraderie, "an intimacy missing in a big venue."

I listened and Bernie continued.

"You know, I started playing music when I was four years old.... I had a strict upbringing.... I met George Clinton at a barbershop in Plainfield, New Jersey; my wife introduced us—it's where George formed his Doo-Wop group called The Parliaments."

Bernie laid out a beautiful story, referring to that barbershop as *the heart of the scene.*

I started standing in front of 77 White in March 1979 when the Mudd Club was the heart of what was happening. I knew what he was talking about.

I talked to Dawn Silva and her recollections serve this story well. She "can still see the stage and the steel curtain rolling up and down" and still remembers how "the audience sway had its own tempo."

We kept talking and I felt a connection, that *sense of camaraderie* based on having been there. I remembered where I was standing that night; I closed my eyes and could still see the Brides of Funkenstein onstage. I could feel the beat and I could hear that *one voice* loud and clear. I opened my eyes and said, "Boy that was a great show," but I think she already knew that.

Almost Fucking

Nearly three weeks into September, the *never knowing what's next* ride continued. Barely twenty-seven, I continued flirting with heroin but by now heroin was flirting back. Still, something was always missing and my balance was always off. I wasn't sure if it was just me wondering what was going on or whether everybody was walking the same fine line. It was hard to tell the difference between moving forward and moving closer to the edge. Chain in hand, I just kept sending people thru the door.

Ten minutes later, I found myself leaning on the sink in the second-floor bathroom; there were six other people inside. Two were up against the wall, almost fucking, and everyone else was getting high. I lit a cigarette and fond memories of all the bathrooms and

Richard Boch, bathroom portrait with red leather tie, 1980, by Marcia Resnick.

toilets in town came flooding back. When someone passed me a vial of coke I dumped a pile on my fist and snorted it up in one blast. When the top of my head settled down I looked around and said, "Thanks."

Bad Behavior

I leave Mudd and cab it over to Laight Street. Sturgis is spinning records, Krystie's behind the bar and Marcia Resnick's standing in front of it. Anita Pallenberg is in the back, and John Belushi is on his way out. I have nearly a gram of cocaine wrapped up in a fifty and I'm not sure where it came from. Coked up and frozen, drifting thru the blue haze of cigarette smoke, I'm wishing for a speedball. Maybe two dozen people are in the place and everybody looks easy; at this hour or any, bad behavior has little meaning. With few boundaries other than messing with the Hells Angels, I hit on a security guy from The Ritz instead. Dumb and wasted, long dark hair and beautiful in the right light, he's got Bensonhurst or Bay Ridge written all over him. I walk over, mumble in his ear for thirty seconds and he follows me out the door.

The next time I look at a clock it's noon and I'm lying on my living room floor; the fifty's wiped clean, lying on the kitchen table, and Bensonhurst is in the shower. The speedball wish never came true and ten hours of crash time later I'm back at 77 White.

Chipmunks

Eighteen months and counting—it sounds like nothing, but when you're in your twenties it's a good chunk of life. Fall 1980, I was still hooked on my job and all that came with it, but I wanted to start doing more than the door. When I realized all I had to do was ask and all Steve had to do was say okay it seemed I was on to something. I had one or two ideas, and the only budget I needed was a stack of drink tickets.

I set up a last-minute after-party for the Pretenders following their September 24 show at the Palladium. I left the door at 1 A.M. and worked the room, the basement and the bathroom. Chi Chi assumed her role as director of second-floor admissions and Aldo stayed

Vitas Gerulaitis, Cynthia Heimel, Stiv Bators and John McEnroe, post-concert Pretenders party, Mudd Club second floor, 1980, by Kate Simon.

outside working security. McEnroe and Gerulaitis were upstairs hiding behind Roy Orbison-style sunglasses; Chrissie was probably hiding out with Kate. Everyone else was hiding in plain sight—just along for the ride and free drinks.

A week later, I started booking guest DJs for the new plexiglass booth, putting the club's low-tech second-floor renovation to good use. I kicked off the series with Stephen Saban of the *SoHo Weekly News*, a safe bet with a steady hand and a decent record collection.

Tonight I've lined up a wild card: Ricky Sohl at the turntables and Teri Toye as the almost able assist. Dusty Springfield, The Monkees, *Cher's Greatest Hits* and the Chipmunks covering Blondie's "Call Me" are all on the playlist. Ricky's segues are smooth and clean, and Teri's only dropped two or three records on the floor. It's a performance piece—Lucy and Ethel, slapstick and serious at once—and it's working out beautifully. Alice Himelstein's at the bar, laughing out loud as the tiny Chipmunk voices struggle with Giorgio Moroder's arrangement. It's the yin and yang of White Street's Next Wave-No Wave soundtrack and a hard one to top.

Three minutes and thirty seconds later, the Chipmunks settle down, Alice stops laughing and opens her big black bag. She reaches inside, digs around and introduces the second floor to the world of pharmaceutical amyl nitrite. Not your standard disco/sex club variety, these *poppers* snap with a heart-pounding, room-spinning burst of high school acid-trip laughter. It's a de-evolutionary moment, and it's difficult to say if we've reached a new high or low. I walk over to Ricky and ask him to play "Baby Don't Go." He tells me to calm down.

By 4 A.M., Alice is in a corner with Gary and Mary Lou Green. Everyone else is sitting down, trying to stand or heading for the door. I grab one of the yellow boxes of amyl and start to leave with a guy from New Jersey named Tim. Danny Fields stops me and tells me he looks too *Blueboy* but at this point who even cares. I just hope he's gone by noon.

Okay When It Isn't

The door's become routine, the chain sometimes opening on its own. Making sure my friends get in is easy—knowing who they are, still the hard part. I'm starting to catch the *anything can happen* moments before they arrive. I've begun to realize there has to be an endgame. Heroin, even just a line, makes everything okay when it isn't, and *more okay* when it is. I finally understand that working the Mudd Club door is a very hard job.

A few people know what that's like, and legendary Limbo King Mike Quashie is one of them. The former Lou Reed associate and onetime opening act for Led Zeppelin was part of *the scene*; he worked the door at a long-ago Greenwich Village joint called Salvation. When Mike Quashie steps out of a cab and sees me, his smile is big and real.

Photographers and co-conspirators Nan Goldin and David Armstrong are standing at the chain but have no idea what a crazy job this is. After a quick low-key hello, I follow them upstairs as they disappear into a bathroom. Cookie Mueller, a Goldin muse, is already sitting on a toilet, ready for a close-up.

Back on the street, one of those good-looking bridge-and-tunnel kids—whose name I've never known and probably never will—is standing alone in the crowd. I let him into the Clash *Rude Boy* party two months ago; he likes to get wasted and fuck, so he's coming in again.

Chi Chi and Gennaro have the night off and Aldo's working outside with me. Debi Mazar's inside dressed in a suit and porkpie hat,
"working" at the foot of the stairs. She's easily distracted but
runs a tight ship; besides, no one argues with a fifteen-year-old
gatekeeper. I turn around, tell Aldo I'll be back in ten and head
inside to find the kid from Queens whose name I'll never know.

Tiepolo and Turtles

I pass Eric Goode on the second floor, spot bridge-and-tunnel boy
near the bathroom and hand him a drink ticket. He asks me "What's
up," and I tell him I'm working. He appears confused by my answer
and so am I.

Eric and Shawn Hausman are still hanging near the bar; I pass by,
saying little more than hello. They've gotten used to me at the door
and I've gotten to know them as the guys who live around the corner.

Tonight they're talking with Ricky and Teri. She barely knows
Eric from Parsons School of Design but she likes him and wastes no
time turning on the Teri Toye charm. Steve soon joins the conversation and from a safe distance it feels like I'm watching bad late-
night television.

Eric and Shawn were eager for something to do and Steve was always eager to do something. The Mudd Club basement, sorely in need
of a makeover, became Eric and Shawn's first commission. There were
no rules when it came to design, demolition or construction, and a
Tiepolo reproduction ceiling and trompe l'oeil marble floor sounded perfect. They asked Steve if they could cut a hole in the ceiling and without a second thought he said, "Sure." Working day and
night, the whole project took about a week.

Eric and Shawn made a great team. Following the Mudd basement
redo, they did some of their best "early" work on a project called
The Club with No Name, located far west on Twenty-fifth Street.
Like everything else happening in late-night New York it was "completely illegal." Small and dark, the place was a cross between an
after-hours club and the Bronx Zoo Reptile House. Stephen Saban
spoke of it fondly in his *SoHo News* article "Night of the Iguana."

Three years later, in September 1983, Eric and Shawn, along with
Eric's brother, Christopher Goode, and a fourth partner, Darius
Azari, went on to create a nightlife masterpiece called Area, just

four blocks from 77 White. I stopped by occasionally and after way too many drinks I'd beg Jodie, the backroom DJ, to play Elvis' "Suspicious Minds."

Eric's involvement and partnership in various restaurants, hotels and clubs grew steadily while Shawn's design career went from big-time dream to bigger-time reality. Neither will forget the basement job on White Street.

Today Eric Goode describes himself as a "hard-core world traveler and crazy conservationist." His Turtle Conservancy and far-flung adventures are the rewards of a wild life that keeps giving. Sitting across a table, he's echoing and retooling the words of Marcia Resnick, telling me he always thought of the Mudd Club as "a democratic society once you got past Richard Boch." I almost laugh, and take it as a great compliment.

Roller Coaster

Later that same night I'm back upstairs when Jack Casady pulls me aside and asks if his band, SVT, can play a free show at the Mudd Club. It's a great offer, Wednesday after next works for the band, and a 3 A.M. set sounds about right. I'll talk to Steve and make sure it happens.

The next night, Andi shows up with a test pressing of "Chinese Chance," the single she recorded back on August 9 at Electric Lady Studios. DJ David cues it up and it sounds beautiful ringing thru Mudd's PA system. It's a hit, at least in our minds, and the B-side cover of Pete Townshend's "Nothing Is Everything" holds its own with the original. Andi's happy and the song remains forever part of our connection. Everyone's dancing and David gives "Chinese Chance" a second spin.

Looking around, the place is filling up. I've been keeping things tight at the door and Chi Chi's keeping an even tighter grip on the second floor. *Just off the bus* and barely legal performance artist David Ilku is trying to get upstairs; Chi Chi lets him down easy with a smile and the old standby, "Sorry hon, not tonight." I'm outside smoking, minding my own business, trying not to watch.

I send more people in, one or two at a time. I turn around and do a double take when drummer Michael Shrieve steps out of a cab with Mick Jagger. They've just been to see Keith Jarrett perform, figured the

Mudd Club an easy late-night pit stop, and headed downtown. I open the chain, they both say hello and walk in. No one seems to notice.

Michael Shrieve's claims he's "a tourist" when it comes to Mudd, but he's been coming around White Street since the beginning. A little over ten years earlier, he was a teenage phenom, joining Santana in 1969 and playing drums on their first eight albums. He's been everywhere from Max's Kansas City to Max Yasgur's farm and now he's hanging with the Stones. Tonight, Charlie Watts set him up on a date with Mick. A tourist he's not.

Jagger's another of those onetime teen phenoms. The last time I saw him at Mudd he was incognito, bearded and in the company of Iggy Pop. Tonight he's cleaned up and clean-shaven, dressed in jeans and a sport jacket, and headed straight upstairs. A stop at the bar and a few girls circle for a closer look—heads turn but nobody really cares. Five minutes later, he's in the bathroom, an hour later, he's gone.

Running around, uptown and down, Shrieve calls it a "New York nightlife roller coaster."

How Long

When I tried to slow that coaster down I looked forward to *paint, eat, sleep*. I thought the Mudd Club would always be around and I planned on surviving a seventh season; I was looking forward to another new and happy year. I couldn't see any further, but that was far enough.

Opening the chain, asking how many, I stood there staring into the headlights of a cab coming down Cortlandt Alley. After a while, Nico came outside looking for her friend, the Squat Theater's "entertainment curator," Janos Gat. I lit a cigarette and kept staring down the alley. Minutes later, I wandered upstairs and found Ricky and Teri in full glam dementia—lipstick, dark shadow and black velvet berets. They were standing near the front windows, leaning on some invisible means of support, talking to Marcia Resnick. Steve walked over, said something and the four of them disappeared. The bartender passed me another beer, and I went back outside. Nico was still looking for Janos. I stood there wondering how long I'd be staring down Cortlandt Alley.

Richard Sohl and Teri Toye perfectly accessorized, second floor Mudd, 1980, by Marcia Resnick.

Finally, John Lurie steps outside to get some air and I snap out of it. He lights my cigarette and I stop wondering, start working and we keep talking.

Boris Policeband is standing in the street at the back of the crowd, a head taller than everyone else. I give him a wave to come inside and he shakes his head *no*. I wave again and he shakes *no* again. John cracks up and goes inside. Boris seems happy where he's standing but I'm not sure if I am.

Now, not even 1 A.M. and it's busy. The streetlight's bright and it feels like a sunny day. Gary and Alice get out of a cab at Broadway and wander toward the door. Kirk Baltz, the actor who loses his ear in *Reservoir Dogs*, arrives with Alice's neighbor, Billy Gross. Five hours earlier, we all started the night with dinner at her place: vodka and pot, spaghetti, salad and garlic bread, but now I'm hungry again. I need a hot dog from Dave's and a few lines of coke; whichever comes first, but preferably in that order. In the meantime, I'll keep working, staring at the usual variety of a hundred-odd people I don't know and never will. Before finishing that thought, the captivating, often sweet but occasionally scary and bottle-smashing International Chrysis saunters her way thru the crowd. Besides looking particularly glamorous in a beyond-trans, beyond-gender kind of way, she's one of the few faces I've seen before. Chrysis seems relatively calm, and I let her in. Former Rolling Stones producer Andrew Oldham, visiting White Street for the first time, gets out of a cab a minute later. His is a face I've never met so I introduce myself and take him upstairs. Another legend and Mudd regular, Giorgio Gomelsky, whose earlier involvement with the Rolling Stones *and* the Yardbirds included promotion, management and production, is already inside. Talking to both of these guys makes me feel that *I was there*; everyone else makes me feel *here and now*.

Artist Judy Levy, who's at the club every night, arrives with author and former *High Times* chief Larry "Ratso" Sloman. Steven Davis, a young architect who jogged by in spring '79 and wondered *what's going on*, follows them in. (Back then we hadn't yet seen a jogger inside and I thought perhaps we should.)

When I turn around Keith Haring is in front of me on the other side of the chain. Maybe I can ask him to get me a hot dog and I'll try and forget about the coke.

Tonight's turned into the kind of New York night that gets me hungry for more than sex, junk food or drugs; it's another beautiful bright-light constellation coming together at 77 White.

October 1980, Saturday morning, 6 A.M. I'm headed home alone but I'm not feeling lonely. I'll start a new painting, and try to sleep. I'll eat something when I wake up. Then I'll head back to the Mudd Club—and so will *everyone* else.

That's when we heard the news.

Closed

The original Danceteria, Jim Fouratt and Rudolf Piper's legendary joint on West Thirty-seventh Street, closed on October 5, 1980. It never seemed any more or less illegal than any other unlicensed late-night club with blocked fire exits, but that didn't seem to matter. The police and the fire departments, the State Liquor Authority and maybe even the FBI raided the place and shut it down. Jim and Rudolf safely circled the block in a limo; stage manager Rico Espinet escaped out a back door, hopped in and provided the grim details to Danceteria's fearless leaders.

I was working on White Street when the news landed on the front steps. The staff spent a night in jail and twenty-four hours later they were back in play, flooding the nightlife job market. Poet and writer Max Blagg, handcuffed to Keith Haring as part of an employee roundup, chain gang-style, lived to tell and kept on writing. Haring had a brief stint at the Mudd Club door in his future while Danceteria "admissions director" Haoui Montaug followed his own celebrity doorman trajectory. Danceteria's fall season never happened but Jim and Rudolf already had another plan. All I could say was "Good luck."

Missing

A week later, the story of a nightclub raid and closure was already old news and Haring seemed unfazed by the handcuffs and the night in jail. He'd been in New York for about two years when Danceteria opened and closed but didn't sit still for long.

Arriving from Pittsburgh in 1978, Keith wound his way thru the School of Visual Arts and became one of the original "members" of Club 57. He's been showing up at the Mudd Club, on his way to becoming a hero and frontrunner of the new guard. He's a sweet guy, and just like Jean-Michel, he's a star before he's a star.

Eventually reaching a wider audience than anyone could've imagined, Keith commandeered the black unused ad panels on the walls of New York's subway system and the art world took notice. Large-scale playground murals followed, along with a show at the newly opened Tony Shafrazi Gallery in SoHo; in 1983, Haring was included in the Whitney Biennial. One year later, he spotted me in Little Italy, sharing a pizza with Gary. He ran home and came back with two printed bandannas: invitations to the first "Party of Life," May 16, 1984, at the Paradise Garage. They're beautiful and I still have mine, but so much else is missing.

Different Speak

Haring and Basquiat were part of a world we knew; two blocks south of Canal was heart and home. The moment was brief but its consequence and revelation still rule; still speaks to the now. Standing at the door of 77 White, I was part of that moment and that world. Despite my own doubts and confusion, I watched lightning strike one more time.

The Mudd Club was ready to ride the *next wave*—the entire New York art scene on the cusp of reinventing itself—again. Happening in and on the street, it's what Diego Cortez predicted and hoped for. Patti Astor, an early champion of Hip-Hop, was only months away from setting up the first Fun Gallery while dealer and Mudd regular Tony Shafrazi already was seeing dollar signs and planning his next move. There seemed no limit to possibility and no end in sight. Punk moved Post and Post was moving New Wave. The "writing" of Rauschenberg and Jasper Johns was the cursive of a different era. Graffiti and Hip-Hop was a new language and a different *speak*; Haring, Basquiat and the kids from the Bronx and Brooklyn moved it forward. White Street was still in play and the Mudd Club had a full cycle left.

***

I keep showing up for the job but there's surely more to me and, hopefully, my future. I need to get out of whatever I've gotten into but ambivalence leaves me trapped and cocaine has me jumpy—heroin and equivocation helps me hide whatever else is going on.

White Street, Murray Street and One University Place aren't the problem and I can't even blame the drugs. It might feel like high school, but it's not. Maybe I need a fresh approach to my job and to leave the basement and bathroom hookups behind. Maybe staying out till 9 or 10 A.M. just doesn't work. Maybe I'm thinking too much or maybe I'm not thinking at all. There are a lot of maybes but as yet, no answer.

Summer 1980 is over and my birthday party in Montauk was one short month ago. I'm *only* twenty-seven and everything should be easy—shouldn't it? Tomorrow's another day but so was yesterday and today. Tonight I'm back for another round, standing at the door of 77 White. I'll be fine.

Mudd Times

VOL. CXX.   WEDNESDAY, OCTOBER 22, 1980   FREE

GROUPIES CRUSHED BY STEEL GATE AT MUDD

SECURITY EXPERTS AMAZED

Special to The Mudd Times

NEW YORK, New York, Oct. 17 — Four young women, carried away by the emotion of being close to their rock idol, Kristian Hoffman, of the Swinging Madisons, stormed past Mudd Club guards in an attempt to bring the band back for an encore. For a few moments they were able to hold up a two thousand pound steel garage door as it crushed their frail young bodies. Experts in the field of crowd control had seen this only at the site of religious miracles or in cases where people have lifted automobiles off the bodies of loved ones. Frightened guards had brought down the curtain which is driven by a ten horse-power motor but the young women pushed it up and away, twisting it like a pretzel. Dr. Mudd commented later that it was a shame that young people couldn't apply this type of energy towards athletics.

EVENT FORECAST

Steel Pulse
WEDNESDAY, OCT. 22

Playboy Bunny Lounge Party
THURSDAY, Oct. 23. Enjoy a true playboy cocktail party. Guys dress calm and collected like Hef. Girls, of course, come as bunnies and receive free champagne.

Wendy & the Roll-ons
FRIDAY, Oct. 24. All girl band, expert in the lyrics of feminine toiletry products.

Laughing Woman
FRIDAY, Oct. 24. Radley Metzger, rarely shown film about a wealthy sadist who stages torture games in his roman villa. Showing at 10:00 p.m. sharp

Del Byzanteens
SATURDAY, Oct. 25.

Magazine Benefit
TUESDAY, Oct. 28. Poetry Readings. Max Blagg, Peter Cherchez, Tuli Kupferberg (with Lannes Kenfield & the Revolting Theatre), Taylor Mead, John Perrault, Barry Yourgrau. Films. Red Grooms, Catherine Mercier, Susan Pitt, Peter Wallach. Live music by Sweet Heart Roland. Starts at 9:30.

Halloween
FRIDAY, Oct. 31. Shox Lumania. The Lumanian sect will lead a special Halloween celebration, a volk festival in the spirit of Octoberfest. Heavy accent on Eastern European embroidered dresses, clogs, pigtails and leiderhosen.

Steel Pulse, first show in the USA, Mudd Club 1980, by Allan Tannenbaum.

One Spliff Down

The fall season marked the return of the long tweed coat. Other than
adapting to the cool weather, my routine remained the same. I slept
till the afternoon, worked on a series of messy new paintings,
smoked a lot of pot and got hungry. I was unsuccessful when it came
to avoiding heroin.

Wednesday, October 22, 1980. I finished dinner at One U, hailed
a cab, headed south on Broadway and got out at White. The street was
still quiet—just a small group of people outside. An hour later I
was hard at work.

I should've known what was coming, considering the minor chaos
that accompanied Burning Spear, but the crowd showed up early and
caught me off guard. The chains were open and twenty people started
talking to me at once, explaining why they *should* be on the guest
list. Then someone handed me a monster spliff; someone else handed
me another one. I held onto both, politely told everyone "Get the
fuck off the steps." I closed the chains and started negotiations.

Steel Pulse, the Rastafari roots Reggae band from Birmingham,
England, was making its American debut at the Mudd Club. Their
alignment with British Punk gave them a reputation and a following. The dreads, the smoke and the Rastaspeak were out in force by
midnight, and by 1 A.M., the sweet-beat rhythm carried a message
of love and revolution across the floor and through the room. Back
outside I fired up the first spliff. The music kept playing and I
couldn't tell if I was stoned, losing my mind or just enjoying myself. One spliff down, but it was early.

Uncompleted One A.M.

The rest of the night I was in a state of lost and sometimes found.
I was home before daylight; Thursday 11 P.M. back at the door. Friday I played it on repeat but the weekend was still mine. Gennaro
was still at the door and a sense of joy still fueled the Mudd Club
dance floor. More times than not, that joy was contagious.

The week happened fast and it's Wednesday night again. SVT ar-
rive after a gig on Long Island and Jack Casady's already upstairs.
The band's van is parked in the alley and, according to drummer Paul
Zahl, it feels as though they're "on a late-night Kamikaze raid."

With "two admittedly loud amps, drums and a microphone" the stage is set and ready. Brian Marnell's mission—that the band doesn't leave town until they play the Mudd Club—is nearly accomplished.

The second floor's crowded, and Danny Fields is near the bar telling Casady that he "came to see the best dressed man in Rock 'n' Roll." Jack looks sharp in a sport jacket and black shirt, but it's a look far removed from Jefferson Airplane's 1968 heyday when Jean-Luc Godard captured their thwarted-by-the-cops New York City rooftop performance. Like a night at Mudd, Godard's uncompleted *One A.M.* (which deciphers as *One American Movie*) was a trippy slice of a soon-to-be lost golden time.

The French New Wave, Psychedelia and the Mudd Club: three decades and zero degrees of separation. Now it's 1980, 3:30 A.M., I turn around and walk over to Steve. The band needs more drink tickets and it's almost showtime.

Ten minutes later, I grab Tina L'Hotsky, float downstairs, and move toward the front of the stage. The steel security gate curtain rolls up and Jack's bass lets out a growl that rattles the building—the Mudd *breakfast crowd* has no idea what they're in for. SVT opens with "The Last Word," and, as Paul Zahl likes to say, "We tidal wave the place." Forty minutes later, they close it down with a beautiful version of Marnell's "Heart of Stone."

SVT are in the van by 6 A.M., headed for San Francisco. I'm gone by 7, headed who knows where.

Noon Every Night

October is passing by for the second time in my Mudd Club career. DJ David's getting itchy about something, and I'm getting crazier by the minute. Steve's getting more reclusive, elusive and vague—calling on the wall phone and speaking in tongues, appearing and disappearing. The weather's getting cold and the long tweed coat is making regular appearances at the door. I've been staying out till noon almost every night.

Two years after the club opened, a lot of the regulars were still coming around. A few gave up; some got lost along the way. The ghosts, the no-name kids and the one-night stands—sometimes I remember them all. Mudd was still crowded and the drugged-out morning haze of the second floor was thicker than ever. I stood near the

Anya and Diego. Then is where we came from, 1979, by Bobby Grossman.

bar watching what Jo Shane called the gorgeous swirl of Mudd Club gestalt and it seemed to be out of control. I wasn't sure what was happening or whether it was just me.

Later that night, Pierre came by and we went downstairs. He offered me a few lines of his brown, allegedly *Persian* dope. I walked out of the basement, across Eric and Shawn's trompe l'oeil marble floor, and went back to the door. Seven seasons and counting, time was trying hard to stay on my side. I wasn't cooperating.

Shitty Grade-B Movie Star

Tuesday, November 4, I was busy working the door and Ronald Reagan was busy getting elected. The well-meaning peanut farmer was on the way out. Apathy, drugs and a touch of lunacy left me blind—tears admittedly came in retrospect.

Jimmy Carter was a good man who sucked at being president. Reagan was America's perfectly awful choice. I voted for Carter and we all lost, I did another line and ordered another drink. I was back to work on Wednesday as if nothing had changed. The new administration was a relapse waiting to happen, ready to move against any line of freethinking. The moral hypocrisy of conservatism was mounting a new assault, and Reagan's soon-to-be royal court was lined with deep pockets. Politics was losing its service ideal while offering the conservative right a new hero; everyone else faced a problem.

"I Had the Real Thing"

Several nights later, freethinking icon Robert Rauschenberg stopped by the club. We avoided talking politics and went directly for the trash. I'd met Bob several times prior and had been to his house on Lafayette Street, but this was one of his first visits to the Mudd Club. I got him a drink, introduced him to Steve and the three of us went up to the third floor. I smiled, sitting in the company of one of the greatest artists of our time while he and Steve made small talk. When all realized that the coke on hand was limited, the conversation slowed and we went our separate ways: Bob went back downstairs, I wandered back outside, and Steve did his usual thing and disappeared. Rauschenberg remained one of my heroes; getting acquainted didn't fuck that up. Steve later complimented me for my ability to "recognize Rauschenberg arriving at the door dressed like a bum."

Out on the street, a crowd was still waiting. Anita Pallenberg was walking out the door when she turned around and spit out the words, "I don't need this shit, I had the real thing." She headed for a cab with a wounded and pajama-clad Richard Lloyd trailing and flailing behind her. I didn't even try to say good night.

A short time later, *SoHo News* editor and future *Paper* magazine publisher David Hershkovits wandered off in the direction of home after another long night of "drinking, dancing to Blondie songs and chasing girls." It was already late when Chris Parker and French Chris arrived and headed upstairs. Parker, newly minted star of Jim Jarmusch's *Permanent Vacation*, was talking fast, gesturing about something, while French Chris wasn't doing much of anything other than smoking a cigarette and looking pretty.

Actress Rosemary Hochschild and director Michael Oblowitz were leaving when Rosemary stopped and said something I couldn't decipher; Michael asked out loud if she told me and I answered, "Told me what?" but they already had disappeared. Lynette came outside a minute later and asked what I was doing.

I didn't have an answer.

The night was doing its best to keep going and so was I. The street was getting quiet until I heard the grunt and cry of drunken sex coming from Cortlandt Alley. I had to laugh; the grunting sounded familiar. I refused to look.

By now, it was well after 3 A.M. Andi was pouring herself into a cab, Lori and Joe were leaving and I headed inside to see what Ricky and Teri were up to. Jo Shane was still upstairs, and Gary was deep in conversation with Vicki. He was asking her about the guillotine and she was telling him that she never learned how to knit. I felt as though I'd been here before and didn't get involved.

I went downstairs, talked to DJ David. He told me Jim Fouratt and Rudolf were trying to put something together in midtown; he told me I should talk to Jim but I had my doubts and should've held on to them. Problem was, I hadn't yet figured out there's no such thing as *should have*.

I walked onto the dance floor and stood there looking around. White Street *still* felt like home; what wasn't always clear was how I felt about myself.

Angel

I know it's coming but I just can't see it. I'm too busy working, painting and getting high. Trying to sleep, I finally doze off and it's already time to get up.

Somewhere in between all that and everything else, there's a new place to cop. Poet Gregory Corso, a member of the Beat Generation's inner circle, has a furnished room on the second floor of the Chelsea Hotel, complete with a bathroom, a TV and a heroin dealer named Angel. Gregory's about fifty, a little crazed and more than a little manic. Angel's a good-looking tattooed Latino who sits on the bed with the drugs, the money and a gun. Together they offer a kind of old-school bohemian charm that's missing from most shooting galleries and crash pads around town. The room becomes *the* place to get off, nod out and catch up with old friends; for a small group of artists, musicians and *Vogue* cover girls who love heroin, it's as close to perfect as it gets.

I stop by before work—I'm there and I'm gone. I stop by after, I have more time to get high, lie around on the floor and stare at the ceiling. If the nod doesn't take me too far away, I'll be home before the morning rush.

Luckily for those involved, the Corso Room had a short shelf life and only lasted two or three months. There were no sad good-byes, and Angel never had to shoot anyone; considering the fucked-up dead-end scene, that was a miracle. Gregory stopped by the club on occasion but I never saw Angel again. It would've been nice, but I didn't really care. I was starting to feel that way about a lot of things.

What Just Happened

Walking to work, the November nighttime cool keeps me moving. I have a moment to myself but my mind won't stop talking. I step inside the door, look around and the place is empty. It's early but something's different. DJ David looks over and smiles.

Little more than a week after the Mudd Club's second anniversary, DJ David Azarch told Steve he's leaving—and now he's telling me. He's taking a job with Jim and Rudolf, who are reopening the Peppermint Lounge, hoping to put a new spin on the birthplace of the Twist.

I hear what he's saying but I'm having a hard time processing it. Listening to David talk about his conversation with Steve, I'm fading in and out, and all I can say is "Wow" and "Really." David's my friend and has been since the beginning. He says I should come with him. I can barely speak but I tell him that we're part of *this* place.

I reach across the bar, take hold of the bottle of Rémy Martin and fill a plastic cup. The bartender looks at me but I'm well past responding. I walk away and stop at the foot of the stairs. I step outside and take a deep breath. A minute later I ask David to tell Jim I'm ready to leave the Mudd Club.

I have no idea what just happened.

The Only Thing Left to Do

Later that week, David had another meeting with Jim and Rudolf. He told them I wanted to talk and Jim just smiled; the following afternoon, I went to West Forty-fifth and had my conversation. The only thing left to do was talk to Steve. I went home, tried to take time to think about what I was doing, but I didn't have it. I went to work that night, and it all went down.

I was alone at the foot of the stairs, just inside the front door, when Steve walked in. I told him we needed to talk and he stopped. I looked at him and said, "I'm leaving in two weeks to work the door at the Peppermint Lounge." It just spilled out of me. He never saw it coming, and I'm not sure I did until I said it out loud.

Steve turned away, turned back, and asked, "How much are they paying you?" There was no plan and all I could say was, "It's a done deal." After nearly twenty-one months and the phone call that changed everything, the conversation lasted less than ten minutes. I lit a cigarette; Steve walked away and disappeared. I stood there trying not to cry.

I stuck around those next two weeks, and stayed close to the door. I still couldn't believe what was happening. I wasn't sure if I saved myself or fucked everything up, if it was about the money, or the drugs I couldn't stop doing. Maybe I needed a change or maybe that gorgeous swirl of Mudd Club gestalt truly *was* out of control.

The end of November 1980. I was gone.

***

It's been years since the Mudd Club officially opened, since I wandered in on my way home. Together with Gary Kanner, Pat Wadsley and Steve Miller, we followed the noise to White Street. We found a DJ playing Rock 'n' Roll and a dance floor that never stood still. It was a big dark box of a room that *allowed* for anything to happen. When I looked around, *everyone* was there.

The Mudd Club seduced me the moment I stepped inside and within months I was working the door. Gary couldn't stay away, and Pat knew she had to write about it. Steve Miller remembers more than one night of *lucky to be alive*. I fell in love with the place. It put its mark on me, and in a crazy way I've returned the favor.

A few brief moments—I thought those nights might last forever.

Spring 1978, Diego Cortez and Anya Phillips gave the push and shove that helped get it started. Steve Mass was the genius Doctor Mudd who kept it going, and everyone who stepped past the chain became part of it. I stood at the door and ran around inside—a twenty-one-month, white light experience. I never missed a night of work, and spent most of my nights off on White Street. To this day, I've never been sure if I was ready to leave the Mudd College of Deviant Behavior when I did; and I've never let the memories disappear. There was no surprise ending. It was just too much and too beautiful to hold on to.

As Marcus Leatherdale likes to say, "It was far more than we realized at the time."

***

Brooklyn, Queens, Long Island and Connecticut—the road to New York City. The nine blocks between Murray Street and White was the neighborhood, 1979 and 1980, the Golden Age. Time passed but I still love the red wide-wale cords that Brian Jones wore on the cover of *High Tide and Green Grass*.

PROGRESS, DEDICATION, INITIATIVE AND INTENSITY is the motto printed on my Mudd Club ID. If you were there, you knew. If you weren't, it's a great story.

Steve Mass and the widest lapels known to man,
third floor Mudd, 1981, by Kate Simon.

EPILOGUE/
AND
THEN

I grew up with *Surrealistic Pillow* and *Rubber Soul*. *The Velvet Underground and Nico* was the dark heavy blanket, the nightmare and the dream. Then *Horses* came along and everything changed.

Life in New York City turned *anything goes*: beautiful, fast, reckless. The consequences still seemed minor and occasional if at all. Everyone I knew was hanging on to a sense of freedom born of the sixties, out of control by the seventies. Getting high and fucking around—nearly all of us were guilty. A version of common sense prescribed a Quaalude and a cocktail, the inevitable blackout burying any possibility of shame. Cocaine and heroin tried their best to level things out. Before long, the minor consequences weren't.

The Mudd Club appeared out of nowhere, opened its doors, and sat on the cusp of a changing world. For the first three years of its short life the place was on fire, and by 1981 the club had a *real* third floor, an art gallery and a new staff, mostly poached from Club 57. It was still crowded but the vibe was different. The irony became more obvious.

In spite of the change it was still the Mudd Club, and I kept going whenever I could. Then in 1982 it started a slow fade, and by 1983, the fire was out.

By then I was taking my own slow fade. Five months later, I looked in the mirror and knew it was time. That's the short of it.

Here's the rest.

***

Monday, December 8, 1980, started out fine. Lynette was hanging out at the loft, Gary was rolling a joint, and I was busy figuring out what album to play. Abbijane and DJ David were on their way over to help decorate the Christmas tree. The TV was on, and that's when we heard the news.

John Lennon was shot outside his home about one hundred blocks north of Murray Street. I called David and asked him to stop by One University and pick up a bottle of Rémy. I called Mickey, and he said it was okay. I hung up the phone and cried.

Within twenty-four hours, I was back working the door at the Peppermint Lounge; and by late December, I was getting buried. There was nothing special about my new job and I was in trouble. The only thing I could do was let it play out and try to catch *last call* at Mudd. On Wednesday, December 10, that's what I did.

I got into a cab and headed for White Street. Well past 3 A.M., Captain Beefheart and His Magic Band were onstage: Don Van Vliet— a.k.a. the Captain—riding high on the morning end of a night. He blew my brains out and half a dozen songs later it was over. I headed for the second floor, walked up to the bar and the bartender pulled a beer out of the bathtub. I was feeling bad. John Lennon was two days gone and I was working at a mobbed-up Rock 'n' Roll shithole in midtown. At least I was still drinking for free.

It Never Felt Like Home

The *original* Peppermint Lounge opened in 1958, and for the next couple of years it was just another West Forty-fifth Street dive. Then in 1960, a guy named Chubby Checker helped establish a dance craze called the Twist, and the house band added a *Peppermint* version. That's when Sinatra, Marilyn, Jackie Kennedy and, eventually, the Beatles walked thru the door.

In the mid-sixties, the Peppermint lost its liquor license and was shut down due to various infractions. It returned in the seventies under the name Hollywood, reclaiming itself as a dive. Its final incarnation, before going Peppermint again, was GG Barnum's Room. The place lasted a few years and featured trapeze-flying male go-go dancers, along with assorted androgynies and drag queens offering entertainment, conversation and moderately priced blowjobs. The clientele consisted of the people who paid to love them, and tourists who liked to watch. I went once, bought a drink and felt like a tourist. I left alone.

The club and its various alter egos had a shadowy past and a dubious reputation linked to drugs, vice and organized crime. None of that was ever going to change.

November 1980, The Peppermint Lounge *re*-opening night was a madhouse. Jim Fouratt and Rudolf looked pleased, but something felt wrong. The people behind the scenes were somewhere between creepy and sinister, smiling through clenched teeth, and keeping an eye on the rest of us. The club itself was a series of rooms and open spaces that didn't *speak* to one another. I had a bad feeling from the start but now it was too late. The only thing to do was to wander into the bathroom, snort up a few lines of anything and try not to think—the same way I handled most situations.

After two weeks, I was on autopilot. David Azarch was in the DJ booth and appeared to be happy. Gary worked the entrance to the VIP room and Pat Wadsley was my partner at the door. Lynette Bean, Krystie Keller and former Danceteria employee Cathy Underhill were behind the bar, and future Chelsea gallerist Lisa Spellman (taking a break from running around Mudd in pajamas) was the cover charge-collecting cashier. Despite the familiar and semi-familiar faces, it never felt like home.

I stood outside, surrounded by a set of velvet ropes with a clipboard in hand. I checked off names from time to time and fucked around as much as possible. With the exception of a few old friends and the usual variety of slumming celebs, the crowd on West Forty-fifth was more rock idiot and less of a downtown No Wave/art world mash-up. Jim and Rudolf's relationship with the club was short-lived (allegedly run off by mob henchmen) and it wasn't long before the new Pep existed solely as a music venue.

Downtown '81 *and* Beyond Words

December 1980 and Christmas season was in full swing. Sad-looking Salvation Army Santas were ringing bells, sneaking cigarettes and collecting money along Lower Broadway. Canal Street was still dirty and jammed with traffic, and Dave's Luncheonette was still serving grease to the late night-early morning Mudd Club crowd. I was feeling lost up on West Forty-fifth Street, trying to get past the

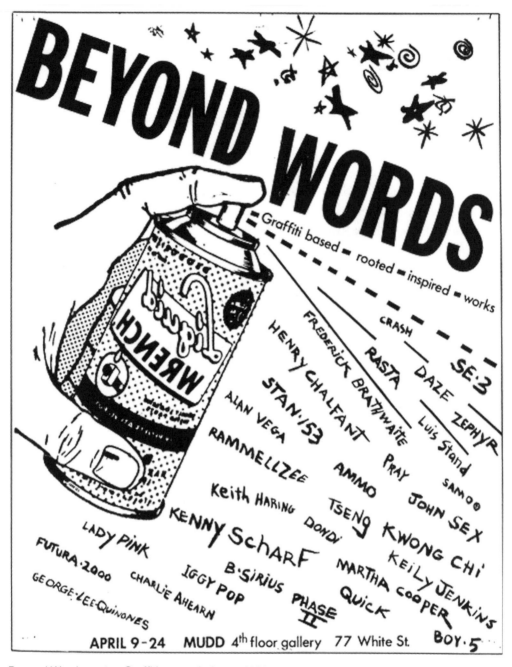

Beyond Words poster, Graffiti moves indoors, 1981.

denial and accept the facts: I made a bad move, I missed celebrating the holidays at Mudd, and White Street was still home turf.

By then *Downtown '81*, a movie starring Jean-Michel Basquiat, written and produced by Glenn O'Brien, co-produced by Maripol and directed by Edo Bertoglio, was headed into production. The story, the faces and places were all familiar, and the cast and crew already had filmed scenes inside and outside the Mudd Club. They shot the go-go bar scene at Diamond Lil's, a dingy topless and sometimes bottomless bar located on Canal near Cortlandt Alley. Heavy on atmosphere and talent, Lil's was the kind of place where a dancer could earn an extra dollar blowing out a candle with her pussy.

DNA, James White and the Blacks, Walter Steding, Kid Creole and the Coconuts and a version of Blondie were all part of the *Downtown '81* soundtrack. I knew everyone involved but the action passed me by.

Filming was soon completed but finances fell apart and the project didn't see a release date for nearly twenty years. Michael Zilkha, the entrepreneurial former head of ZE Records, came to the rescue and Maripol got involved in postproduction. *Downtown '81* premiered at Cannes in 2000 but by then, Jean-Michel was gone. Art world success and excess were only partly to blame.

In early 1981, Steve Mass opened a gallery on the Mudd Club's third floor. Diego Cortez had just curated the show called *New York New Wave* at PS1 in Long Island City that included everyone from Haring and Basquiat to photographers Kate Simon and Robert Mapplethorpe.

Immediately following PS1, Keith Haring put together the *Lower Manhattan Drawing Show* at Mudd. *Beyond Words* opened shortly after, April 9, at Mudd. Fab Five Freddy and Futura 2000 were involved as both curators and participants, and the show blew the doors of the graffiti world wide open.

Once again, Mudd was at the forefront and I couldn't help feeling I missed something. I felt sad not to be part of it. People forgot I was a painter and for a while I did too: I messed up, trading the door of 77 White for drugs, sex and alcohol. Now I was trying it on Forty-fifth Street but it was a losing game, a waste of time.

Brick Wall

During those early months of 1981, I spent a lot of time running around inside the Peppermint Lounge when I was supposed be tending the door. I saw some great live music and did more than my fair share of drugs. I lounged with Pat Wadsley in the VIP on a Saturday night where we laid ourselves down on a dirty, carpeted floor and snorted coke with Mick Jagger and Charlie Watts. Pete Townshend stood around and watched. No one else paid any attention.

Jean-Michel Basquiat, *TV Party*,
"The Beatnik Show," 1980, by Bobby Grossman.

A few weeks later I sat on the bar alongside the dance floor making out with Robert Rauschenberg. Nina Hagen was onstage, I was allegedly working and Bob was just having fun. We were both tripping on something.

I had sex in a broom closet with a *bi-closeted* musician who was prettier than most of the girls in the club. The behavior was careless, the sex was casual, and it happened more than once. The closet was right outside the upstairs office, but we never got caught. I thought all of it was great fun, that it meant something—though I wasn't sure what.

By the time May 28, 1981, rolled around I was ready to say *Fuck it*. Every night for over two weeks, I left the door for thirty minutes, went down the street to Bond's Casino and listened to The Clash tear the place apart. They were at their peak, and I was ready to crash. That brick wall was right in front of me, the small world getting smaller.

On June 19, 1981, just days after The Clash finished their Broadway run, Anya Phillips died of cancer. As fierce as she was, she'd been sick for more than a year and couldn't hang on. I never really knew her and there were times when she frightened me, but for Anya—Punk icon and instigator, Mudd Club force and member of the Radical Three—I have the greatest respect.

By the end of June I was running blind and wasn't thinking. I still believed getting high was part of whatever job I had. I didn't give a shit about the Peppermint Lounge and the feeling no doubt was mutual. I left the Mudd Club to work with Jim and Rudolf, and wound up working for a bunch of mob lackeys and gofers. The only compensation, besides getting paid, was seeing bands like the Cramps, X, Bush Tetras, and Echo and the Bunnymen. Even Philip Glass, The Raybeats, and the Jim Jarmusch/James Nares/Luc Sante collaboration, Del-Byzanteens, played the Pep.

In the end, it didn't matter. Lightning had already struck a second time and it wouldn't strike again. I lasted a little over seven months on West Forty-fifth and was fired for being out of control. I got in a cab, copped some dope and headed back downtown.

On my own, I was treading water and needed a fresh start. I called Jerry Brandt for a favor, and he offered me a job working the door of the VIP lounge at The Ritz. The only problem: I considered myself *an important person* and got just as lost as Ron Wood, Robert Kennedy, Jr., or any of the models, actresses or soon-to-be-discarded child stars crashing inside. I hung out on the balcony,

Did you say
the Mudd Club
is free !!
227-7777

Desperate times, 1982.

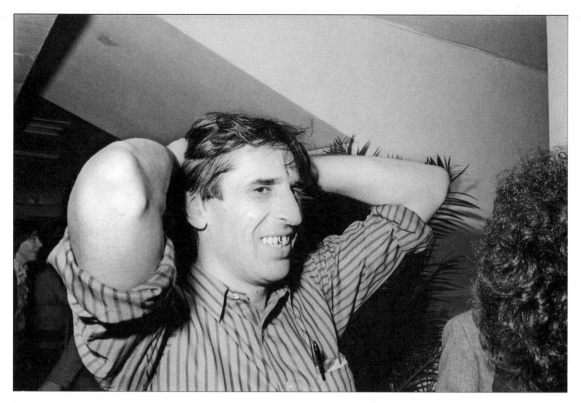
Mickey Ruskin showing off his elbows. Chinese Chance, One University Place, 1979, by Allan Tannenbaum.

stood on my chair, and listened to Kraftwerk. I went to the dressing room and said hello to the bands I knew. The job only lasted a few weeks and I left without any hard feelings. I headed to One University, ordered a drink and asked for a dollar's worth of quarters—Pac-Man had just arrived.

Some weeks later, Larry Wright came to my rescue and hired me as a colorist at his Mulberry Street print shop. Larry, always the comedian, likes to say I came to him "to dry out after all the drugs people put in my pockets." It's a version of the truth, even though no one, especially me, was even close to drying out. I worked with Larry for five months and I'm forever grateful.

Another Home

In the early fall of 1981, Mickey Ruskin hired me as the dining room manager at One University Place. I was back in the thick of it, and my hospitality skills once again were put to good use. I had a job I loved, and the place felt like home.

Mickey, an accidental visionary, was truly one of the all-time great saloonkeepers. He was my friend, became a mentor of sorts and always told me I "had it" if and when I wanted to open a joint of my own. Mickey treated me as family—with generosity and patience. There was no one like him.

A year after I left the Mudd Club, New York was still an adventure. I was still hanging with Ricky, Teri, Andi and Ron. Gary and I were still *Richard and Gary,* and Laura Kennedy of Bush Tetras was still living at the loft and still "dating" Claudia Summers. Ricky Sohl, finishing up a stint as Iggy Pop's keyboard player, was soon to become a member of Nina Hagen's band. Pierre was still selling the brown Persian dope and when he wasn't, Alphabet City was open for business. Allen Lanier and his wife Dory were living at One Fifth Avenue and their apartment was another home away from home.

Whenever the Pretenders came to town I dropped everything.

When 1981 came to a close, the world I knew was still hanging out at One University Place. Everybody was drunk or stoned and I thought I was Superman. I still believed my own bullshit and it hadn't yet hit the fan. The brick wall was still at least an inch away. I was still telling myself, and anyone who asked, that everything was fine.

***

When 1982 rolled around, nothing slowed down but some things started to change. I started to hear rumors that became fact. The "rare cancer" described in a 1981 *New York Times* article was the warning shot. Hearing that Klaus Nomi was sick but doing his best to maintain his career and health became a heartbreak. Few of us had any idea where we were headed.

I heard the word GRID (gay-related immune deficiency), but I was unresponsive. Despite years of anonymous sexual encounters and one-night stands I didn't see a connection, my worst experience being a case of the clap. I believed drugs were my own business and the few shared needles an on-the-spot but necessary choice. By year's end GRID had come to be known as AIDS (acquired immune deficiency syndrome), as the disease had now been found outside the gay community. Our once carefree attitude toward drugs and sex was forever lost in a nightmare; past behavior became suspect, even among ourselves. Fear and panic set in: those who suffered were made outcasts by those seeking blame. Stones were thrown, morals questioned, and ha-

Poetry and spoken word poster, 1980.

tred soon followed. The only compassion and support came from those of us who realized it could happen to anyone.

I kept trying to ignore it, praying it would stop. Drugs and apathy, along with my gift for denial, kept my head in the sand. I was anything but safe.

My life still centered around the loft on Murray Street while my after-hours activity included AM PM, a late-night/early-morning drug den located down the block. The Zodiac on Mercer Street was the after-work default destination. In either place, drunken (and now high-risk) sex was easy to find.

I was still working for Mickey, and the bar and dining room at One University were always full. You could sit in a booth with a de Kooning, a Rivers or a Schnabel hanging on the wall behind you, and order a club steak for dinner with a half-gram of coke and a few lines of heroin for dessert. Despite an ongoing mix of beauty and grime, the high-end bohemian highlife was in its final phase.

At home I continued painting, selling a few new pieces to Solveig and my friend Susan. I was catching more daylight and less of the 10 A.M. cocaine freeze; still, there was always a dime bag of dope in my pocket. At work I tried balancing things out with very dry Beefeater martinis "in a tall glass with a lot of ice." By midnight, I was all over the place, and by 2 A.M., one of the bartenders usually tried to cut me off. Mickey Ruskin, never the voice of moderation, pulled me aside and explained, "Six martinis doesn't make for a good manager." I looked at Mickey without looking at myself and replied, "I only had four or five."

By April 1982, Mickey finally sent me on a trip to the Bahamas with his wife Kathy keeping me company. I was supposed to dry out but I copped and got high as soon as I got to Nassau. I bought a bottle of Stolichnaya thinking that Beefeater might be the problem, and somewhere between a stash of 10mg blue Valium, cocaine and the beach, I managed to forget about heroin. I met up with a rugby player from the Canadian national team and a hustler from the Midwest. We drank, gambled and fucked our way thru the next ten days. I returned to New York refreshed and ready to dive back in but unprepared for what was in store.

On September 2, Tom Baker died from a heroin overdose. Cookie Mueller was there and tried to save him but it was too late. Sunday afternoon, the following weekend, people gathered at One University to tell stories about Tom. I showed up with Lisa Rosen; we sat and listened and no one called me Richie.

At the end of 1982, Mickey Ruskin fired me, but kept me around to scout locations for his next project. He remained a loyal and forgiving friend.

No Longer a Reason

Twenty blocks south, the Mudd Club was well past what Glenn O'Brien called "its later days when the cool crowd had kind of stopped going there." Despite the deteriorating cool factor, Glenn still dropped by to check things out and so did I. It was hard not to.

Finally, the *slow fade* started speeding up and I lost track of what was going on at 77 White. Steve Mass often stayed at home, watching what was happening at the door and elsewhere via closed-circuit security cameras—a pastime more voyeurism than distrust. The world of Mudd was getting smaller too, and if it were possible, even stranger. There was no longer a reason to stop the cab at White Street.

Christmas party invitations and New Year's Eve announcements never got mailed. Maybe Steve lost interest or maybe it was time. There was no swan song, no crash and no burn. The Mudd Club limped into January, and before long it was over.

Then in the spring of 1983, everything fell apart.

I was tired and lost and I felt like shit. The drugs and alcohol finally got to me, and people were starting to notice. I was unemployed and dating a three-hundred-dollar-an-hour call girl named Loren Desire. Generous to a fault but a bit delusional, she thought I was boyfriend material. She believed Valium and champagne could cure my gin and heroin "bug." She thought we had a future; I didn't.

The Party Was Over

Deep in the nod, I stepped back from the edge; I never wound up at the wrong end of a dream. On April 14, 1983, I woke up and heard the news: my friend Pete Farndon died in the bathtub of his London home from an overdose of heroin. He was thirty years old; his wife Conover phoned and told me what happened. A few hours later, it was on TV.

Find rocker dead in bath

London (AP)—Bass guitarist Pete Farndon, 30, a former member of the Pretenders rock group, was found dead in the bathtub at his west London home, police said yesterday. A spokesman at Scotland Yard said Farndon's body was discovered Thursday in the bath by his wife, Canover. The spokesman said the cause of death was drowning. But he said authorities were investigating a possible drug link.

Pete Farndon

Farndon left the Pretenders 10 months ago after a dispute with two other members, singer Chrissie Hynde and drummer Martin Chambers. Less than 48 hours after the breakup, the group's lead guitarist, James Honeyman-Scott, died of a cocaine overdose.

Pete Farndon, dead in bath, the saddest day, 1983, courtesy Richard Boch.

It had been just four years after I started working at the Mudd Club and a little more than three years since I'd met Pete. I already knew it was time to say good night but I kept waiting for a sign—and Pete Farndon's death was the turning point. It's when I started to see and hear, and finally started to listen.

One month later, on May 16, 1983, Mickey Ruskin died during an early morning poker game at his apartment on West Twenty-third Street. His wife Kathy called to let me know. He was fifty years old and his next project was never going to happen.

That night everyone headed for One University, but the party was already over. I stayed for an hour and headed home. It was the end, and survival had become less theoretical. One week later, I headed to Mount Sinai Hospital for a seven-day detox.

On August 6 that same year, Klaus Nomi died of complications from AIDS. It was only five years earlier that he'd thrilled the crowd at 1978's "New Wave Vaudeville" with a song from the 1877 opera *Samson and Delilah*. A year later, 1979, he was singing the "Nomi Song" and Lou Christie's "Lightning Strikes" at the Mudd Club.

For me, fear didn't truly set in until 1985 when Rock Hudson's death became front-page news. Closer to home it was Ricky Wilson of the B-52's. By then I knew I was at risk and I had to do something different. I still had a chance. The next chapter was unwritten.

Lucky

It's strange and unpredictable, the places we found and find ourselves. When the dust finally began to settle Steve Mass was dealing with tax problems and serving weekends in jail. Ross Bleckner, once again, owned 77 White Street, and I was starting over, still figuring things out.

I was twenty-nine years old—struggling but still standing. I had my friends, my parents still loved me, and I somehow managed to hang on to my loft. I was looking for a job and trying to paint. I was trying to smile and occasionally succeeding. I was attempting to put things into perspective, make some changes and move forward. I put away the razor blade and the mirror, the needle and the spoon—and in 1987 I put the cork in the bottle. Considering the hours spent in bathrooms, basements and abandoned buildings, I was lucky to be alive.

No Dry Eyes

Cookie Mueller spent the rest of the decade writing about what she loved and what she didn't. She died in November 1989 of an AIDS-related cause. Far from the last, the disease was ravaging the downtown community along with cities and countries around the world. A funeral service was held at the St. Mark's Church; her lover and soul mate Sharon Niesp sang the blues. I sat in a pew with Gary and Anita Sarko. There were no dry eyes, no answers and as yet, no cure.

On June 3, 1990, Richard "Ricky" Sohl was napping in his bedroom on Fire Island. He never woke up—his death the result of complications from an untreated childhood bout with rheumatic fever. Louie Chaban called me from the Island, I called Andi and she called Patti. Our hearts break.

That spring, Steve Mass opened a restaurant on Church Street called Cannes 46. It was two blocks and almost a decade removed from where the Mudd Club stood. Three months later, and still very much thinking of Ricky, I celebrated my thirty-seventh birthday at Cannes with a dinner for twenty-five. Steve served the birthday cake and I blew out the candles. The guests included a number of people I came to know and truly love at the Mudd Club—that number, in my life today.

The following week, I walked back to Cannes 46 and told Steve he should hire me as a manager. His response: "Why do I need a manager?" In less than a year, the place was closed.

Steve at some point moved to Germany and, in 2001, opened a place in Berlin called the Mudd Club. I never went there, never knew much about it, and now it too is gone.

I Still Get That

My parents passed away in 2000. The loss was overwhelming and I still miss them. By that time Gary and I had been drifting apart for more than a decade. When the towers got hit on 9/11 I was asleep on Murray Street, three blocks away. My building shook and the windows rattled. The world became a different place. I sold the loft in 2004, after having lived there for twenty-seven years.

Steven Davis, the young architect who jogged down White Street in 1979, helped design the National September 11 Memorial and Museum. He still loves New York and speaks with great enthusiasm about the Mudd Club.

In 1995, the Solomon R. Guggenheim Museum mounted a mid-career retrospective of Ross Bleckner's work. A decade later, he sold the building at 77 White Street for six million dollars. The new owners converted the floors into luxury condominiums and the sales prospectus noted the building's "historical significance."

In March 2009, Abbijane died suddenly. In October, Alice Himelstein died after a ten-month battle with cancer. Laura Kennedy died in 2011. We spoke on the phone a few times but hadn't seen each other in nearly a decade. That same year, I walked into a restaurant in upstate New York and someone yelled, "Hey, Richard from the Mudd Club!" My friends looked at me and asked, "Do they mean you?" I laughed.

"Yeah, I still get that."

Lost and Found

It's been a while but I still think about Pete, Mickey and Ricky. I think about the friends I lost, the friends I found and the friends who never went away. I think about life in New York City, how it changed, and how it continues. I think about how lucky I was. How lucky I am.

I know my life would be different if I hadn't seen that poster with the address *77 White Street*. I'd be a different person if I hadn't followed that winding road and eventually hit that wall.

Thirty-odd years after the Mudd Club closed I still see the crowd waiting outside. I see myself running around the second floor, hiding out in the bathrooms and jumping around on the dance floor. I still remember how the place felt like home the first time I walked thru the door. The moment seems brief but for a few short years 77 White was the heartbeat—and the heart of the scene.

Today I'll hear a song and remember where I've been. I'll hear another song and think about where I'm going. I open a box of old photographs and some things look familiar—other things don't even seem real. A few of the pictures make me feel older and younger at once. I'll recognize my family and friends, but sometimes it's hard to recognize myself. That's when I turn down the music, look away, and try to move forward. Other times I close my eyes and try to sleep.

Heading south on Broadway, White Street flashes by. Time gets buried but the memories survive. I drift back and forth—then and now, now and then. I look at a painting from 1980 and recall standing before it in my studio on Murray Street. I'd light another joint and get ready for work. An hour later, I'd walk up Broadway to Franklin Street, cut thru Cortlandt Alley to White, and step inside. When the lights went down and the music came on, I'd light a cigarette, grab a beer and step out. Soon the crowd would be backed up into the street, Iggy's "Lust for Life" pounding the dance floor. Today people walk past but have no idea.

***

I went to see Joey Arias perform last summer. He laughed, saying, "We probably know each other longer than anyone else here." I saw my friends, the Bush Tetras, celebrate thirty-five years of making music; Blondie recently celebrated forty. Backstage at Hot Tuna I said hello to Jack Casady. He lowered his glasses, smiled and said, "You're still alive." I laughed. "Looks like we both are."

I went to John Lurie's opening in Chelsea and his paintings were beautiful. Michael Holman was there and so was Delphine Blue. I sat down for dinner with Lisa Rosen, Walter Robinson, Vicki Pedersen and filmmaker Sara Driver. It was Pat Place's birthday; Linda Yablonsky showed up late. I ran into Robert Molnar on the street and he's still amazed I'm writing this book. Louis Chaban offers enthusiasm and encouragement while Diego Cortez remains *curatorially* curious about the endeavor. David Azarch lives a few blocks from me on the city's far Upper West Side, and Chi Chi and Johnny remain Chi Chi and Johnny. Joey Kelly is the singer in a band; he's still a lovable guy.

In October 2015, Anita Sarko said good-bye. In April 2017, Glenn O'Brien passed away after a long illness. For the rest of us and for the moment, time is on our side.

I speak to Andi Ostrowe every day; she still works for Patti Smith and Patti still *is*. Phoebe Zeeman (now Fitch) has a place in upstate New York; she made me dinner on the eve of my last birthday. Claudia Summers lives in Chelsea with Amos Poe. Marcus Leatherdale has been living in Portugal.

Lynette just sent me some 1980 Polaroids; she lives in Spokane and looks forward to a trip back east. Diane Dupuis, a nature-loving artist, is often seen chasing bears and squirrels in her rural Connecticut backyard.

My friend Solveig is living in the Southern California desert and I'm godfather to Pat Wadsley's daughter. I spoke to Jo Shane a few days ago and I saw Marcia Resnick a few weeks ago. A book of Marcia's photos was released last year. Allan Tannenbaum just published his fourth book of photographs; I wrote the sidebar to the nightlife section. Bobby Grossman is busy working on a book of his own.

My childhood friend Louis Minghinelli and his wife Jackie split their time between Long Island, Florida and NYC. Steve Miller, living in Amsterdam for five years, recently returned to the U.S. and is living in Connecticut. Teri Toye *officially* became Teri Toye, gave up her modeling career and returned to Iowa. Big Ron built a home in Mexico and still travels the world. Kate Simon is still taking pictures and still calls me *RB*. We often talk about life and what it all means.

The guy who dumped me in 1977 with a late-night phone call is alive and well and living in San Francisco; we're happy to have reconnected and occasionally speak on the phone. The cowboy from Chicago—never heard from again.

Gary Kanner is an artist. He still lives in New York City. Today, after years of damage and needed repair, our friendship continues.

Everyone else I see or speak to from time to time.

The Phone Call Reprise

November 2015. I'm cooking dinner and watching *ABC World News* when my phone starts ringing. I don't recognize the number; neither does the phone. I pick up anyway and hear someone say, "Hello, this is Dr. Mudd."

Steve Mass arrived in town to lend his name and support to a Bowery Mission benefit aptly billed as a "Mudd Club Rummage Sale." He's asking for my help. Over the course of three weeks, and thirty-five years after the fact, Steve finally tells me what a great job I did working the door of 77 White. We talk about things we never talked about before. Our connection finally becomes a friendship.

Today, Steve travels back and forth from Berlin, hoping to once again settle in New York.

***

By now I've waited a lot longer than ten minutes. I took my time writing it all down. I look back without getting lost, happy to remember those twenty-one months. It's taken a while but I finally stopped hiding and stopped worrying about fitting in. I look in the mirror and—other than a bit of *age*—everything is okay.

ACKNOWLEDGMENTS

The encouragement, support and collective memory of all those friends and associates who made this book possible, I can never thank you enough. These pages keep us close and move us forward.

Lori Barbaria was the first to tell me I could do this. Tim Broun, Andi Ostrowe, Kate Simon and Claudia Summers lent me their ear and never stopped listening. Ray Adams, Diane Dupuis, Phoebe Fitch, Michael Holman, Gary Kanner, Pat Place, Vicki Pedersen, Lisa Rosen, Jo Shane and Pat Wadsley were always there, then and now. Michael Wilde helped reacquaint me with the English language and Ira Silverberg encouraged me to keep writing. There would be no story to tell if it wasn't for Steve Mass.

Animal X, Joey Arias, Emily Armstrong, Patti Astor, David Azarch, Cedric Baker, Ivan *Ivan* Baker, Joe Barbaria, Ron Beckner, Edwige Belmore, Adele Bertei, Max Blagg, Dike Blair, Ross Bleckner, Delphine Blue, Mark Boone Jr., David Bowie, Fred 'Fab 5 Freddy' Brathwaite, Jerry Brandt, Ernie Brooks, Robin Bruch, Bebe Buell, Leo Carlin, Neke Carson, Louie Chaban, James Chance, Leee Black Childers, Don Christensen, Cheetah Chrome, Tessie Chua, Brien Coleman, Diego Cortez, Jayne County, William Coupon, Bruce Crocker, Ronnie Cutrone, Sharon D'Lugoff, Steven Davis, Edit De'Ak, Deerfrance, Brooke Delarco, Maria DelGreco, John Doe, Johnny Dynell, Sara Driver, Tim Ebneth, Suellen Epstein, Marianne Faithful, Melvone Farrell, Danny Fields, Jim Fouratt, Patrick Fox, Chris Frantz, Jane Friedman, Julie Glantz, Henny Garfunkel, Eric Goode, Bette Gordon, Bobby Grossman, Vince Grupi, Randy Gun, George Haas, Carrie Haddad, Debbie Harry, Kim Hastreiter, Shawn Hausman, Wayne Hawkins, Lisa Helmholz-Adams, Mona Helmholz, David Hershkovits, Gail Higgins, Rosemary Hochschild, John Holmstrom, Francine Hunter McGivern,

Richard Boch, author, 2016, by Kate Simon.

Pat Irwin, Pat Ivers, Jim Jarmusch, Roxanne Jefferies, Jefferson Airplane, John Jennings, Betsey Johnson, Nathan Slate Joseph, Larry Kaplan, Lenny Kaye, Stephanie Kaye, Krystie Keller, Joey Kelly, David Kinigson, Lynette Bean Kral, Solveig Lamberg, Dory and Allen Lanier, Marcus Leatherdale, Judy Levy, Rebecca Litman, Hal Ludacer, Colette Lumiere, John Lurie, Marina Lutz, Valden Madsen, Gerard Malanga, Monique Mallory, Richard 'Handsome Dick' Manitoba, Marilyn, Maripol, Michael Maslin, Larry Mass, Debi Mazar, Dolette McDonald, Maureen McLaughlin, Legs McNeil, Taylor Mead, Barry 'Scratchy' Meyers, Sylvia Miles, Nancy Miller, Steve Miller, Louis Minghinelli, Eric Mitchell, Robert Molnar, Mary-Ann Monforton,

Elliot Murphy, Michael Musto, James Nares, Natasha, Donald Newman, Nico, Klaus Nomi, Judy Nylon, Michael Oblowitz, Glenn O'Brien, Peter Occhiogrosso, Anita Pallenberg, Deb Parker, Rudolf Piper, Charles Patty, Nick 'Berlin' Petti, Dustin Pittman, Amos Poe, Dee Pop, Iggy Pop, Linda Psomas, Joann Pugliese, Howie Pyro, Ramones, Lou Reed, Marcia Resnick, Barry Reynolds, 'Boy Adrian' Richards, Lynne Robinson, Walter Robinson, Danny Rosen, Roxy Music, Colter Rule, Yvonne Ruskin, Anita Sarko, Kenny Scharf, David Scharff, Robert Schnur, Susan Sedlmayr, Scott Severin, Jackie Shapiro, Michael Shrieve, Dawn Silva, Cynthia Sley, Patti Smith, Stephen Dennis 'Smutty' Smith, Lisa Spellman, Phyllis Stein, Gretchen Stibolt, Walter Steding, Justin Strauss, Betsy Sussler, SVT, Talking Heads, Allan Tannenbaum, Marvin Taylor and The Fales Library at NYU, The Clash, The Brides of Funkenstein, The Pretenders, Phyllis Teitelman, Regine Thorre, Tami Toye, Teri Toye, Bob Tulipan, Cathy Underhill, Chi Chi Valenti, Arturo Vega, Brent Ward, John Waters, Sally Webster, Tina Weymouth, Wendy Whitelaw, Bernie Worrell, Tom Wright, X, Linda Yablonsky and Paul Zahl—your recollections, words and music, paintings and film spoke to me, and helped piece this story together.

Emily Armstrong, Ron Beckner, Rhonda Corte, William Coupon, Lisa Genet, Bobby Grossman, Bob Gruen, Alan Kleinberg, Lynette Bean Kral, Marcus Leatherdale, Maripol, Eugene Merinov, Dustin Pittman, Eileen Polk, Marcia Resnick, Ebet Roberts, Kate Simon, Robin Schanzenbach, Chris Stein, Billy Sullivan, Allan Tannenbaum and Nick Taylor—your images document and celebrate the Mudd Club moment that was 1979 and 1980.

Marina Lutz and Howie Pyro, your archives of pertinent and important miscellany are truly a gift.

Tom Baker, Jesse Chamberlain, Pete Farndon, Alice Himelstein, Laura Kennedy, Cookie Mueller, Mickey Ruskin, Richard DNV 'Ricky' Sohl and Abbijane—you will forever be a part of me.

To *everyone*—thank you.